ENGLISH LANGUAGE SERIES

TITLE NO 10

An Introduction to English
Transformational Syntax

ENGLISH LANGUAGE SERIES
General Editor: Randolph Quirk
Title no:

INVESTIGATING ENGLISH STYLE 1
David Crystal and Derek Davy

THE MOVEMENT OF ENGLISH PROSE 2
Ian A. Gordon

A LINGUISTIC GUIDE TO ENGLISH POETRY 4
Geoffrey N. Leech

AN INTRODUCTION TO 7
MODERN ENGLISH WORD-FORMATION
Valerie Adams

COHESION IN ENGLISH 9
M. A. K. Halliday and Ruqaiya Hasan

AN INTRODUCTION TO ENGLISH 10
TRANSFORMATIONAL SYNTAX
Rodney Huddleston

MEANING AND FORM 11
Dwight Bolinger

An Introduction to English Transformational Syntax

RODNEY HUDDLESTON

Reader in Linguistics
University of Queensland

LONGMAN

LONGMAN GROUP LIMITED *LONDON*
Associated companies, branches and representatives throughout the world

© Longman Group Ltd 1976

First published 1976
Third impression 1979

Cased ISBN 0 582 55061 0
Paper ISBN 0 582 55062 9

Printed in Great Britain by
Spottiswoode Ballantyne Ltd.
Colchester and London

for JOAN

Foreword

There have been a good many short books on English grammar and – in the past fifteen years – a good many short books on transformational-generative grammar. Such activity in no way implies duplication and redundancy. It testifies rather to the abiding and intense interest in these subjects; to the impossibility of writing the definitive short book on either of them; to the fact that every treatment – well, almost every treatment – adds a new and welcome dimension, dealing with some aspect in a more satisfactory way, or fulfilling more nearly the needs of certain readers. And of course, so far as transformational-generative theory is concerned, the activity testifies to the most agreeable fact of all: to the new ideas, new research, new interaction of minds and disciplines that continue to endow TG with the excitement of the frontier spirit.

Rodney Huddleston takes on the sobering task of providing us with a new book on both fronts: a new introduction to English grammar as illuminated by the insights of TG; and a new introduction to transformational theory as applied to the complexities of English grammar. He brings to the work not only exceptional intellectual powers but also an exceptionally rich and deep range of studies pursued at several universities – especially Cambridge (where he read modern languages), Edinburgh (where he did a PhD in the linguistics of French), and University College London (where he conducted a Government-sponsored research programme in computational linguistics applied to English scientific writing). Latterly, with a senior appointment at the University of Queensland, he has faced the problem of synthesizing the bewildering flood of recent and current contributions to linguistic theory in all parts of the world – and of doing so in such a way as to make the synthesis both comprehensible and relevant to the needs of students engaged in thinking about their native language. This book is a direct product of his work in the classroom and we can be confident that its impact will be as revelatory to readers as to those who are fortunate enough to be in daily contact.

And the volume makes a most welcome and timely addition to this series. As English has increasingly come into world-wide use, there has arisen an acute need for more information on the language and the ways in which it is used. The English Language Series seeks to meet this need and to play a part in further stimulating the study and teaching of English by providing up-to-date and scholarly treatments of topics most relevant to present-day English – including its history and traditions, its sound patterns, its grammar, its lexicology, its rich variety in speech and writing, and its standards in Britain, the USA, and the other principal areas where the language is used.

University College London   RANDOLPH QUIRK
June 1975

Preface

This book is intended as an introduction to the general theory of transformational-generative grammar, with extensive and systematic exemplification from selected areas of English. I have used the term 'syntax' rather than 'grammar' in the title because I do not deal in detail with all aspects of the theory: phonology and semantics are considered only to the extent necessary to make clear how the grammar as a whole is organized and how the syntactic component fits into this larger framework. The book is an introduction in the sense that it presupposes no previous knowledge of transformational grammar and that it aims to put the reader in a position to tackle the more advanced literature reporting on research of the last few years: with this aim in view I have tried to give a faithful and clear account of those aspects of the theory and the analysis of English that are generally taken for granted in the advanced literature. It is not an introduction to linguistics as a whole: it does not, for example, cover historical and comparative linguistics, and it deals with only one approach to grammatical theory, that which developed out of work by Noam Chomsky in the mid-fifties; however, no knowledge of other modern approaches is required for an understanding of the book, and I have assumed only minimal acquaintance with traditional grammar.

A number of friends and colleagues were kind enough to read a preliminary draft: Barry Blake, Ray Cattell, Bob Dixon, Chris Hauri, Dick Hudson, Steve Johnson, John Lyons, Peter Matthews, Akira Ota and Randolph Quirk; I am very grateful to them for the suggestions they made for improving it, though they are not of course to be held responsible for its remaining shortcomings. I wish also to thank Cecily McDonald, who typed several draft versions, and my wife, for her help in correcting the proofs and her patience and encouragement during the writing of the book.

Brisbane
June 1975

R H

Table of Symbols and Notational Conventions

*   asterisk: indicates a deviant sentence, *p* 9.

( )   parentheses: enclose optional element in a rule, *p* 42.

{ }   braces: enclose alternative elements in a rule, *p* 42.

[ ]   square brackets: enclose syntactic or phonological features, *p* 149.

[.]ₛ   labelled brackets: enclose a constituent belonging to the category S, etc, *p* 102.

/ /   obliques: enclose phonological units, *p* 29.

/   oblique: is used (a) in context-sensitive phrase structure rules, *p* 44; and (b) to abbreviate examples: *He is very tall/*taller* abbreviates the two sentences *He is very tall* and **He is very taller.*

→   arrow: is used in rewrite rules, *p* 35.

⇒   double arrow: is used in transformational rules, *p* 73.

∅   zero: indicates the absence of any element, *p* 74.

marks sentence boundary, *p* 36.

SPACED SMALL CAPITALS mark an important technical term at its first introduction.

UNSPACED SMALL CAPITALS indicate emphasis.

italics are used for (a) citation of linguistic forms, and (b) terminal symbols, *p* 36.

bold face focuses attention on a particular part of a cited example.

CAPITAL ITALICS indicate contrastive stress in cited examples.

Phonological symbols:

/p/ as in *pie*	/f/ as in *few*	/ɛ/ as in *pet*
/b/ ,, ,, *buy*	/v/ ,, ,, *view*	/æ/ ,, ,, *pat*
/t/ ,, ,, *toe*	/θ/ ,, ,, *thigh*	/a/ ,, ,, *palm*
/d/ ,, ,, *doe*	/ð/ ,, ,, *thy*	/ɒ/ ,, ,, *pot*
/k/ ,, ,, *kilt*	/s/ ,, ,, *seal*	/ɔ/ ,, ,, *pawn*
/g/ ,, ,, *gilt*	/z/ ,, ,, *zeal*	/u/ ,, ,, *put*
/m/ ,, ,, *my*	/h/ ,, ,, *he*	/ə/ ,, ,, *sofa*
/n/ ,, ,, *nigh*	/w/ ,, ,, *we*	/eɪ/ ,, ,, *wait*
/l/ ,, ,, *lie*	/i/ ,, ,, *peat*	/aɪ/ ,, ,, *might*
/r/ ,, ,, *rye*	/ɪ/ ,, ,, *pit*	/ɛə/ ,, ,, *mare*

References in the text and notes to other works give the author, date of publication and, where relevant, page number(s) – *eg* Chomsky (1957:93); full bibliographical details can be found on *pp* 261–7.

Contents

Foreword		vii
Preface		ix
Table of Symbols and Notational Conventions		xi
1	Aims and Scope of Transformational-Generative Grammar	1
2	Syntax in Relation to Semantics and Phonology	23
3	Phrase Structure Grammars	35
4	Transformational Grammars	47
5	A Fragment of a Transformational Grammar	57
6	Syntactic Structure and Meaning	82
7	Recursion	93
8	Aspects of the Grammar of Complementation	111
9	Syntactic Structure and Illocutionary Force	127
10	Syntactic Features and the Lexicon	147
11	Phonology and Morphology	158
12	The Interpretation and Ordering of Rules	172
13	Universal Grammar	196
14	A Reconsideration of Auxiliary Verbs	211
15	Grammatical Functions	226
16	Syntax and Semantics	248
Bibliography		261
Index		269

Chapter 1

Aims and Scope of Transformational-Generative Grammar

In this chapter we shall be considering such questions as what it is that the generative grammarian seeks to describe and explain, what constitutes his data, what kinds of criteria are relevant in determining which of two rival grammars is the better, and so on. Most of the remaining chapters will then be concerned with investigating and exemplifying the general form that a generative grammar should take, the theoretical concepts it must incorporate, if it is to meet its objectives. However, it should not be expected that a complete and precise delimitation of the field can be provided in advance, so that a number of the points discussed in this introductory chapter will necessarily be dealt with in a provisional or fairly superficial way: some of these will then be taken up again in the course of the subsequent more formal investigation.

1.1 Competence and performance

Chomsky has characterized a generative grammar of a language as an explicit description of 'the ideal speaker-hearer's intrinsic competence'. A person's LINGUISTIC COMPETENCE is his tacit knowledge of his language. We attribute knowledge of a language to a person to account for his ability to use the language, to produce and understand utterances in it. Clearly this ability does not require any CONSCIOUS knowledge: one can learn a language without any formal instruction, and even where a native speaker does receive such instruction it covers only a minute fraction of the structure of the language and is given after the learner has already acquired the ability to use it on a large scale. The knowledge that underlies a person's ability to use his language is thus only TACIT – and it is the grammarian's aim to acquire conscious knowledge of the speaker-hearer's tacit knowledge.

It is evident that a person's ability to use his language involves being able to produce and understand NEW utterances, ones he has never spoken or heard before. A language cannot be equated with any set, however large, of utterances that have actually occurred, utterances produced by specific individuals using the language at specific times and places: it is much more abstract than this. This much is obvious; but we shall not want to identify a language with a set of POTENTIAL utterances either. Consider examples [1] and [2]:

(a modal is always followed by an infinitive without the "to") no tense e.g., can be, can give, should be, should give

6 Modals: (pres. tense) will, can, shall, may, must, ought
(past tense): would, could, should, might, must, ought
They all indicate possibility or probability, ∴ future to

[1] *I was hoping that you – would you tell him the news for me?*
[2] *I was hoping that you would tell him the news for me*

[1] exhibits the phenomenon known as 'anacoluthon', the change from one grammatical construction to another leaving the first incomplete. This phenomenon is quite common in spontaneous speech, and therefore there can surely be no question of denying that [1] is a 'potential utterance', that it could occur. Nevertheless, speakers of English are aware (or can in general easily be made aware) that [1] differs significantly in status from [2] – and an adequate description of (a speaker-hearer's knowledge of) English must express this difference in status. Since utterances of both types undoubtedly do occur, we cannot characterize this difference in status in terms of the notion 'potentiality of occurrence'. Instead we introduce the theoretical concept of a WELL-FORMED SENTENCE, and say that [2] but not [1] belongs to the set of well-formed sentences of English.

This brings us to the distinction Chomsky draws between linguistic competence and LINGUISTIC PERFORMANCE. The former is tacit knowledge of the language, the latter the use of the language in concrete situations. 'Sentence' is a concept that belongs to the theory of competence, while 'utterance' belongs to performance. In the case of an utterance of [2], there would be a direct and (relatively) simple relationship between utterance and sentence, whereas there is no sentence or sequence of sentences corresponding to an utterance of [1]. Not all utterances are utterances of sentences, and this is one important reason for keeping the concepts theoretically distinct. Notice that if someone uttered [1] we would not take this as evidence that he had an imperfect knowledge of English; rather we allow that a person's use of his language may not directly reflect his knowledge of it.

Ultimately the linguist (or linguist-cum-psychologist) must aim to account for the actual use of language, but the latter is dependent on the complex interaction of a variety of factors, so that there are methodological advantages in tackling some of them separately: competence is just one such determining factor. We shall thus not regard all properties of utterances as attributable to the structure of the language used in making them, but will set as an intermediate, limited goal the task of accounting for those that are: this is the task of a generative grammar. Since it is actual utterances produced in specific situations that constitute the most obvious data for linguistic analysis, it will help delimit the scope of generative grammar if I explain here the main features of such utterances that will NOT be accounted for in a description of competence. But it must be emphasized that in pruning away these features to yield a more manageable object of study we are not suggesting that they are unimportant or not susceptible to systematic investigation: Chomsky's claim is that competence provides a coherent object of study and that progress in this more limited field is a logical prerequisite for serious work towards a comprehensive theory of linguistic performance – that one cannot profitably study the use of language without some significant understanding of linguistic form or structure.

Aspects = Perfect (pres. perf, past perf, future perf.)
Progressive (pres. prog., past prog., future prog., future perf prog.)
(futures always include modals)

(a) First of all, we shall regard some features of utterances as simply errors of performance, irrelevant to underlying competence. Such will be anacolutha, as already mentioned, slips of the tongue, hesitation noises and pauses, and so on. Speakers differ quite considerably in the closeness of the match between their utterances and sentences of the language they are speaking (those with a closer match being typically regarded as more articulate, though there is a good deal more involved in articulateness than just this). Moreover, a single person's performance will vary according to his psychological and physical state, the match between utterance and sentence being typically less close when he is affected by fatigue, anxiety, anger, intoxication, not to mention various patho-logical conditions. It is reasonable to say that we do not want to regard these things as forming part of the subject matter for a study of the structure of language, and the distinction between performance (use) and competence (knowledge) provides the rationale for excluding them, for editing out errors and extraneous noise – for a certain 'idealization' of the data. The principle of idealization is not a controversial one and is invoked in any discipline con-cerned with the description of complex empirical phenomena – though there may be disagreement over just how much idealization is justified. But, lest the use of the term 'error' here create any misconception, let me stress that we shall not regard utterances like *It's me* or *John is older than me* as involving per-formance errors because they conflict with the rule for the choice between *I* and *me* found in some older prescriptive grammars: where there is conflict between the data and the rules of a grammar the onus is on the grammarian to show that the error is in the data rather than in the grammar (*cf* 1.5) – and this onus certainly cannot be discharged in examples like these, where *It's me* is the form normally used by many speakers.

(b) Most speakers of English would probably be inclined to think of an utterance, considered from the point of view of the speech signal, as a sequence of sounds – a sequence of consonant and vowel sounds (I simplify the discussion here by ignoring features of intonation and stress overlaid upon the consonants and vowels). However, if we were to carry out an acoustic analysis of a normal utterance we should find that there is in general no sharp division between the sounds: we should not be able to point to a precise place where, say, a consonant ends and a following vowel begins. In actual utterances, then, the sound units are not discrete, but merge into each other. Nevertheless, this non-discreteness is to be regarded as a feature of performance that has no counterpart in com-petence, in linguistic structure: as far as sentences are concerned, the intuition that the phonetic units come in discrete successive segments is a valid one.

There are in fact two kinds of discreteness to be recognized: besides that applying to successive units in a sentence, there is discreteness in the inventory of units in the language. And again this type of discreteness is not found in actual performance. Suppose we ask whether two utterances are 'the same' or 'different'. The term 'utterance' is in fact ambiguous: it can be applied to an ACT of speech or to the PRODUCT resulting from such an act, the physical sound

SAAD = simple, active, affirmative, declarative
Sentence   sentence

Metalanguage or metalinguistics = terminology used to talk
                                              about lang-

produced. An utterance-act will be performed by a particular person at a particular time and place, so that if we take these particular circumstances into account each utterance-act will be a unique event, different from every other utterance-act. But even if we ignore these circumstances of the act and consider only utterance-products, the uniqueness remains: sensitive instruments will be able to detect some acoustic difference between the products of different utterance-acts. Yet clearly it would be absurd to deny the possibility of repeated utterances of the same sentence: the conventions for the use of language are such that physically different utterances can count as linguistically the same. A spoken utterance-product is a stretch of physical sound; a sentence is not: it is an abstract theoretical construct. The phonetic description of a sentence will represent it as a sequence of discrete units, each defined in terms of an inventory of discrete properties. In performance the sounds will not only merge into each other in succession but will also show continuous variation along some of the relevant dimensions of classification, such as height of tongue in the case of vowels. Some of the physical properties of utterances will be accounted for by reference to the phonetic structure of the sentence being uttered, but not all; apart from those relating to non-discreteness, we shall also discount those depending on the particular, idiosyncratic shape of a person's vocal tract, resulting in his individual voice quality. The task of providing a principled basis for determining which physical properties of utterances are to be discounted in a competence grammar is one for the theory of phonology and need not concern us here: for present purposes it is sufficient to establish the abstract, non-physical nature of the sentence.

(c) A third limitation of scope is that the grammar will describe the meanings of sentences in abstraction from their use in any particular situation. One aspect of this limitation involves the distinction between meaning and reference. Many linguistic expressions can be used to refer to non-linguistic objects and phenomena. For example, I can refer to the four-wheeled contraption in my garage by using the expression *my car:* there is an obvious distinction between the LINGUISTIC FORM *my car* and the OBJECT that I drive about in. Expressions used to refer to things outside themselves are called REFERRING EXPRESSIONS, and the things they refer to are called their REFERENTS. Now it is an important fact about the use of language that a single referring expression may have different referents in different situations. Consider, for example, sentence [3]:

[3] *I was reading in the library*

The word *I* can refer to as many different people as there are speakers of English; in any particular utterance of [3], *I* will refer to some specific individual, whoever it is who happens to be making the utterance. But this variation in the referents of *I* is a matter of performance. In considering sentences in abstraction from their situation of utterance the generative grammarian is not interested whether *I* is used to refer to John Smith, Bill Jones or whoever: from the point

Determiners = signals for nouns:
articles: a, an, the   indef. pron (some, many)
poss pron: my, his   cardinal num (one, two)
demon. pron: this, that   ordinal num (first, 2nd, next, last)
                              ∅ (zero pro) - none before proper nouns

of view of the grammar there is just one word *I* with a constant set of linguistic properties. Similarly, the expression *the library* can be appropriately used to refer to a vast number of different rooms or buildings: in a given UTTERANCE of [3] the speaker (assuming he is using it normally, as opposed to citing it as a linguistic example, etc) will have in mind a specific one of these, but whether it is a certain room in the house where he lives, the municipal library in the town where he is staying, the library in the school, college or university where he is a student or teacher, or some other possibility, will have no bearing on our description of SENTENCE [3]. Different utterances of [3] may differ, then, in respect of the referents of *I* and *the library* (not to mention differences in the time periods in which the reading is said to have taken place – periods prior to the time, whenever that happens to be, at which the utterance takes place), but we shall say that in each case the same sentence has been used.

Conversely a single referent may be referred to in different situations by means of different linguistic expressions. For example, Harold Wilson might be referred to as *I, you, the Prime Minister, The Leader of the Opposition, my husband, the bloke on the right smoking a pipe*, etc, depending on who is speaking, who is being addressed, when the utterance takes place (relative to the elections of 1964, 1970 and 1974), and so on. But clearly we would not wish to say that all these expressions have the same meaning. We accordingly make a distinction between MEANING and REFERENCE, such that the difference between the *I* in an utterance of [3] spoken by Harold Wilson and that in one spoken by Mary Wilson is one of reference not meaning, while that between Harold Wilson's *I* and his wife's *my husband* is one of meaning not reference. Reference, as we have seen, is dependent on various features of the situation of utterance, but meaning is not – it is a property of sentences or smaller expressions independent of their use on any particular occasion. In generative grammar we aim to describe the meanings of sentences and their parts, but not to specify the referents of linguistic expressions as used in particular situations.

To distinguish these two concepts of meaning and reference is not, however, to deny that they are closely related. Although the referent of an expression depends on various aspects of the situation of utterance, it also depends on the meaning of the expression. There is, for instance, a very large set of objects that I can refer to, in normal use of language, with the expression *the library*, but it does not include the jacaranda tree in my garden, the boot of my car, and an indefinite number of other things: the set is circumscribed by the meaning of the word *library*. Data concerning the referential use of expressions will therefore be relevant to the study of meaning. There is an analogy here with the point made under (b) above: just as the phonetic description of a sentence will account for some but not all of the articulatory, acoustic and auditory properties of a normal utterance of it, so its semantic description will account for some but not all aspects of the normal referential use of various parts of it.

It is important to add, however, that although the linguistic structure of a sentence does not fully determine the referents of the expressions within it, it does to a large extent determine whether two expressions can or must have the same referent, *ie* be COREFERENTIAL. This may be illustrated by examples like

[4] i *John taught himself*
   ii *John taught him*
[5] i *When she got home, Mary had a bath*
   ii *She said that Mary had a bath*

In [4], the choice between the reflexive pronoun *himself* and the non-reflexive *him* depends on whether the teacher and the one taught are or are not the same: *John* is coreferential with *himself* in [i] but non-coreferential with *him* in [ii]. Both [5i] and [ii] have an interpretation where *she* refers to someone other than Mary, but [i], unlike [ii], can also be understood with *she* and *Mary* coreferential. This difference is related to the different linguistic structures of the sentences: in [i] but not [ii] *she* is inside a clause that is subordinate to the following one containing *Mary*. The generative grammarian is not concerned with whether *she* refers to Pat Smith, Jill Jones, etc, but he must state whether it can refer to the same person as *Mary*, because this is something the speaker-hearer knows about the sentences in abstraction from their use in any particular situation. We shall be looking further into coreference in Chapters 6 and 16.

In confining our attention to sentences as opposed to utterances produced in concrete situations, we shall also ignore certain aspects of the speaker's intentions. Suppose, for example, John says to his wife on some occasion, *I'm incredibly thirsty;* it may well be that in uttering this sentence his intention is less to impart information as to how he is feeling than to suggest or request that his wife get him a drink – but this is not part of the meaning of the sentence. Similarly, one might say, *May I ask why you're here?* with the intention of eliciting the reason for the addressee's being in the place where the utterance takes place, rather than to find out whether one has permission to ask a certain question. Nevertheless, from the point of view of the sentence considered in isolation, it does have the meaning of a request to be told whether or not the speaker may ask his question. What these examples illustrate is that the generative grammarian is concerned with what SENTENCES mean as opposed to what SPEAKERS mean when they use them – or, to put it another way, he considers only the idealized situation where the speaker means just what he says, where what the speaker means is identical with what the sentence that he uses means. This point will be taken up in Chapter 9.

More generally, we can say that a generative grammar will describe the phonetic form and the meaning of all the sentences in the language, but will not concern itself with the reasons why a speaker selects one sentence rather than another in a given situation. It should be emphasized in this connection, however, that there is a high degree of independence between sentences and the situations in which they are used. There are, it is true, some situations where conventions circumscribe quite narrowly what it is appropriate to say (for example, when two people are being introduced to each other for the first time), but there are others where it is left very widely open, as in intellectual discussion and so on.

Transformations : add
delete
transpose
substitute
or combine any number of these

(d) A fourth aspect of performance that is discounted in the study of competence is the difference between the roles of speaker and hearer. A generative grammar does not describe the process by which a person produces or interprets an utterance – it does not describe PROCESSES at all. The grammar is quite neutral as between speaker and hearer: it accounts for the knowledge a person has of the structure of his language, and this knowledge is a STATE, independent of the person's role as speaker or hearer in any given speech situation. I shall develop this point in 12.1.

(e) Finally, Chomsky has argued that certain limitations on the possible complexity of utterances are attributable to non-linguistic factors and are consequently not relevant to a study of competence. One obvious case of this is the limitation on the overall length of the utterance. One general type of sentence construction in English consists of a sequence of clauses linked by a co-ordinating conjunction such as *and: The first day they went to the beach, the second they spent at the party congress and on the last day they did a tour of the town.* Here there are three clauses coordinated, but there would be no difficulty in devising examples where the number of clauses was four, five, six, . . ., and so on. How far in fact can we go on? The generative grammarian's answer would be that as far as the structure of the language is concerned, there are no limits on the number of clauses that can be coordinated. The fact that there is bound to be some limit on the number of clauses coordinated in any sentence that could actually be uttered is not incompatible with this claim because the limiting factors (the need to break off for food and rest, for example) are not specific to the use of language, but apply to any kind of human activity. And it is precisely because the constraints are so general that it would be inappropriate to treat them as part of the subject matter of a theory of language structure, a theory of grammar. They are thus held to be limitations on the class of possible or potential utterances, not on the class of well-formed sentences – a further reason for keeping these two concepts distinct. The example considered here is doubtless a fairly trivial one, but it has important consequences. For to accept that there are no linguistic limits on the number of clauses that can be co-ordinated within a sentence is to accept that there are no linguistic limits on the number of different sentences in the language, *ie* that there is a (literally) infinite set of well-formed sentences. We shall see in Chapter 7 that this has a significant bearing on the kind of formal apparatus that we need in a generative grammar.

The principle that there are limitations on performance that are not specifically linguistic is invoked in certain more interesting, and more problematical, cases than that of coordination. Consider, for instance, the construction exhibited by the following set of examples:

[6] i *The man that you describe is no longer alive*
   ii *The man that the woman that you describe wanted to marry is no longer alive*
   iii *The man that the woman that the policeman that you describe had arrested wanted to marry is no longer alive*

Phrase Structure Rules = tell how to produce any
                                   (SAAD sentence in English
DSS = Deep structure string (or DSS)

A fairly standard analysis of [i] would say, among other things, that *that you describe* is a subordinate – more specifically, a relative – clause which belongs inside the NP (noun phrase) *the man that you describe*, this NP being the subject of the main clause *the man that you describe is no longer alive*. Thus we have a clause inside a NP, which is subject of a larger clause. In [ii] this pattern is repeated: *that you describe* is a relative clause inside the NP *the woman that you describe*, which is itself subject of another relative clause, *that the woman that you describe wanted to marry*, which in turn belongs in the NP *the man that the woman that you describe wanted to marry*, this being, finally, the subject of the whole clause [ii]. In [iii] the pattern is carried one stage further: this time we have three relative clauses, the smallest being inside the subject NP of the next larger, which is inside the subject NP of the largest of the relative clauses, this being then inside the subject NP of the main clause.

What are the limits on this type of construction? Certainly they are very much more severe than with coordination: it is doubtful whether even [iii] would make a fully acceptable utterance and it would require not a little effort of imagination to devise an acceptable example with four relative clauses arranged in this pattern. However it can again be argued that the constraints are not strictly linguistic, but are explicable in terms of more general factors – in this case psychological factors (such as memory limitations) rather than the physiological ones that we saw to operate in the coordination example. In hearing [iii] we meet a sequence of verb phrases *had arrested, wanted to marry, is no longer alive* and we are likely to have difficulty in keeping track of the structure so that we can see what the subject of each of these is. An analogy is often drawn here with mental arithmetic: most people would find it beyond them to multiply in their head two such large numbers as, say, 473288 and 61835714. But my failure to find the correct answer here would not mean that I do not know how to multiply: it is simply that such cases are too complex for me to be able to cope with (I could manage if I had the use of paper and pencil to overcome the effects on my performance of my memory limitations). The point of the analogy is to suggest that the psychological factors involved here affect the whole range of our mental activities: if the limitations are not specific to linguistic behaviour, this justifies our discounting them in a grammar designed to account for specifically linguistic knowledge.

Limitations of memory and such factors are also undoubtedly responsible for many of the 'errors' I spoke of in point (a). Typical is the following attested example:

[7] *The fine structure of the capsule in the few bacterial forms examined show similarities with the sheath of blue-green algae*

The subject of the main clause here is the singular *structure*, but instead of the singular verb *shows* we find the plural *show:* the lack of agreement between subject and verb here is doubtless due to the fact that there is a considerable distance between them and that the nearest noun preceding the verb is the plural *forms*.

Partitive = part of a group
eg., three of the boys
        any of the food

To conclude this discussion of competence and performance, let me emphasize again that in limiting the scope of generative grammar in the ways suggested we are not denying the desirability of constructing a more comprehensive theory of performance; indeed some recent work in transformational grammar has extended its scope somewhat beyond that outlined above. Nor is there reason to assume that there is a clear-cut distinction between those aspects of performance that reflect underlying competence and those that are determined by other, not strictly linguistic factors – but this undermines neither the theoretical nor the methodological value of the distinction.

1.2 Sentences and their structure

We have said that a generative grammar aims to describe the speaker-hearer's linguistic competence. What sort of information can we expect such a grammar to give? In the first place, we shall expect it to distinguish the sentences of the language from non-sentences – to distinguish [8] from [9], for example.

> [8] i *Bill sent his daughter to the doctor*
> ii *It seemed that John had made a mistake*
> iii *The children went home*
> [9] i **Bill elapsed his daughter to the doctor*
> ii **That John had made a mistake seemed*
> iii **The childs goed home*

The examples in [8] are WELL-FORMED, those in [9] DEVIANT (or 'ill-formed') – the standard convention is to use an asterisk to indicate deviance. The term 'sentence' is itself sometimes used in the sense of well-formed sentence (I intended it in this sense in the last section), but it is also frequently extended to cover examples like [9], so that it is not contradictory to speak of a deviant sentence.

Not all examples are as clear-cut. The status of [10], for instance, is open to doubt and disagreement, and many other borderline cases could be cited.

> [10] i *What she wouldn't condescend to was to take a job as a governess*
> ii *He didn't want to be regarded importunate*
> iii *John was closely resembled by all of his sons*

Such cases undoubtedly pose problems for the grammarian, but again it is worth emphasizing that the lack of a sharp division between well-formed and deviant sentences does not invalidate the theoretical distinction. There are indefinitely many examples which we are able to classify without hesitation as well-formed or deviant, and this ability in itself guarantees that there is a genuine distinction here: it is not dependent on there being a hard and fast line between the two classes. The crucial fact is that we can classify NEW examples: it is not a question of our simply being able to attach the appropriate label to a determinate list of examples whose classification we have memorized. This means that we are able to operate with the concepts of well-formedness and deviance, and these concepts thus unquestionably have a place in an account of our linguistic competence. The principle involved here is an important one; we shall see that it applies also to a number of other important distinctions that are needed in generative grammar.

I shall return in 1.3 to the concept of a well-formed sentence; in the meantime we can work with a rough intuitive understanding of it. We have agreed, then, that one thing a grammar of a language should do is to specify what are the well-formed sentences of that language. But clearly the speaker-hearer knows a great deal more about the well-formed sentences of his language than that they ARE well-formed; most importantly and obviously he knows what they mean. As a starting-point, therefore, we may define the tasks for a grammar as: (a) To enumerate the well-formed sentences in the language; (b) To associate with each of them one or more meanings.

The meanings will in principle be given in the form of SEMANTIC REPRE-SENTATIONS, though in the present state of semantic theory there is relatively little understanding or agreement concerning an appropriate systematic framework in terms of which meanings can be formally stated; what is said about meanings in this book will consequently be quite informal. As for (a), the sentences will be given in the form of PHONETIC REPRESENTATIONS specifying how they are pronounced (subject to the limitations mentioned on p 4). For example, the phonetic representation of [8i] would show it as beginning with a consonant characterized by voicedness (vibration of the vocal cords), closure of the lips, and so on, followed by a vowel segment articulated with the tongue and lips in such and such a position, . . .: phonological theory provides a general framework of classificatory dimensions in terms of which the individual segments can be described. Since phonology is not a major concern of this book I shall continue, for convenience, to cite sentences in their standard orthography, but this is not how they would be given in a formal grammar. In generative grammar, as in modern descriptive linguistics generally, speech is regarded as primary, writing as secondary and to a significant extent derivative from speech. There are several reasons for assigning priority to speech. Firstly, there are lots of languages (for example, many Australian aboriginal languages) for which no standard written form exists. Secondly, in communities where there is a standard writing system the child learns to use the spoken medium before the written, and whereas some never master the latter, remaining illiterate, no physically normal child fails to learn to speak if he lives in the society of others. A further point is that a writing system is relatively open to control and change by governmental decree and the like, whereas speech would be highly resistant to deliberate interference of such a kind. In Turkey, for example, a system using the Roman alphabet replaced the earlier Arabic script in 1926, and in China there are currently proposals to adopt an alphabetic system in place of the present character script: the very possibility of such a change implies the priority of speech, since the only possible basis for the alphabetic system would be the consonant and vowel units manifested in speech. This brings us to the structural primacy of speech, which may be illustrated by comparison of forms like *stab, pelt, font* with **stb, *plt, *fnt*. The former set are English words, while the latter are not – and could not be, because they violate the rules governing possible word forms in English; in particular they violate the rule that a word contain at least one vowel. Now the terms 'vowel' and 'consonant' are commonly applied to both classes of sounds and classes of letters, but whereas the difference between vowel and consonant SOUNDS is an intrinsic one, that between vowel and consonant LETTERS is derivative from the difference in sound. By this I mean that the two classes of sounds are distinguished by their inherent phonetic properties, by the way they are pronounced (very roughly we can say that the articulation of consonants, unlike that of vowels, involves some narrowing or closure at some point in the pharynx or mouth), whereas vowel and consonant letters are defined in terms of the speech sounds they represent, not in terms of the way they are written. Considered purely as marks on paper, for example, the letter *e* is more like *c* than it is like *i:* what it shares with the latter is its function of characteristically standing for a sound of a certain type. The rule that words must contain a vowel is thus essentially and primarily a rule of spoken English: the fact that written words must contain a vowel letter can be explained only in terms of the logically prior rule governing possible combinations of sounds. More generally, the intrinsic properties of sounds play a role in determining their possible combinations whereas those of letters do not. Another example is found in *spit, stand, skit* versus **sbit, *sdand, *sgit:* again there is nothing in the shape of the letters to distinguish *b, d, g* from *p, t, k*, and the rule at issue here involves the phonetic properties voiced and voiceless, with **sbit*, etc, violating the rule that a consonant following *s* must be voiceless. The intrinsic properties, of sounds are thus of much greater significance for the determination of linguistic form than those of letters, and phonology must occupy a much more central place in linguistics than 'graphology'.

Sentences are identified by their phonetic representation rather than by the combination of a phonetic and a semantic representation: each different phonetic representation enumerated by the grammar constitutes a unique sentence. A sentence is then AMBIGUOUS precisely when it is associated with two or more semantic representations. Conversely, a single semantic representation may be associated with two or more different sentences, which are then said to be PARAPHRASES (*cf* Chapter 6). For example, [11] is ambiguous, meaning roughly either 'Mary looked intensively' or 'Mary appeared hard', whereas [12i] and [ii] are paraphrases.

[11] *Mary looked hard*
[12] i *Give it to the girl that John's talking to*
    ii *Give it to the girl John's talking to*

The correspondence relations between sentences and their meanings are extremely complex: the existence of ambiguity and paraphrase is just one facet of this complexity. To describe them at all systematically we shall need to set up levels of representation intermediate between the semantic and the phonetic so that instead of moving in one step from meaning to pronunciation we will proceed in smaller, more manageable steps via these intermediate levels. For example, we will give an analysis of each sentence as a string of words classified in terms of 'parts of speech' and 'grammatical categories' (to use, for the moment, traditional concepts and terms). The ambiguity of [11] is then due to the fact that *hard* belongs to both the adverb and adjective classes and that *look* occurs in construction with either – note that *She looked carefully*, *She looked cruel*, *She worked hard* all lack the ambiguity. The paraphrase relation between [12i] and [ii] is accounted for by the rule that the relative pronoun *that* is optionally omissible except when it has the function of subject – compare *Give it to the girl that is talking to John* with the deviant **Give it to the girl is talking to John*. Concepts like adverb, adjective, relative pronoun, subject, are not definable in either phonological or semantic terms (see Chapter 2 for development of this general point), but belong to the theory of syntax. We can now revise our earlier statement of the tasks for a generative grammar, saying that it should assign one or more STRUCTURAL DESCRIPTIONS to each well-formed sentence in the language, where a structural description consists of a combination of a semantic and a phonetic representation, together with various intermediate levels of representation. This book will be concerned primarily with the form and justification of a subset of these intermediate representations, and secondarily with the nature of their relationship to the 'outer' levels of semantics and phonology.

1.3 The concept of a well-formed sentence

Given the central role played by this concept in our statement of the tasks for a generative grammar, it will be worth attempting some clarification of it at this stage. In view of what has been said of the distinction between competence and performance, it is not necessary to labour the point that well-formedness cannot be defined in terms of occurrence in some actual 'corpus', *ie* collection of utterances. Lots of sentences that are used are deviant, like [7], and conversely many well-formed sentences will never be found used in any corpus because of their excessive length or complexity. Nor, for the same reasons, can we define the concept in terms of potentiality of occurrence.

A second point is that in classifying a sentence as well-formed or deviant the linguist is not passing any value judgment on it. The grammar will be formulated as a set of rules, but these are not to be construed as rules for good speaking (or writing): they are simply descriptive statements about the structure of the language. There are two cases where confusion may arise over this issue. One involves sentences of 'non-standard' dialects, such as *Me and him are going together*, *I ain't got none* and so on. Well-formedness is a relative concept, not an absolute one. It is trivially obvious that a sentence like *Je ne l'ai pas vu* is well-formed in (*ie* relative to) French, but not in English, but the same point holds less trivially for dialects: *Me and him are going together* is well-formed in some dialects of English but not in the standard dialect. Well-formed and deviant should not therefore be equated with the schoolteacher's 'correct' and 'incorrect', which are relative just to the standard dialect. *I haven't any* and *I ain't got none* are both well-formed, but relative to different dialects; from a linguistic point of view there is no question of one of them being 'better' than the other: the greater prestige attaching to the first is not due to any intrinsic linguistic merits but to the fact that it is the form belonging to the dialect used by the socially and educationally privileged.

A second case where the linguist is sometimes mistakenly thought to be making value judgments involves phenomena like metaphor, as in

[13] *Macbeth does murder sleep*

In classifying this as deviant, we are not making any judgment about its literary effectiveness: the tasks of the generative grammarian and the literary critic are quite distinct. Notice, incidentally, that examples like [13] show that deviant sentences are not used only through accidental error (as in [7], presumably): in linguistic performance, as in other forms of social behaviour, rules may be deliberately violated.

Examples of this kind bring us to my third point: the relation between well-formedness and meaningfulness. Here we must begin by distinguishing between literal and non-literal meaning. [13] is meaningless under a literal interpretation of *murder* and *sleep*: the sentence is obviously quite different in status from, say, *Macbeth does murder his enemies*, and we account for this difference by saying that [13] violates the rule that the object of *murder* be human. The same general principle applies to the following examples of Chomsky's, often cited in discussions of well-formedness:

[14] *Golf plays John*
[15] *Colourless green ideas sleep furiously*

Again we will establish rules governing the combination of verbs with different types of subjects and objects, and of nouns with classes of adjectival modifier, rules that are followed in perfectly normal sentences like *John plays golf* and *Revolutionary new ideas appear infrequently* – rules that capture the speaker-hearer's tacit knowledge of the difference in status between these sentences and those like [14] and [15] where the rules are violated. Violation of such rules does not necessarily make a sentence uninterpretable; with [13] the context makes it fairly easy to find an interpretation, but it is also possible to devise plausible interpretations for [14] and [15]. The former, for instance, might be said by John's disgruntled wife, aggrieved at what she regards as his obsession with golf: it is as though he is addicted to it in such a way that his behaviour appears to be controlled by the obsession. But the crucial point is that to interpret sentences like [13–15] requires a creative, innovative effort of the imagination such as is not needed with well-formed sentences, where the interpretation follows from quite general rules for combining the literal meanings of the component words according to the grammatical structure uniting them. A meaningless sentence will be deviant but not all deviant sentences will be uninterpretable.

This is further evident from examples like:

[16] *John breaked the window
[17] *John tends losing his temper
[18] *Which film were you annoyed because you had missed?

These are indisputably deviant, but there is no difficulty in finding an interpretation for them – and here it can be derived simply from the literal meanings of the components of the sentence. It follows that even if we exclude metaphorical and other non-literal meanings, deviance cannot be defined in terms of any logically prior notion of meaningfulness.

We noted in 1.2 that a grammar will provide an analysis of sentences at a series of linguistic levels: semantic, syntactic and phonological. To qualify as well-formed, a sentence must not violate any of the rules involving the combination of the different types of units at the various levels. We can distinguish different kinds of rule depending on such things as the type of unit they involve, and we can then differentiate among deviant sentences according to the kind of rule or rules they violate. Examples [13–15] violate what are known as SELECTIONAL RESTRICTIONS, which we may roughly and provisionally characterize as restrictions on the permitted combination of words in such grammatical relations as subject-verb, verb-object, etc – *golf* cannot combine with *play* in the subject-verb relation and so on (*cf* Chapters 4, 10, 16 for further discussion). [16–18] violate different kinds of rule: [16] the rule specifying that the past tense of *break* is *broke*, [17] the rule specifying that *tend* (in contrast to *keep*, for example) takes a following infinitive not a gerund (thus *to lose*, not *losing*), [18] the rule determining what elements can be questioned in an interrogative sentence. Or a sentence used by a speaker with a foreign accent might violate a number of phonological rules while observing all the syntactic and semantic rules. Thus in addition to directly providing a structural description for each well-formed sentence in the language, a generative grammar will also indirectly specify, in a large class of cases, the nature of the deviance of ill-formed sentences. (It is worth commenting briefly here on the terms 'grammatical' and 'ungrammatical'. These are sometimes used as equivalent to 'well-formed' and 'deviant' respectively, but for various historical reasons that we shall be considering later they are often used in a narrower sense, where violation of a semantic rule does not render a sentence ungrammatical. If, for example, we believe that selectional restrictions are semantic rather than syntactic, we could say that [13–15] are grammatical, in this second sense of the term. It is important to distinguish the substantive issue of whether the restrictions are semantic or syntactic from the purely terminological one of how we define the term 'grammatical'. In this book I have accordingly preferred to use the unequivocal terms 'well-formed' and 'deviant', qualifying them with 'semantically', 'syntactically' etc, where appropriate.)

The final distinction I want to mention is that between deviant sentences and well-formed ones that express factually absurd propositions. Examples like

[19] *The cross-eyed elephant slept in the hotel bed*
[20] *My cat saw the weakness in the traditional definition of 'noun'*

will be regarded as linguistically well-formed. People might well characterize them as absurd or nonsensical, but this does not have to be accounted for by linguistic theory. Generative grammar aims to describe the ideal speaker-hearer's knowledge of his language, not his knowledge of the world. The fact that elephants are not cross-eyed and do not normally sleep in hotel beds, that cats do not have the necessary conceptual powers to evaluate definitions of 'noun', is something we know about elephants and cats respectively, not about the WORDS *elephant* and *cat*. Unless we draw a distinction between knowledge of language and knowledge of the world there can clearly be no separate field of linguistics: to analyse the words *elephant* and *cat* we would need to call in the zoologist, and so on. We use language, of course, to talk about the world and consequently properties of things in the world are often relevant to the linguistic analysis of the words denoting them; we shall regard it as part of the meaning of *cat*, for example, that it denotes an animal – and as part of the meaning of *cheese*, say, that it denotes an inanimate object, so that *The cheese saw the weakness in the traditional definition of 'noun'* will not be regarded as linguistically well-formed. Just how to draw the distinction between knowledge of language and knowledge of the world is a matter for semantic theory, and hence beyond the scope of this book: here it is sufficient to say that such a distinction is assumed in all work on generative grammar, although there is a good deal of variation among different writers (especially in the matter of selectional restrictions) as to where they implicitly draw the boundary; I see no reason to expect the cut-off point to be sharply defined.

In his original discussion of the concept of well-formedness, or grammaticalness, as he at first called it, Chomsky defined a grammatical sentence as one that is 'acceptable to a native speaker' (1957:13). However, one should not expect that the acceptability judgments of a speaker will correspond directly to the theoretical concept of well-formedness: there is no reason to assume, for example, that he will spontaneously make the distinctions discussed above and base his judgment exclusively on what the linguist takes to be purely linguistic considerations – for example, well-formed sentences of great complexity or those expressing absurdities may be judged unacceptable whereas certain types of deviant sentences for which plausible interpretations can be found may be judged acceptable. Accordingly in later work Chomsky distinguishes the notions 'well-formed' and 'acceptable' as belonging to competence and performance respectively; ideally the speaker-hearer's judgments about the acceptability of utterances will reflect directly the well-formedness or deviance of the sentences uttered, but in the case of such judgments, as in the ordinary use of language, the actual relationship between performance and competence will be much less direct.

1.4 'Generative' grammar

A GENERATIVE grammar is one that is fully explicit. This means that the reader of the grammar is not required to use any knowledge of the language being described or any intelligent guesswork in determining what the grammar says about any given sentence – whether or not it is well-formed and, if so, what its analysis is at all levels: this information must be retrievable in a purely mechanical way. As Chomsky and Halle put it (1968:60):

> The rules of the grammar operate in a mechanical fashion; one may think of them as instructions that might be given to a mindless robot, incapable of exercising any judgment or imagination in their application. Any ambiguity or inexplicitness in the statement of the rules must in principle be eliminated, since the receiver of the instructions is assumed to be incapable of using intelligence to fill in gaps or to correct errors. To the extent that the rules do not meet this standard of explicitness and precision, they fail to express the linguistic facts.

It is evident that traditional grammars do not remotely approach complete explicitness. In particular, they rely heavily on the reader's ability to generalize, extrapolate from a few examples. Consider, for instance, the following passage from Jespersen (1909–49), undoubtedly one of the best of the large comprehensive grammars:

> There are two kinds of questions: 'Did he say that?' is an example of the first kind, and 'What did he say?' and 'Who said that?' are examples of the other. [. . .]
>
> In questions of the second kind we have an unknown quantity x, exactly as in an algebraic equation; we may therefore use the term x-QUESTIONS. The linguistic expression for this x is an interrogative pronoun or pronominal adverb. The pronouns are seen in these examples: Who said that? | Which of the boys said that? | Which boy do you mean? | Which do you like best, tea or coffee? | Which way shall we turn? [ie to the right or to the left?] | What did he say? | What woman was bold enough to say that? | Whose child is he? | [. . .] (Part V, pp 480–1)
>
> The interrogative adverbs call for few remarks: when did it happen? | where did it happen? | how did it happen? (p 493)

To a significant extent the reader is required to do his own analysis. If he has reasonable intelligence and some knowledge of the language, he will doubtless be able to classify in the intended way other questions like *Have you finished?*, *With whom were you talking?*, etc, but in so doing he has to make extensive use of his intelligence and knowledge. Given that it is the speaker-hearer's knowledge of his language that we are aiming to describe, however, it makes sense to say that it should not be necessary to draw on that knowledge in interpreting the description. Intelligence and knowledge are obviously required in WRITING the grammar, but we want to write it in such a way that there is no doubt about what it says. How this can be achieved will become clear when we embark on the formalization of grammatical rules in Chapter 3.

Explicitness is a matter of goals, and it is hardly to the point to criticize traditional grammarians for failing to meet a goal they did not set themselves. Nevertheless, there are significant advantages to be gained from adopting a generative approach. First there are what may be called 'descriptive' gains. Writing a grammar necessarily involves a great deal of trial and error: on the basis of a sample of data we formulate a hypothesis and then test the predictions following from the hypothesis against further data, modifying or rejecting it in the case of conflict. The more explicit the hypothesis, the easier it is to check and thus to detect errors whose recognition can lead to the formulation of an improved hypothesis. There is no doubt that attempts over the last fifteen years and more to write generative grammars covering various selected areas of English, say, have added greatly to our (non-tacit) knowledge of the language. Secondly there are 'theoretical' gains. The theoretical concepts that the linguist makes use of in his description, whether traditional ones like noun, clause, word, interrogative, inflection, auxiliary verb and so on, or new ones, can only be explicated by reference to the role they play in grammatical description: they cannot be defined independently (see Chapter 2 for exemplification of this point); it follows that the more explicit our grammars are, the more precise will be our explication of these concepts and the greater will be our understanding of the way language works.

1.5 The evaluation of grammars and the nature of linguistic data

The final question I wish to consider in this introductory chapter is what kind of criteria we can use to determine how successful a proposed grammar is. These criteria are of two basic kinds, according as they relate to the EXTERNAL ADEQUACY of the grammar, ie its correspondence with the data (which are 'external' to the grammar itself), or to its INTERNAL ADEQUACY, its simplicity. I shall take these in turn.

Let us begin as usual with some very simple cases.

[21] i *Yesterday I musted go to town   ii Yesterday I had to go to town
[22] i The cat chased the mouse   ii The mouse chased the cat

Suppose someone wrote a grammar in which [21i] was classified as well-formed or [ii] as deviant, or in which [22i] and [ii] were analysed as paraphrases. We would have no hesitation in dismissing the grammar as wrong: it conflicts with the data and thus fails to meet the condition of external adequacy. This then raises the question of what kinds of data we can test the grammar against. Firstly, there are the data provided by the ordinary use of language – actual utterances, the situations in which they take place and the responses, linguistic or non-linguistic, that they evoke. Secondly, there are native speakers' judgments about their language. These may be about such questions as the following: Is [21i] an acceptable utterance? Are a given pair of utterances utterances of the same sentence or of different sentences? Can *he* and *John* be coreferential in *He was ill but John didn't know it?* Is *John thinks she is taller than she is* ambiguous between an interpretation 'the height John thinks she has is greater than the height she actually has' and one where John is said to have the contradictory thought 'she is taller than she is' (leaving aside interpretations where the two occurrences of *she* are non-coreferential)? Could I without self-contradiction assert *John expected to intimidate Bill* and deny *Bill expected to be intimidated by John* or assert *John wanted Bill to brief Guy* and deny *John wanted Guy to be briefed by Bill* (*cf* Chapter 8)? If I ask *When did your mother arrive?*, am I seeking to elicit information as to whether you have a mother, and if so whether she has arrived, or simply information about the time of her arrival (*cf* Chapter 9)? And so on.

Most of the literature in transformational grammar relies exclusively on the writer's own judgments – it is comparatively rare for a writer to invoke actually attested examples or to back up his own judgments with properly documented reports of judgments elicited from a sample of native speaker informants. This differs from the practice and theory of many scholars working outside this field. The large 'classical' grammars of English by Curme, Jespersen, Kruisinga, Poutsma and others were based on massive collections of examples taken from readily available books and periodicals, and more recently – in what is often referred to as 'structural linguistics' – it was argued that reliance on native speaker judgments was incompatible with a properly scientific approach to linguistic analysis; a clear statement of this position can be found in Allen (1957:18):

> It is true that the linguist's gospel comprises every word that proceeds from his informant's mouth which cannot by definition, be wrong: but it is no less true that, as a matter of principle, whatever the informant volunteers ABOUT his language (as opposed to IN it) must be assumed to be wrong – he is not after all a linguist (or if he is he will quite probably be a useless informant!)

The two principal reasons for rejecting such a restrictive view of the linguist's data are as follows. Firstly, since a generative grammar aims to be completely explicit, we cannot be satisfied with simply citing a handful of attested examples of a given construction, leaving it to the reader to generalize from these. An explicit grammar will enumerate EVERY well-formed sentence; this means that we must go beyond those actually attested in the data provided by ordinary use of language: excluding judgments from our data leaves us without empirical checks on the validity of our extrapolations from the attested examples. Secondly, practically nothing of interest can be said about meanings if we restrict our data in this way. If we discount native speaker judgments we shall have to rely on observable features of the situation in which utterances take place. And indeed the approach to meaning of some of the leading American structural linguists was along these lines: one finds the meaning of a linguistic form, be it word, phrase or whatever, defined as the feature common to all the

situations in which it is used. Yet the assumption behind such a definition –
that there is, in fact, an observable common feature to all the situations in
which a given word is used (beyond what is common to situations in which
any word is used) – has never been justified, and seems quite patently mistaken.
It could not even be shown to hold for relatively simple cases of 'concrete'
nouns like *dog*, *table*, *grass*, let alone more difficult words like *true*, *since*, *never*.
I observed earlier that the use of language is characterized by a remarkably
large degree of freedom from situational constraint (this is an important
difference between human language and many animal communication systems).
We can talk about dogs or whatnot when none are present. We are not constrained to talk about things in the immediate spatio-temporal situation of
utterance: we can speak of the past and the future, of what is far away, of things
like centaurs and unicorns which have no existence in the real world. Not
surprisingly the theory that the meaning of a form is the feature common to the
situations in which it is used led to no new insight in semantics, which tended
to be regarded by American structural linguists as falling outside the scope of
linguistics proper.

In defining a grammar as a description of the speaker-hearer's tacit knowledge
Chomsky makes clear the mentalistic character of the subject matter of generative grammar, and there is no reason to suppose that we shall be able to describe
this knowledge if we restrict our data to the observable physical properties of
ordinary utterances and of the situations in which they take place. This is not
to deny that there are dangers and serious problems in the heavy reliance on
data derived from introspection, for introspection of any kind is notoriously
prone to error (for this reason it is regrettable that so many writers apparently
rely exclusively on their own judgments). There are, moreover, lots of cases
where judgments are uncertain – as with [10], for example – and here there is
bound to remain some indeterminacy in evaluating a grammar according to its
match with the data. Nevertheless, it must be emphasized that there is a vast
amount of such data that is quite clear and beyond dispute, and we can certainly
proceed a long way in our investigation of the form of grammars while remaining within the limits of secure and uncontroversial judgments.

Let us turn now to the second condition that a successful grammar must meet,
that of internal adequacy. Here we are concerned with its simplicity, more
precisely with the question of whether it expresses the LINGUISTICALLY SIG-
NIFICANT GENERALIZATIONS about the language. We can approach this important notion via an obvious and elementary example based on the following
data:

[23] i *Tom is very old*   [24] i *Tom is older than Joe*
    ii *Tom is very tall*   ii *Tom is taller than Joe*
   iii *Tom is very smart*   iii *Tom is smarter than Joe*
   iv *Tom is very clever*   iv *Tom is cleverer than Joe*
[25] **Tom is very older*   [26] **Tom is old than Joe*

If we replace *old*, *tall*, *smart*, *clever* in [23] by *older*, *taller*, *smarter*, *cleverer* from

[24], or vice versa, we get deviant sentences like [25] and [26]. Any grammar meeting the condition of external adequacy must therefore distinguish between the words that can occupy the position after *very* in [23] and those that can occur before *than* in [24]. Suppose we have two grammars, G_1 and G_2, which both do this, so that they can correctly classify [23] and [24] as well-formed, [25] and [26] as deviant. G_1 just gives separate lists of members for the two classes: *old*, *tall*, *smart*, *clever*, . . ., for the first, *older*, *taller*, *smarter*, *cleverer*, . . ., for the second. G_2 on the other hand gives a list of members for the first class but not the second: it states instead that each member of the second class consists of a member of the first class with the suffix *-er* added. This statement expresses a significant generalization about the relationship between the two classes, a generalization which is not formulated in G_1, where the reader is left to find it for himself by comparing the two classes. We accordingly reject G_1 for failure to meet the condition of internal adequacy. (As given, the above rule from G_2 is in fact TOO general for external adequacy: whereas *Tom is very intelligent* is well-formed, **Tom is intelligenter than Joe* is deviant, and so on. We must distinguish between adjectives whose comparative is formed by adding *-er* and those which take a preceding *more;* but here too we must generalize – on the basis of the number of syllables and so on – instead of merely listing. There will still remain a few exceptions like *bad* versus *worse*, *good* versus *better;* but we shall not abandon the regular or general rules just because they have exceptions: we merely exclude the exceptions from their domain of applicability.) The notion of a linguistically significant generalization will be further exemplified and developed as we go on. We shall see that it plays a central role in the justification of the theoretical concepts introduced: the apparatus we make use of in constructing a generative grammar must be such as to allow these generalizations to be explicitly expressed.

Evaluating grammars is a negative process in the sense that we reject a grammar if it conflicts with the data or misses a generalization expressed in a competing grammar that is equivalent in respect of external adequacy: we can show a grammar to be wrong, but we cannot show it to be ultimately or absolutely right. A grammar is like a theory in this respect: theories can be falsified but not proved correct, for we can never be sure that further evidence will not be found requiring the modification of a theory which has so far withstood efforts to disprove it. Moreover we must bear in mind that generative grammar is in its infancy, even though it can draw on a long tradition of linguistic description; the vast complexity of natural languages is such that we can at present hope to achieve external adequacy on only a very limited scale: a 'complete' grammar is not a realistic goal. Instead of trying to achieve external adequacy on the maximum possible scale, generative grammarians have been concerned with increasing the internal adequacy of grammars accounting for a relatively small proportion of the data. This strategy – which it is particularly necessary to adopt in an introductory book like this – is better suited to increasing our understanding of the nature of language and is thus of much greater theoretical interest.

In American structural linguistics of the forties and fifties there was a wide-spread preoccupation with developing procedures of analysis which could be applied to a collection of data to give a grammar of the language. This preoccupation was understandable in view of the importance attached to describing the numerous hitherto unanalysed Amerindian languages, many of which were in danger of dying out. Presumably no one would deny the validity of giving trainee linguists instruction in 'field methods', guidance on how to go about analysing an unknown, unrecorded language; but Chomsky argued that this is not the kind of thing that general linguistic THEORY ought to be concerning itself with. There is no hope of developing mechanical DISCOVERY PROCEDURES such that a computer, say, could be programmed to apply them to a collection of data given as input, so as to yield as output the correct grammar of the language. If we cannot be sure that a certain grammar, however arrived at, is secure against modification in the light of new evidence, there is no hope of achieving the much more ambitious goal of specifying explicit procedures for arriving at an impregnable grammar. Other disciplines, even the physical sciences, do not set themselves such goals, and it would be quite unrealistic to adopt them in linguistics. The central questions for linguistic theory, Chomsky claimed, are thus not 'How can we discover the correct grammar for any given language?' but rather 'What general form should a grammar take if it is to match the data adequately and express significant generalizations about the structure of the language?' and 'What precise and rigorous criteria can we use for determining the better of two rival grammars that are equivalent in respect of external adequacy?'. These, then, are the questions we shall be investigating in the following chapters.

But first I should add a brief historical note. The theory of transformational grammar has undergone significant modifications since it was first put forward in the late fifties. Four main versions may be distinguished: the first two I shall refer to as the *Syntactic Structures* and *Aspects* (*of the Theory of Syntax*) versions – after the major works in which they are expounded – while the remaining two are known as the 'Extended Standard Theory' and 'Generative Semantics'. These last two include rival proposals as to how the *Aspects* theory should be modified, with some scholars, including Chomsky himself, advocating the former, others, notably Lakoff, McCawley, Postal, Ross, the latter. The development may thus be shown schematically as follows:

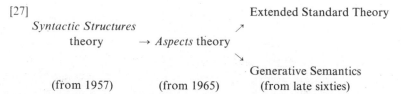

[27]   Extended Standard Theory
   Syntactic Structures   ↗
      theory   → *Aspects* theory
                                ↘
                                Generative Semantics
   (from 1957)   (from 1965)   (from late sixties)

To a large extent the modifications have involved adding new apparatus to the theory to make it able to handle a progressively wider range of phenomena. For this reason I have in the following chapters adopted a largely chronological form of exposition: Chapters 2–5 present and exemplify the major features of the *Syntactic Structures* theory; Chapters 6–13 are based primarily on *Aspects* and work elaborating that theory and applying it in the description of various areas of English; Chapters 14–16 deal mainly with post-*Aspects* work, with the last discussing briefly some of the differences between the Extended Standard Theory and Generative Semantics. Much of what has been said in this introductory chapter holds for all versions; the main exception is that in the early work the study of meaning was held to fall outside the scope of generative grammar and the mentalistic concept of linguistic competence had not been developed – in *Syntactic Structures* the use of language is contrasted not with knowledge of language but simply with linguistic 'form'.

Notes

On competence and performance see Chomsky 1965:3–15, Fodor and Garrett 1966. Campbell and Wales 1970 distinguish between 'grammatical' competence (competence in Chomsky's sense) and 'communicative' competence, which is more comprehensive, covering also the relation of 'appropriateness' between a sentence and the situation or context in which it is used: they make the point that a speaker's tacit knowledge of his language includes knowing what classes of context a sentence is appropriate to. To adapt an example from Katz 1972:8, *rabbit* and *bunny* would be alike (save for their phonological properties) in a description of grammatical competence but not in one of communicative competence. On the role of context in the interpretation of utterances, see Chomsky 1966a:29. A strong criticism of Chomsky's notion of competence is to be found in Derwing 1973, Chapter 8.

On well-formedness and grammaticalness, see Chomsky 1957:13–17, 1961b:227–39, 1965:148–53, Bazell 1964, Katz 1964, G. Lakoff 1969, Haas 1973a, Householder 1973. On the evaluation of grammars, see Chomsky 1957:49–60, 1961b:219–227, 1965:18–47. On problems stemming from the use of introspective data, see Quirk and Svartvik 1966, Bolinger 1968, Greenbaum and Quirk 1970, Bever 1970, Labov 1971 (which also deals with the question of idealization), Derwing 1973. The idea that the meaning of a form can be identified with the features common to the situations in which it is uttered can be found in Harris 1951:34.

Chapter 2

Syntax in Relation to Semantics and Phonology

My primary concern in this book will be with the syntactic component of a grammar rather than with the grammar in its entirety. The purpose of the present chapter is therefore to establish the distinctness of syntax from the 'outer' components of semantics and phonology. Again it is not possible to give in advance a precise delimitation of the domain of syntax, but the discussion will give a preliminary idea of the nature of syntactic concepts, which can then be developed and modified as we attempt, from Chapter 3 onwards, to construct a generative model of syntax.

2.1 Syntax and semantics

In his early work, as I have observed, Chomsky took a somewhat narrower view of the scope of generative grammar than that outlined in Chapter 1: most importantly, he excluded the study of meaning. He contrasted meaning with 'form', and emphasized the lack of any simple correlation between them, arguing from this that form should be studied independently of meaning. In *Syntactic Structures* Chomsky drew a distinction, within the general theory of language, between the theory of linguistic form and the theory of the use of language; the complex correlations between form and meaning were held to fall within the province of the theory of language use, while generative grammar was intended purely as a theory of linguistic form. The aim at this early stage, accordingly, was to generate the well-formed, or grammatical, sentences of a language and to describe the syntactic and phonological structure of each. As we noted in 1.3, well-formedness is clearly not a semantic notion.

In this section I want to illustrate the independence of syntax from semantics by demonstrating the non-semantic nature of a number of important concepts we shall make use of in our description of English syntax. The first two, 'noun' and 'subject' are taken over from traditional grammar, although the account given of these concepts in many traditional grammars is deficient precisely because it fails to give proper recognition to the complexity of the relations between syntax and semantics.

A noun is commonly defined as 'the name of a person, place or thing'. This is an attempt to define the syntactic concept of noun in terms of meaning, but it is easy to see that it does not provide satisfactory criteria for determining whether a given word is a noun or not, in the sense in which 'noun' is in fact used in both traditional and modern grammars. If 'thing' in the definition is interpreted as 'physical object' (a concept which presumably does have a place in semantic theory) the definition is clearly inadequate since many words invariably classified as nouns – *arrival, insanity, strife*, and so on – do not denote physical objects. And if 'thing' is interpreted more widely such that the above are no longer counterexamples, then the definition is circular and vacuous, because there is no independent way of determining what a 'thing' is: knowing whether a word denotes a thing in the sense intended in the definition presupposes a knowledge of whether or not it is a noun. The notion of 'thing' here is much more in need of explication than the concept being defined. (We might also add that the notion of 'name' is likewise in need of clarification.)

There is no semantic property common to all nouns and no non-nouns: noun is not a semantic category. To explain what a noun is, we must introduce the important concept of DISTRIBUTION. Essentially, the distribution of a linguistic element is the set of positions it can occupy in well-formed sentences. A standard technique for investigating distribution is to make substitutions in various positions in a sentence: for example, we might take a sentence like *My bicycle surprised the visitor* and consider what expressions could be substituted for, say, *my* without yielding a deviant sentence: *your, the, a, some*, etc, but not *hilariously, ought*, etc. Then it is an aspect of the distribution of *your* that it can occupy this particular position, and negatively it is an aspect of the distribution of *hilariously* that it cannot, and so on. Now the motivation for establishing a syntactic category noun (and the same holds for verb, adjective, etc) is that it enables us to bring generality into our distributional statements. Instead of separately listing all the words that can fill the position after *my*, all those that can follow *your*, those that follow *the*, and so on, we establish a construction consisting of a determiner followed by a noun, where *my, your, the*, etc belong to the category determiner, *bicycle, house, arrival, insanity*, etc to the category noun. 'Noun' is accordingly the term applied to a set of words alike in their distributional properties. Distributional likeness is not of course an all-or-nothing matter: *boy* and *truth*, for example, are partly alike in distribution, partly different, so that while both can fill the blank position in '*She's frightened of the* __', only *boy* can fill that in '*They ignored the* __ *who came to dinner*', and so on. But we shall handle this phenomenon by establishing subcategories: *boy* and *truth* will both belong to the general category noun, whereas only *boy* will belong to the subcategory human noun.

This distributional conception of noun, verb, and the like means that it is impossible to define them independently of their role in the grammar. A noun is the category that can combine with a preceding determiner to form a noun phrase (as in *my bicycle, the visitor*), a noun phrase is the category that can combine with a preceding verb to form a verb phrase (as in *surprised the visitor*) or with a following verb phrase to form a sentence (*My bicycle surprised the visitor*), and so on – these statements are of course merely illustrative, not

exhaustive. We cannot give a definition of the form 'A noun is . . .' where the
'. . .' contains no other syntactic terms; noun is a theoretical concept and is not
definable independently of the theory. This may appear circular, but it must be
remembered that we have an abundance of data against which to check our
grammar empirically and this provides in effect a way of breaking out of the
circle: if we classified *annihilate* as a noun we would be claiming that sentences
like *They regret the annihilate* are well-formed, a claim that is clearly falsified
by the data of native speaker acceptability judgments.

Let us turn now to the second example of the lack of direct correspondence
between syntactic and semantic concepts, the example of 'subject'. This is a
somewhat different kind of concept from noun, noun phrase and the like.
Whereas these latter are CATEGORIES, subject is a syntactic FUNCTION or
RELATION. In our example *My bicycle surprised the visitor*, we categorize both
my bicycle and *the visitor* as noun phrases because of their common distributional properties, but they have different functions in the sentence: *my bicycle*
stands in the relation of subject to the whole sentence, *the visitor* in the relation
of object. As with noun, we cannot define subject independently of other
theoretical terms; instead of attempting to define it at this stage, therefore, I
shall simply review, briefly and informally, three places in the syntax where
reference must clearly be made to the concept subject. These are: the order of
elements in declarative and interrogative sentences; the person and number in
the verb; the distinction between nominative and accusative case in pronouns.

(a) There is undoubtedly a systematic relationship between pairs of sentences
like

[1] i *John can swim*   [2] i *Can John swim?*
   ii *John likes Bach*   ii *Does John like Bach?*

such that we will regard the sentences in [2] as the interrogative counterparts of
the declaratives in [1]. One major difference (though not the only one) between
the two types of sentence lies in the linear order of the elements: there is an
element – call it 'X' – which in the interrogative occurs immediately after the
(first) auxiliary verb but in the declarative precedes the verb. Thus the concept
X must surely play a role in the statement of the syntactic relationship between
declaratives and interrogatives. 'Subject' is then simply the name regularly used
instead of 'X'.

(b) Consider next the following data:

[3] i *My brother likes music*   [4] i **My brother like music*
   ii *My brothers like music*   ii **My brothers likes music*

The choice between *likes* and *like* depends on whether a certain element in the
sentence – call it 'Y' – is singular or plural. In [3i], Y is *my brother*, in [ii] *my
brothers;* note that if we replace singular *music* by plural *sonatas* the change
has no effect on the choice between *likes* and *like*. 'Subject' is then again the

term commonly used instead of 'Y'. The verb is said to agree with the subject, so that both *my brother* and *likes* are classified as singular, *my brothers* and *like* as plural. (The agreement in fact involves person as well as number – *likes* occurs only with a third person subject, not with first person *I* or second person *you*.)

(c) Similarly, syntactic function is relevant to the choice between *I* and *me*, *he* and *him*, etc. In straightforward examples like *I saw him* and *He saw me* we have the so-called nominative case forms *I* and *he* in subject function, the accusative case *him* and *me* in object function. In sentences containing *be* as main verb the nominative pronouns are sometimes found in positions other than that of subject, as in *It is I*, etc, where *it* is subject by criteria (a) and (b): witness *Is it I?*, **It am I*. But obviously this shows only that there is no one-to-one relation between subject and nominative: it does not invalidate the general point that subject function is one of the determining factors in the choice of case.

Let us turn now to the relation between this syntactic concept and meaning. Traditional semantic characterizations of subject are of two main kinds: those that identify the subject with the 'actor'; and those that invoke the notion of 'topic'. It is easy to show, however, that neither approach provides an adequate definition of the intended syntactic concept.

There is undoubtedly a large set of sentences where the referent of the subject expression can reasonably be said to be the actor, the 'doer of the action'. In *John ate the apple, John murdered Bill, John ran up the hill*, for example, we can agree that John has the role of actor. But there are also innumerable sentences that do not express any action at all, so that the notion of actor is simply not applicable to them: *The bicycle belongs to John, That book looks like mine, He has brown hair*, and so on. Nevertheless such sentences certainly contain subjects: *the bicycle, that book, he*. A second difficulty arises with so-called 'passive' sentences like *The apple was eaten by John*. Here there is action, and it is performed by John, precisely as in the 'active' counterpart *John ate the apple*. But in the passive sentence it is *the apple*, not *John*, that is subject in the sense in which we used this term in discussing points (a–c) above, witness *Was the apple eaten by John?*, and so on. (In the light of examples like these, some traditional grammars make a distinction between 'grammatical' subject and 'logical' subject, such that in *The apple was eaten by John, the apple* would be grammatical subject, *John* logical subject. I shall have more to say about this distinction in Chapter 4 and 15.2; here it is sufficient to observe that the notion actor correlates more closely with logical than with grammatical subject, but it cannot serve as a definition even of the former because of the many sentences like those above where no action at all is expressed.)

The subject can likewise not be identified with the topic of the sentence, in the sense of 'what the sentence is about'. A pair of examples where a difference in subject does seem to correlate with a difference in topic is [5]:

[5] i *This violin is easy to play sonatas on*
   ii *Sonatas are easy to play on this violin*

It has been claimed that the main difference between these is that while [i] asserts something about a certain violin, [ii] is about sonatas. If this is correct, it would give some support to the identification of subject with topic, for *this violin* is subject of [i], *sonatas* of [ii]: note that *is* agrees with singular *this violin*, *are* with plural *sonatas*, that the interrogatives are *Is this violin . . .?*, *Are sonatas . . .?*. But again, counterexamples are plentiful. *Nothing satisfies Mary* is surely not saying something about 'nothing', namely that it satisfies Mary: the sentence is likely to be interpreted as being about Mary. Similarly *I can see your petticoat* would typically be used to say something about the addressee's petticoat (that it is showing) rather than to make an autobiographical statement, yet *I* is the subject, not *your petticoat*. And it would be difficult to make sense of the claim that *Who said that?* and *Close tabs were kept on all the radical students* were about 'who' and 'close tabs'. The latter is not even a coherent semantic concept. *Tabs* is part of the idiom *keep tabs on*, so that it does not have an independent meaning and could thus not qualify as topic. The notion of topic is in fact an extremely elusive one because of the difficulty of obtaining reliable data about what the topics of particular sentences are: informants tend to differ very much in their judgments, and it seems likely that the topic may vary according to the context of the sentence in the larger discourse. Moreover it is questionable whether a sentence should be said to have always just one topic: is it not plausible to say that *In the USA, presidential elections are held every four years* is about both the USA and presidential elections, or *John shot Mary* about both John and Mary? It is in any case clear from the examples cited that the subject cannot be satisfactorily defined as the topic of the sentence.

Further examples of the highly indirect relation between syntactic and semantic concepts will arise in the course of the following chapters, as in the discussion of tense and aspect (5.1) or mood (5.1 and Chapter 9). The moral to be drawn from them is that syntactic concepts must be defined by the role they play in the syntax, not in semantic terms. In a comprehensive study of language, part of the linguist's task will be to describe the relations between meanings and syntactic structures, but clearly he will not be able to do this satisfactorily unless he recognizes the distinct natures of the two kinds of concepts. Grammatical tradition has provided us with a large stock of syntactic terms, most of which are semantically suggestive; we shall continue to use many of these terms, but we must beware of allowing the labels to mislead us about the nature of the concepts in question.

To conclude this discussion of the independence of syntax from semantics I shall examine the concept of MORPHEME. This is the term applied to the smallest unit of syntax, the elements of which words are constituted. For example, *singers* is analysable into the three morphemes *sing*, *er* and *s*, *untie* contains the two morphemes *un* and *tie*, while words like *cat* and *dog* each consist of a single morpheme. Traditional grammars describe word structure in terms of such notions as root (*sing*, *tie*, etc), prefix (*un-*), suffix (*-er*, *-s*): the general term morpheme was introduced in modern structural linguistics, and much attention was given to developing this concept, especially in the work of Bloomfield and his followers. Bloomfield himself defined it as a meaningful form 'which bears no partial phonetic-semantic resemblance to any other form' (1933:161). Different sentences may exhibit partial phonetic-semantic re-semblances, *ie* be partially alike in respect of both pronunciation and meaning. There is such partial likeness between, say, *The cat died* and *The dog died*. On the basis of these partial likenesses and partial differences we can correlate elements of meaning with segments of the phonetic representation. We thus regard the total meaning of *The cat died* as deriving in some systematic way from the meanings of *the*, *cat* and *died* – we are prepared to attribute a meaning not just to the sentence as a whole, but also to smaller units of which it is com-posed. With *died* we can continue the analysis one step further while remaining within the realm of meaningful units: *died* bears a partial phonetic-semantic resemblance to *die*, *dies*, *dying* on the one hand, and to *smile*, *snored*, etc on the other, so that *died* can be divided into the meaningful units *die* and *d*. *Die* itself can be segmented into still smaller phonetic units, but these do not independently carry meaning, and the same holds for *cat* and *the*: accordingly there are just four morphemes in the example sentence, *the*, *cat*, *die* and *d*.

We should note in passing that there is a tacit assumption here that we pay attention only to 'significant' as opposed to 'fortuitous' resemblances. Consider, for example, the forms *cat* and *rat*. The phonetic resemblance between them is obvious, but surely they are also partially alike semantically (the common component of animateness makes them closer in meaning to each other than either is to, say, *truth*); nevertheless all linguists will agree that the phonetic-semantic resemblance here is not morphemically significant: we shall not seg-ment *rat* into 'morphemes' *r* and *at*. Countless other examples of fortuitous partial resemblances could be adduced: *dog* and *frog*, *nephew* and *niece* and so on. It follows that Bloomfield's 'definition' does not in itself provide explicit criteria for determining whether an element is a morpheme or not. Which resemblances we regard as significant and which as fortuitous will depend on the role we want the morpheme to play in the total grammar.

According to Bloomfield, then, the morpheme is the smallest meaningful unit. This can be accepted in the great majority of cases – but not in all. For there are examples of elements whose status as morphemes is not disputed even though they cannot validly be said to have any independent meaning. One standard example is the infinitival marker *to*, as in *I have to depart now*; another is the auxiliary *do* of *They do not speak Greek*, etc. The occurrence of these elements is fully determined by the syntactic construction and they cannot therefore make an independent contribution to the meaning of the sentence. In the first example, *to* is required after *have* (in its 'obligation' sense) – contrast **I have depart now* or *I must depart now*, where *must*, unlike *have*, takes an infinitive without *to*. Notice that it would not do to take *have to* as a minimal syntactic unit, a single morpheme; one obvious argument against such an analysis is that the two parts are not always adjacent, witness *Have I to depart now?*. *Do* is likewise required in certain types of negative construction – compare

[6] i *They speak Greek*   [7] i *They do not speak Greek*
    ii *They will speak Greek*   ii *They will not speak Greek*

To negate [6i] we must add *do* as well as *not* (**They speak not Greek* being deviant), but [ii] is negated by *not* alone. The difference in meaning is the same in both pairs and hence *do*, which occurs in [7i] but not [ii], cannot have any meaning of its own. We conclude that *to* and *do* (as used in the above constructions) do not themselves express any separate component of meaning, and hence that they cannot be regarded as meaningful units. Yet their status is clearly different from that of the same sound sequences occurring as the boldface portions of, say, *afterwards* and *John is doodling* – and this is precisely why we want to treat them as units of syntax, in particular as morphemes. Then since the *to* of *I have to depart* and the *ter* of *afterwards* (which will normally be phonetically alike) cannot be distinguished as meaningful versus meaningless, we must provide another basis for the distinction.

We can do this by again invoking the notion of distribution. Consider the following data:

[8] i /bɪldɪt/   (*Build it*)   [9] i */bldt/   •
  ii /stɪkswɪlhɛlp/ (*Sticks will help*)   ii */ftɪkswɪlhɛlp/
  iii /bɪlwɪltɛltɪm/ (*Bill will tell Tim*) iii */bɪltɛltɪmwɪl/
  iv /brɪkswɪlhɛlp/ (*Bricks will help*) iv */blɪkswɪlhɛlp/

The obliques indicate that the symbols they enclose represent phonological units: /b/ represents a voiced bilabial stop, and so on; the standard orthographic versions of the sentences in [8] are as shown. The examples in [8] are well-formed, those in [9] clearly deviant: what kind of GENERAL statements can we make that will account for this difference between the two sets? We can exclude [9i] by a rule governing the distribution of consonants: no sentence may consist of, or even begin with, a sequence of four consonants. [9ii] is deviant because it violates general constraints on initial consonant clusters: in such a cluster with one of the voiceless stops /p/, /t/, and /k/ as the second element, the first consonant can only be /s/. In these two cases, and countless others like them, we can formulate general rules governing the distribution of phonological units on the basis of their inherent properties – properties like that of being a vowel or a consonant, voiced or voiceless, a stop or a fricative, and so on. But there is no rule of this kind that will account for the difference in well-formedness between [8iii] and [9iii]: the latter does not violate any phonological constraint on the way units may combine. What we must do here is establish *Bill*, *will*, *tell* and *Tim* as elements and formulate rules governing their distribution: these elements are of a different kind from /b/, /ɪ/, etc, for their distribution is not determined by their phonological properties. These new elements are units of syntax. Similarly [9iv] will be excluded as deviant simply because there is no syntactic unit *blick*; there is no phonological reason why there should not be, for this form does not violate any phonological constraint on the distribution of /b/, /l/, /ɪ/ or /k/ – the example shows, rather, that not every phonologically well-formed sequence of units constitutes a syntactic unit.

We can establish the need for two quite different types of linguistic unit, then, without invoking the notion of meaningfulness at all. Some constraints on well-formed sentences can be covered by general rules governing the distribution of units based on properties relating to the way they are pronounced or the way they sound, whereas other constraints can only be formulated in terms of a different type of unit whose distribution is not determined by such properties. In general these units of syntax will be meaningful, but not in all cases: meaningfulness is not a necessary condition for 'morphemehood'. This again illustrates the independence of syntax from semantics: the morpheme is a syntactic unit, not a semantic one, and is not definable in terms of the semantic notion 'meaningfulness'.

Let us now reconsider our earlier example in the light of this revised concept of the morpheme. We shall still analyse *died* as a sequence of two morphemes, but now the justification will be based on distributional criteria. Thus we can establish the following distributional 'proportionalities':

[10] *die* : *died* : : *expire* : *expired* : : *snore* : *snored* : : . . .
[11] *died* : *killed* : : *dying* : *killing* : : . . .

That is, the distributional difference between *die* and *died* is the same as that between *expire* and *expired*, and so on: for example, only the first member of each pair can fill the blank position in such structures as '*He will __ soon*', and only the second that in '*He __ last night*'. Similarly the distributional difference between *died* and *killed* matches that between *dying* and *killing*, witness the well-formedness of *They killed John* and *They are killing John* compared with the deviance of **They died John* and **They are dying John*. The justification for dividing *died* and *dying* into the morpheme sequences '*die + d*' and '*die + ing*' is that we can exclude both these deviant sentences with a single rule about the distribution of the morpheme *die* instead of having one rule for *died* and another for *dying*, as would be necessary if the two words were treated as distinct unstructured minimal units at the syntactic level. And isolating a recurrent morpheme *d* in *died*, *expired*, *snored* enables us to exclude **He will died/expired/snored soon* by a single rule governing the distribution of *d* instead of having separate rules for *died*, *expired* and *snored*.

Notice finally that it is distributional considerations, not meaning, that justify our positing internal syntactic structure within idioms, such as *kick the bucket*, in the sense of 'die'. In its idiomatic use, *kick*, *the* and *bucket* do not make independent contributions to the meaning (it is precisely for this reason that the expression is classified as an idiom) and are thus not individually meaningful, but they are nevertheless separate syntactic units. We need to treat *kick* as a verb in order to be able to account for such matters as the position of the past tense marker, as in *John kicked the bucket*, not **John kick the bucketed*.

2.2 Syntax and phonology

Having established, on distributional grounds, the need for two distinct types of linguistic unit, phonological and syntactic, let us now turn briefly to the relationship between them. On the basis of our initial examples in [8], it might be thought that the relationship is simply one of composition, that the morpheme *brick*, for example, is composed of the four phonological units, or PHONEMES, /b/, /r/, /ɪ/ and /k/ occurring in that order. Not all examples are so straightforward, however, and we shall consequently need to allow for a less direct relationship between morphemes and phonemes.

We noted above that the distributional difference between *die* and *died* is the same as that between *expire* and *expired*, and this provided the basis for extracting a common syntactic element *d* from *died* and *expired*. Now exactly the same distributional difference is to be found in such pairs as *laugh* and *laughed*, *start* and *started*. But if we segment the second member of each pair we find that there are phonological differences in the endings (though they happen not to be reflected in the orthography): in *died* we have /d/, in *laughed* /t/ and in *started* /ɪd/. How then shall we account for this difference? A crucial point to note is that the choice between the three endings is determined by phonological properties of the preceding unit. Thus /ɪd/ occurs when the preceding morpheme ends in one of the alveolar stops /t/, /d/: *waited, planted, landed, plodded*, etc, the ending /t/ occurs after a voiceless phoneme (other than a /t/): *jumped, kissed, sacked;* and the ending /d/ occurs after any voiced phoneme (other than another /d/): *rubbed, slammed, resigned, moved, cried*. For this reason we shall not want to regard the difference between the three endings as a matter of syntax: at the syntactic level we shall ignore the phonologically determined difference and analyse all the above forms as containing the same morpheme, which I shall henceforth represent as *Past*. It is in terms of this unit that we formulate general distributional rules accounting for the deviance of **He will died/laughed/started* and the well-formedness of *He died/ laughed/started last night*, and so on, instead of having separate rules for the three endings.

There is thus no reason to require that a morpheme have a constant phonemic shape: it is a more abstract unit than this. We shall then include within the grammar a set of MORPHOPHONEMIC rules, whose function is precisely to specify the phonemic form of morphemes. At the syntactic level, *died, laughed* and *started* will be represented as '*die + Past*', '*laugh + Past*', '*start + Past*', and the morphophonemic rules will relate these to the corresponding phonological representations.

Given this conception of the organization of a grammar, we shall also assign to the morphophonemic section the rules specifying the phonemic shape of irregular past tense forms like *sang, took, went*, etc. At the syntactic level we shall again represent these as '*sing + Past*', '*take + Past*', '*go + Past*': this is necessary if we are to handle constraints on the distribution of *sang, took, went* by the same general rules as apply to *died, laughed* and *started*. Obviously there is nothing new or controversial in the claim that all these forms have something in common: all grammars will analyse them as past tense forms. I have gone beyond this elementary observation in two respects. Firstly, I have suggested that the JUSTIFICATION for extracting a common element *Past* is that this enables us to formulate generalizations about the distribution of the forms: the shared distributional properties of *died, sang*, etc are accounted for in a single statement about the distribution of *Past*. Secondly, generalizing from the regular forms where this element corresponds to a discrete part of the phonological representation (the final voiced alveolar stop in *died*, etc) I have proposed that all the past tense forms be REPRESENTED syntactically as containing the morpheme *Past* in word-final position.

The syntactic description of a sentence will thus analyse it into a sequence of morphemes, and the morphophonemic section of the grammar will give rules that convert this to the appropriate phonological representation. The part of the latter that corresponds to a particular morpheme is said to be the phonological REALIZATION of that morpheme. Typically, as in our original example of *The cat died*, each morpheme will have a separate meaning and a separate phonological realization. But this will not always be the case: just as it is pointless to ask which part of the total meaning of *I have to depart* belongs to the morpheme *to*, so is it pointless to ask which part of the total phonological representation of *I took the bus* belongs to' *Past* (or *take*): the morphemes in the sequence '*take + Past*' are simply realized jointly rather than discretely. A more extreme example is the comparative form *worse*, as in *a worse film*. At the syntactic level we shall represent this as '*bad + er*', again for distributional reasons: the distributional difference between *bad* and *worse* matches that between *short* and *shorter*, etc, witness *a very short/*shorter film, a very bad/*worse film; a far shorter/*short film than usual, a far worse/*bad film than usual*, and so on. But it would be quite unrealistic to divide the phonological representation of *worse* into two parts, the first a realization of *bad*, the second of *er*. The important point, then, is that the morpheme is not identifiable in either semantic or phonological terms: it is a unit of syntax.

Its lack of phonological identifiability is further apparent in such past tense forms as *cut, hit, put*, which do not differ phonologically from the corresponding present tense forms (except in the third person singular, where we have *cuts, hits, puts* for the present). Thus *I put out the cat* is ambiguous, interpretable as referring to either past or present – compare *John put out the cat* versus *John puts out the cat*. We still represent the past tense forms as containing the morpheme *Past*, so that their ability to occur in the same set of positions as other past tense forms is accounted for by a single general rule governing the distribution of *Past*. The fact that '*put + Past*' is pronounced /put/ is of no more syntactic significance than the fact that '*take + Past*' is pronounced /tuk/: both will be handled by special morphophonemic rules. The inclusion within the grammar of morphophonemic rules specifying the same phonological realization for the past and present tenses of these verbs will then account, obviously, for the ambiguity of sentences like *I put out the cat* in contrast to the lack of this ambiguity in *I took out the cat*.

Plural number in nouns exhibits the same kind of variation in phonological realization as past tense in verbs. It will accordingly be handled in an analogous way: we set up a morpheme *Plural* (henceforth abbreviated *Plur*) and include in the morphophonemic component rules specifying how it is phonologically realized. With regular nouns like *foxes*, *cats*, *dogs*, there are three different endings, the choice between them being determined by the phonological properties of the preceding phoneme: /ɪz/ occurs after sibilants, as in *foxes*, *crazes*, *crashes*, *garages*, *watches*, *judges;* /s/ after voiceless non-sibilants, as in *cats*, *pups*, *socks*, *cliffs;* /z/ after voiced non-sibilants, as in *dogs*, *heads*, *prams*, *peas*, *clues*. In irregular nouns it may have no discrete realization, as in *men*, *mice*, *geese*, etc (*cf* the past tense forms *sang*, *took*, . . .), or it may have no effect at all on the pronunciation, as in *sheep: I caught the sheep* is ambiguous between plural and singular just as *I put out the cat* is between past and present.

In the morphemic representations that I shall be proposing, morphemes will be symbolized by their normal orthographic form, except for a few special cases like *Past* and *Plur;* morpheme boundaries will henceforth be indicated not by '+', as above, but simply by a space. We shall look further into the relations between syntax and phonology in Chapter 11, where we shall see that there is a more appropriate way of representing morphemes in a formal grammar, but the above informal convention will best suit our purposes in the meantime.

My aim in this chapter has been to argue for the independence or autonomy of syntax. Syntax is independent from semantics and phonology, in the sense that syntactic units, categories, functions are not identifiable in semantic or phonological terms. To argue thus is not to deny that there are significant relations between syntax and semantics or phonology, but to suggest that they are typically quite complex and indirect. In the *Syntactic Structures* theory, the relations between syntax and phonology are handled in the morphophonemic section of the grammar, while those between syntax and semantics are held to be a matter of the use of language and are thus not described in the grammar itself.

Notes

On the independence of syntax from semantics, see Chomsky 1957:92–105. Palmer 1971:34–40 gives further examples of the indirect relation between form and meaning. The distributional approach to grammatical description was developed long before the advent of generative grammar: it is characteristic of much work in modern structural linguistics, especially that of Bloomfield and his followers, Bloch, Harris, Hockett, etc (commonly known as neo-Bloomfieldians) in America. Harris 1951 is one of the most thoroughgoing applications of it – and it is worth noting that Chomsky was originally a student of Harris's. This approach is often contrasted with that of much traditional grammar as 'formal grammar' versus 'notional grammar' – see Lyons 1968:134–57.

On the morpheme, see Lyons 1968:180–94; also my Chapter 11 below. The expression 'duality of patterning' is widely used for the property of language whereby it is structured in terms of two distinct types of unit, phonological and syntactic (another term for it is 'double articulation'); it is clearly one of the most fundamental properties of human language (*cf* Hockett 1958:574–5). Comprehensive descriptions of past tense and plural formation in English can be found in Quirk *et al* 1972:104–21 and 172–87.

Chapter 3

Phrase Structure Grammars

We are now ready to embark on a more formal investigation of the syntactic component of a generative grammar – where a generative grammar, it will be recalled, is one which is fully explicit. To achieve this level of explicitness, we shall write the grammar in the form of rules that can be thought of as instructions for constructing the sentences of the language and associating each with its structural description. The question we shall consider, therefore, is what kind of rules we need for this purpose.

In *Syntactic Structures* Chomsky outlined three models of grammar incorporating different answers to this question; they are known as finite state grammar, phrase structure grammar and transformational grammar. The aim of the comparison was to demonstrate, by pointing out the shortcomings of the first two, the need for the more complex apparatus included in the third. It is not necessary for our purposes here to examine the finite state model, the most elementary but least adequate of the three; there are, however, a number of reasons why it will be worth our while considering the phrase structure model even though it is not the one Chomsky finally adopts. In the first place, the type of rule used therein is also included in the transformational model, which differs from it in allowing for a different and more complex type of rule in addition: discussing the phrase structure model first will therefore considerably facilitate our presentation of the transformational model in Chapter 4. Secondly, the phrase structure model also has a good deal of intrinsic interest inasmuch as it can be regarded, to a considerable extent, as a formalization of the approach to syntax adopted by American structural linguists in the forties and fifties, in particular by the so-called neo-Bloomfieldians.

We can best begin by taking a very simple example of a phrase structure grammar, such as is given in [1]:

[1] i   S → NP VP   vi Det → *the*
   ii   VP → V NP   vii NS → *cat*
  iii   NP → Det N   viii NS → *mouse*
  iv   N → NS *Plur*   ix VS → *catch*
   v   V → VS *Past*

This grammar consists of nine PHRASE STRUCTURE RULES. ('Phrase structure' will henceforth be abbreviated 'PS'.) Each rule is an instruction to 'rewrite' the symbol on the left of the arrow as the string of one or more symbols given on the right. The symbols used in the grammar are divided into two discrete sets (apart from the arrow): NON-TERMINAL symbols occur on the left of some rule or rules, TERMINAL ones do not. The terminal symbols represent morphemes, the non-terminal ones syntactic categories (with the following abbreviations: S = sentence, NP = noun phrase, VP = verb phrase, V = verb, Det = determiner, N = noun, NS = noun stem, VS = verb stem).

Such rules permit the construction of sentences in a purely mechanical way (thus by a 'mindless robot') in accordance with our goal of complete explicitness. The procedure is illustrated in [2], where the succession of 'strings' of symbols given in column A constitutes what is called a PS DERIVATION (column B is added simply to facilitate discussion).

	[2] Column A	Column B
i	#S#	
ii	#NP VP#	By rule [1i]
iii	#NP V NP#	,, [1ii]
iv	#Det N V NP#	,, [1iii]
v	#Det N V Det N#	,, [1iii]
vi	#Det NS *Plur* V Det N#	,, [1iv]
vii	#Det NS *Plur* V Det NS *Plur*#	,, [1iv]
viii	#Det NS *Plur* VS *Past* Det NS *Plur*#	,, [1v]
ix	#*the* NS *Plur* VS *Past* Det NS *Plur*#	,, [1vi]
x	#*the* NS *Plur* VS *Past* the NS *Plur*#	,, [1vi]
xi	#*the cat Plur* VS *Past the* NS *Plur*#	,, [1vii]
xii	#*the cat Plur* VS *Past the mouse Plur*#	,, [1viii]
xiii	#*the cat Plur catch Past the mouse Plur*#	,, [1ix]

# indicates sentence boundary. S is designated as the INITIAL SYMBOL of the grammar, reflecting the fact that we are concerned with devising a grammar to generate sentences. Thus all PS derivations generated by this grammar (and others we shall consider) have #S# as the first line. Each subsequent line in a derivation derives from the one preceding it by one application of a PS rule. Line [2ii] derives from [2i] by rewriting S as NP followed by VP according to rule [1i]; line [2iii] derives from [2ii] by rewriting VP as V NP by rule [1ii], the initial NP of [2ii] being simply copied down unchanged into line [iii]. And so on: in moving from one line to the next we replace just one symbol, and copy the remainder unchanged; in column B I have shown which rule has been applied to derive each line other than the first from the one preceding it. A derivation is complete, or terminated, when its last line contains no non-terminal symbols. The last line of the derivation can then be converted into the appropriate phonological representation by means of morphophonemic rules, specifying for example that the morpheme sequence '*mouse Plur*' is realized as /maɪs/, and so on. [2xiii] will be converted into the phonological representation corresponding to *The cats caught the mice* (see Chapter 11 for the form of these morphophonemic rules – here we shall be concerned solely with the syntactic

rules). The sentences that can be constructed by following the rules of a given grammar are said to be GENERATED by that grammar.

In addition to generating a set of sentences, such a grammar will automatically assign a structure to each. For example, the syntactic structure assigned to the sentence *The cats caught the mice* by grammar [1] may be represented as in diagram [3].

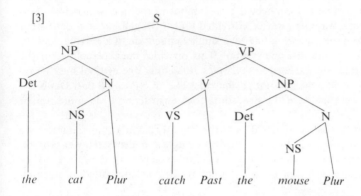

This kind of representation is known as a PHRASE-MARKER (henceforth 'PM'). It plays an important role in Chomsky's theory and is consequently worth examining in some detail; I shall quickly outline the mechanical procedure by means of which a PM can be obtained from a PS derivation and introduce some terminology for talking about the structure of PMs, and then turn to their interpretation and significance.

PM [3] can be formed from the derivation [2] in the following way. We begin by inspecting each pair of successive lines in the derivation, ignoring the boundary markers #. We ask whether the first symbol is the same in each line of the pair; if so we draw a line between them and compare the second symbols; if these are identical we join them up and move to the third symbol – and so on. Similarly, we compare the final symbols; if they are identical we join them up, and compare the penultimate ones, and so on. The results of applying this procedure to the first four lines in [2] is given in diagram [4], which can easily be extended to cover the remaining lines.

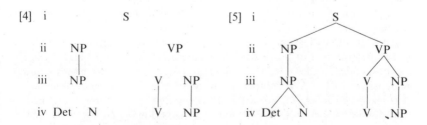

In each non-terminal line there will then be exactly one symbol that is not connected to an identical symbol in the line next below: in [4i] it is S, in [ii] VP, in [iii] the first NP, and so on. We then join this single symbol in each line$_i$ to all the symbols in line$_{i+1}$ which have not already been connected to a symbol in line$_i$. Thus the S in [4i] is joined to NP and VP in [ii], VP in [ii] to V and NP in [iii], etc. This gives diagram [5] above, again incomplete.

The procedure requires that at the stage illustrated in [4] there be only one symbol in each line not connected to a symbol in the line next below. This condition will always be satisfied provided that: (a) Each line in a derivation is derived from the preceding line by a single application of a PS rule; and (b) each PS rule rewrites just one symbol. This provides the explanation for the major constraint on the form of PS rules: that only one symbol may be rewritten per rule. We thus do not permit rules like 'V NP → VS Past Det N': if such a rule were included the procedure for constructing PMs could not be applied.

To convert [5], duly completed, into the PM [3] is then a simple matter: we delete any symbol that is directly joined to a single and identical lower symbol, and extend the lines in the obvious way. For example, we delete the NP of line [5ii] and extend the line from S to join up with the leftmost NP of line [iii], and so on.

It will be clear from the above informal outline that, given a set of PS rules of the form illustrated in [1], PMs can be generated by means of a fully explicit and mechanical procedure. I have broken it down into separate minimal steps, but the reader will have no difficulty in bypassing the intermediate stages [2], [4] and [5] and constructing PMs directly from the PS rules, for instance by interpreting rule [2i] as an instruction to join up S to a lower NP on the left and VP on the right, and so on. I shall comment further on this matter later; here it is worth observing, in explanation of Chomsky's adoption of the apparently more laborious procedure, that in his original research on the formalization of grammatical theory he drew on, and contributed to, various branches of mathematics – in particular, the notion of a rewrite rule, a rule for replacing one string of symbols by another in the construction of a derivation as exemplified above in the discussion of [2], is taken over from the mathematical theory of rewriting systems. (Indeed, the basic term 'generate' is itself taken from mathematics.) A considerable amount of his early work in generative grammar was devoted to a highly formal investigation of the properties and capacities of PS grammars interpreted as sets of rewrite rules; this work belongs, however, to the branch of linguistics known as mathematical linguistics and will not be discussed here.

A PM (or 'tree-diagram', as it is sometimes called) consists of a two-dimensional arrangement of labelled NODES connected by lines or branches. The topmost node (labelled S in [3]) is called the ROOT. For any two nodes A and B, A DOMINATES B if A lies on the shortest path joining B to the root node or if A is itself the root. In [3], for example, the node labelled *cat* is dominated by four nodes, labelled NS, N, NP and S; *Past* is dominated by V, VP and S;

and conversely the node labelled V dominates three nodes, VS, *catch* and *Past*.
More particularly, node A IMMEDIATELY DOMINATES B if there is no
intermediate node on the shortest path joining B to A. By analogy with
genealogical trees, B is said to be a DAUGHTER of A if A immediately dominates
B, and B and C are said to be SISTERS if they are both daughters of A. Again
using [3] as example, VS immediately dominates *catch*, the daughters of S are
NP and VP, V is sister to a node labelled NP, and so on. The nodes which do not
dominate any others are the TERMINAL NODES. They are ordered from left
to right and form the TERMINAL STRING of the PM; the terminal string of
[3] is thus *the cat Plur catch Past the mouse Plur*.

Consider now the interpretation and justification of this form of representing
syntactic structure. What kind of information does the PM give about the
sentence?

In the first place, the terminal string of the PM gives an analysis of the
sentence into a linear sequence of morphemes. I have already presented distributional arguments for assigning a morphemic structure to sentences as well
as a phonological structure and need not repeat them here. The phonemes in the
phonological representation will obviously be linearly ordered: this reflects
(subject to the qualifications mentioned on *p* 3) the temporal order in performance of an utterance of the sentence. The linear order of the morphemes then
determines that of the phonemes. But it must be remembered that the two levels
are related by morphophonemic rules, and in the interests of generality we
allow for certain sequences of morphemes to be realized non-discretely (*cf p* 32).
The position of *Plur* to the right of *cat* (which results from the PS rule 'N → NS
Plur') accounts automatically for the position of the phoneme /s/ relative to
/kæt/ in the phonemic representation, while the irregularity of *mice* is handled
by a special morphophonemic rule. The temporal sequence of speech provides
the ultimate explanation for the linear aspect of syntactic representations; the
latter, however, are abstractions, theoretical constructs, and there is no requirement that the linear order of morphemes should stand in a one-to-one relation
with the temporal order of corresponding sections of an utterance of the sentence. The linear aspect of the syntactic representation is nevertheless much
more directly related to properties of phonological structure than to the
meaning. The syntactic order may be semantically significant inasmuch as
differences in order may correlate with differences in meaning, as in *He can
swim* versus *Can he swim?;* but in describing the meanings of these sentences
we shall not regard them as different linear arrangements of the same set of
semantic elements: we shall differentiate them rather in terms of semantic
notions like 'statement' and 'question' (*cf* Chapter 9).

In addition to specifying the morphemes in a sentence together with their
linear order, the PM also represents the hierarchical structure of the sentence.
It is intuitively obvious that certain morphemes in the string belong together
more closely than others – that they combine to form units intermediate in size
between the morphemes and the sentence as a whole. The 'word' is one type
of unit of this kind: clearly *Past* belongs more closely with *catch* than with *the*,

and we can account for this by saying that *catch* and *Past* combine to form a single unit, or CONSTITUENT, as do *cat* and *Plur* or *mouse* and *Plur*. And the same point holds for words: the second *the* in our example belongs more closely with the sequence *mouse Plur* than with *catch Past*, so that we shall want to regard *the mouse Plur* but not *catch Past the*, as a constituent. The PM indicates explicitly what the constituents of the sentence are – namely, all the morphemes (these are the 'ultimate' constituents), and each sequence of morphemes that can be traced to a node in the tree. Thus in [3], *cat* and *cat Plur* are both constituents, but *the cat* and *Past the* are not. The constituents represented by the nodes immediately dominated by S, *ie: the cat Plur* and *catch Past the mouse Plur* are said to be the IMMEDIATE CONSTITUENTS (ICs) of the sentence, and similarly *the* and *cat Plur* are the ICs of *the cat Plur*, and so on.

The labels attached to the non-terminal nodes of the PM specify the syntactic category of the constituents. In [3], for example, *the* is assigned to the category Det, *cat* to NS, *cat Plur* to N, and so on. ('Noun' is used for a category of words, while 'noun stem' is applied to that part of a noun which remains when any inflectional endings have been removed; analogously for verb and verb stem.) This aspect of the representation expresses what is known as the IS A relation (not a very elegant term, but one widely used in the literature): *the* 'is a' determiner, *cat Plur* is a noun, and so on. It will be noted that in [3] *Plur*, unlike such morphemes as *the* and *cat*, is not assigned to any category: this is because it is distributionally so unlike any other morpheme that setting up a syntactic category here would not permit the expression of any significant generalization.

The IC and categorial aspect of the syntactic structure of a sentence is much less directly reflected in its pronunciation than is the linear aspect. This is evident from the existence of many ambiguities attributable to the fact that different structures are associated with the same sequence of morphemes. The example given on *p* 11, *Mary looked hard*, is one such: in one interpretation *hard* belongs to the category adjective, in another it is an adverb. An example involving differences of IC structure is *Jill attacked the man with a knife*. This has the interpretations 'Jill attacked the man who had a knife' and 'Jill used a knife in her attack on the man' (compare the passive counterparts *The man with a knife was attacked by Jill* and *The man was attacked by Jill with a knife*). In the syntactic structure corresponding to the first interpretation *the man with a knife* forms a single constituent (a NP), but in the second it does not – the VP *attacked the man with a knife* will here be analysed into three ICs, the verb *attacked*, the NP *the man* and the prepositional phrase *with a knife*. It does not follow, however, that there is no systematic relation at all between the pronunciation and the categorial constituent structure: on the contrary, the latter plays a crucial role in determining such phonological properties of the sentence as stress. We accordingly find examples where different syntactic structurings of a single sequence of morphemes are also phonologically distinct. For example the single written form *She told me about the new doctor's degree* has the two interpretations 'she told me about the new doctorate' and 'she told me about the degree of the new doctor', but in speech these would normally be differentiated, with the main stress falling on *doctor's* in the first interpretation, *degree* in the second. Syntactically, the structures differ in that in the first case *doctor's degree* forms a constituent, but in the second it does not, the ICs of *the new doctor's degree* being here *the new doctor's* and *degree;* (a full account of the two syntactic structures would be out of place at this point, but see Chapter 14 for further discussion of the possessive construction).

However, as I emphasized in Chapter 2, the correlation between syntactic structure and meaning or pronunciation is too complex for us to be able to appeal directly to semantic or phonological factors in justifying our syntactic analyses: the constituents and categories we set up will be justified by their role in enabling us to formulate generalizations about the way morphemes combine in well-formed sentences. Having the constituent category NP, for example, enables us to account by means of a single general rule for the deviance of *Cats the caught the mice* and *The cats caught mice the* in contrast with the well-formedness of *The cats caught the mice* – the one rule 'NP → Det N', putting the determiner before the noun, applies twice in derivation [2]. Notice that what we have to exclude is not the linear sequence 'N Det' (which is found for example in the structure of *He told people the truth*, where the noun *people* is followed by the determiner *the*) but the constituent structure in which N and Det occur in that order as ICs of a single constituent. It is likewise in the interests of generality that we shall allow for NPs consisting of a single word – a proper noun, say, or a pronoun, as in *John gave it to Bill*. In traditional grammar, the term 'phrase' is normally restricted to expressions containing more than one word, but within the present framework there are compelling reasons for treating *John, it, Bill*, etc, as NPs along with *my uncle, the money, the man who had defended him*, etc. We can see this by comparing two grammars, G_1 and G_2, where G_1 analyses *John, it, Bill*, etc as nouns only, while G_2 analyses them as both nouns and NPs. There are a number of positions in a sentence where there is a choice between expressions like *John* and those like *my uncle:* subject, direct object, object of a preposition, and so on. G_1 will have to say: (a) The subject may be either a NP or a N; (b) The direct object may be either a NP or a N; (c) The object of a preposition may be either a NP or a N; and so on. G_2 on the other hand will say that subject, direct object, object of a preposition, etc, are NPs and a NP may consist either of a N alone or of a N combining with other elements. In G_2 one either-or statement does the work of three in G_1. We accordingly reject G_1 for failing to meet the condition of internal adequacy (*cf* 1.5): the fact that we get the same choice in three places is left for the reader to infer by comparing the three rules, whereas the generalization is explicitly formulated in G_2, for the choice is handled by a single rule.

In 2.1 I distinguished between the concepts of syntactic category (such as NP, N, V) on the one hand and syntactic function (such as subject, direct object) on the other. Now the labels attached to the non-terminal nodes of a PM are all category labels. The difference in function between *the cats* and *the mice* in our example sentence is, however, deducible from the fact that they occupy different positions in the tree. There is therefore no need to complicate the rewrite rules in order to have them introduce functional labels into the PMs, for all the necessary information is effectively contained in PM [3] as it stands. It would be redundant to insert the labels subject and direct object to differentiate the functions of *the cats* and *the mice* given that they are already differentiated by their position: 'subject' is simply equivalent to 'the NP which is an IC of S'; and 'direct object' to 'the NP which is an IC of VP'. This interpretation brings out the relational nature of these functional concepts – note that we would not normally say that in *The cats caught the mice, the cats* is a subject, but rather that it is the subject of the sentence. Similarly the traditional functional term 'predicate' does not figure in PM [3]; instead we use the category term VP and define the predicate relation as that holding between the VP and the S of which it is an IC. I shall discuss this treatment of syntactic functions more fully in Chapter 15, where I also consider the correctness (here simply assumed) of the traditional division of a sentence like *The cats caught the mice* into two ICs, *the cats* and *caught the mice*, rather than three, *the cats, caught* and *the mice*.

In the light of these observations we can make a distinction between two types of technical terms that are used in linguistic discussions. The terms which figure directly in the structural representations generated by the grammar I shall call PRIMITIVES; those that do not, but which are definable by reference to the representations and derivations, are by contrast NON-PRIMITIVES. We are thus treating syntactic categories as primitives, functions as non-primitives. It is probably true to say that the majority of the technical terms used in traditional grammars to classify sentences or parts of sentences will turn out to be non-primitive in generative grammar: 'compound sentence', 'complex sentence', 'clause', 'subordinate clause', 'relative clause', 'declarative clause', 'phrase', 'word', 'root', 'inflection', are among many examples that could be cited, and a number of these will be discussed in the following chapters – as remarked in 1.4, the adoption of a formalized, generative approach is a significant help in explicating and evaluating many such traditional concepts.

Let us now consider more carefully the form of rules needed to generate sentences together with the appropriate PMs. Grammar [1] generates only four different PMs: [3], one with *cat* and *mouse* interchanged, one with two occurrences of *cat*, one with two of *mouse* – the only place where the grammar allows for a choice is in the rewriting of NS. We can extend it in two obvious ways: by adding rules introducing further morphemes and, more interestingly, by adding rules to account for further syntactic constructions. Thus rule [1iv], 'N → NS *Plur*', caters only for plural nouns; we can introduce singulars by the rule 'N → NS'. These two rules are partially similar and can be merged into a single composite rule 'N → NS (*Plur*)', where parentheses indicate optionality: N is rewritten as NS optionally followed by *Plur*. Similarly, if we replace [1ii] by 'VP → V (NP)' we allow for both 'transitive' VPs like *caught the mice* and 'intransitives' like *died*. A second abbreviatory convention is the use of braces to enclose alternatives, so that [1vii] and [viii] can be merged as 'NS → {*cat*, *mouse*}'. These devices are used in the following grammar:

[6] i   S → NP VP   v   N → NS (*Plur*)
     ii VP → V (NP)   vi   NS → {*cat, mouse*}
     iii V → VS *Past*   vii Det → {*the, some*}
     iv NP → Det N   viii VS → {*catch, die*}

[6] generates far more terminal strings than our first grammar – 144, to be precise. Among them, however, are many that should be excluded from an adequate grammar of English because the corresponding sentences are unacceptable: *the cat die Past the mouse, the mouse Plur catch Past*, and so on. A crucial weakness of [6] is that it fails to account for differences in the distribution of *catch* and *die*. What is needed is a subclassification of verbs or verb stems: we must somehow incorporate the traditional distinction between transitive verbs like *catch*, which take an object NP, and intransitives like *die*, which occur alone. Using only the type of rule introduced so far, we might try revising the grammar in the way shown in [7], where 'V_{trans}' stands for transitive Verb, 'VS_{trans}' for transitive verb stem, and so on.

[7] i   S → NP VP   iv–vii: as in 6
     ii   viiia VS_{trans} → *catch*
           VP → $\begin{Bmatrix} V_{trans} \text{ NP} \\ V_{intrans} \end{Bmatrix}$ viiib $VS_{intrans}$ → *die*
     iiia V_{trans} → VS_{trans} *Past*
     iiib $V_{intrans}$ → $VS_{intrans}$ *Past*

The braces in rule [ii] again indicate alternatives, though this time the alternatives are placed one above the other: the rule is an abbreviation of the two subrules 'VP → V_{trans} NP' and 'VP → $V_{intrans}$'. (Whether alternatives are written one above the other or one after the other is of no significance, but in the latter case they must be separated by commas; the usual practice in the literature is to place them one after the other only when they are terminal symbols.)

Grammar [7] is an improvement on [6] in that it excludes unwanted strings like *the cat die Past the mouse*, etc. But it would be a mistake to interpret [7] as in fact subclassifying verbs. It accounts for the distributional differences between *catch* and *die*, but it does so by assigning them to different primary categories, not to different subcategories of the primary category verb. It will be recalled that the procedure for constructing PMs requires that each PS rule rewrite a single symbol at a time; from a formal point of view, then, 'V_{trans}' and '$V_{intrans}$' are treated as single symbols: they have no internal structure and hence no formal partial similarity to each other. Note that the PM the grammar assigns to *the cat catch Past the mouse*, say, is [8], not [9]. Interpreting [8] in the way described above, we see that *catch* is said to be a transitive verb stem and *catch Past* a transitive verb, but they are not also categorized as verb stem and verb respectively: [7] does not contain symbols for these more general categories.

Whereas [6] expresses only the likeness between *catch* and *die*, [7] expresses

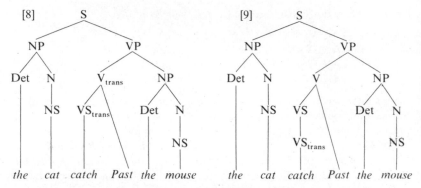

only the difference: what we want is a grammar that will express both. The likeness is evident from the fact that both combine with the morpheme *Past* (and various other verbal inflections to be introduced later). The failure of [7] to express this likeness is clear in rules [iii*a–b*]: *Past* is introduced by two separate rules instead of by a single rule dealing with the structure of verbs in general. To remedy this deficiency we add to the formal apparatus used in [6] and [7] by allowing for CONTEXT-SENSITIVE PS rules. Consider grammar [10], where [iii*b*] is such a context-sensitive rule, all the others being by contrast CONTEXT-FREE:

[10] i   S → NP VP
　　 ii   VP → V (NP)
　　iii*a*   V → VS *Past*
　　iii*b*   VS → $\left\{ \begin{array}{l} \text{VS}_{\text{trans}} / \underline{\hphantom{xx}} \textit{Past} \text{ NP} \\ \text{VS}_{\text{intrans}} / \underline{\hphantom{xx}} \textit{Past}\# \end{array} \right\}$
iv–viii: as in [7]

We have seen that one line of a PS derivation is obtained from the preceding line by rewriting a single symbol. A context-free rule is applicable to ANY string containing the symbol on the left of the arrow. Rule [iii*a*], for example, is thus equivalent to an instruction to replace a line 'X V Y' by 'X VS *Past* Y' where X and Y are arbitrary substrings. A context-sensitive rule, on the other hand, applies not to any string containing the symbol to be rewritten, but only to the subset of such strings in which the symbol occurs in the context specified on the right of the oblique. The first subrule of [iii*b*], *ie* 'VS → VS$_{\text{trans}}$ / ___ *Past* NP', accordingly replaces a line 'X·VS *Past* NP Y' by 'X VS$_{\text{trans}}$ *Past* NP Y'. Note that the symbols on the right of the oblique occur in both the upper and lower of the pair of lines related by the rule; the marker '___' indicates the position in the upper line of the symbol being rewritten: immediately to the left of the substring '*Past* NP', and so on. If a phrase structure grammar (PSG) contains one or more context-sensitive rules, it is said to be a CONTEXT-SENSITIVE PSG, and a CONTEXT-FREE PSG is one where every rule is context-free. Grammars [1], [6] and [7] are accordingly context-free, grammar [10] context-sensitive.

[11], suitably completed, is an example of a PS derivation generated by grammar [10].

[11] i #S#
 ii #NP VP#
 iii #NP V NP#
 iv #NP VS *Past* NP#
 v #NP VS$_{trans}$ *Past* NP#
 vi #Det N VS$_{trans}$ *Past* NP#
 vii #Det N VS$_{trans}$ *Past* Det N#
  . . .
 xiv #*the cat catch Past the mouse*#

Only the first subrule of [10iii*b*] can apply to line [11iv]: the second applies only where the VS occurs to the left of the substring '*Past*#', *ie* when there is nothing between *Past* and the sentence boundary. This means that the grammar will not generate such strings as *the cat die Past the mouse*. *The mouse catch Past* will similarly be excluded by virtue of the fact that *catch* is assigned to the category VS$_{trans}$, which is allowed by the first subrule of [iii*b*] as a rewriting of VS only where there is a following NP. [10] thus avoids the deficiency noted in grammar [6]. Rule [10iii*a*] expresses the generalization that *Past* can occur in all verbs, so that the grammar remedies the deficiency of [7]. The procedure outlined earlier will convert derivation [11] into PM [9] above, which classifies *catch* as both a VS$_{trans}$ and a VS: the lower label shows the difference between *catch* and *die*, while the higher label captures the more general likeness between them.

It will be evident that grammars [7] and [10] generate exactly the same set of terminal strings; they are accordingly said to have the same WEAK GENERATIVE CAPACITY. Where they differ is in the structures they associate with the strings – in their STRONG GENERATIVE CAPACITY. Grammars [6] and [10], on the other hand, differ even in weak generative capacity, since the former generates some strings that the latter excludes. The terms 'weak' and 'strong' are suggestive of the fact that in evaluating a grammar by determining whether it generates the desired set of terminal strings (or, ultimately, sentences) we are applying a weak criterion of adequacy in comparison with that involved when we consider the structures assigned to them. The distinction is similar to that drawn in 1.5 between external and internal adequacy. In the present example the distinctions are in fact equivalent: we prefer [10] over [6] by the criterion of external adequacy ([6] generates sentences which are unacceptable) and [10] over [7] by the criterion of internal adequacy ([7] misses the generalization concerning verb structure). When the scope of generative grammar is widened to include semantics, however, the distinctions are no longer equivalent: data relating to meaning will be relevant to external adequacy but not to weak generative capacity.

To conclude this chapter, let me briefly summarize the main points we have made. (a) A PM form of representation of syntactic structure identifies the morphemes that are the minimal constituents of the sentence, specifies their linear order, groups them into layers of larger constituents and classifies the constituents in terms of a set of syntactic categories; I have attempted to present some of the justification for adopting a form of syntactic description involving these notions. (b) PMs can be generated by a grammar consisting of PS rules. The PMs can be constructed from the rules in a wholly mechanical way: intelligence is needed to devise and evaluate the rules, but not to use them to construct PMs – this is a task that can be performed by a mindless robot. (c) A context-sensitive PS grammar is able to capture various syntactic generalizations that are not expressible in a context-free one, and is accordingly to be preferred as a model of the syntactic component.

Notes

On PS grammars, see Chomsky 1957:26–33, Kimball 1973:1–17; on strong and weak generative capacity, Chomsky 1965:60–2. A survey of work in mathematical linguistics is given in Wall 1971. It will be noted that the term 'context' is used in this chapter in a somewhat different sense from that of 1.1, where it was applied to the situation in which an utterance takes place; this double use, quite standard in the literature, is unlikely to cause confusion. My definition of 'dominate' reflects the most widespread usage of the term since the mid sixties; in earlier work (*eg* Chomsky 1961a, Postal 1964c) a node was said to dominate the complete sequence of terminal elements traceable to it but not the separate elements – *eg* in [3]; 'V' would dominate '*catch Past*', but not '*catch*' or 'VS'. The argument against introducing functional labels into PMs is given, for example, in Chomsky 1965:68–74. On the distinction between what I have called primitive and non-primitive terms, see Matthews 1965.

Chapter 4

Transformational Grammars

The aim of this chapter is to demonstrate that PS rules are not powerful enough to provide an adequate description of the syntax of English and that the deficiencies noted can be overcome by introducing rules of a new kind, called transformations. I shall, in other words, be arguing for the replacement of the PSG model of syntax outlined in Chapter 3 by a transformational (TG) model. A PSG consists exclusively of PS rules and assigns to each sentence a syntactic structure in the form of a SINGLE PM (except in the case of syntactically ambiguous sentences), whereas a TG consists of a set of PS rules plus a set of transformational rules and assigns to each sentence a SERIES of PMs, varying in the level of abstraction involved.

The argument will take the same logical form as that used in Chapter 3 to justify the introduction of context-sensitive rules. There we saw that a context-free PSG could account for the differences between transitive and intransitive verbs but could not at the same time express the significant likeness between them. Here we shall examine pairs of sentences and show that a PSG can handle the differences between the members of each but not the likeness, the systematic relation between them. I shall give three examples: active/passive pairs like *The storm frightened the child* and *The child was frightened by the storm;* declarative/imperative pairs like *You pamper yourself* and *Pamper yourself!;* and pairs (for which no standard traditional terms are available) like *It was difficult for John to annihilate the insects* and *The insects were difficult for John to annihilate.*

Consider first the differences and similarities between the active sentence [1] and its passive counterpart [2].

[1] *The storm frightened the child*
[2] *The child was frightened by the storm*

We have seen that the principal syntactic notions incorporated into the PSG model are morpheme, linear order, IC structure and distributional category. And it is clear that the difference between [1] and [2] can be described easily enough in terms of these notions: the sets of morphemes they contain are partially different (*eg: by* occurs in [2] but not [1]), the linear position of the morphemes *storm* and *child* is different, and so on. What of the similarity between them? The similarity that comes first to mind is doubtless a semantic one: the sentences are paraphrases inasmuch as it would, for example, be inconsistent to assert one while denying the other (*cf* Chapter 6 for further remarks on paraphrase). But since we have argued for the independence of syntax from semantics this paraphrase relation is not directly relevant to our present concern, which is to devise a generative model of syntax. What we need to show is that there is a systematic syntactic relation between [1] and [2] that cannot be expressed by means of PS rules. The task of the syntactic component is to describe the way morphemes combine to yield well-formed sentences; we can therefore show [1] and [2] to be syntactically related by comparing them with deviant sentences like [3–6].

[3] *The storm frightened the fact*
[4] *The fact was frightened by the storm*
[5] *The storm died the child*
[6] *The child was died by the storm*

The data of [1–6] illustrate the point that a sentence with the structure 'NP_1 passive verb *by* NP_2' is well-formed only if there is a well-formed sentence 'NP_3 active verb NP_4', where $NP_1 = NP_4$, $NP_2 = NP_3$ and the verb stem is the same in both. It is for this reason that we are entitled to say that there is a significant syntactic relation between [1] and [2], and we shall accordingly want to formalize the idea that the subject of the active somehow 'corresponds' to the agent of the passive ('agent' being the traditional functional term for the NP following *by*) and the object of the active corresponds to the subject of the passive. The highly elementary apparatus available in a PSG does not suffice to handle this type of correspondence. A traditional grammar would typically describe the relation between actives and passives by saying that a passive is 'formed from' an active by moving the active object into subject position, adding *by* before the active subject and moving it into agent position, and inserting the passive auxiliary *be*. There is no doubt that this traditional account is in essence correct, but it is clear that the procedure given in Chapter 3 for constructing sentences by means of PS rules does not allow for operations involving the movement of an element from one part of the structure to another: to formalize this kind of operation we shall need transformational rules.

To establish this point more rigorously, let us consider how we might handle the data of [1–6] given only the apparatus of PS rules. As a first step I will propose rules that will generate [1] and [2]; then I will discuss the modifications needed to ensure that [3–6] are excluded. *Was* in [2] is the past tense form of the passive auxiliary *be* and will be analysed in the familiar way as '*be Past*'. The *frightened* following *was* is traditionally called a 'past participle'; in regular verbs (such as *frighten* itself) and in some irregular ones too (*eg catch*), the past participle and past tense forms are phonologically identical, but there are also irregular verbs where the two forms are distinct – compare past tense *took* (as in *John took the cat*) with past participle *taken* (as in *The cat was taken by John*). We therefore need to distinguish the two forms in our morphemic representations. This is obvious in the case of *take*, for if we represented the past participle as '*take Past*' the morphophonemic rules would convert this to /tʊk/, resulting in the generation of unacceptable sentences like **The money was took by John*. And we shall likewise distinguish them in the case of *frighten*, so that we can formulate the proper generalizations about the distribution of past tense forms (*eg* that they cannot occur after the passive auxiliary) and past participles (*eg* that they cannot occur in such a context as '*John __ the cat*'). The morpheme symbol most usually adopted for the past participle inflection is '*en*' (suggestive of its realization in *taken*, *eaten*, etc: the past tense morpheme is never realized in this way). *Frightened* will therefore be represented in [1] as '*frighten Past*' and in [2] as '*frighten en*'. Grammar [7], completed in an obvious way, will generate PMs for sentences [1] and [2] that incorporate this analysis; they are given in [8] and [9] respectively.

[7] i   S → NP VP

ii   VP → $\left\{ \begin{array}{l} \text{V NP} \\ \text{PAux V PP} \end{array} \right\}$

iii   V → VS $\left\{ \begin{array}{l} Past \ / \ \text{NP} \ \_\_ \\ en \ / \ \text{PAux} \ \_\_ \end{array} \right\}$

iv   PAux → *be Past*

v   PP → *by* NP

vi   NP → Det N

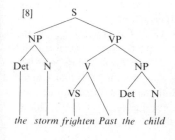

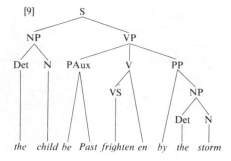

'PAux' stands for passive auxiliary, 'PP' for prepositional phrase. Rule [7iii] is context-sensitive, specifying that the main verb V takes the ending *Past* when it occurs immediately after the subject NP, as in [8], and the ending *en* when it follows the passive auxiliary, as in [9].

We must now adjust the grammar so that it will handle the difference in well-formedness between [1] and [2] on the one hand, [3] and [4] on the other. The latter violate what we have called a 'selectional restriction' (*cf p* 14), a restriction on permitted combinations of lexical items in various syntactic constructions. Take the active pair first. Here we need to say that *frighten* (like *annoy*, *please*, *worry* and many other verbs) can combine with a following animate noun, such as *child*, *dog*, *man*, etc, but not with an inanimate noun, such as *fact*, *storm*, *turnip*. We could cater for this restriction by adding the following rules to grammar [7]:

[10] i $N \rightarrow \left\{ \begin{matrix} N_{anim} \\ N_{inan} \end{matrix} \right\}$

ii $VS \rightarrow \left\{ \begin{matrix} VS_a \, / \, \underline{\quad} \; Past \; Det \; N_{anim} \\ VS_b \, / \, \underline{\quad} \; Past \; Det \; N_{inan} \end{matrix} \right\}$

[10i] subclassifies nouns as animate or inanimate; *child* would then be given as a possible rewriting of N_{anim}, *fact* of N_{inan}. The context-sensitive rule [ii] subclassifies verb stems according to the type of noun they combine with. *Frighten* would be assigned to the VS_a subclass (by a rule '$VS_a \rightarrow$ *frighten, annoy, please*, . . .') but not to VS_b, and consequently [3] would not be generated.

Now the important point to note is that [10ii] subclassifies VS on the basis of the type of noun which FOLLOWS (as is evident from the position of the '__'). This means that it will not enable us to block [4], for in the passive the restriction is that *frighten* cannot combine with a PRECEDING inanimate noun. We shall accordingly need another rule to handle the passives:

[11] $VS \rightarrow \left\{ \begin{matrix} VS_a \, / \, N_{anim} \; PAux \, \underline{\quad} \\ VS_b \, / \, N_{inan} \; PAux \, \underline{\quad} \end{matrix} \right\}$

Instead of allowing us to formulate a generalization concerning the restriction violated in [3] and [4], the PSG model forces us to deal separately with the active and passive instances of the restriction; instead of a general definition of the subcategory VS_a, the grammar gives a disjunctive definition: VS_a is the subcategory of VS that occurs either in the context '__ *Past* Det N_{anim}' or the context 'N_{anim} PAux __'. There are of course large numbers of selectional restrictions like that involving *frighten* (a second example is found in pairs like *The boy saw the mouse, The mouse was seen by the boy* versus **The fact saw the mouse*, **The mouse was seen by the fact*), so that the amount of duplication necessitated by treating the active and passive types separately would be enormous.

The argument does not rest wholly on selectional restrictions, however, for basically the same problem arises with [5] and [6]. I have already given rules that will distinguish between transitive and intransitive verbs in active sentences – we used a context-sensitive rule to subclassify verb stems according to whether or not there was a NP following. This will serve to exclude [5] but is irrelevant to [6]: in the passive what matters is the preceding context – *die* cannot follow PAux (note that *die* can occur before a *by* phrase, as in *He died by the roadside*). It will therefore be necessary to define the transitive and intransitive subclasses independently for active and passive sentences.

The weakness of the PSG model here has to do with strong generative capacity, with internal adequacy. We can devise PS rules that will generate [1] and [2] while excluding [3–6], but they fail to express the important generalization that a passive sentence is well-formed if and only if the corresponding active is well-formed – the reader has to discover this for himself by comparing pairs of rules like [10ii] and [11]. The generalization cannot be expressed because the PSG model does not allow for the formalization of the notion 'corresponding active and passive sentences'.

It was this kind of deficiency that the transformational model was designed to overcome. It does so by assigning to each sentence a syntactic structure consisting of a sequence of PMs. For example, the fragment of grammar that I shall be presenting in Chapter 5 (extended very slightly in an obvious way) will assign to *The storm frightened the child* the pair of PMs shown in [12], and to *The child was frightened by the storm* the sequence of PMs [13i–iv] (where VGp stands for verbal group, Aux for auxiliary, Prep for preposition and Tns for tense inflection).

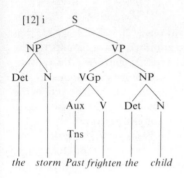

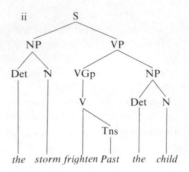

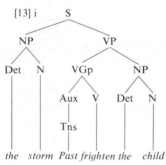

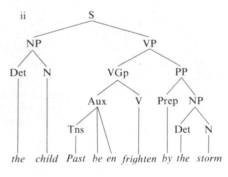

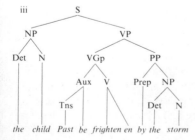

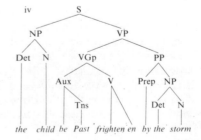

The sequence of PMs assigned to a sentence constitutes its TRANSFORMATIONAL DERIVATION. The first PM in the sequence is a representation of the DEEP (or UNDERLYING) STRUCTURE of the sentence, while the last PM represents its SURFACE STRUCTURE. The deep structure PM is generated by PS rules in the familiar way, and each subsequent PM in the sequence derives from the one preceding it by the application of a transformational rule. The model may be shown diagrammatically as follows:

[14]

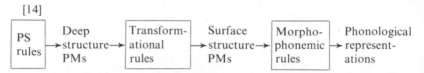

Looking now at the transformational derivations [12] and [13], we see that the two PMs [12i] and [13i] are identical. The grammar thus accounts for the likeness between the two sentences in a direct and straightforward way: they are derived from the same deep structure. The difference is attributed to the effect of a transformation, which we shall call Passivization, that applies in the second derivation but not the first, converting [13i] into [13ii]. The Passivization rule moves the original object NP *the child* into subject position, the original subject NP *the storm* into final position, adding *by* before it, and inserts *be* and the past participle inflection *en* into the auxiliary constituent. It thus formalizes the essence of the traditional account of the passive given above. There is one important difference, however. The latter deals with the formation of passive sentences from active sentences, whereas a transformational rule converts one PM into another, not one sentence into another. The reason for modifying the traditional notion can be seen by considering the passive counterpart of such a sentence as *They have seen her* – which is not *Her have been seen by they*, but *She has been seen by them*. If we regarded a transformation as a rule changing one sentence into another, we would have to complicate it very considerably in order to get the right form of the pronouns and of the auxiliary verb *have*, and so on, and we would thereby miss significant generalizations: it is not just a property of passive sentences that the subject pronoun is in the nominative case, and therefore the choice between *she* and *her* should not be handled in the Passivization rule, but in a separate general rule applying to actives and passives alike.

It will be noted that in the deep structure the tense inflection *Past* occurs immediately after *the storm* and is moved later in the derivation to the position it occupies in surface structure (and that *en* is introduced in [13ii] to the left of *frighten*, being subsequently moved to its right). A detailed explanation and justification of this analysis will be given in Chapter 5; my reason for giving the derivations in the above form even at this stage is that I wish to make it clear from the outset that transformations operate on PMs not sentences. We show the likeness between a passive sentence and its active counterpart not by deriving the former from the latter, but by assigning them identical representations at the level of deep structure. It is then at this deep structure level that we handle selectional restrictions and the distinction between transitive and intransitive verbs. We formulate rules along the lines of [10] (adjusted on account of the position of the *Past* morpheme) to exclude the insertion of *frighten* before an inanimate noun, and these will now serve to exclude both [3] and [4]: we do not need separate rules for the latter because actives and passives are not differentiated until a later stage in the derivation. Similarly we can express the generalization that in deep structure *die* cannot take an object NP: the one statement will account for the deviance of both [5] and [6].

Let me turn now to a second classic example of the capacity of TG to express generalizations that cannot be formalized in the less powerful PSG model. Here we shall be concerned with the relation between an imperative sentence like *Pamper yourself!* and its declarative counterpart *You pamper yourself.* A PSG can handle the obvious syntactic difference between them, that the second but not the first contains initial *you,* but is not able to account satisfactorily for a significant likeness between them, namely that the object pronoun in both is reflexive. The distribution of reflexive pronouns, those ending in -*self* or -*selves,* is illustrated in the following data:

[15]			[16]		
	i	*I pamper myself*		i	*I pamper me
	ii	*You pamper yourself*		ii	*You pamper you
	iii	*He pampers himself*		iii	*He pampers him*
	iv	*I pamper him*		iv	*I pamper himself
	v	*You pamper me*		v	**You pamper myself*
	vi	*He pampers you*		vi	**He pampers yourself*
	vii	*Pamper yourself!*		vii	**Pamper you!*
	viii	*Pamper him!*		viii	**Pamper himself!*

(The asterisk in [16vii] applies to the imperative reading, where the sentence has the same intonation as [15viii]; in such an exchange as 'A: *You ought to pamper me more.* B: *Pamper you? Certainly not.*', we simply have a different sentence, for the intonational properties of a sentence are as relevant to its identification as the consonants and vowels. This so-called 'echo'-form *Pamper you?* is irrelevant to the point at issue.) Suppose we have at our disposal only the apparatus provided by the PSG model, so that each sentence will be assigned just one PM. The PS rules will have to distinguish the declarative sentences [15i–vi], all of which begin with a NP, from the imperatives [vii–viii], which begin with a V. Instead of having as the first rule 'S → NP VP', with obligatory NP, we shall need 'S → (NP) VP', with optional NP: it is selected in the derivation of the declaratives but not of the imperatives. Once we do this, however, we make it impossible to give a general statement governing the distribution of reflexive pronouns: we need one statement for the declaratives and another for the imperatives. For declaratives we shall say that if the subject and object NPs are different in person (or number), the object cannot be a reflexive pronoun; if subject and object are alike in person (and number), the object is obligatorily reflexive in the first and second person, optionally reflexive in the third person (note that both members of pair [iii] are well-formed; they differ in meaning, of course, with subject and object coreferential in [15], but not in [16]). For imperatives we shall say that if the object pronoun is second person it must be reflexive, otherwise non-reflexive. These two statements are totally unrelated, which implies that the selection of reflexives in imperatives is determined by a quite different principle from that which holds for declaratives.

TG, on the other hand, enables us to handle the selection of a reflexive pronoun in a statement that generalizes over both declarative and imperative sentences. The deep structure of both [15ii] and [vii] will be essentially as shown in [17] (again, as with [12] and [13], the reason for putting the tense element on the left of the verb in deep structure will be given in Chapter 5).

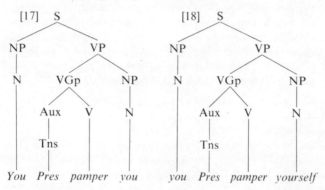

A transformational rule of Reflexivization converts [17] to [18]: the reflexive pronoun is introduced (obligatorily for first and second persons, optionally for third) when subject and object are identical. The same general rule applies to imperatives and declaratives alike (and also interrogatives, etc). At a later stage in the derivation of [15vii], but not of [15ii], a further transformation deletes the subject *you*. The analysis can be thought of as formalizing a quite traditional statement that *you* is 'understood' as subject of imperative sentences, a statement which again cannot be expressed within a PSG framework. It will be noticed, however, that the argument I have given for postulating *you* as subject in the deep structure of [15vii] is based not on the meaning of the sentence but on syntactic considerations – it enables us to formulate a general rule determining the distribution of reflexives.

My final example, based on [19], can be dealt with more briefly.

[19] i   *It was difficult for John to annihilate the insects*
    ii *The insects were difficult for John to annihilate*
   iii **The insects were difficult for John to annihilate the flies*
   iv **John annihilated*

Here we shall say that in the deep structure of both [i] and [ii] *the insects* is object of the verb *annihilate;* in the derivation of [ii] it is subsequently removed from this position by a transformational rule (*cf* Chapter 15). This analysis permits us to account for the well-formedness of [i] and [ii] and the deviance of [iii] and [iv] by means of the generalization that in deep structure *annihilate* takes an object. [iii] is deviant because the deep object position, being pre-empted by *the insects,* cannot be filled by *the flies* (*annihilate* does not allow two non-coordinate objects, as is evident from **John annihilated the insects the flies*), and [iv] is deviant because there is no object at all. But in a PSG, where no allowance is made for abstract deep structures, the rule we use to distinguish [i] and [iv] will not also handle [ii] and [iii] – for these we will need an immensely complex rule that takes account of the type of adjective in the position of *difficult* (contrast *The players were eager for John to annihilate the insects*) and the type of subject in the main clause (in order to differentiate between [iii] and *It was difficult for John to annihilate the flies*).

A PSG assigns just one PM to each (unambiguous) sentence; since this PM forms the input to the morphophonemic rules, we can apply the term 'surface structure' to it (*cf* diagram [14]) and contrast the PSG and TG models of syntax by saying that PSG describes only the surface structure of sentences while TG describes both deep and surface structure (and the relationship between them). The surface structure is not of course directly observable – we utter sounds not tree diagrams – but it is nevertheless comparatively closely related to the speech signal: in the surface structure of [19ii] *the insects* is initial, not final, in the terminal string, and this matches the position of the corresponding part of the signal; in the surface structure of [15vii] there is no *you* in subject position, and this accounts for the fact that there is no *you* pronounced; and so on. The examples discussed in this chapter demonstrate the need to go beyond the surface structure and posit syntactic representations that are a good deal more abstract (*ie* considerably more indirectly related to the signal). If we try to generate the surface structure directly by means of PS rules, our description is bound to remain unrevealing, to miss many intuitively obvious generalizations about the language – it will miss them precisely because they are not generaliza- tions about surface structure.

Chomsky's demonstration of this point in *Syntactic Structures* is of particular historical importance because the kind of analysis that was being proposed in structuralist grammars of the time, especially those of the neo-Bloomfieldian linguists, was in effect very similar to that provided by a PSG. The major notions in neo-Bloomfieldian grammar were morpheme, IC structure and distributional class: no allowance was made for the more abstract structures that Chomsky advocated. There can be no doubt that Chomsky's adoption of a generative framework contributed crucially to this advance: the shortcomings of the type of description that analyses a sentence into a hierarchical arrangement of constituents and assigns them to various classes emerged in the course of his investigation of the form of rules implicit in such a conception of grammar.

Notes

On the motivation for adding transformations to the grammar, see Chomsky 1957:34–91, 1961*a*, 1962, Postal 1964*a*. The arguments from English demonstrate the superiority of TG over PSG in terms of strong generative capacity; Postal 1964*b* gives an argument based on weak generative capacity. It is an oversimplification to regard PSG as a complete formalization of neo-Bloomfieldian syntax – the latter allowed, for example, for 'discontinuous constituents' and for more complex correlations between syntactic functions and categories such that in a faithful formalization the former would have to be primitive terms too. There is no reason to believe, however, that the extra power permitted by these two factors could remedy the shortcomings of PSG; for a somewhat polemical account of the relations between PSG and structuralist theories of syntax, see Postal 1964*c*. The terms 'deep' and 'surface' structure were not used in the early transformational literature, but no harm will come from my anticipating the later and now standard terminology.

It is not strictly true to say that a passive sentence is well-formed if and only if the corresponding active is – contrast, for example, *This book costs a dollar* and **A dollar is cost by this book*. The fact that there are some exceptions (for the treatment of which, see Chapter 10) does not mean, however, that we do not need to account for the systematic relation that holds in the regular cases.

Chapter 5

A Fragment of a Transformational Grammar

The aim of this chapter is to present an example of a transformational grammar of the kind proposed in *Syntactic Structures*. In 5.2 I shall give the PS and transformational rules needed to generate positive declarative sentences containing the range of verbal forms shown in column A of [1] (see next page), and then extend the grammar in 5.3 so as to account for the interrogative and negative counterparts of such sentences. 5.1 will prepare the ground for the subsequent presentation of the formal rules by discussing the surface structure of the verbal forms, especially their morphemic analysis; I shall also add some informal comments on the relation between the syntactic forms and meaning, and on the traditional terminology widely used to classify the forms.

Some of the forms may sound somewhat strained when considered in isolation but, given appropriate contexts, they are widely judged to be acceptable – for example, form [xxxi] (with *build* substituted for *see*) might be found in such a sentence as *The Opera House will have been being built for ten years soon.* It may be that we should allow for dialect differences relating to the well-formedness of [xxv–xxxii], but certainly there are many speakers who accept them all, and it is this dialect that I shall be discussing.

5.1 A preliminary classification of the verbal group

The thirty-two forms will be classified as belonging to the category 'verbal group' (VGp), this term being distinguished on the one hand from 'verb', a category applying to single words, and on the other from 'verb phrase' (VP), which includes the object NP, etc, as well as the VGp. In *John will see Mary*, therefore, *will see Mary* is a VP, *will see* is a VGp, *will* and *see* are both verbs. The last verb in the VGp will be referred to as the 'main verb', the others as 'auxiliary verbs'.

Column B of [1] analyses the VGps as strings of morphemes: these representations will constitute part of the terminal strings of the surface structure PMs, and the latter form the input to the morphophonemic rules specifying the phonological realizations. I shall simplify by ignoring subject-verb agreement, so that the representations do not distinguish (*He*) *sees* from (*They*) *see*:

[1]

	A. ORTHOGRAPHIC FORMS	B. SURFACE STRUCTURE MORPHEMIC REPRESENTATIONS	C. CLASSIFICATION					
			Finiteness	Tense	Mood	Perfect aspect	Progressive aspect	Voice
i	*sees*	*see Pres*	Finite	Pres	N/Mod	N/Perf	N/Prog	Active
ii	*saw*	*see Past*	Finite	Past	N/Mod	N/Perf	N/Prog	Active
iii	*will see*	*will Pres see*	Finite	Pres	Modal	N/Perf	N/Prog	Active
iv	*would see*	*will Past see*	Finite	Past	Modal	N/Perf	N/Prog	Active
v	*has seen*	*have Pres see en*	Finite	Pres	N/Mod	Perfect	N/Prog	Active
vi	*had seen*	*have Past see en*	Finite	Past	N/Mod	Perfect	N/Prog	Active
vii	*will have seen*	*will Pres have see en*	Finite	Pres	Modal	Perfect	N/Prog	Active
viii	*would have seen*	*will Past have see en*	Finite	Past	Modal	Perfect	N/Prog	Active
ix	*is seeing*	*be Pres see ing*	Finite	Pres	N/Mod	N/Perf	Progress	Active
x	*was seeing*	*be Past see ing*	Finite	Past	N/Mod	N/Perf	Progress	Active
xi	*will be seeing*	*will Pres be see ing*	Finite	Pres	Modal	N/Perf	Progress	Active
xii	*would be seeing*	*will Past be see ing*	Finite	Past	Modal	N/Perf	Progress	Active
xiii	*has been seeing*	*have Pres be en see ing*	Finite	Pres	N/Mod	Perfect	Progress	Active
xiv	*had been seeing*	*have Past be en see ing*	Finite	Past	N/Mod	Perfect	Progress	Active
xv	*will have been seeing*	*will Pres have be en see ing*	Finite	Pres	Modal	Perfect	Progress	Active
xvi	*would have been seeing*	*will Past have be en see ing*	Finite	Past	Modal	Perfect	Progress	Active

xvii	is seen	be Pres see en	Finite	Pres	N/Mod	N/Perf	N/Prog	Passive
xviii	was seen	be Past see en	Finite	Past	N/Mod	N/Perf	N/Prog	Passive
xix	will be seen	will Pres be see en	Finite	Pres	Modal	N/Perf	N/Prog	Passive
xx	would be seen	will Past be see en	Finite	Past	Modal	N/Perf	N/Prog	Passive
xxi	has been seen	have Pres be en see en	Finite	Pres	N/Mod	Perfect	N/Prog	Passive
xxii	had been seen	have Past be en see en	Finite	Past	N/Mod	Perfect	N/Prog	Passive
xxiii	will have been seen	will Pres have be en see en	Finite	Pres	Modal	Perfect	N/Prog	Passive
xxiv	would have been seen	will Past have be en see en	Finite	Past	Modal	Perfect	N/Prog	Passive
xxv	is being seen	be Pres be ing see en	Finite	Pres	N/Mod	N/Perf	Progress	Passive
xxvi	was being seen	be Past be ing see en	Finite	Past	N/Mod	N/Perf	Progress	Passive
xxvii	will be being seen	will Pres be be ing see en	Finite	Pres	Modal	N/Perf	Progress	Passive
xxviii	would be being seen	will Past be be ing see en	Finite	Past	Modal	N/Perf	Progress	Passive
xxix	has been being seen	have Pres be en be ing see en	Finite	Pres	N/Mod	Perfect	Progress	Passive
xxx	had been being seen	have Past be en be ing see en	Finite	Past	N/Mod	Perfect	Progress	Passive
xxxi	will have been being seen	will Pres have be en be ing see en	Finite	Pres	Modal	Perfect	Progress	Passive
xxxii	would have been being seen	will Past have be en be ing see en	Finite	Past	Modal	Perfect	Progress	Passive

N/Mod = Non-modal, N/Perf = Non-perfect, N/Prog = Non-progressive, Progress = Progressive both are given as '*see Pres*'; the question of how to handle agreement within a TG will be taken up in Chapter 11.

Column C gives a classification of the VGps along six dimensions. Finiteness distinguishes the thirty-two forms from various others not given in the table: all those shown are finite in contrast to non-finite forms like *to see, having been seen*, etc. Each of the other dimensions partitions the forms into two sets of sixteen. These dimensions cut across each other in such a way that no two of the forms listed have the same classification in all five. The various classes can be defined quite straightforwardly in terms of the morphemic composition of their members; for example a perfect VGp is one containing the morpheme *have* plus the morpheme *en* as suffix to the following word, while a non-perfect VGp is definable negatively as one that does not contain both these elements – compare perfect *has seen* ('**have** *Pres see en*') with the corresponding non-perfect *sees* ('*see Pres*'). For this reason we do not need to treat the class labels as primitive terms: they will not figure in the rules and representations of the formal grammar. In view of the direct relation between the classification and the morphemic analysis, I shall discuss them together, examining in turn each of the six dimensions of contrast.

I Voice: active versus passive

This dimension can be disposed of quickly, since we have already discussed it in Chapter 4. The voice contrast clearly affects the structure of the whole sentence, not just the VGp: the passive of *John saw Mary* is *Mary was seen by John*, not *John was seen Mary*. As far as the VGp is concerned, a passive VGp differs from the corresponding active by containing the extra morphemes *be* and *en*, the latter being suffixed to the word following *be:* compare passive *was taken* ('**be** *Past take en*') with active *took* ('*take Past*'). The term 'voice' is widely used in the grammars of different languages for systematic contrasts involving the relation between the surface-structure subject and the verb, especially when there is an accompanying difference in the verb or VGp. In clauses expressing an action, the NP functioning as surface subject typically has the role of 'actor' (and hence is the 'active' participant) in the active voice, *eg:* **John** *attacked Peter*, and the role of 'patient' (the 'passive' participant) in the corresponding passive, *eg:* **Peter** *was attacked by John*. It must be emphasized, though, that this difference in the semantic role of the surface subject does not serve to define active and passive sentences. Sentences like *Everyone knew the answer* and *The answer was known by everyone* do not express the action of an actor on a patient, but they will nevertheless be classified as active and passive respectively because they exhibit the same syntactic contrast as the *attack* pair. In accordance with the principles of Chapter 2, we define active and passive sentences in syntactic terms – a passive sentence is one in whose derivation the Passivization transformation applies. The correlation that holds in action clauses between the semantic notions 'actor' and 'patient' and the surface subjects of actives and passives is to be understood as simply providing a basis for naming the syntactic classes. I shall return in Chapter 13 to the theoretical issues involved in the contrast I have drawn here between defining and naming; in the meantime it should be borne in mind that it will apply to our discussion of the remaining dimensions too.

II Tense: past versus present

Past-tense and present-tense VGps are defined as those containing the respective morphemes *Past* and *Pres* suffixed to the first word in the group. The classification differs from that adopted in most traditional grammars in recognizing only two tenses instead of the usual three: there is no future tense. The traditional future form *will see* is analysed as a present tense, differing from *sees* not in tense but in mood. To justify this analysis, let us first examine the contrast between the uncontroversial forms *saw* and *sees*, and then consider *will see* in the light of our findings. Tense is an area where the relations between syntax and semantics are highly complex, and where it is therefore particularly important to distinguish clearly between the concepts needed in description at the two levels; to facilitate this I shall use TENSE as a syntactic concept, and TIME as a semantic one. What kind of semantic differences correlate with the syntactic contrast between past and present tense?

(a) The primary semantic function of tense is to indicate the relation between the time at which the sentence is uttered and the time of the action, event, state or whatever it might be (henceforth simply 'action/state'), that is expressed in the main verb. Consider the following elementary examples:

[2] *John died of cancer*
[3] *Mary lives in Sydney*

The past tense in [2] indicates that the time of John's dying of cancer is past relative to the time of speaking, and the present tense in [3] that Mary's living in Sydney is present relative to the time of speaking. Past time is time before the moment of utterance, present time is inclusive of it – 'inclusive of', rather than 'co-extensive with', of course, since the time during which Mary lives in Sydney will clearly be much greater than the time taken to utter sentence [3]. The same applies in a case like *John shaves at night:* this would normally be used to assert that John habitually shaves at night – he need not be in the act of shaving when the sentence is uttered, but the time during which he is said to be in the habit of shaving at night does include the moment of utterance, and this is why the present tense is used. Similarly, in *Oil floats on water*, oil is asserted to have a certain property, and the time during which it has this property again includes the time of utterance – presumably it extends indefinitely on either side of it, but the factor determining the choice of present tense is simply that the period, however long, includes the moment of speaking.

The first qualification to this elementary account is that a present tense can be used when the time of the action/state is later than that of the speech act, as in *Mary leaves for London next week*. Here the expression *next week* indicates that the leaving is future relative to the time of speaking, but the verb *leaves* is a present tense form, identical with that in *Mary leaves for London every Friday night*, where both tense and time are present. This use of a present tense with future time reference is restricted to cases where the action/state is in some way already arranged or scheduled – contrast the above with *Mary has a nervous breakdown soon unless she takes things easier*. A second qualification involves the so-called 'historic present', as in *And then this girl comes up to me and asks for a light*: here the tense is again present but the action/state is in past time. This is a stylistic device found in certain types of literary or conversational narration – the purpose is characteristically to make the narrative more vivid by assimilating its time to that of the speech act. The present tense is most often used to indicate present time and we can regard this as its basic meaning, but far from there being a one-to-one correlation between them, we see that a syntactic present tense can also be associated in certain circumstances and styles with past or future time – which makes it essential to keep tense and time conceptually distinct.

(b) In indirect reported speech the contrast between past and present tense has a somewhat different semantic function. (The traditional term 'indirect reported speech' is in fact too narrow, but it will suffice for present purposes.) Suppose that at some point in time John utters [4]; I could subsequently report this event by means of [5], [6] or [7].

[4] *Mary has three children*
[5] *John said: 'Mary has three children'*
[6] *John said that Mary had three children*
[7] *John said that Mary has three children*

[5] is a 'direct' report, [6] and [7] 'indirect'. I am concerned with [6] only in the interpretation where it is an indirect report of [4] (it could also be used to report an event where what John said was *Mary had three children*, in which case it would stand in exactly the same relation to the latter sentence as [7] does to [4]). The past tense *had*, in the intended interpretation of [6], thus corresponds to the original present tense *has*. This phenomenon is often called 'backshifting': an original present tense is backshifted to a past under the influence of the past tense of the reporting verb *said*. [7] shows that backshifting is not obligatory, so that the question arises: what is the difference in meaning between [6] and [7]?

Semantic past, present and future are relational concepts: we are concerned with the temporal relation between the action/state and some point of reference. Normally, as in the cases considered under (a) above, it is the speech act itself that serves as this point of reference, but in indirect reported speech there may be a choice of reference point. Diagram [8] shows schematically the relations between the state and events in [4–7]: A is the state of Mary's having three children, B is the event consisting of John's uttering [4], and C is the event of my uttering [5], [6] or [7]. Having three children is a state which typically lasts for a considerable time, so we may assume that A is temporally inclusive of B and C, as shown in [8]. It is of course because A is inclusive of B that John uses a present tense form in [4]. Now the difference between [6] and [7] is that [6] has B as reference point while [7] has C. The present tense in [7] expresses the fact that A is inclusive of C, in accordance with the basic meaning of a present tense. In [6], A is also inclusive of the reference point, but because the latter (B) is itself past relative to C (the actual utterance of [6]), backshifting applies to give a past tense instead of a present. Notice that [6] is a more 'faithful' report of [4] than

[8]

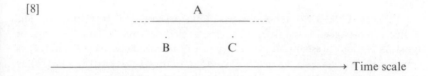

[7] is, for both [4] and [6] express the relation between A and B, whereas in [7] I relate A directly to C. It would be inappropriate for me to use [7] rather than [6] if I knew that at some point between B and C Mary had ceased to have three children (owing to some fatal accident, say). To see this more clearly, consider a case where the analogue of A is of short duration. If John's speech act was, for example, *It is three o'clock*, I could appropriately report this a couple of hours later with *John said that it was three o'clock*, but not *John said that it is three o'clock*: it may remain (roughly) three o'clock for a few minutes but not for a couple of hours. It is never inappropriate to use the backshifting construction, but as this last example demonstrates, it is appropriate to use the non-backshifting type only if one assumes that A stands in the same relation to C as to B – and it is because this is the reporter's assumption, not the original speaker's, that I characterized [6] as a more faithful report than [7].

According to this analysis, the semantic function of the tense contrast between [6] and [7] is somewhat different from that of the one between [2] and [3]. Additional support for distinguishing a backshifted past tense like *had* in [6] from an ordinary one like *died* in [2] is provided by the behaviour of the auxiliary verb *may*. If John says *May I smoke?*, I can report this subsequently with *John asked whether he might smoke;* but I cannot express the fact that yesterday I was allowed to smoke during an examination by, say, **I might smoke during yesterday's examination. Might* occurs freely as a backshifted past tense of *may*, but not as an ordinary past. Nevertheless, where both uses are possible there will never be any difference in phonological realization, and hence we shall represent both in the same way in the surface structure PM. *Died* in [2] is analysed as '*die Past*'; *had* in [6] as '*have Past*'; *might* in *whether he might smoke* as '*may Past*'.

We are now in a position to consider the traditional future tense, *will see*. The major reason for departing from the traditional analysis is that the contrast we have been examining between forms like *sees* and *saw* is found also between *will see* and *would see*. This is evident from examples like [9–16].

[9] *The box didn't open very easily* (*then*)
[10] *The box doesn't open very easily* (*now*)
[11] *The box wouldn't open very easily* (*then*)
[12] *The box won't open very easily* (*now*)
[13] *John said that Mary knew French*
[14] *John said that Mary knows French*
[15] *John said that Mary would be selected*
[16] *John said that Mary will be selected*

[9–12] involve the use of tenses discussed in (a) above, [13–16] that in (b). The difference between [9] and [10] is the same as that between [11] and [12], one of past time versus present time. Similarly, the difference between [13] and [14] as reports of *Mary knows French* is the same as that between [15] and [16] as reports of *Mary will be selected*. In these and innumerable other examples, then, the difference between *would* and *will* is just the same as that between *saw* and *sees* and similar pairs. We will accordingly handle them both as differences in tense, representing *would* as '*will Past*' and *will* as '*will Pres*', just as we represent *saw* as '*see Past*', *sees* as '*see Pres*'. Notice also that these analyses are required to permit general distributional statements about the tenses: we want to exclude **John sees her yesterday* and **John will see her yesterday* by the same rule of incompatibility between *yesterday* and *Pres*, and so on.

It follows from these morphemic analyses that *will* combines with either *Past* or *Pres* – instead of being mutually exclusive with them, as it should be if it were to be appropriately regarded as the marker of a third tense. Instead of a three-way contrast *will* versus *Pres* versus *Past*, we have two two-way contrasts, *Pres* versus *Past*, selection of *will* versus non-selection of *will*. These contrasts cut across each other, as shown in [17]:

[17]	*Pres*	*Past*
will selected	*will see*	*would see*
will not selected	*sees*	*saw*

The contrast between the two columns is one of tense, while that between the rows will be handled under mood, to which I shall return presently.

III Progressive aspect: progressive versus non-progressive
Progressive VGps are marked by the morphemes *be* and *ing*: as with the *be* and *en* of passive VGps, they occur in separate words – compare progressive *is seeing* ('*be Pres see ing*') with its non-progressive counterpart *sees* ('*see Pres*'). The main semantic function of the progressive is to indicate that the action/ state is being considered not in its totality, but at some point or period of time intermediate between its beginning and its end. *They were having lunch when John arrived* says that the lunch activity was 'in progress' at the time of John's

arrival: the sentence is not concerned with the whole of the lunch activity, but just with that temporal segment of it that was contemporaneous with John's arrival. Similarly with a present-tense progressive like *Mary is waiting for you in the garden:* we focus on that segment of the waiting that coincides with the time of speaking, rather than on the complete period of Mary's waiting. This is not to say that in the non-progressive we necessarily do consider the action/ state in its totality. We clearly do in a case like the earlier *John died of cancer,* but there are other cases where we may not, *eg: Mary was able to speak fluent French, so we soon extricated ourselves from the difficulty.* Although we have a past tense *was* here, there is no implication that at the time of my uttering the sentence Mary no longer has the ability to speak French: I am not concerned with the ability in its temporal totality, but just that period of it relevant to the events under narration. The point is that the progressive explicitly marks focus on an intermediate part of the action/state rather than on the whole of it, whereas the non-progressive is simply neutral, or 'unmarked' with respect to this semantic contrast.

The relation of *was seeing* to *is seeing* is the same as that of *saw* to *sees:* the two contrasts, past versus present and progressive versus non-progressive, are independent of each other, as shown in [1]. Some older grammars use the term 'tense' in a very broad sense such that each of [li–xvi] counts as a distinct tense. It is now more usual to restrict tense to syntactic contrasts in the verb or VGp whose basic semantic function is to indicate the location in time of the action/ state, especially its location relative to the time of utterance. The contrast between *saw* and *sees* is then clearly one of tense, whereas that between *saw* and *was seeing* is not: we speak of this as a contrast of 'aspect'. This term will be found used for a variety of contrasts: not just for that between an action/state viewed in its totality versus one viewed at an intermediate point, but also between completed and non-completed actions/states, between those that are habitual or repeated and those that are not, and so on. The terms habitual and non-habitual aspect will indeed be found in many grammars of English, but it must be emphasized that the semantic contrast habitual versus non-habitual is not systematically expressed by any syntactic contrast in the VGp – in particular not by the progressive aspect system. The non-progressive *John shaves at night* will generally be interpreted as habitual, but *He drives it past mid-off* (as said in a cricket commentary, for example), *I declare this meeting open, I have no money on me at the moment,* etc, will be non-habitual; and similarly we find progressives correlating with both habitual and non-habitual actions/states – compare *John is always teasing Mary* with *John is mowing the lawn at the moment.*

Two last brief points on the progressive. First, examples where there is reference to future time, such as *I was leaving tomorrow* (roughly equivalent to 'I was scheduled to leave tomorrow') or *John is joining us later,* involve a different use of the progressive from that discussed above, and provide still further evidence of the complexity of the tie-up between meaning and syntactic form. Secondly, not all non-progressive clauses have acceptable progressive counterparts. *This parcel contains the relevant documents, Mary has two brothers, 'John forced Peter to resign*' entails '*Peter resigned*' are examples: replacing *contains*, *has*, *entails* by *is containing*, *is having*, *is entailing* yields anomalous sentences.

IV Perfect aspect: perfect versus non-perfect

As noted above, perfect VGps are marked by the morphemes *have* and *en*, occurring in successive words, while non-perfects lack these elements. The morpheme *en* occurs in both perfects (*has seen*) and passives (*was seen*). We represent *seen* as '*see en*' in both cases because there is no verb whose 'perfect participle' and 'passive participle' differ; if we gave different morphemic representations we would have to duplicate the realization rules relating '. . . *en*' to the phonological representations.

The contrast between *had seen* and *has seen* is one of tense, like that between *saw* and *sees*, or the main verbs *had* and *has* in, say, *John had/has a headache*: pairs like those in [9–16] can be paralleled by *John had finished then* versus *John has finished now* or *John said Mary had been to Rome* versus *John said Mary has been to Rome* (as reports of John's utterance of *Mary has been to Rome*). *Had seen* is accordingly a past perfect, *has seen* a present perfect. At this stage I follow the most usual terminology, treating the contrast of *has seen* and *sees* as one of aspect – but with some misgivings, for it is very much concerned with the temporal location of the action/state and thus might more appropriately be regarded as an auxiliary tense system. For example, in *John has been ill* versus *John is ill*, the illness is in past time and present time respectively. *Sees* contrasts with *saw* as present tense versus past, and with *has seen* as non-perfect aspect versus perfect. Semantically the difference between *saw* and *has seen* can be described in terms of the notion 'current relevance': in both cases the seeing is in past time, but with *has seen* the seeing also has relevance to the present time. Consider, for example, the difference between *John broke his leg* and *John has broken his leg*. The first simply reports a past event, whereas in the second we are concerned with the past event of leg-breaking and also with its current effects – the sentence would typically be used while John is still incapacitated. With this form, therefore, there is both a past time component and a present time component: the past component is associated with the action/state itself and is syntactically expressed by the selection of perfect aspect, the present component is associated with the effects, consequences or whatever, and is syntactically expressed by the selection of present tense. I should add that this is a much simplified account of a difficult and complex matter: I shall be looking more carefully into the syntax and semantics of the perfect in Chapter 14.

V Finiteness: finite versus non-finite

In the first instance, the distinction of finite versus non-finite applies to verbs, *ie* the separate words of the VGp. Finite verbs are those ending in one or other of the tense morphemes *Past*, *Pres*. The term 'finite' is used because the forms are 'limited' to one or other tense, whereas the non-finites are not: note that in *She believed him to be in Paris* and *She believes him to be in Paris* the single non-finite form *be* is used where in the finite constructions *She believed that he was in*

Paris and *She believes that he is in Paris* we have the contrast between *was* and *is*, so that *be* is not temporally limited in the way *was* and *is* are.

Non-finite verbs can be divided into three types according as they end in *ing*, *en* or neither. The morphemes *Past*, *Pres*, *ing* and *en* are mutually exclusive; no verb contains more than one. I shall refer to them as the verbal 'inflections', and to the remaining part of the verb as the 'stem'. This gives the following set of verb classes and structures:

[18]

CLASSIFICATION		STRUCTURE	EXAMPLES		
Finite {	present tense	stem *Pres*	*see/sees*	*am/is/are*	*kill/kills*
	past tense	stem *Past*	*saw*	*was/were*	*killed*
Non-finite {	infinitive	stem	*see*	*be*	*kill*
	ing-form	stem *ing*	*seeing*	*being*	*killing*
	en-form	stem *en*	*seen*	*been*	*killed*

I use the traditional term 'infinitive' for the form consisting of stem alone; it is often accompanied by the special marker *to*, as in *He hopes **to** see her*, but not always: witness *He may **be** ill, He let himself **be** cheated*. The *ing*-form is traditionally called the 'gerund' or 'present participle' – we need not go into the difference between these, for we certainly want only a single morphemic representation since there is never any difference in phonological realization. The traditional name for the *en*-form is 'past participle'. I adopt the structural labels for these last two forms to avoid the false impression that the relation of *seeing* to *seen* is the same as that of *sees* to *saw*.

It will be noticed that there is a certain amount of 'homonymy', *ie* identity of realization, between the finite and non-finite forms. We have already noted (*p* 48) that the past tense and *en*-form of regular (and some irregular) verbs are homonymous – hence the appearance of *killed* in two places in [18]. To determine whether a given occurrence of *killed* is a past tense or an *en*-form, we need only replace *kill* by a verb like *see* or *take* where the forms are not homonymous: if we do this in *John killed it* and *John has killed it* we get *John saw/*seen it* and *John has seen/*saw it* respectively, showing that the first *killed* is past tense, the second an *en*-form. Similarly there is widespread homonymy between the infinitive and the present tense when the latter is not third person singular – *be* is the only verb where there is no homonymy here. But the same kind of test allows us to classify the *know* of *They know the language* and that of *They may know the language* as respectively present tense and infinitive: compare *They are/*be careful* and *They may be/*are careful*.

The above classification can be extended quite straightforwardly to VGps, and also to clauses. If the first word of a VGp is finite, the whole VGp will be classed as finite, otherwise as non-finite; and then a finite clause is one containing a finite VGp, and so on. There can be no more than one occurrence of a tense inflection in any VGp, and it will always be in the first word – note the position of the morphemes *Past* and *Pres* in column B of [1]. The rules to be given in this chapter generate only finite clauses, which is why non-finite VGps like *to see*, *having seen*, etc, are omitted from table [1]; some non-finite constructions will be examined in Chapter 8.

VI Mood: modal versus non-modal

Modal VGps are marked by the presence of one of the modal auxiliaries, *will*, *shall*, *can*, *may*, *must* and two or three others; non-modal VGps simply lack such an element. The syntactic property that most clearly distinguishes the modal auxiliaries from other verbs is that they have only finite forms; since only the first verb in a VGp can be finite, this means that a modal can occupy only the first position in a VGp, and hence that we cannot have two modals in the same VGp: *John may will leave tomorrow*, *You will may have it when you've repaid your debts*, *John must can swim* are quite clearly deviant. We saw above that *will* combines freely with *Past* or *Pres;* now we see that it is mutually exclusive with *can*, *may*, *shall*, *must*, etc: this establishes beyond doubt that it belongs to the same distributional category as the latter, not the former. Modals are also distinguished from other verbs by the fact that they do not exhibit subject-verb agreement: compare *He has gone* versus *They have gone* or *He likes Bach* versus *They like Bach* with *He can/will swim* versus *They can/will swim*.

These properties delimit the class of modals syntactically: let us now turn briefly to questions of meaning. The term 'mood' is traditionally applied to systems of syntactic contrasts whose primary semantic function has to do with the level of the speaker's assurance in the factuality of what he is saying. The 'neutral' mood is typically associated with assured factual statements and the various non-neutral moods involve qualifications to or departures from this. There are in fact three quite separate areas of English syntax where the term mood is widely used:

(a) The contrast between declarative, interrogative and imperative clauses, as in *You are generous*, *Are you generous?*, *Be generous!*, respectively. The declarative is the unmarked mood here, being typically used to make statements, whereas interrogatives are usually associated with questions, imperatives with requests, commands, etc. This mood system will be the topic of Chapter 9.

(b) The contrast between non-modal and modal VGps, which is our present concern. The non-modal is the neutral mood, while the modal auxiliaries typically express qualifications of the kind exemplified in [19] and [20].

[19] i *That is the doctor*	[20] i *The match starts soon*	
ii *That will be the doctor*	ii *The match will start soon*	
iii *That must be the doctor*	iii *The match must start soon*	
iv *That may be the doctor*	iv *The match may start soon*	

[19i] is a factual assertion. [19ii] is a prediction; it is not yet known with certainty that that is the doctor, but the speaker is predicting that when the facts are revealed it will turn out to be so. In [19iii] the speaker is basing his claim on inference: he does not have direct certain knowledge that that is the doctor, but he is led by reasoning to conclude that it is. [iii] is probably slightly less assured than [ii], but both are clearly much more confident than [iv], where there is simply a possibility that that is the doctor: *may* marks the greatest qualification to the assertion in [i]. Analogous remarks hold for the examples in [20]. Notice that in [19] the time of that being the doctor is present, while in [20] the time of the match starting is future: the examples show that futurity can be expressed without the use of *will* and that *will* can be used to make predictions about the present. These semantic facts lend further support to the earlier distributional arguments for treating *will* as a modal rather than as a future tense marker.

As before, the semantic contrasts exhibited in [19–20] provide the basis for naming these auxiliaries as modals, not for defining the syntactic class. In this area too there is nothing like a one-to-one correlation between the semantic and syntactic categories. In the first place, the sort of qualification to an assured factual assertion that we find in [ii–iv] can be expressed by quite other syntactic devices – adverbs like *necessarily*, *probably*, *possibly*, *perhaps*, etc, or complex sentence constructions like *It is possible that that is the doctor*, and so on. Secondly, the modal auxiliaries are also used with significantly different meanings from those considered – compare *I won't answer him*, negated willingness or intention rather than prediction, *You must be more careful in future*, obligation or requirement rather than inference, *You may smoke if you wish*, permission rather than logical possibility. These examples illustrate what is often called the 'root' meanings of the modals in contrast to their 'epistemic' meanings in [19–20] ('epistemic' because they are concerned with the nature or limits of the speaker's knowledge of the proposition in question). Ambiguities may then arise between the two types, as in say, *You must be very quick:* 'I am logically forced to the conclusion that you are very quick' (epistemic *must*) or 'I want you to be very quick' (root *must*); [20iii] and [iv] are in fact also ambiguous in this way.

(c) Finally mood is applied to the contrast exemplified in

[21] *If John is there tomorrow, he will see her*
[22] *If John were there tomorrow, he would see her*

Semantically these differ in the speaker's assessment of the chances of fulfilment of the condition expressed in the *if* clause: they are assumed to be more remote in [22] than in [21]. *Is* and *will* in [21] are in the 'indicative' mood, *were* and *would* in [22] in the 'subjunctive' mood (note the difference between this *would* and those of [11] and [15]). With subjunctive conditional clauses, the possibility of fulfilment is often so remote as to be excluded altogether (as in *If I were you*, . . .), but there is not necessarily any assumption of counterfactuality – in *What would you do if I gave you the money?* I am not ruling out all possibility of giving you the money. Except in the first and third person singular of *be*, there is homonymy between the subjunctive and the past tense indicative: *were* in [22] contrasts with the *was* of, say, *John was there yesterday*, whereas with other verbs there would be identity of phonological realization – compare *If John came tomorrow, . . .* and *John came yesterday*. The subjunctive is of quite limited distribution, occurring primarily in conditional constructions like [22]; it is also found after the verb *wish*, as in *I wish he were here*. Some of the modals occur in the subjunctive in independent clauses as well: compare indicative *It may rain* with subjunctive *It might rain*, where the former suggests a greater possibility of rain than the latter. Non-modal subjunctive VGps, however, occur only in subordinate clauses: *would see* in [22] could be replaced by *might see* or *could see* but not by *saw* – note, for example, that Macbeth's *If it were done when 'tis done, then 'twere well it were done quickly* is not well-formed in present-day English.

5.2 A grammar for positive declarative sentences

Let us now turn to the task of constructing a grammar that will generate sentences containing forms [li–xxxii]. Since the main interest in this chapter is on the VGp, I shall ignore all but the very simplest constructions in other parts of the sentence. The model introduced in Chapter 4 consists of two sets of rules, PS rules which generate the deep structures, and transformations which convert these into surface structures. We have already argued that active–passive pairs should not be differentiated in deep structure, which means that our PS rules need distinguish only sixteen types of VGp. The following rules will do this:

[23]   i   S → NP VP
       ii   VP → VGp NP
       iii   NP → N
       iv   VGp → Aux V
       v   Aux → Tns (M) (*have en*) (*be ing*)
       vi   Tns → {*Past, Pres*}
       vii   M → {*will, can*, . . .}
       viii V → {*see*, . . .}
       ix   N → {*John, Mary*, . . .}

(The major simplification referred to above is in [ii], which allows only for transitive VPs, and [iii], which allows only for NPs consisting of a single noun.) Rule [iv] divides the VGp into a V, standing for what I have been calling the main verb, and Aux(iliary), a cover term for all elements in the VGp preceding the main verb. Rule [v] introduces an obligatory tense element (recall that we are here dealing only with finite, *ie* 'tensed' clauses), which is then rewritten in [vi] as either *Past* or *Pres*: [vi] formalizes our claim that English has a two-term tense system. The remaining elements on the right of rule [v] are optional. If M (modal auxiliary) is selected we get a modal VGp, otherwise a non-modal one; if the pair of morphemes *have* and *en* are selected we get a perfect VGp; if *be* and *ing* are selected we get a progressive one. The options and alternatives in [v] and [vi] allow for sixteen different combinations of elements, corresponding to the sixteen types of active VGp we are aiming for. Note that although the modal and aspectual auxiliaries are optional, their relative order is fixed: the modal always precedes the perfect auxiliary, which in turn precedes the progressive auxiliary. The linear order of M, *have* and *be* in [v] will allow for the generation of *can have seen, has been seeing*, while excluding **has could see, *is having seen*, and so on.

All that remains to be explained in [23] is the linear position of the elements Tns, *en* and *ing* in rule [v]. [23] will generate strings in which the inflectional morphemes occupy different positions from those they have in the representations given in column B of [1]. For example, [23] generates [24], not [25] (corresponding to [lxv], *will have been seeing*):

[24] . . . *Pres will have en be ing see* . . .
[25] . . . *will Pres have be en see ing* . . .

[24] is part of the deep structure, [25] part of the surface structure: since they differ, we shall need a transformational rule to convert [24] into [25], and similarly with other sentences. This is the rule that relates PMs [12i] and [ii] of Chapter 4 and also [13ii–iv]. Why do we not have the PS rules insert these elements directly into the positions they occupy in surface structure?

We have seen that each verb consists of a stem alone or a stem plus one of the four inflections. But just which inflection it has, if any, depends on where it occurs in the VGp. If it is the first word, it will have a tense inflection; if it follows a modal, it will consist of the stem alone; if it follows the perfect auxiliary *have*, it will end with *en;* and so on. To account for this dependence we would need context-sensitive rules, so that instead of [23iv], [v] and [vii] we would have [26].

[26] i VGp → (M) (Perf) (Prog) V

ii   V → VS $\left\{ \begin{array}{l} \text{Tns} / \text{NP} \_\_ \\ / \text{M} \_\_ \\ en / \text{Perf} \_\_ \\ ing / \text{Prog} \_\_ \end{array} \right\}$

iii Prog → *be* $\left\{ \begin{array}{l} \text{Tns} / \text{NP} \_\_ \\ / \text{M} \_\_ \\ en / \text{Perf} \_\_ \end{array} \right\}$

iv Perf → *have* $\left\{ \begin{array}{l} \text{Tns} / \text{NP} \_\_ \\ / \text{M} \_\_ \end{array} \right\}$

v   M → MS Tns

vi MS → {*can, will,* . . .}

(where Perf, Prog, VS and MS stand for perfect auxiliary, progressive auxiliary, main-verb stem and modal stem respectively). These rules will generate the surface morphemic representations for [li–xvi] (and exclude deviant strings), but the highly repetitive nature of them shows clearly that important generalizations are being missed. Instead of a general rule inserting Tns as suffix to the first word in the VGp, [26] has four separate rules introducing Tns in this position; similarly it has three rules accounting for the absence of a suffix on the next word after a modal, and two introducing *en* on words following the perfect auxiliary. [26] shows the kind of rules we would need if we adopted the PSG model, and its inability to express these generalizations is further evidence of the inadequacy of that model.

Notice, moreover, that [26] accounts only for the active forms. Once we accept that *John saw Mary* and *Mary was seen by John* have the same deep structure, it is evident that the surface position of the inflections cannot be determined at the level of deep structure, *ie* by the PS rules. [26ii] will put the tense element on the right of *see* here, which is its surface position in the active *John saw Mary*, but not in the passive *Mary was seen by John*. And the same would apply to *ing* in the pair *was seeing, was being seen:* [26ii] inserts it on the right of *see*, which is the surface position it has in the active, not the passive.

The ultimate position of the inflections cannot be specified directly by the PS rules, therefore. [23v] does, however, express the generalization that *have* is associated with *en*, *be* with *ing*, and that the relative order of the tense, perfect and progressive inflections is as shown.

So much for the PS rules [23]; we must turn now to the transformational component of the grammar. A transformation, like a PS rule, relates an 'input' to an 'output', but whereas with PS rules input and output are strings of symbols (lines in PS derivations), with transformations input and output are both full PMs. A transformation accordingly has two parts: a STRUCTURE INDEX defining the class of PMs to which the rule can apply, and a STRUCTURE CHANGE, specifying how the output PM differs from the input.

The structure index for the Passivization rule is

[27] X — NP — Aux — V — NP — Y

Passivization can apply to any PM which is ANALYSABLE in the way shown in [27], where the elements separated by dashes are the TERMS of the structure index. The notion of analysability depends on the 'is a' relation discussed in Chapter 3. A PM is analysable as in [27] if its terminal string is divisible into six substrings, such that the second 'is a' NP, the third is an Aux, the fourth a V, the fifth a NP; the first and last substrings can be anything at all: this is the meaning of the 'variables' X and Y. [28] shows a PM analysed in accordance with this index. Here the first and last substrings are empty – a special case of being 'anything at all'. X and Y are included in [27] because in other sentences there may be expressions in these positions: for example, the deep structure of *Mary will have been seen by John at the races* will differ from [28] in having *at the races* as the sixth substring.

[28]

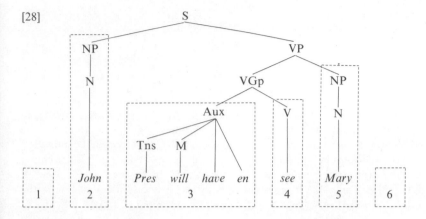

Adding now the structure change, we get the complete rule [29].

[29] PASSIVIZATION   X — NP — Aux   —   V — NP — Y
     (Optional)   1   2   3   4   5   6 ⇒
                     1   5   3+be en   4 by+2 6

The rule interchanges the positions of the NPs in terms 2 and 5, adds the morphemes *be* and *en* to the auxiliary constituent, and adds the morpheme *by* in front of the NP in the position of the original term 5. Applying this to [28] gives

[30]

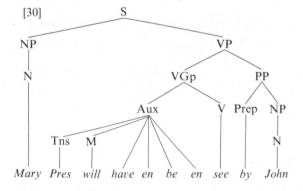

I shall leave until 12.4 a systematic account of how the structure change works – by that time we shall have introduced a sufficient variety of transformations to illustrate the principles involved; in the meantime we shall be able to get by with a rough grasp of the general idea.

The only other transformation needed to generate the positive declarative sentences we are concerned with is 'Affix Hopping', the rule that moves the inflectional affixes to their surface position:

[31] AFFIX HOPPING
(Obligatory)

$$X - \begin{Bmatrix} \text{Tns} \\ ing \\ en \end{Bmatrix} - \begin{Bmatrix} \text{M} \\ have \\ be \\ \text{V} \end{Bmatrix} - Y$$

1	2	3	4	$\Rightarrow$
1	$\varnothing$	$3+2$	4	

The braces enclose alternatives, just as in PS rules. [31] applies, therefore, to any PM containing any one of Tns, *ing* or *en* immediately to the left of any one of M, *have*, *be* or V. The rule moves the affix to the right of term 3. The symbol $\varnothing$ ('zero') indicates that the position occupied by term 2 in the input PM is empty in the output (the original term 2 appears instead on the right of term 3). PM [30] is analysable in accordance with the structure index of [31] in the following way (I save space by giving only the terminal string):

[32]

Mary Pres will have en be	*en*	*see*	*by John*
1	2	3	4

Term 2, *en*, is actually mentioned in the rule, while term 3, *see* stands in the 'is a' relation to V, which figures in the index of the rule. Applying the rule gives a PM which can again be analysed to meet the index as shown in [33].

[33]

Mary Pres will have	*en*	*be*	*see en by John*
1	2	3	4

Thus a second application moves *en* around *be*, and finally a third application moves *Pres* around *will* to yield a surface structure terminating in '*Mary will Pres have be en see en by John*'. The transformational derivation for the sentence *Mary will have been seen by John* will thus consist of five PMs terminating in the strings shown in [34].

[34] i *John Pres will have en see Mary*
    ii *Mary Pres will have en be en see by John*
    iii *Mary Pres will have en be see en by John*
    iv *Mary Pres will have be en see en by John*
    v *Mary will Pres have be en see en by John*

[i] comes from the PS derivation, [ii] is derived by Passivization, the remainder by Affix Hopping. For two derivations showing full PMs, see [12] and [13] of Chapter 4 (to generate the NPs in the latter we would need to add 'NP → Det N', etc to the PS rules).

The transformations are ordered so as to apply at successive stages in a derivation. For example, Passivization is ordered before Affix Hopping, for as noted above the ultimate position of the inflectional affixes cannot be specified until the voice of the sentence has been determined. The rules are classified as OPTIONAL or OBLIGATORY, an obligatory transformation being one that must apply at its appointed stage in the derivation if the PM is analysable in accordance with its structure index. Passivization is optional, so that both active and passive surface structures will be generated; Affix Hopping is obligatory, so that [30] is not accepted as a well-formed surface structure – it is only an intermediate stage in the derivation.

5.3 Interrogative and negative sentences

The next task is to extend the grammar to cover the interrogative and negative counterparts of the sentences we have accounted for so far. I shall here deal only with 'yes/no' interrogatives (so called because of the type of answer they invite), as opposed to 'wh' interrogatives like *Who saw Mary?*, *Who(m) will John see?*, etc. A sample of declarative-interrogative pairs is shown in [35], where the Roman numbering matches that of [1].

[35]

	DECLARATIVE	INTERROGATIVE
i	*John sees Mary*	*Does John see Mary?*
ii	*John saw Mary*	*Did John see Mary?*
iii	*John will see Mary*	*Will John see Mary?*
vi	*John had seen Mary*	*Had John seen Mary?*
x	*John was seeing Mary*	*Was John seeing Mary?*
xiv	*John had been seeing Mary*	*Had John been seeing Mary?*
xviii	*Mary was seen by John*	*Was Mary seen by John?*
xix	*Mary will be seen by John*	*Will Mary be seen by John?*

Let us temporarily leave aside cases [i] and [ii], which raise the problem of accounting for the special auxiliary verb *do* that appears in the interrogative. In other cases (including all of [iii–xxxii], not just those shown in [35]) the only difference between the interrogatives and declarative counterparts is in the word order. There are two ways in which we could generate structures with the interrogative word order: we could add PS rules introducing the relevant elements on the left of the subject NP in deep structure (the PS solution); or we could generate the interrogatives with the same word order in deep structure as declaratives and add a transformation that moves the relevant elements around the subject NP to yield the surface order (the transformational solution). It is easy to show that the latter is much the better.

The PS solution would require that the first PS rule have essentially the following form:

[36]
$$S \rightarrow (Tns \begin{Bmatrix} M \\ have \\ be \end{Bmatrix}) \; NP \; VP$$

This allows for the option of M, *have* or *be*, plus the tense element (which I continue to put on the left), to precede the subject NP: if this option is selected we get an interrogative, otherwise a declarative. The trouble with [36] is that it necessitates revising the rules for VGp and Aux, replacing the simple context-free versions [23iv] and [v] with highly complicated context-sensitive rules. For Aux, for example, we would need

[37]

$$\text{Aux} \rightarrow \begin{cases} \text{Tns (M) } (have\ en)\ (be\ ing) & / \ \# \ \text{NP} \ \underline{\quad} \\ (have\ en)\ (be\ ing) & / \ \text{M NP} \ \underline{\quad} \\ en\ (be\ ing) & / \ have\ \text{NP} \ \underline{\quad} \\ ing & / \ be\ \text{NP} \ \underline{\quad} \end{cases}$$

The first subrule applies to declaratives, cases where the subject NP is in sentence initial position, the remaining three to interrogatives, depending on which of M, *have* and *be* has been selected from [36]. The lack of generality is evident: instead of a single rule giving the structure of Aux, we have four separate rules – the grammar has to state four times that *ing* is associated with progressive *be*, three times that *en* is associated with perfect *have* and is optionally followed by *be ing*, and so on. We have here a further example of a case where the PS rules can account for the differences between a pair of constructions, declarative and interrogative, but not for the similarity and systematic relationship between them. (Notice, moreover, that complex as they are these amended PS rules do not account for the surface word order in passive interrogatives like [35xviii]: as the passive auxiliary *be* is not present in deep structure it cannot be placed in initial position by the PS rules.)

The transformational solution overcomes these difficulties. The many common syntactic properties between declaratives and interrogatives are accounted for by using the rules of [23] to generate the deep structures of both types, and the difference is attributed to the optional application of a transformation that changes the order of elements. A provisional formulation of this rule is as follows:

[38] INVERSION
(Optional)

$$\text{NP} - \text{Tns} \begin{Bmatrix} \text{M} \\ have \\ be \end{Bmatrix} - \text{X}$$

$$\begin{array}{ccc} 1 & 2 & 3 \ \Rightarrow \\ 2+1 & \varnothing & 3 \end{array}$$

This moves term 2 to initial position; the X in term 3 stands for a variable as usual: what occurs after term 2 need not be specified in detail because it is irrelevant to the operation of the rule. [38] will convert a PM terminating in [39] into [40] (corresponding to [35vi]):

[39]

John	Past have	en see Mary
1	2	3

[40]

Past have John		*en see Mary*
2 + 1	∅	3

The *en* associated with *have* is subsumed under the variable X: it is not carried to front position along with *have*, for in both declarative and interrogative *en* will be attached to *see* by the Affix Hopping rule. Transformation [38] formalizes the intuitive statement that interrogatives are formed from declaratives by reversing the order of the subject and the first auxiliary verb. As I emphasized in Chapter 4, however, in the formal theory of TG a transformation does not change one sentence into another, but one syntactic representation, *ie* one PM, into another: a sentence is defined by its final phonological form (*cf* 1.2), whereas the applicability of a transformation has to be defined in syntactic terms. I shall frequently follow the widespread practice of saying, for example, that *Had John seen Mary?* is derived by Inversion from *John had seen Mary*, but this is to be understood as an informal shorthand way of saying that the two sentences derive from a common underlying structure, with Inversion applying in the transformational derivation of the former but not the latter.

If we order Inversion so that it applies after Passivization, it will cover cases where the *be* of term 2 is the passive auxiliary, as well as those where it is the progressive. The transformational derivation for *Was Mary seen by John?* will thus be as in [41] (simplified, like the other derivations given in this chapter, to show only terminal strings instead of the full PMs that would be generated by the grammar).

[41] i   *John Past see Mary*   [by PS rules]
    ii *Mary Past be en see by John* [by Passivization]
    iii *Past be Mary en see by John* [by Inversion]
    iv *be Past Mary en see by John* [by Affix Hopping]
    v   *be Past Mary see en by John* [by Affix Hopping]

It remains now to deal with interrogatives like *Does/did John see Mary?* which contain the auxiliary *do*. There are four types of construction in which this auxiliary occurs: interrogatives, negatives, emphatic positives and certain anaphoric constructions. The last three are exemplified in [42–44] respectively.

[42] *They do not speak French*
[43] *She DID hear him*
[44] *John likes Bach and so does Peter*

In [43] the auxiliary carries heavy stress (indicated in the notation by capitalization), marking a contrast with the corresponding negative – note that in *She HEARD him* the contrast is not with the negative but with some other lexical item than *hear*, such as *see*. What is meant by 'anaphora' will be explained in Chapter 16; at this point it is sufficient to note that *so does Peter* in [44] is equivalent to *Peter likes Bach* – the use of *do* and *so* avoids the repetition of material from the preceding clause. Other anaphoric constructions where *do* is found are answers to questions (A: *Do you know John?* B: *Yes, I do*), question 'tags' (*John doesn't speak French, does he?*), and so on. *Do* differs from the modal, aspectual and passive auxiliaries in that it cannot combine with any other auxiliary verb – compare *Can John speak French?* versus **Does John can speak French?*; *They have not arrived* versus **They do not have arrived; She IS working* versus **She DOES be working; John was killed and so was Bill* versus **John was killed and so did Bill*. Since the passive auxiliary is not present in deep structure, the occurrence of *do* is not predictable at that level; we will accordingly insert it by a transformation, *Do* Support, ordered to apply after Passivization. This approach will also allow us to formulate a single rule for *do* that will cover all four of the above constructions, thereby giving a general account of its incompatibility with the other auxiliaries.

In *Does/did John see Mary?* the tense inflection is suffixed to *do* not *see*, so that it will have to be moved from its underlying position. This can be achieved by amending the Inversion rule, and ordering *Do* Support to apply later in the derivation.

[45] INVERSION
(Optional)

$$\text{NP} - \left\{ \text{Tns} \begin{Bmatrix} \text{M} \\ \textit{have} \\ \textit{be} \end{Bmatrix} - \text{X} \atop \text{Tns} \quad - \text{V X} \right\}$$

$$\begin{array}{ccc} 1 & 2 & 3 \Rightarrow \\ 2+1 & \varnothing & 3 \end{array}$$

[46] *Do* SUPPORT   X   — Tns — Y
(Obligatory)   1   2   3 ⇒
               1   *do*+2   3
Condition: X ≠ W {M, *have*, *be*, V}

[45], besides doing the work of the earlier [38], also moves to front position a tense inflection immediately to the left of V. [46] then introduces *do* as 'support' for any tense element which does not follow M, *have*, *be* or V. The 'condition' in the rule is to be interpreted as part of the structure index, *ie* as part of the specification of the class of PMs to which the rule applies. It says that the variable X preceding Tns must not be ('≠') W followed by any one of M, *have*, *be* or V, where W is another variable standing for any string of elements. The derivation of *Did John see Mary?* will then be as follows:

[47] i *John Past see Mary*   [by PS rules]
    ii *Past John see Mary*   [by Inversion]
   iii *do Past John see Mary* [by *Do* Support]

The four transformations we have introduced apply in the order Passivization, Inversion, Affix Hopping, *Do* Support. We have already seen why Passivization must be the first of these: it introduces the auxiliary *be*, which may be moved by Inversion, and which must be in the structure when the inflectional affixes are moved to their surface position by Affix Hopping. We order Inversion before Affix Hopping to prevent *Past* being moved round *see* in [47] and the like: note that [47i] satisfies the structure index for Affix Hopping whereas [ii] does not. Inversion is ordered before *Do* Support because it creates the environment which requires the insertion of *do:* the declarative counterpart of *Did John see Mary?*, ie: *John saw Mary*, has no *do*. And finally Affix Hopping must precede *Do* Support or else [46] would insert *do* before every tense inflection; [41iii], for example, satisfies the index for *Do* Support, so that we would get wrong results if the rule were allowed to apply at this stage of a derivation.

Negatives can be dealt with more quickly, because the problems they raise are very similar to those associated with interrogatives. I shall consider only simple constructions marked by the presence of *not* in the VGp – this excludes negatives like *Nothing satisfies her, I saw neither John nor Bill*, and also contracted forms like *John hasn't seen Mary*. [48] gives a sample of positive/negative pairs.

[48]

	POSITIVE	NEGATIVE
i	*John sees Mary*	*John does not see Mary*
ii	*John saw Mary*	*John did not see Mary*
iii	*John will see Mary*	*John will not see Mary*
vi	*John had seen Mary*	*John had not seen Mary*
x	*John was seeing Mary*	*John was not seeing Mary*
xiv	*John had been seeing Mary*	*John had not been seeing Mary*
xviii	*Mary was seen by John*	*Mary was not seen by John*
xix	*Mary will be seen by John*	*Mary will not be seen by John*

Comparison of [48] with [35] shows striking similarities between negatives and interrogatives: again we find it is just forms [i] and [ii] that require the insertion of *do* and, more generally, the surface position of *not* in the negative declaratives of [48] is the same as that of the subject NP *John* in the interrogatives of [35]. Thus just as the position of *John* in the latter will be accounted for by transformation rather than by PS rules, so will that of *not:* we add rule [49] to the grammar.

[49] *Not* PLACEMENT
(Optional)

$$NP - \left\{ \begin{array}{l} Tns \left\{ \begin{array}{l} M \\ have \\ be \end{array} \right\} - X \\ Tns \qquad - V X \end{array} \right\}$$

$$\begin{array}{ccc} 1 & 2 & 3 \Rightarrow \\ 1 & 2+not & 3 \end{array}$$

The derivation of *John was not seeing Mary* and *John did not see Mary* will now be as follows:

[50] i *John Past be ing see Mary*   [by PS rules]
   ii *John Past be not ing see Mary*   [by *Not* Placement]
  iii *John be Past not ing see Mary*   [by Affix Hopping]
   iv *John be Past not see ing Mary*   [by Affix Hopping]

[51] i *John Past see Mary*   [by PS rules]
   ii *John Past not see Mary*   [by *Not* Placement]
  iii *John do Past not see Mary*   [by *Do* Support]

Note that [51ii] does not satisfy the index for Affix Hopping, so that *Do* Support applies instead. *Not* Placement is ordered before Affix Hopping so as to prevent the latter applying to [51i]; it must of course be ordered after Passivization, so that *not* will be correctly placed in *Mary was not seen by John*, etc.

Negative interrogatives like *Had John not seen Mary?* can be generated by the above rules with *Not* Placement ordered before Inversion:

[52] i *John Past have en see Mary*   [by PS rules]
   ii *John Past have not en see Mary*   [by *Not* Placement]
  iii *Past have John not en see Mary*   [by Inversion]
   iv *have Past John not en see Mary*   [by Affix Hopping]
    v *have Past John not see en Mary*   [by Affix Hopping]

One slight modification must be made to cater for *Did John not see Mary?*: instead of 'V X' in term 3 of [45] we shall need '(*not*) V X'.

A TG breaks down the generation of a sentence into significantly more stages than a PSG, and to this extent the individual sentence derivations are more complex. But it is the simplicity of the grammar, of the rules, that is of interest, not that of the separate derivations. After all, the simplest derivation for *Had John not seen Mary?* would be achieved by including in the grammar the rule 'S → *Had John not seen Mary?*': simple, but totally unrevealing. Having many separate steps in the various derivations enables us to express the systematic resemblances and relationships between different sentences; the rules relating the successive stages in a derivation will typically apply in the generation of a great range of sentences and thereby express general regularities in the language.

Notes

There is a large literature on the verb in English. Among the best general studies are Palmer 1965 and Allen 1966; a concise account of the dimensions discussed in 5.1 is Twaddell 1960; see also Quirk *et al* 1972, Chapter 3. Lyons 1968:304–17 has a valuable discussion of the general linguistic categories of tense, mood and aspect. The contrast between subjunctive *were* and indicative *was* is not made by all speakers; in dialects having *was* for both, the distinction between *If he is there tomorrow*, . . . and *If he was there tomorrow*, . . . will be analysed (at least in surface structure) as one of tense rather than mood. Many grammars also apply the term subjunctive to forms like *be* in *It is essential that you be here when she arrives*; this, however, is simply the infinitive form, and I am aware of no reason for treating it together with the *were* of *If he were here* as a single mood in modern English.

The rules given in 5.2–3 follow closely those proposed in Chomsky 1957. The major features of this analysis of the auxiliary verbs were accepted in virtually all transformational studies of English in the first ten years or so of TG, and are indeed still accepted by many scholars; I shall be discussing a fairly radically different alternative in Chapter 14. The term 'VGp' I have imported from outside the transformational literature; Chomsky used 'Verb' instead, distinguishing this from 'V', which had the same interpretation as in my rules; many works avoid the VGp category by making Aux a daughter of S. The main reason for recognizing Aux as a constituent, consisting of all the verbal elements except the main verb, is that this permits a simpler formulation of Passivization (see [29]) than would be possible if VGp were rewritten directly as 'Tns (M) (*have en*) (*be ing*) V'. My formulation of Affix Hopping is not quite correct, since as it stands there is nothing to prevent its applying to its own output to move the same affix more than once, yielding *Mary will have be see Pres en en by John*, instead of [34v], and so on; Chomsky's version overcomes this problem by the use of word boundaries.

Alternative terms for 'structure index' are 'structural analysis' and 'structural description' (commonly abbreviated SD, with SC standing for structure change). On the formal structure of transformational rules, see Chomsky 1961*a*, Kimball 1973.

Chapter 6

Syntactic Structure and Meaning

The task of a generative grammar according to the *Syntactic Structures* theory was to generate the well-formed sentences of a language and describe the syntactic and phonological structure of each, but the description of their meaning was, as I have said, regarded as a matter for a separate theory of language use. Moreover, the division of the syntax into PS and transformational components was based on non-semantic considerations. In his original investigations of the adequacy of the theory of PSG, Chomsky noted that there was a class of very elementary sentences whose syntactic structure could apparently be handled more or less satisfactorily by this model – sentences that were 'simple' (in the technical sense of containing only one clause), active, positive, declarative, and so on. The shortcomings of PSG became evident when one tried to extend the grammar to cover sentences containing more than one clause as well as simple ones, passives as well as actives, interrogatives and imperatives as well as declaratives, negatives as well as positives, and so on. It was this that provided the motivation for adding transformational rules to the grammar. As we have seen, the addition of transformations did not involve the abandonment of PS rules, but rather a narrowing of their scope and function. Instead of a vastly complex set of PS rules that would directly generate the full range of different sentence structures found in a language, Chomsky envisaged a relatively small and simple set of PS rules generating a highly restricted class of basic structures associated fairly directly with the elementary sentences – KERNEL SENTEN-CES, as he called them. The more complex structures of non-kernel sentences were then derived from the basic structures by various transformations. The kernel/non-kernel distinction reflects the intuition that sentences like *John saw Mary* are somehow more 'basic' than *Mary was seen by John, Did John see Mary?*, etc. It is not quite the case that transformations played no role in the generation of kernel sentences. We saw, for example, in the discussion of the English auxiliary, that there are good grounds for generating the verbal affixes in a different position in deep structure from that which they occupy in surface structure, and this means of course that Affix Hopping will apply in the derivation of *John saw Mary* and the like. Kernel sentences were thus defined as those in whose generation no OPTIONAL transformation applies. Nevertheless, in spite of such differences in the position of affixes, the deep and surface structure of a kernel sentence were very alike – and the possibility was not excluded that in some languages they might be identical. In this conception of syntax, then, the role of the PS rules was to generate a highly restricted set of elementary structures, while that of the transformations was to operate on these to yield the full, more varied, more complex set of structures found in the language.

The first proposals for extending the scope of generative grammar so as to include semantics were made in a paper published in 1963: 'The structure of a semantic theory', by J. J. Katz and J. A. Fodor. There was certainly no question here of eliminating the distinction between linguistic form and use of language: the effect was rather to enrich the conception of formal structure by including a semantic level. The aim was to devise explicit rules which would assign semantic representations to sentences – representations that would account for such semantic relations between sentences as paraphrase, entailment, inconsistency, and so on. Katz and Fodor began with the very plausible assumption that the meaning of a sentence depends in part on the lexical items it contains, in part on the syntactic structure uniting them. Thus in

[1] *The dog chased the man*
[2] *The dog bit the man*
[3] *The man bit the dog*

the difference in meaning between [1] and [2] is attributable to the lexical difference *chase* versus *bite*, whereas that between 2 and 3 is attributable to the different syntactic arrangement of the same set of lexical items. This distinction provided the basis for the division of the semantic component into two subcomponents: a DICTIONARY, which gives the meanings to the lexical items, the minimal meaningful units in the sentence, and a set of PROJECTION RULES, which assign meanings to the larger units and ultimately the sentence as a whole, by combining the meanings of the lexical items in ways which take account of the syntactic structure.

A discussion of the form of Katz–Fodor dictionary entries and projection rules would be outside the scope of this book; the question I want to investigate here is, rather: What aspects of syntactic structure play a part in determining the meaning of a sentence? The above simple example demonstrates that one obvious and important contribution is made by the syntactic relations or functions – subject, object and so on. In [2], the semantic roles of 'actor' and 'patient' are filled by the dog and the man respectively, whereas they are reversed in [3]: this clearly correlates with the fact that *the dog* and *the man* are respectively subject and object in [2], object and subject in [3]. We have defined the syntactic functions in terms of the positions of categories in PMs, subject being the NP that is daughter of S, and so on; and since the syntactic structure of a sentence takes the form of a sequence of PMs, the syntactic functions in a sentence are identifiable at different stages in its derivation, from the deep to the surface level. In examples like [2] and [3] this is of little interest, because here the deep and surface functions are identical. There are, however, many cases where this is not so, where the effect of a transformation is to alter the syntactic functions in a sentence. And in all such cases it emerges that it is the deep structure functions that determine the semantic roles. We have so far come across only three transformations that change the syntactic functions, but they will serve well enough to illustrate the principle. One is Passivization: in *The man was bitten by the dog*, according to the analysis we have given, *the man* has the same surface function, subject, as in [3], and the same deep function, object, as in [2]. And clearly the semantic role is the same as in [2], not [3]: the man is understood as patient. A second function-changing transformation is the one that deletes *you* to yield imperative sentences like *Pamper yourself!*. Here there is no subject at all in surface structure, but I argued in Chapter 4 that we need to recognize a *you* in deep structure subject position – and this correlates with the fact that the semantic role of actor is filled by the addressee. Thirdly, in the brief discussion of the sentence *The insects were difficult for John to annihilate* I suggested that there is a transformation that removes *the insects* from its position of deep structure object to *annihilate*: in surface structure *annihilate* has no object, yet clearly we understand the sentence in such a way that the insects have the role of patient relative to the action of annihilating. Several other function-changing transformations will be added later, and they will all follow this pattern.

To avoid possible misunderstanding here, I should emphasize that I am not claiming that there is a constant semantic role associated with each deep grammatical function – that the deep subject invariably identifies the actor, the deep object the patient, say. We noted in 2.1 that many clauses do not express actions (*eg: He has brown hair*, *The bicycle belongs to John*, etc), so that the notion of actor will not be applicable in such cases, even though there is a subject: the distinction we have since introduced between deep and surface subject does not affect this point. In saying that it is the deep structure functions that determine meaning we are making the weaker but nevertheless important claim that the rules which relate the syntactic structure of a sentence to its meaning will interpret the semantic role of an element on the basis of its function in deep structure, not in surface (or intermediate) structure. Thus in *John annihilated the insects*, *The insects were annihilated by John* and *The insects were difficult for John to annihilate* there is a constant semantic role associated with *the insects* and this is attributable to the fact that it has the same syntactic function relative to *annihilate* in the deep structure: the surface structure differences are irrelevant to our interpretation of the semantic relation between *the insects* and *annihilate*.

It is worth emphasizing that this correlation between deep syntactic function and semantic role played no part in the original arguments in favour of TG over PSG, nor in the justification of particular deep structure analyses. As remarked above, the arguments for including transformations in the grammar were based on the inability of a PSG to distinguish well-formed sentences from deviant ones by means of rules expressing significant generalizations. The analyses of passives, imperatives, and so on proposed in Chapter 4, for example, were justified by the fact that they enabled us to express general distributional statements, not by any appeal to the semantic relation between verbs and noun phrases.

The same point holds in the special case of ambiguous sentences, such as *I like Bill more than Tom*. The ambiguity is accounted for by showing that the sentence is transformationally derived by deletion of repeated material from two different deep structures, one containing the clause *I Pres like Tom*, the other *Tom Pres like Bill* (compare *I like Bill more than I like Tom* versus *I like Bill more than Tom likes him*). The semantically significant relations between the elements are here apparent in deep structure, but obscured in surface structure. The ability of TG to account in a principled way for a much greater range of structural ambiguities than PSG counted as an added argument in its favour – but again the role of transformations in accounting for ambiguities was not invoked in the general explication of the different functions of the PS and transformational components, nor in the primary justification of particular syntactic analyses. The claim that *I Pres like Tom* occurs in the deep structure of *I like Bill more than Tom* in one of its derivations, and *Tom Pres like Bill* in that of the other, is based primarily on the same kind of distributional argument as we have been using in the analysis of non-ambiguous sentences. For example, we want to distinguish the well-formed *Bill smiles more than Tom* from the deviant **Bill smiles more than the storm:* only if we postulate deep structures containing the clauses *Tom Pres smile* and *the storm Pres smile* can we handle this distinction by the same rules as we use to generate the simple sentence *Tom smiles* while excluding **The storm smiles*.

We have claimed that the projection rules which yield a representation of the meaning of a sentence must take account of the syntactic functions in deep structure, but can ignore those in all subsequent PMs in its transformational derivation. To what extent, we must now ask, does this hold also for the contribution to meaning of other aspects of syntactic structure?

Certainly not for all, if we accept the grammar of Chapter 5, which, as I have said, closely follows that proposed in *Syntactic Structures*. There we derived pairs like *John saw Mary* and *John didn't see Mary* from a common deep structure *John Past see Mary*, so that if the semantic rules took only the deep structure into account they would fail to assign distinct meanings to these sentences. Similarly, *John saw Mary* and *Did John see Mary?* were derived from the same deep structure and the difference in mood, crucial to the meaning of the sentences, was introduced by transformation: any viable semantic rules, therefore, would have to look beyond deep structure and take account of the contribution to meaning of the optional Inversion transformation.

Let us look more closely at the syntactic analysis of negatives, however. The argument for having a *Not* Placement transformation was that *not* cannot be inserted directly into its surface structure position by PS rule without significant loss of generality in the statement of permitted combinations of auxiliary verbs. Consider, for example:

[4] i *John will not have been seeing Mary*
  ii *John has not been seeing Mary*
  iii *John is not seeing Mary*
  iv *John does not see Mary*

In [i] *not* is on the left of *have*, in [ii] on the right; in [ii] it is on the left of *be*, in [iii] on the right. To handle these facts directly in the PS component would require one rule for the case where there is a modal; another for the case where there is no modal, but a perfect *have;* a third for the case where there is neither a modal nor *have*, but a progressive *be;* and a fourth for the case where there is no modal, no *have* and no *be*. Instead of our earlier rule for Aux, repeated here as [5], we would need something like [6].

[5] Aux → Tns (M) (*have en*) (*be ing*)

$$[6] \ \text{Aux} \rightarrow \text{Tns} \begin{cases} \text{M (\textit{not}) (\textit{have en}) (\textit{be ing})} \\ \textit{have (not) en (be ing)} \\ \textit{be (not) ing} \\ \textit{(not)} \end{cases}$$

This argument establishes that we should not use PS rules to insert *not* in its surface position – but it does not follow that they should not insert it in any position. An alternative analysis to that presented in Chapter 5 would be one where the PS rule for VGp is [7] and the *Not* Placement transformation [8].

[7] VGp → (*not*) Aux V

[8] *Not* PLACEMENT
   (Obligatory)

$$\text{NP} - not - \begin{cases} \text{Tns} \begin{cases} \text{M} \\ \textit{have} \\ \textit{be} \end{cases} - \text{X} \\ \text{Tns} \quad - \text{V X} \end{cases}$$

1	2	3	4	⇒
1	∅	3+2	4	

Here *not* is optionally introduced into deep structure by [7] and then moved to its surface position by [8]. Whereas the earlier *Not* Placement rule was optional the new one is obligatory: if there is a *not* in the input PM it must be shifted round term 3. In the analysis of Chapter 5 the choice between positive and negative sentences was handled by the optionality of the *Not* Placement rule, in the new analysis by the optionality of *not* in rule [7].

 Both analyses enable us to express the generalization about the combination of auxiliary verbs formulated in rule [5]. And when one considers a wider range of negative sentences it emerges that the second analysis has certain advantages over the first. Note, for example, the following contrasts in well-formedness:

 [9] *He does not always/often speak*
 [10] **He does not never/scarcely/seldom speak*
 [11] *He always/often/never/scarcely/seldom speaks*

In the new analysis of negatives, we can exclude [10] while generating [9] and [11] by assigning *always, often, never, scarcely, seldom* to a category 'Preverb' (so called because of its most usual position) and making the PS rule that rewrites Preverb sensitive to the presence or absence of *not* in the context (see *p* 179 for a formalization of the necessary rules). This solution is not available if *not* is not introduced until after all the PS rules have applied, and for this reason the second analysis came to be adopted in preference to the original one.

The significance of this revision from a semantic point of view is that the contrast between positive and negative sentences is now represented in deep structure. The original version of *Not* Placement had been MEANING-CHANGING, inasmuch as the difference in meaning between pairs like *John did not see Mary* and *John saw Mary* was attributable to the fact that the rule applied in the first but not the second: up to the stage of application of the rule their derivations had been identical. In the revised grammar, however, the difference in meaning between the sentences is attributable to the selection or omission of *not* in the rewriting of VGp by rule [7]. It is still the case that *Not* Placement applies in the first and not the second, but this is simply a consequence of the difference introduced earlier in the derivation by rule [7]: since the new *Not* Placement is an obligatory rule it cannot be the source of any contrast. Accordingly we shall say that it is MEANING-PRESERVING.

A somewhat similar revision was proposed for imperatives. In Chapter 4 I analysed declarative *You pamper yourself* and imperative *Pamper yourself!* as deriving from a common deep structure '*you Pres pamper you*', with a *You* Deletion transformation applying in the derivation of the imperative. Since the two sentences clearly differ in meaning, this transformation was not meaning-preserving. The revision here involved introducing the abstract morpheme *Imp(erative)* into the deep structure of imperatives, this morpheme serving as a 'trigger' for the *You* Deletion rule. Its structure index will now read '*Imp – you – VP*', so that it is no longer applicable to the declarative structure. The difference in meaning between imperative/declarative pairs is now attributable to the presence or absence of *Imp* in deep structure, not to the application or otherwise of the *You* Deletion transformation, which accordingly is no longer meaning-changing. I should add that the rule remains optional, because *you* can in fact occur as surface subject of an imperative. *You mow the lawn*, for example, can be interpreted as either a declarative or an imperative: it could be used to make a statement or a request; compare *You mow the lawn too often* and *You mow the lawn – I'm too busy*. That there is a syntactic distinction here, not just a semantic one, is evident from the fact that the constructions are overtly differentiated both in the negative, where declarative *You don't mow the lawn (often enough)* contrasts with imperative *Don't you mow the lawn (– I want to do it)*, and also when the verb is *be*, as in declarative *You are careful* versus imperative *You be careful;* moreover, the difference would typically be marked, in speech, by stress and intonation: in the imperative the *you* must be strongly stressed.

The introduction of a purely abstract morpheme like *Imp* does not involve any real extension of the general theory, for I emphasized from the start that morphemes are syntactic units, not directly identifiable in phonological terms. The syntactic arguments for positing an *Imp* morpheme in deep structure were based as usual on distributional considerations. Certain adverbs do not occur in imperative clauses (**Hardly/scarcely/seldom mow the lawn!*) and some verbs are apparently excluded too (witness **Suffer from diabetes!* and the like – I shall take up this point in Chapter 15): in the revised analysis these restrictions can be handled by context-sensitive rules that block the selection of the relevant class of adverb or verb in a structure containing *Imp*. Similar arguments can be given for positing an abstract *Q(uestion)* morpheme in the deep structure of interrogatives – see 9.2 for detailed discussion.

· Now it was claimed that the kind of revision I have presented here for the analysis of negatives and imperatives was needed in all cases where in the early work a transformation had been meaning-changing. This leads, then, to what is commonly referred to as the Katz–Postal hypothesis (after the influential work, Katz and Postal 1964, in which it was developed): that all transformations are meaning-preserving. The importance of the changes as far as the semantic component is concerned will be obvious, for if the transformations introduce no semantically relevant differences among sentences they can be completely ignored by the semantic rules. Wherever two sentences differ in meaning, they will differ in deep structure; the meanings of sentences will thus be determinable from their deep structures, which will form the sole syntactic input to the semantic rules. The proposed interrelation between the various sets of rules is shown diagrammatically in [12].

[12]   INITIAL STRING:

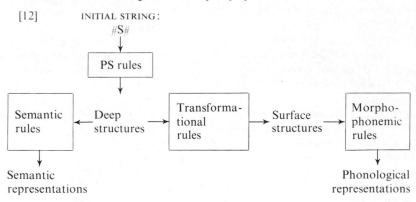

This is only a first approximation to the organization of the *Aspects* version of the theory, but the modifications I shall introduce later will not affect the general point being made here: that the only part of a syntactic derivation that has semantic relevance is the deep structure.

The elimination of meaning-changing transformations makes the task of devising semantic rules significantly less formidable than it would be if they had to operate on complete syntactic derivations. One suspects, indeed, that this may have carried rather more weight in the widespread acceptance of the revised model than the purely syntactic arguments of the type I have illustrated. It should nevertheless be borne in mind that Katz and Postal claimed that in all the transformations they considered (and they were quite numerous) there were syntactic arguments for a reformulation in which they ceased to be meaning-changing: this is theoretically important because if one accepts purely semantic arguments for deep structure analyses the independence of syntax will be lost.

There was indeed one modification of syntactic theory introduced in the *Aspects* model in 1965 whose justification was apparently purely semantic. Let us consider again how we can handle the distribution of reflexive pronouns. According to the analysis suggested in Chapter 4, they are not present in deep structure but are introduced by a Reflexivization transformation which sub-stitutes such a pronoun for an object NP that is identical to the subject. *John shaved himself*, for example, would derive from '*John Past shave John*'. One argument in favour of this analysis over one where reflexive pronouns are intro-duced by PS rules into the deep structure is based on selectional restrictions. We want the grammar to generate *The dog frightened itself* while excluding **The fact frightened itself;* if we inserted reflexive pronouns by PS rule, we could not show that the deviance of the latter sentence is due to the general restriction that *frighten* cannot take an inanimate object – we could not exclude it by the same rule as blocks **The storm frightened the fact.* A second argument for the transformational introduction of reflexive pronouns will be given in Chapter 8, where we shall see that what determines whether a NP is reflexivized is its position not in deep structure but in some PM later in the derivation, after various other transformations have already applied. Notice, however, that in addition to *John shaved himself* we also find *John shaved John*. This type of sentence is admittedly somewhat unusual, but read with an appropriate stress pattern it is widely judged to be acceptable, with an interpretation where the shaver and the one shaved are different persons who happen to have the same name. (Compare *That box must accompany that box* said as the speaker points out two different boxes.) It may be that *John shaved John* can also be interpreted with the two *John*'s coreferential, but the crucial point for our argument here is that it has a meaning where they are not. It follows that if both *John shaved himself* and *John shaved John* are derived from the one deep structure '*John Past shave John*' the Reflexivization transformation must be optional and meaning-changing.

To avoid this kind of problem, Chomsky introduced what he called REFERENTIAL INDICES, markers attached to the referring expressions in a sentence. The deep structures of the two sentences will now be differentiated as, say, '*John$_i$ Past shave John$_i$*' and '*John$_i$ Past shave John$_j$*'. The indices are not intended to represent actual referents, for we are dealing with sentences, not specific utterances of them: their function is just to show identity or difference of reference. This is why it is sufficient to use variables, like subscript i, j, etc: two or more items marked with the same index variable are coreferential and items with different indices are non-coreferential. We can now reformulate Reflexivization so that it applies only if the two NPs have the same index. The difference in meaning between the two sentences above will now be attributable to the identity versus non-identity of the indices attached to *John* in deep structure, not to the application versus non-application of the Reflexivization transformation, which thus ceases to be meaning-changing. Referential indices are used not just to handle reflexive pronouns: they also play a role in a number of other rules involving identity between NPs. For example, the derivation of *John went out and bought a newspaper* from *John went out and John bought a newspaper* (see Chapter 7) is dependent on the two deep structure occurrences of *John* having the same index, and so on.

The introduction of referential indices made it possible to retain the Katz–Postal hypothesis in the face of a substantial class of apparent counterexamples. However, it was not justified on independent syntactic grounds, and this innovation consequently represented a departure from the strictly autonomous syntax of the earlier model: syntactic transformations are now required to meet the semantic condition that they preserve meaning. I shall return to this issue in Chapter 16.

The elimination of meaning-changing transformations involved a considerable modification in the respective roles of the PS and transformational rules; I observed above that in the *Syntactic Structures* theory the PS rules were designed to generate a highly restricted set of PMs associated fairly directly (*ie* via a small number of transformations effecting quite minor structural changes) with the surface structure of kernel sentences. The concept of a kernel sentence, defined as one in which no optional transformation applies, was intended to capture the intuition of a basic or elementary sentence. But in the amended theory the match between kernel sentences and intuitively basic ones is more or less eliminated – notice, for example, that *Did John see Mary?* and *John did not see Mary* no more involve optional transformations than does *John saw Mary;* the common properties of the three sentences are still accounted for at the deep structure level, but their relation at this level is now one of partial likeness, not complete identity. It follows that the concept of kernel sentence no longer has any real significance, and it has been more or less dropped from the theory. I should add that the intuitive notion of a basic sentence is an extremely elusive one, and even in the grammar as it was before the above revisions were introduced it could hardly be said to be formalized satisfactorily by the concept of kernel sentence. Why should we say, for example, that *John did not see Mary* is non-basic, a derivative of *John saw Mary*, whereas *John could see Mary* or *John saw Mary very often* are basic? It is doubtless a mistake to think in terms of a division of sentences into two types, basic and non-basic. What is needed is a concept of varying complexity, with sentences ranging from very simple to highly complex; and we must surely allow that the complexity of a sentence will depend on the interaction of a whole variety of structural factors instead of being determined simply by whether or not any optional transformation applies in its derivation.

In the *Aspects* theory, by contrast, the function of the PS rules is defined by their role in generating structures that provide the input to the semantic rules. (We shall see in due course that these structures are not generated by PS rules alone, but the latter nevertheless retain a crucial role here.) The concept of deep structure now assumes a much greater significance than before (the term 'deep structure' was not in fact used in the early theory, as I have remarked: in *Syntactic Structures*, for example, Chomsky talks rather of the 'kernel strings' or 'underlying strings' from which sentences derive). The deep structure of a sentence contains all the syntactic (including lexical) material that determines its meaning, so that sentences differing in meaning will necessarily differ in deep structure. The role of the transformations is then to convert these deep structures, which determine meaning, into the corresponding surface structures, which determine pronunciation.

To conclude this discussion, let me comment briefly on the way 'meaning' is to be understood in the present context. It is used in a somewhat narrower sense than in the work of many writers on language, some of whom insist that no two different sentences can be completely identical in meaning. Here we shall allow for two sentences to have the same meaning – to be PARAPHRASES or STYLIS-TIC VARIANTS. *John took off the record* and *John took the record off*, for example, will be regarded as differing syntactically but not semantically. (They will both derive from *John Past take off the record*, with an optional transfor-mation called Particle Shift applying in the second to move *off* around the object NP.) Similarly, *Mow the lawn* will have the same semantic representation as the imperative reading of *You mow the lawn*, and *The man was bitten by the dog* the same as *The dog bit the man*. We thus ignore possible differences in emphasis (as in the imperative pair) or topic (if it is maintained that the passive sentence is about the man, saying what happened to him, the active one about the dog, saying what it did), and so on. Such differences would seem to be of a significantly different kind from those between *The dog bit the man* on the one hand and *The man bit the dog* or *Did the dog bite the man?* or *The dog didn't bite the man*, etc on the other, and they have been regarded by Katz and his col-leagues as falling outside the scope of a semantic theory. The latter is seen as having to do with relations like entailment, contradiction, consistency, and so forth. When considered from this point of view the active and passive sentences are equivalent: each entails the other, it would be inconsistent to assert *The dog bit the man* while denying *The man was bitten by the dog*, and so on. Recent work in generative grammar, however, has attempted to broaden the scope of seman-tic theory to include such matters as topic and the like: I shall accordingly be returning to this question in Chapter 16.

Notes

The fullest account of the semantic component of the grammar can be found in Katz 1972; Chapters 1 and 8 discuss the scope of semantic theory. In the *Aspects* theory it is normally assumed, not only that if two sentences differ in meaning they will differ in deep structure, but also that if a sentence is ambiguous it will have as many different deep structures as meanings: see Jackendoff 1972:5–10 for discussion of this point. On kernel sentences, see Chomsky 1957:45, 1965:17–18. Referential indices are introduced in Chomsky 1965:144–6.

My account of the revision of the treatment of negatives draws on Lees 1961:17–19; see also Klima 1964 – these two works are among the most extensive descriptions of English within the *Syntactic Structures* framework. On imperatives, see Katz and Postal 1964:74–9, Bolinger 1967a, Huddleston 1971:49–60, Stockwell *et al* 1973:633–71; and on reflexives Lees and Klima 1963, Postal 1964a (and works cited in Chapter 16).

Chapter 7

Recursion

7.1 Recursive grammars

In this chapter we shall be concerned with the analysis of sentences containing more than one clause, *eg*

[1] *John writes poetry and Mary plays the piano*
[2] *Everyone expects that Jill will say something*

These illustrate constructions known respectively as COORDINATION and EMBEDDING (or subordination). The main difference is that in [1] the whole sentence consists of a SEQUENCE of clauses whereas in [2] one clause is INCLUDED (or embedded) in the other. Very rough PM representations are [3] and [4].

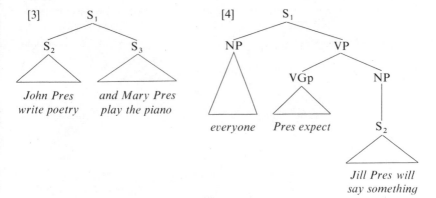

(I introduce here two widely used informal notational devices: the triangle permits one to avoid specifying details of the structure that are irrelevant to the point under discussion, and the numerical subscripts enable one to refer to specific nodes when they are not uniquely identifiable by their category label. Neither the triangles nor the subscripts figure in the formal representations generated by the grammar.) In PM [3], the coordination relation holds between S_2 and S_3, each being coordinate to the other; in PM [4], S_2 is subordinate to S_1. Notice that in PM [3] there are three S nodes, in PM [4] only two: *everyone*

expects does not form a constituent, any more than it does in, say, *Everyone expects a recession.*

An important and distinctive characteristic of coordination is that there is no linguistic limit to the number of clauses that can be coordinated in a single construction. [1], for example, could be extended by adding *and Tom paints and George makes pottery*, and so on. The grammar must therefore be able to generate subtrees [5], and so on indefinitely.

[5]

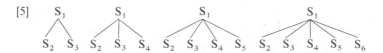

We accordingly need an infinite number of rules, 'S → S S', 'S → S S S', 'S → S S S S', and so on. Since the grammar must nevertheless be finite (for our aim is to provide a model of the grammar internalized by the speaker-hearer, who could not acquire a system that was not finite) we must add to the formal apparatus introduced so far the notion of a RULE SCHEMA, a means of specifying a set of rules without listing them individually. Thus we include in the grammar the rule schema 'S → S^n, where $n \geq 2$': this says that for any integral number n greater than or equal to 2 there is a PS rule rewriting S as a sequence of n Ss, *ie* the schema specifies the infinite set of rules 'S → S S', 'S → S S S', etc.

To handle the embedding in PM [4], all we need is a PS rule that introduces S as daughter to NP. The grammar of 5.2 can therefore be extended along the following lines:

[6] i $S \rightarrow \left\{ \begin{array}{l} S^n; \text{where } n \geq 2 \\ NP\ VP \end{array} \right\}$

  ii VP → VGp NP

  iii NP $\rightarrow \left\{ \begin{array}{l} (\text{Det})\ N \\ S \end{array} \right\}$

([i] and [iii] will be later amended slightly, but this will not affect the general principle.) Such a grammar is said to be RECURSIVE, in that it allows for the same rules to reapply indefinitely many times within a single derivation. Suppose, for example, that to the initial string #S# we apply the rule 'S → NP VP', producing #NP VP#, then apply [ii] to get #NP VGp NP#, and then apply the second subrule of [iii], so that the resultant string is #NP VGp S#: at this point we can reapply [i] – and we can proceed in this way without limit. I argued in 1.1 that the number of different sentences in a language is infinite, and it is now clear that [6] (suitably completed) will indeed generate an infinite set of sentences, even though the grammar is itself finite. It will do so for two reasons: it contains a rule schema specifying an infinite set of rules, and the rules can reapply indefinitely often to their own output.

It is worth observing that in the *Syntactic Structures* theory, Chomsky located the devices permitting the grammar to generate an infinite set of sentences not in the PS component, as I have just done, but in the transformational component. This was in keeping with his conception of the respective functions of the two components, which I described in Chapter 6. Sentences containing more than one clause were not regarded as forming part of the kernel, and the PS rules generated only a highly restricted, and finite, set of elementary structures. PMs like [3] and [4] were generated by a special type of transformation, known as 'generalized', or 'double-base', transformations: these operated on a pair of PMs as input, combining them to give as output a single composite PM. For example, [4] might have been derived by combining the PMs terminating in *everyone Pres expect something* and *Jill Pres will say something*. In this model the transformational derivation of a sentence does not consist of an ordered sequence of PMs, as it does in the *Aspects* theory, but has a more complex structure (which we need not go into here). In the change to the *Aspects* theory, generalized transformations were eliminated: all transformations are now 'singulary': they operate on a single PM as input. This change was necessary if the deep structure was to contain all the syntactic information relevant to semantic interpretation. For to derive the meaning of [2] we need to know more than that it contains the clauses *everyone Pres expect something* and *Jill Pres will say something:* we need to know the syntactic relationship between them in order to distinguish [2] from *Jill will say that everyone expects something.*

The shift of the recursive power of the grammar from the transformational to the PS component was also justified by certain purely syntactic arguments concerning the operation of transformational rules. We have seen that the transformations are ordered relative to each other, that Passivization is ordered to apply before *Not* Placement, and so on. In the *Aspects* theory, the order of application of these rules is further governed by the principle of the TRANS-FORMATIONAL CYCLE. To construct a transformational derivation beginning with a certain deep structure, we first apply the rules, in order, to that part of the tree dominated by the most deeply embedded S node, then we run through the rules again applying them to the second most deeply embedded S, and so on until we reach and process the root S. For example, in constructing a derivation from PM [4] we would apply the transformations first to S_2, and then work through the rules again with S_1 as the domain of operation. There is one pass through the transformations, one 'cycle', for each S, beginning with the lowest and ending with the highest. Ample exemplification of the cyclic application of transformations will be given in Chapter 8, and a more careful presentation and justification of it in 12.3; here the main point to note is that this condition on the order of application of transformations is quite straightforward to state formally within a theory where PMs like [4] are generated directly by the PS rules, but creates considerable problems for formalization in one that allows generalized transformations: this then supports the semantic case for eliminating the latter.

I began this chapter by saying we would be concerned with sentences containing more than one clause – but the term 'clause' itself has not figured in the PMs proposed. This is because we do not want both 'sentence' and 'clause' as primitive terms: to introduce 'clause' as a node label would involve pointless complication of the PS rules. Suppose, for example, we wanted to say that *John writes poetry* and *and Mary plays the piano* in [1] and *that Jill will say something* in [2] (or, more properly, the structures underlying these) were clauses, not sentences, so that all the S nodes in [3] and [4] except the root ones would be replaced by 'Cl'. Such structures can be generated if we substitute [7] for [6i] and Cl for S in [6iii].

[7] i $S \to Cl^n$; where $n \geq 2$
   ii $Cl \to NP\ VP$

The trouble with [7] is that it does not allow for the 'layering' of coordination. Consider the contrasting structures of [8–10].

[8]   *John writes poetry, Mary plays the piano, and George makes pottery*
[9]   *John writes poetry and Mary plays the piano, but George has no artistic interest at all*
[10] *John writes poetry, but George has no artistic interest at all and Mary has very little*

In [8] we simply have a coordination with three members, but in [9] the first two clauses are coordinated to form a constituent which is in turn coordinated to the third clause, and in [10] the last two clauses form a larger unit that is coordinated with the first. [6i] accounts for this quite straightforwardly, generating the respective subtrees [11–13], but [7] can cope only with examples like [8] where there is just one layer of coordination.

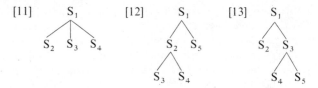

Similarly, having Cl rather than S in [6iii] would not allow for examples like *Everyone expects that Jill will say something and that there will be an almighty row*. The crucial point is that, as far as their DISTRIBUTION is concerned, there is no difference between a unit consisting of NP VP and one consisting of a coordination of such units. In general, any clause can be replaced by a coordination of clauses, and it is precisely this fact that is expressed by rule [6i].

Another way of introducing Cl as a primitive term, one that overcomes this last objection, would be to replace [7i] by [14] (retaining [7ii]).

[14] $S \to \begin{Bmatrix} S^n; \text{ where } n \geq 2 \\ Cl \end{Bmatrix}$

This formalizes a quite common analysis wherein a simple form like *John died*, say, is said to be a sentence consisting of one clause. (But it also carries over this description to *John writes poetry* in [1]: the argument given above shows that it is mistaken to reserve the S label for the root node.) There are two objections to this proposal. Firstly, it is more complicated than the original, [6], since it contains an extra category symbol and an extra rule ([14] plus [7ii] replace [6i]), and there will be no simplification elsewhere in the grammar to compensate for this. The Cl symbol is just redundant. Secondly, it is a misuse of the formal apparatus to introduce a category distinction to handle what is really a difference in internal structure, rather than distribution – as noted above, a unit consisting of NP VP and a coordination of such units are alike in their distribution. Notice in this connection that the coordination relation may hold between smaller units, as in *The butcher and the baker are a pair of twisters*. Here we shall say that the subject NP consists of a pair of coordinate NPs: there is no more reason to make a category distinction between S and Cl than there is here between *the butcher and the baker* on the one hand and *the butcher* on the other. Distinguishing S and Cl would thus lead to a proliferation of similar distinctions elsewhere in the grammar, so that the resultant complication and redundancy would be very considerable.

I conclude, therefore, that there is no justification for distinguishing between sentence and clause as primitive terms in syntactic theory (though I shall continue to use 'clause' as a non-primitive term, defined, essentially, as a sentence having NP and VP as daughters). It is worth observing, however, that the term 'sentence' is used in two different, though related, senses in generative grammar. (a) There is, firstly, the sense we have just been considering where, like 'noun phrase', 'verb', etc, it is applied to a syntactic category. (b) Secondly, there is the sense it has when we say that the task of a grammar is to generate all and only the well-formed sentences of the language and to assign one or more structural descriptions to each of them. Here each different final phonological representation generated by the grammar counts as a distinct sentence. The connection between (a) and (b) is evident: each sentence of type (b) is associated with a deep syntactic structure (more than one if it is ambiguous) in the form of a PM whose root node is labelled 'sentence' in sense (a). But the correlation is not one-to-one: in *Everyone expects that Jill will say something* the embedded clause is a sentence of type (a), but not (b). (More precisely, the deep syntactic structure corresponding to it is a type (a) sentence but the phonological representation corresponding to it is not a type (b) sentence.) This lack of equivalence, though not formulated in this way of course, undoubtedly provided the major motivation for the traditional distinction between clause and sentence, but various other factors were involved as well.

I have discussed this question at some length as an example of the way the generative approach, by its emphasis on formalization, or explicit rules, permits a greater precision in the explication of the theoretical concepts used in grammatical description. In the remainder of this chapter I shall review, briefly and informally, some of the main types of coordinate and subordinate constructions in English; this will provide a framework for a more detailed study in Chapter 8 of one quite small area of the grammar, illustrating more clearly the explanatory power of deep structure and transformations.

7.2 Coordination

There are three topics within this area that I want to consider: the transformational reduction and restructuring of coordinate constructions; the deep structure of coordinate NPs; the syntax of the coordinating conjunctions, *and*, *or*, *but*.

Strings of coordinate Ss can be generated by the rule schema 'S → Sⁿ'. Suppose that the PS derivation then proceeds in such a way that two coordinate Ss dominate partially identical subtrees. An example might be *John Pres be ing study law and Tom Pres be ing study medicine*, where the two clauses have different subject and objects but identical VGps. In such a case the second VGp is optionally deleted, so that the one deep structure underlies both [15i] and [ii].

[15] i *John is studying law and Tom is studying medicine*
     ii *John is studying law and Tom medicine*

There are several reasons why the transformational solution to [15ii], which derives it by deletion from (the structure underlying) [i], is better than the PS solution, which would generate *and Tom medicine* directly by the PS rules. The transformational solution enables us to block deviant sentences like **John died and Tom medicine* or **John frightened Mary and Peter the fact* by the same rules as exclude **Tom died medicine* and **Peter frightened the fact*, whereas these obvious generalizations would be lost in the PS solution. Moreover, in the transformational solution the PS rules can expand each S in the structure independently of the others, whereas in the PS solution blocking the above deviant examples would require PS rules sensitive to the context formed by a neighbouring coordinated sentence, with a consequent vast and probably unmanageable increase in the complexity of the PS rules. Then there is the added bonus that the transformational solution accounts for the paraphrase relation between [i] and [ii]: *and Tom medicine* is understood quite differently in [15ii] than in, say, *John failed law and Tom medicine*.

Somewhat more complex than the relation between [15i] and [ii] is that between the following pairs, where again [ii] derives from [i] in each case.

[16] i *John$_i$ liked Tom$_j$ and Mary$_k$ liked Tom$_j$*
     ii *John$_i$ and Mary$_k$ liked Tom$_j$*

[17] i *John$_i$ was tired and John$_i$ was hungry*
     ii *John$_i$ was tired and hungry*

[18] i *John$_i$ went out and John$_i$ bought a newspaper$_j$*
     ii *John$_i$ went out and bought a newspaper$_j$*

As in [15] there is deletion from one clause of material that is identical with part of the other clause (the identity including that of referential indices). This time, however, there is not simply deletion, but also a certain amount of restructuring of the tree: the transformations yield PMs containing the co-ordinate NPs, AdjPs (adjective phrases) and VPs, [19–21].

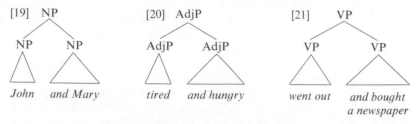

For in surface structure the first IC division in [16ii] is not *John* plus *and Mary liked Tom* but *John and Mary* plus *liked Tom*, and similarly with the others. Again, it is worth considering the argument for a transformational solution to the [ii] sentences, deriving them by deletion and restructuring from [i], as opposed to a PS solution, which would require rule schemata like 'NP → NP^n', 'AdjP → AdjP^n', 'VP → VP^n'. The strongest evidence comes from sentences like *John wandered into the field and was attacked by the bull*. Once it is agreed that passives are derived by transformation from underlying actives rather than by special PS rules, it is clear that *was attacked by the bull* (more precisely, *Past be en attack by the bull*) cannot be a VP in deep structure, and therefore *wandered into the field and was attacked by the bull* cannot be one either. Within the theoretical framework that we have established, then, there is no plausible alternative to the transformational solution. The underlying structure will be *John$_i$ Past wander into the field and the bull$_k$ Past attack John$_i$;* Passivization applies to the second clause, making its subject identical to that of the first, at which stage it can be removed by the deletion rule.

Just as in [15ii] we have deletion without restructuring, so we find cases of restructuring without deletion:

[22] i *Manchester City defeated Wolves and Manchester United were beaten by Sunderland*

ii *Manchester City and Manchester United defeated Wolves and were beaten by Sunderland respectively*

I have chosen an example here where the NPs coordinated in surface structure have different deep structure functions, *Manchester City* being deep subject, *Manchester United* deep object; this demonstrates that the NP coordination must arise transformationally rather than by PS rules: [i] and [ii] both derive from *Manchester City Past defeat Wolves and Sunderland Past defeat Manchester United*.

However, it is hardly feasible to derive all NP coordinations from underlying clause coordinations – which brings us to the second topic, the deep structure of coordinate NPs. There is no problem in deriving [16ii] from [i], but the transformational solution will not work in cases like *John and Mary are a happy couple, George and Harry look alike,* etc. This is because the putative underlying clauses would be incoherent, as is evident from the deviance of **John is a happy couple,* **George looks alike.* It seems that in cases like these we do need to allow for coordinate NPs in deep structure, and hence for a 'NP → NP$''''$' rule schema. But NP is apparently the only category besides S for which such a schema is needed: all other surface structure coordinations can be satisfactorily handled by the transformational restructuring of clause coordinations.

According to these proposals, there will be two different ways of generating coordinate NPs – by the 'NP → NP$''''$' PS rule schema, as in these last examples, or by restructuring from coordinate clauses, as in [16ii] and [22ii]. This then enables us to account for the ambiguity in sentences like *John and Peter had owned the flat.* In one interpretation they had owned the flat separately (and hence at different times): this interpretation matches the syntactic analysis where it is derived from *John had owned the flat and Peter had owned the flat.* Alternatively, they may have owned the flat jointly, each being individually merely a part-owner, an interpretation which fits naturally the derivation from a single deep structure clause with a coordinate NP subject.

Finally, let me turn to the coordinating conjunctions *and, or, but* (I shall ignore *nor,* for otherwise we would need a long excursus into the syntax of negation). The main point to make is that there can be no mixing of conjunctions within a single layer of coordination. That is, if we have a sequence X Conj$_1$ Y Conj$_2$ Z, where Conj(unction)$_1$ is different from Conj$_2$, there will necessarily be two layers of coordination, one within the other, so that the structure will be like [12] or [13], but not [11]. Sentences [9] and [10] show this layering with *and* and *but;* an example with *and* and *or* is *John must come with us or the guard will be suspicious and we shall not be allowed in.* Here *and* belongs to the lower layer of coordination, *or* to the higher: the structure is again like [13]. The absence of contrasting conjunctions within a single layer can be accounted for if we treat the choice between *and, or* and *but* as a property of the coordinate structure as a whole, rather than of the individual clauses. This can be expressed formally by replacing the earlier 'S → S$''$' with:

[23] i   S → Conj S^n; where $n \geqslant 2$
     ii   Conj → {*and, or, but*}

[23] will generate strings like '*and* S S' '*or* S S S', etc. Transformational rules will then account for the surface position of the conjunctions. The most usual pattern is the one where the conjunction is simply shifted to the left of the last member of the coordination, as in all the examples given so far. But there are three other possibilities. Firstly, *and* may be deleted, yielding sentences like *I came, I saw, I conquered* or *John is studying law, Tom medicine.* Secondly, where the coordination has three or more members the conjunction may appear in all but the first, so that a stylistic variant of example [8] would be *John writes poetry and Mary plays the piano and George makes pottery.* Thirdly, in *or* coordinations, *either* may appear with the first member: there is free variation between *John stole the car or Peter did* and *Either John stole the car*

or Peter did. Both has a similar role in *and* coordinations, but is limited to cases where there are just two members and where deletion and restructuring have applied: *Both John and Mary liked Tom* (derived from [16i]), *John both wrote the introduction and edited the text*, but not **Both John liked Tom and Mary liked Tom*. I should add that [23ii] is too general as it stands: *but* is restricted to coordinations with two members, and only *and* is found in deep structure NP coordinations – examples like *John or Peter stole the money* all derive from underlying clause coordinations.

7.3 Embedding

I shall consider in turn two major types of embedding construction, the first involving 'relative' clauses (as in [24]), the second 'complement' clauses ([25]).

[24] *Mary believed the rumour **which John had started***
[25] *Everyone expects **that Jill will say something*** (=[2])

As a rough first approximation, a complement clause may be thought of as equivalent to the traditional grammarian's 'noun clause'. The transformational literature contains comparatively little work on what are traditionally known as adverbial clauses, as in *John was sacked because he criticized the boss*, and I shall not discuss these: the classification into relatives and complements is thus not here claimed to be exhaustive (but *cf* 15.5).

According to one commonly adopted analysis for relatives the deep structure of [24] would be

[26]

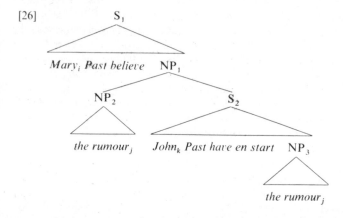

There are two aspects of this that merit discussion: (a) Why do we put NP_3 at the right of S_2 rather than the left, and why have it dominate *the rumour* rather than the pronoun *which*? (b) Why do we recognize NP_2 as a constituent, instead of having NP_1 immediately dominate Det N S?

The first question can be answered with the kind of argument that we used to justify the deep-surface distinction in the first place. We want to show the systematic relation between the relative construction *the rumour which John had started* and the simple sentence *John had started the rumour:* we do so by assigning the relative clause the same underlying structure and accounting for the surface difference by means of transformations. Giving the relative clause the same deep structure as the corresponding simple sentence enables us to express generalizations about the transitivity of verbs and about selectional restrictions which would elude us if we took the deep structure to be *'which John Past have en start'*, and so on. Thus we shall not need special rules to exclude *the man whom/that John died*, *the man whom/that John killed the man*, *the storm which/that John frightened*, etc: they will be blocked by the same rules as block *John died the man*, *John killed the man the man*, *John frightened the storm*.

Given that the deep structure of the relative clause is *'John Past have en spread the rumour'*, we shall need, in the transformational derivation, to substitute a relative pronoun for *the rumour* and shift it to clause-initial position; for present purposes we may assume that both operations are carried out in a single rule, Relativization. The rule can of course apply only where the NP to be relativized is identical to a preceding NP, called its ANTECEDENT; the structure index will thus be, roughly,

$$[27] \ W — [_{NP}NP — [_S X — NP — Y]_S]_{NP} — Z$$
$$\quad\quad 1 \quad\quad 2 \quad\quad 3 \quad 4 \quad 5 \quad\quad\quad 6$$
$$\text{Condition: } 2 = 4$$

Term 2 is the antecedent, term 4 the relativized NP. The variables W and Z allow the NP consisting of the antecedent plus the relative clause (*ie* NP_1 in the case of [26]) to occupy any position in the higher clause (S_1): in [26] this NP is in the direct object position, with W covering *Mary$_i$ Past believe* and Z being empty; in *The rumour which John had started was false* it is subject; and so on. Similarly the variables X and Y allow the relativized NP to occupy any position in the relative clause: in [26] it is direct object, with X covering *John$_k$ Past have en start* and Y again empty; in *the man who came to dinner* it is subject; and so on. The structure index includes a device not found in our earlier examples: the use of brackets with category labels attached as subscripts. The purpose of the brackets labelled S is to stipulate that terms 3, 4 and 5, which they enclose, jointly constitute a sentence: this guarantees that the relativized NP is in a lower clause than the antecedent – when the identical NPs are in the one clause, the rule that applies is not Relativization, but Reflexivization (converting *'the man$_i$ Past hurt the man$_i$'* into *'the man$_i$ Past hurt himself$_i$'*, etc). Similarly the NP brackets enclosing terms 2–5 prevent the rule applying to structures like that underlying *I asked the man$_i$ whether the man$_i$ had finished* to yield *I asked the man whether who had finished*.

The identity condition in [27] holds between NPs, which brings us to question (b), the justification of the NP_2 node in [26]. The latter corresponds to term 2 in [27], and is thus a necessary part of the structure if [27] is in fact correct in specifying the identity condition in terms of NPs rather than nouns. Some evidence that full NPs are involved comes from examples like *a man and a woman who were the happiest of couples*. Here *who* substitutes for *a man and a woman*, which must be a deep structure coordination of NPs (because of the deviance of **a man was the happiest of couples*): there can be no restructuring of a clause coordination here. The identity thus holds between the two occurrences of the NP *a man and a woman*, and since this contains more than one noun it would not be possible to replace NP by N in terms 2 and 4 of [27]. A second point supporting the NP_2 node in [26] is that the relative construction appears to be 'cumulative', in that the antecedent NP may itself contain a relative clause, as in *They were talking about a girl that they had met who could speak a dozen languages*. Here there are two relative clauses which are not coordinated: *that they had met* and *who could speak a dozen languages*. The antecedent of *who* is *a girl that they had met*. Now the PS rule which applies to NP_1 in [26] must be '$NP \rightarrow NP\ S$', and such a rule can obviously reapply immediately to its own output to yield subtrees like [28].

[28]

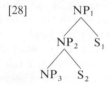

This is just what we want for the present example: S_1 corresponds to *who could speak a dozen languages*, S_2 to *that they had met*. We could not handle this kind of construction if we introduced relative clauses into deep structure by such a PS rule as '$NP \rightarrow Det\ N\ S$'.

So much for the justification of the proposed analysis of [24]. Let us now extend it to cover certain other types of relative construction. First, there is clearly a systematic relation between the members of pairs like

[29] i *the tree which is at the bottom of the garden*
    ii *the tree at the bottom of the garden*

Compare also: *people (who are) fond of animals, someone (who is) intelligent, the man (who was) causing the disturbance, those (who were) interrogated by the police*, where the parenthesized elements are optional. This relationship can be expressed by giving [i] and [ii] the same deep structure and having an optional transformation that deletes the sequence 'relative pronoun Tns *be*' – a transformation often known as *Whiz* Deletion or, less picturesquely, Relative Clause Reduction. As the examples indicate, the *be* deleted may be the main verb or an auxiliary, progressive or passive. The reason for deriving [ii] from [i] rather than vice versa (by a rule of '*Whiz* Insertion') is elementary: [i] is going to be handled anyway by the rules we have already established to deal with [24] and the like, which have no counterparts like [ii].

Consider next the following examples:

[30] i   *the girl who was pretty*
     ii **the girl pretty*
     iii *the pretty girl*

Comparison of [30i] and [ii] might seem to suggest that *Whiz* Deletion should be formulated in such a way that it could not apply to the structure underlying [30i]. This would mean making '*Whiz*' deletable if followed by PP (*at the bottom of the garden*), *ing* or *en* (subsequently moved by Affix Hopping, as in *causing the disturbance, interrogated by the police*), or by the sequence Adj PP (*fond of animals*), but not when followed by Adj alone – except where the antecedent is an 'indefinite pronoun' (*someone intelligent*). But when we take [30iii] into account we see that there is a much better solution. Instead of complicating *Whiz* Deletion in the above way, we allow it to apply to the structure underlying [i] to yield [ii], which then undergoes an obligatory transformation, Adjective Shift, moving *pretty* around *girl* to give [iii] as output. [iii] will thus derive by Relativization, *Whiz* Deletion and Adjective Shift from '*the girl_i* [_S *the girl_i* Past be pretty]_S' (or with *Pres* rather than *Past*, for [iii] is related also to *the girl who is pretty*). As I observed of an earlier example, it would be to miss the point to complain that using three transformations to derive [iii] makes heavy weather of an apparently straightforward construction. Our aim is to formulate rules that express significant generalizations, not to minimize the number of steps in a derivation. Of the three transformations proposed, only Adjective Shift is set up just to handle the Adj N construction – and, as we saw, having this rule permits a more general formulation of *Whiz* Deletion. If we derived [30iii] by a PS rule, 'NP → Det Adj N', we would be unable to show that the relation between *pretty* and *girl* is the same as in the simple sentence *The girl was pretty* (note the shared selectional restrictions in *the angry man/*key* and *The man/*key was angry*).

There is an important type of relative construction differing from those considered so far in that the antecedent NP does not appear in surface structure:

[31] *The cat wouldn't eat what Mary had put on the plate*
[32] *John was mowing the lawn when Mary arrived*

These look quite different from [24], but there is good reason to believe that in deep structure they exhibit the same kind of construction as is shown in [26]. Thus the deep structure of [31] will be [33]. The identification of NP_2 and NP_3 as *the thing* is not to be taken too literally: further theoretical apparatus to be introduced later will permit a preferable and slightly more abstract analysis; the important point for present purposes is that the structure does contain two identical NPs which are more or less equivalent in their semantic and underlying syntactic properties to *the thing* or *that*. One piece of evidence for postulating an underlying antecedent NP is the close relation between [31] and *The cat wouldn't eat that which Mary had put on the plate*: in the relative construction under consideration here, *what* is systematically replaceable by *that which*. Secondly,

[33]

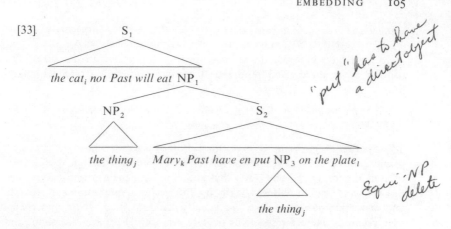

there is evidence from selectional restrictions. *Eat* requires that its object be concrete, not abstract. The object of *eat* in [31] therefore could not be simply a clause, for clauses are abstract – compare **He ate that John had died*, in contrast with *He knew that John had died*, where *know* does allow an abstract object. The position and labelling of NP_3 in [33] is justified by the fact that in simple sentences *put* requires an object NP and a locative phrase: *She put the food on the plate*, but not **She put the food*, **She put on the plate*, **She put*. In the transformational derivation of [31] NP_3, being identical with NP_2, is replaced by a relative pronoun and moved to the front of its clause, just as in the derivation of [24]: Relativization applies to both. In [31], the antecedent NP_2 is subsequently deleted, and this affects the final form of the relative pronoun.

Extending this analysis to [32] gives [34] as deep structure.

[34]

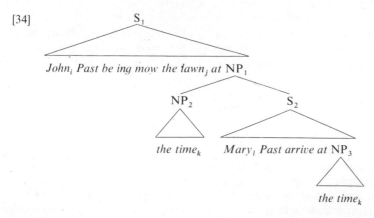

Notice that although we have been arguing on syntactic grounds, these structures also provide appropriate inputs to the semantic rules. In [34], for example, both clauses contain a time phrase: NP_2 specifies the time of John's being in the process of mowing the lawn, NP_3 the time of Mary's arrival – and the fact that $NP_2 = NP_3$ indicates that the two times are the same.

So far I have considered only so-called 'restrictive' relative clauses. The contrast between these and 'non-restrictive' ones is often illustrated with pairs like

[35] *Mary disapproves of students whom she considers promiscuous*
[36] *Mary disapproves of students, whom she considers promiscuous*

[35] says that Mary disapproves of that subset of students whom she considers promiscuous (hence the term 'restrictive') while [36] says that she disapproves of students in general and adds that she considers them promiscuous. The distinction is marked phonologically by differences in intonation and rhythm, and in writing non-restrictives are usually separated from their antecedents by a comma, whereas restrictives usually are not. There are also significant syntactic differences, illustrated in part in the following examples.

[37] *John, who's an engineer, couldn't solve the problem*
[38] *Tom overslept, which made him miss the train*
[39] *Bill will return in a year, by which time the house will be ready*
[40] **George, I met last night, is coming to lunch*

Firstly, only with non-restrictives can the antecedent be a proper noun ([37]) or a clause ([38]). Secondly, only in non-restrictives do we find relative *which* as a determiner ([39]) rather than pronoun. Thirdly, in non-restrictives the relative pronoun is never deletable (contrast [40] with restrictive *The man I met last night is coming to lunch*). Fourthly, the deletion of the antecedent is possible only with restrictives ([31], [32]).

It follows from the first of these points that non-restrictive relative clauses cannot be introduced into deep structure by the PS rule proposed above for restrictives, 'NP → NP S': there is no reason to suppose that the *which* clause in [38] is either daughter or sister to a NP. The most promising alternative that has been suggested is to derive non-restrictives from coordinate constructions. [37], [38] are strikingly similar to *John couldn't solve the problem, and he's an engineer; Tom overslept, and this made him miss the train;* and so on. Indeed, there is an even closer resemblance between [37] and *John, and he's an engineer, couldn't solve the problem,* which might reflect an intermediate stage in the derivation of [37]. It remains to be seen whether this derivation can be sustained, and whether it is possible to formulate a general Relativization transformation that covers both types.

Let us turn now to complement clauses. I shall be dealing at some length with one subtype of these in Chapter 8: what I want to do here, therefore, is to narrow down to this subtype and clear up some points of detail so that in the subsequent discussion the major descriptive and theoretical issues will emerge more sharply.

One type of complement construction looks superficially like a relative. For instance, our earlier relative example [24] (*Mary believed the rumour which*

John had started) is on the surface similar to the complement construction [41], whose deep structure is given below.

[41] *Mary believed the rumour **that John had departed***

[42]

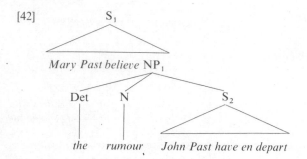

Here there is no antecedent-pronoun relation between *the rumour* and *that*, so that there is no occurrence of *the rumour* in the deep structure of the complement clause S_2, and no reason for treating *the rumour* as constituting a full NP by itself – contrast [42] with [26]. The *that* in [41] is a subordinating conjunction, a marker of the complementation construction, and for this reason is usually called a 'complementizer'; note that there is no corresponding element in the non-embedded counterpart, which is simply *John had departed*. As we have seen, *that* can also serve as a relative pronoun (almost invariably in the restrictive construction) in free variation with *which, who*, etc, and this double use can sometimes be a source of ambiguity: *Mary believed the rumour that John had started* can be interpreted as a paraphrase of [24], with the *that* clause a relative, or of *Mary believed the rumour that John had made a start*, with the *that* clause a complement. Notice, however, that there is only a fairly small subclass of nouns that can take a complement clause: besides *rumour* we find *fact, idea, proposal, suggestion*, etc, but not *depth, dog, man, sincerity, whisky* and countless others; the distribution of relative clauses, on the other hand, is not subject to this kind of constraint. Thus while *the whisky that/which John had drunk* is well-formed, there is no acceptable construction like **the whisky that John had departed*. Semantically there is in [41] some kind of identity relation between the rumour and the whole of the complement clause: the rumour which Mary believed was that John had departed (this is why the subordinate clause is traditionally said to be in apposition to the preceding noun) – and clearly there could not be such an identity relation between the abstract proposition that John had departed and the concrete substance whisky.

Complements most frequently occur, in fact, without any such noun at all, as in

[43] *That John was a spy was obvious*
[44] *Everyone expects that Jill will say something* (=[2])

However, the same kind of underlying structure as [42] has been widely adopted for this type too, with PMs [45] and [46] underlying the above examples.

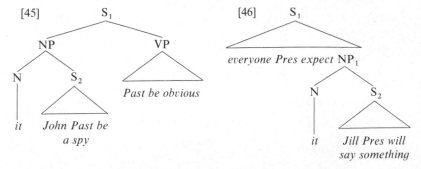

According to this analysis, complement sentences are introduced into deep structure by the rule 'NP → (Det) N S' (rather than the earlier [6iii]), and hence are always sister to a noun at this level. The sister noun may be one of the small class mentioned above, *rumour, fact, idea*, etc, or else the pronoun *it*. Evidence for this *it* comes from examples where it is retained in surface structure:

[47] *It was obvious that John was a spy*
[48] *It is expected by everyone that Jill will say something*

[43] and [47] are paraphrases, and the close systematic resemblance between the two types of sentence argues for a common underlying structure. Note that [47] is only superficially like *I was sorry that John was a spy* (for which there is no counterpart of the form **That John was a spy was sorry*): the syntactic and semantic difference between them can be accounted for in a natural way if we have the complement clause originating in the deep subject in [47]. The surface position of S_2 here is then attributable to the application of a transformation known as Extraposition. A first approximation to this rule is given in [49].

[49] EXTRAPOSITION $X - [_{NP} it - S]_{NP} - Y$
     (Optional)   1   2   3   4   ⇒
                       1   2   ∅   4+3

The effect is to move the complement sentence to the rightmost position in the next higher sentence. In the derivation of [48] from [46], Passivization first applies to move NP_1 into subject position, and then Extraposition shifts S_2 to the far right. Extraposition is optional: if it is not applied to [45], the *it* is removed by a special obligatory transformation to yield [43]; similarly *It Deletion* applies in the derivation of [44] from [46]. It must be conceded that the argument for having a deep structure *it* here is not very impressive (the alternative would be to have deep structures like [4], and to cater for [47] and [48] by a rule of *It Insertion*); this, however, is the analysis that was adopted in the first major transformational study of this construction, Rosenbaum 1967, and in a great deal of the subsequent literature, and I have accordingly thought it best to adopt it here too: it does not crucially affect the arguments that follow.

Complement clauses are subclassified according to the form of their VGp. All examples so far have been finite; others are infinitival ([50]) or 'gerundive' ([51]).

[50] *Everyone expects Jill to say something*
[51] *I hate it raining so much*

Which type occurs depends on the verb in the next higher clause (or if the verb is *be*, on the following adjective). *Contend, tend, enjoy*, for example, take only finite, infinitival and gerundive complements respectively – *John contended that he was right, Bill tends to get irritable, Mary enjoys reading science fiction* but not **John contended to be right, *It tends that Bill gets irritable, *Mary enjoys to read science fiction*. Some verbs or adjectives allow a choice between two types – finite or infinitival for *expect*, for example (as in [44] and [50]); and a few allow all three, *eg: intend*, as in *I intend that John should know, I intended Peter to do it, I intend seeing her tomorrow*. Finite complements are typically introduced by *that* (though it is often omissible); infinitival ones are sometimes introduced by *for*, as in *For John to be late was rare;* and in gerundives the subject NP is often in the possessive/genitive case, as in *She resented John's getting the job* (the case morpheme has a variety of phonological realizations and is usually symbolized as '*Poss*'). The elements *that, for* and *to, Poss* and *ing* are known as complementizers. I shall not go further into these matters, and in what follows I shall simply assume (a) that the complementizers are introduced by transformations, not PS rules; (b) that in non-finite complements the tense element is absent from deep as well as surface structure. The correctness or otherwise of these assumptions does not bear directly on our main concern, which will be with deep and surface grammatical relations in infinitival complement constructions.

Notes

On the shift of the recursive power of the grammar from the PS to the transformational component, see Chomsky 1965:128–47. The change leads to certain problems in constructing PMs from PS derivations by the procedure of Chapter 3 – see Postal 1964c:9–17, and 12.1 below. On the distinction of sentence and clause, see Lyons 1968:170–1, Palmer 1971:70–80.

A general study of coordination can be found in Dik 1968; his Chapter 5 surveys various treatments of coordination within the TG framework. Among the main transformational studies are Gleitman 1965, Lakoff and Peters 1966, Ross 1967:88–108 and 220–2, Dougherty 1970–1, Koutsoudas 1971, Stockwell *et al* 1972:294–418. Quirk *et al* 1972:536–620 gives a detailed non-transformational treatment. A major problem is the relation between coordination and number: note, for example, that the ambiguity of *John and Peter had owned the flat* is found also in *The brothers had owned the flat:* the appeal of the proposal to account for the former in terms of the distinction between S and NP coordination is weakened by its failure to generalize to the latter; see Hudson 1970; McCawley 1968b, 1974a. The term 'conjoining' will sometimes be found in place of coordination; coordination with *and* and *or* are often distinguished as 'conjunction' and 'disjunction' respectively (with 'conjunction' here used in the logician's sense, rather than the traditional grammarian's, for whom it denotes a class of words).

On relative clauses, see Quirk *et al* 1972:864–74 and, for transformational analyses, Smith 1964, Ross 1967, Kuroda 1968, Thompson 1971, Huddleston 1971:210–62, Stockwell *et al* 1972:419–501. Some problems in deriving Adj N constructions by *Whiz* Deletion and Adjective Shift are discussed in Bolinger 1967*b*.

Chapter 8

Aspects of the Grammar of Complementation

In this chapter I want to illustrate in a more detailed and thorough way than in preceding chapters the kind of argumentation that is used to justify transformational analyses. The discussion will also, I hope, bring out the explanatory power of transformational grammar: we shall be examining a range of, on the face of it, unrelated differences in the properties of certain verbs, but the analysis will show that in fact they are related, that they all follow from a single very general difference in the deep structure properties of the verbs.

We shall be very largely concerned with justifying the inclusion in the grammar of two transformations, Equi NP Deletion and Subject Raising (henceforth abbreviated as Equi and Raising). They apply in the derivation of sentences containing non-finite complements, *eg* [1] and [2] respectively.

[1] *John expected to intimidate Bill*
[2] *John seemed to intimidate Bill*

In spite of the apparent similarity between these, I shall be arguing that they differ significantly in their deep structures, which are essentially as follows:

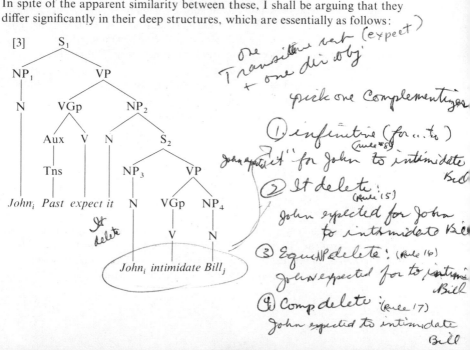

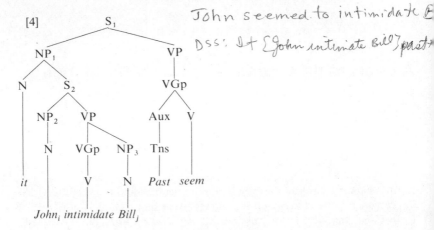

John seemed to intimidate B

DSS: It [John intimidate Bill] past

Both of these contain the complement clause *John intimidate Bill* (= S_2), but in [3] this clause belongs within the object (NP_2) of the higher clause, whereas in [4] it belongs within the subject (NP_1). *Expect* in [3] is thus a transitive verb with NP_2 as its object, while *seem* in [4] is intransitive. There are two occurrences of *John* in [3], one being subject of S_1, the other of S_2; in the corresponding surface structure, however, there is only one *John*, subject of S_1. This change is brought about by the Equi transformation: it deletes a complement clause subject if it is identical with a NP in the higher clause. In the other example there is only one occurrence of *John* in deep as well as surface structure but whereas in the deep structure [4] *John* is subject of S_2, in surface structure *John* is clearly subject of the *seem* clause, ie S_1. The change here is due to the Raising transformation: it moves the subject of the complement clause into the next higher clause. Thus although *intimidate* has no surface subject in either [1] or [2], the reasons are different in the two cases: in [1] the underlying subject of *intimidate* has been simply deleted, whereas in [2] it has been raised out of S_2 into S_1.

As a first approximation, sufficient for our purposes here, the transformations may be formulated as follows:

[5] EQUI NP DELETION: $X - NP - (VGp) - it - [_S NP - Y]_S - Z$

           1   .2   3   4   5   6   7 ⇒

           1   2   3   4   .:   6   7

                 Condition: $2 = 5$

[6] SUBJECT RAISING: $X - [_{NP} it]_{NP} - (VGp) - [_S NP - Y]_S - Z$

           1   2   3   4   5   6 ⇒

           1   4   3   ∅   5   6

The S-labelled brackets stipulate that NP and Y together constitute a sentence, and similarly for the NP brackets in [6]. Term 5 in [5] and term 4 in [6] are thus the initial NPs, and hence the subjects, of the embedded complement clauses. The name 'Equi' is suggestive of the 'equivalence' (identity) relation between the deleted NP of term 5 and the NP of term 2. The parentheses enclosing VGp in each rule may be ignored for the moment: their purpose will become apparent later.

Equi can be applied quite straightforwardly to [3], which matches the structure index in the following way:

[7]

*I	John$_i$	Past expect	it	John$_i$	intimidate Bill$_j$	
	2	3	4	5	6	7

where the first and last positions are empty. Raising, however, does not apply directly to [4]: the latter first undergoes Extraposition (see *p* 108), which gives [8] as output. This matches the structure index for [7] in the way indicated.

[8]

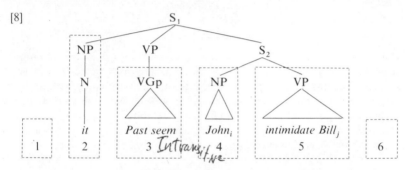

Thus Extraposition shifts the whole complement clause to the right of *seem*, then Raising takes the S$_2$ subject, *John*, and substitutes it for the NP *it* in S$_1$.

Our task now is to justify these analyses. Note that the question we shall be concerned with is 'What evidence supports the analysis?', not 'How was the analysis arrived at?'. As I remarked in 1.5, we cannot prescribe procedures that will mechanically lead to a correct analysis. Writing grammars involves a great deal of trial and error: one formulates a hypothesis, tests its predictions against the data, and amends the hypothesis if its predictions are falsified. In presenting evidence in support of the above analysis of [1] and [2], I shall in effect be illustrating this process of testing. Only if one understands the kind of argumentation involved in justifying analyses, can one then go on to initiate sensible hypotheses of one's own.

One preliminary point to make is that the difference between the deep structures [3] and [4] has semantic plausibility. [3] shows *John* as subject of *expect*, which correlates with the fact that John is understood as 'experiencer' of the expectation. Semantically, *expect* expresses a relation between a person and a state of affairs or event: the former corresponds to NP$_1$, the latter to NP$_2$. In [4], however, there is no direct syntactic relation between *John* and *seem*, and nor is there a semantic relation: John is not experiencer or whatever, relative to the 'seeming'. The experiencer role can in fact be expressed in a prepositional phrase: *John seemed to Mary to intimidate Bill* expresses a relation between Mary and the proposition that John intimidated Bill.

Let us turn now to the main arguments. Given that the status of *John* as SURFACE subject of the higher clause in [1] and [2] is not in doubt, we shall have shown the need for some such rules as Equi and Raising if we can demonstrate that *John* occurs in DEEP structure in the positions shown in [3] and [4]. My line of attack, therefore, will be to consider various differences between *expect* and *seem* which can be accounted for by the hypothesis that they enter into deep structures of the kind illustrated in [3] and [4].

(a) PASSIVIZATION OF THE COMPLEMENT CLAUSE

Consider the following sentences:

[1] *John expected to intimidate Bill*
[9] *Bill expected to be intimidated by John*
[2] *John seemed to intimidate Bill*
[10] *Bill seemed to be intimidated by John*

The crucial difference here is that the two *expect* sentences clearly differ in meaning, whereas the two *seem* sentences are paraphrases, in the sense in which we are using this term (*cf p* 91). With the first pair we could without inconsistency assert one and deny the other, but not so with the second. In the normal use of [10] Bill will presumably have exhibited symptoms, in looks or behaviour, that led the speaker to infer intimidation, but exactly the same holds for [2]: each sentence implies the other. This difference between the pairs is just what our analysis predicts.

Let us first take [2] and [10]. These are both derivable from the one deep structure, [4]. The principal transformations applying in the derivation of [2] are Extraposition and Raising (I shall ignore Affix Hopping and the rule inserting the complementizer *to*). In the case of [10], we first apply Passivization to S_2; this converts [4] into [11].

[11]

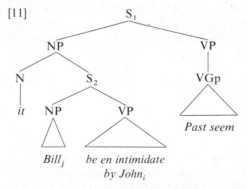

Extraposition now shifts S_2 round *seem*, and Raising moves the subject of S_2, *Bill*, into the subject position of S_1. Adjusting for Affix Hopping and *To*

Insertion we thus have '*Bill seem Past to be intimidate en by John*', the surface structure string of [10]. Recall that the transformations apply according to the cyclic principle. Passivization here applies to S_2, and thus precedes Extraposition and Raising, which cannot apply until the S_1 cycle. The NP moved by Raising is the NP which is in S_2 subject position at that stage in the derivation when Raising applies – thus *John* in the case of [2], *Bill* in [10]. Given, then, this general principle of the transformational cycle, and the rule of Passivization which we have already established on the basis of simple sentences, [10] derives from the same deep structure as [2], with the same rules applying on the S_1 cycle in each case.

The two *expect* sentences, on the other hand, cannot be derived from the same deep structure. We have said that [1] derives from [3] by Equi (plus *To* Insertion, Affix Hopping, *It* Deletion). Suppose we start with [3] and apply Passivization on the S_2 cycle, giving the PM terminating in '*John$_i$ Past expect it Bill$_j$ be en intimidate by John$_i$*'. This clearly does not satisfy the identity condition for Equi, for term 2 is *John*, term 5 *Bill*. In order for Passivization not to make Equi inapplicable, term 2 must be *Bill* too; and this is possible only if *Bill* is subject of S_1 in deep structure. The deep structure of [9] must therefore differ from [3] in having *Bill*, not *John* in NP_1 position – its terminal string is

[12] *Bill$_j$ Past expect it John$_i$ intimidate Bill$_j$*.

And this accounts precisely for the difference in meaning between [1] and [9]: the same thing is being expected in both (there is no difference in NP_2), but they differ in respect of who is expecting it, John ([1]) or Bill ([9]). Leaving aside the minor rules, the derivations of the four sentences may be summarized as follows:

EXAMPLE:	[1]	[9]	[2]	[10]
Deep structure	[3]	[12]	[4]	[4]
S_2 cycle	—	Passivization	—	Passivization
S_1 cycle $\left\{\begin{array}{c} \\ \\ \end{array}\right.$ Equi	Equi	Equi	Extraposition Raising	Extraposition Raising

(b) *There* INSERTION

Let us turn now to a second set of data:

[13] *Some policemen expected to be among the guests*
[14] **There expected to be some policemen among the guests*
[15] *Some policemen seemed to be among the guests*
[16] *There seemed to be some policemen among the guests*

The crucial point here is that [14] is deviant whereas [16] is well-formed, and is, moreover, a paraphrase of [15]. Again, these facts are what our analysis predicts. [15] and [16] are derivable from a common deep structure, whereas [14] is not derivable at all, given the structures and rules we have proposed. To demonstrate this, we must first briefly examine the syntax of *there* in simple sentences.

Consider, for example,

[17] *Some policemen are among the guests*
[18] *There are some policemen among the guests*

The deep structure position of *some policemen* must be the same in each case, as is evident from selectional restriction violations in pairs like *Sincerity is on the table* and *There is sincerity on the table*, and from its common semantic role. *There* has no independent meaning, and it is accordingly plausible to derive [18] from [17] by a rule that moves the underlying subject to the right of the verb and inserts the 'dummy' element *there* to fill the vacated position. This *there* is to be distinguished from the locative adverb that is also spelt *there*, and which clearly does have an independent meaning. The two words are usually phonologically distinct: the dummy element is unstressed and typically has the vowel /ə/ or /ɛ/, the locative is more strongly stressed and has the vowel /ɛə/ – compare them in a sentence where they occur together, such as *There's a mistake there*. Dummy *there* is a NP: the evidence for this claim is that it behaves just like a NP with respect to various transformations. For example, the yes/no interrogative counterpart of [18] is *Are there some policemen among the guests?*. If *there* is analysed as a NP, this will be handled automatically by the Inversion transformation given on *p* 78, whereas the rule would have to be complicated if *there* were not a NP, and there would be no compensatory gains elsewhere. Sentences like [18], accordingly, are among those where the deep and surface subjects are distinct: the deep subject is *some policemen*, the surface subject *there*.

The actual formulation of the transformation introducing *there* poses many problems, and as with other rules discussed in this book, the following is only a crude approximation:

[19] *There* INSERTION: X — NP — VGp — (PP)
         1   2   3   4   ⇒
         1   there   3 + 2   4

The NP of term 2 will not normally be definite: *John and Mary are among the guests* can hardly be transformed into *There are John and Mary among the guests;* in what follows I shall consider only examples with indefinites (on definiteness, see Chapter 15). The rule most frequently applies when the main verb is *be*, but examples like *There remain several problems* show that it would be over-restrictive to mention *be* in the structure index; the deviance of *There consisted one drink of a mixture of liqueurs* demonstrates, however, that [19] is certainly too general as it stands. But the two points relevant to our present limited purposes are not in doubt: *there* is inserted only in subject position and the rule cannot apply when the verb has a direct object. *Some youths broke the windows*, for example, has no well-formed counterpart with dummy *there*: **Some youths broke there the window, *There broke some youths the window*. Notice, however, that *there* can occur under certain conditions in passive sentences, as in *There are now being manufactured some thirty different brands of washing powder by just two major companies;* the fact that these have no active counterparts containing *there* provides the strongest argument for introducing dummy *there* by transformation rather than PS rule, for it shows that the conditions on the insertion of *there* cannot be stated by reference to deep structure: Passivization must apply before *There* Insertion.

Let us now return to [13–16]. [13] and [15] differ only trivially from [1] and [2]; thus [13] derives from [20] by Equi, [15] from [21] by Extraposition and Raising.

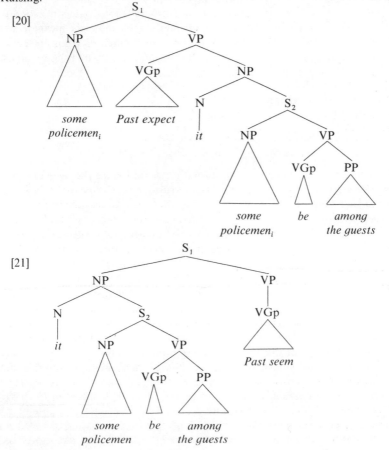

[20]

[21]

Our rules will also derive [16] from [21], thereby accounting for its paraphrase relation with [15]. First, *There* Insertion applies on the S_2 cycle. This moves the original subject *some policemen* into the VP and makes *there* the new subject. Then on the S_1 cycle Extraposition and Raising apply as in the other *seem* sentences, and since at this stage in the derivation the subject of NP_2 is *there*, it is *there* that is raised into the S_1 subject position. We cannot, however, derive [14] from [20]. If *There* Insertion is applied on the S_2 cycle, Equi will not then be able to apply on the S_1 cycle because term 2 of the structure index (*some policemen*) will not be identical with term 5 (*there*). Moreover, *There* Insertion could not apply on the S_1 cycle, because S_1, being transitive, does not satisfy the structure index of [19]. Our grammar will accordingly fail to generate [14], thus correctly excluding it from the set of well-formed sentences.

The argument here is of the same general form as in (a): we show how the analyses we have proposed for the simplest type of *expect* and *seem* sentences interact with rules that we have established INDEPENDENTLY (Passivization in (a), *There* Insertion here) to make correct predictions about the meaning and well-formedness of more complex *expect* and *seem* sentences. Thus no special rules were needed for [9], [10], [14] and [16]: we simply drew on rules that must be included in the grammar anyway.

(c) SELECTIONAL RESTRICTIONS

The third set of data is exemplified in

[22] *The spotlight expected to intimidate Bill*
[23] *The spotlight seemed to intimidate Bill*

The *expect* sentence violates a selectional restriction while the *seem* one does not. There are two facts about selectional restrictions that make the data here give further support to our analysis. First, they have to be stated at the level of deep structure: attempts to handle them at the surface level lead to great loss of generality. This of course was one of the original arguments for making a systematic distinction between deep and surface structure (*cf p* 50). Secondly, noun-verb selectional restrictions (whether the noun is in subject or object position) apply within a single clause: they do not cross clause boundaries. Consider, for example, a sentence like *That John had murdered his cousin didn't emerge until later*. Here there are selectional restrictions holding between *John* and *murder* (contrast *That the storm had murdered . . .*), between *murder* and *cousin* (*That John had murdered the storm . . .*), but not between *John* and *emerge*, or *cousin* and *emerge*. Thus we find innumerable cases where a verb requires that its own subject or object noun be of such and such a subclass, but no cases where a verb imposes such restrictions on the subject or object of another verb. For greater precision let us introduce the concept of CLAUSE-MATE (which we shall also need elsewhere). Two elements are clause-mates within a given PM if and only if there is no S node dominating one of them which does not also dominate the other. In PM [3], for example, *expect* is a

CLAUSE-MATE

clause-mate of *it*, *Past* and the leftmost occurrence of *John*, but not of *Bill*, *intimidate*, and the rightmost occurrence of *John*, for these last three elements are all dominated by S_2, which does not dominate *expect*. We can now say that noun-verb selectional restrictions hold between deep structure clause-mates. This principle is established on the basis of indefinitely many examples (like the one above with *emerge*) where the deep structure subject-verb and verb-object relations are obvious: we can then appeal to the principle to determine these relations in less clear cases, like the infinitival constructions that are our concern in this chapter. [22] shows that we cannot replace *John* in our original example [1] by an inanimate noun like *spotlight*. The restriction clearly holds between *John* and *expect*, not *John* and *intimidate*, for sentences like *The spotlight intimidated Bill* are perfectly acceptable. It follows therefore that *John* and *expect* must be deep structure clause-mates. And this is just what they are shown to be in PM [3]. Conversely, in PM [4] *John* is not a clause-mate of *seem*, so that our analysis predicts that there will be no selectional restrictions holding between them. This prediction is correct: any noun can occur as surface subject to *seem*. (Such a sentence as *The storm seemed to enjoy the concert* is not, of course, a counterexample to the prediction, for the deviance is due to the incompatibility of *storm* and *enjoy* evidenced in the simple sentence *The storm enjoyed the concert*.)

(d) FINITE COMPLEMENTS

Compare next [1] and [2] with examples like

[24] *John$_i$ expected that he$_i$ would intimidate Bill$_j$*
[25] **It expected that John$_i$ would intimidate Bill$_j$*
[26] **John$_i$ seemed that he$_i$ intimidated Bill$_j$*
[27] *It seemed that John$_i$ intimidated Bill$_j$*

Expect and *seem* are among the verbs that can take either finite or infinitival complements. In the finite construction there is significantly less difference between the deep and surface structure than in the non-finite one (because Equi and Raising apply only to the latter). Thus the deep grammatical functions of NPs are more evident in finites than in non-finites. In [24] it is clear that the subject of both *expect* and *intimidate* is *John*, which is what we have claimed about its paraphrase, [1]. In the derivation of [24] the second *John* is replaced by the pronoun *he*, instead of being deleted, as in [1]. Similarly [26] and [27] support our analysis of [2], where we claimed that *John* is underlying subject of *intimidate* but not of *seem*. In the derivation of [27], the complement is moved to the right by Extraposition, but *John* remains in S_2 instead of being raised, as in [2].

At this point I shall leave examples [1] and [2] and continue the justification of Equi and Raising by contrasting a somewhat different pair:

[28] *John told Bill to brief Guy*
[29] *John wanted Bill to brief Guy*

These differ from [1] and [2] in that there is a NP (*Bill*) between the two verbs. However, the difference between [28] and [29] is very similar to that between [1] and [2]. Thus [28] derives by Equi from [30], [29] by Raising from [31].

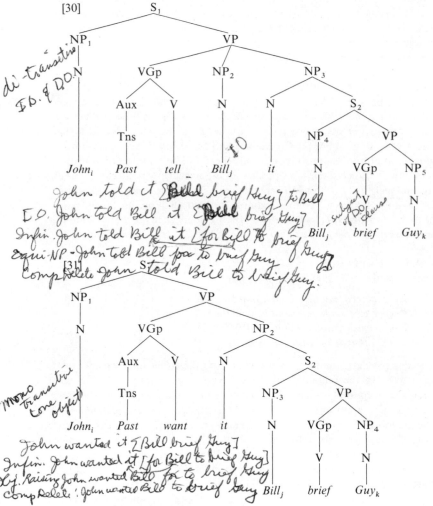

Tell in [30] is 'ditransitive', having two objects (NP$_2$ and NP$_3$), whereas *want* in [31] is simply transitive, with one object (NP$_2$). Again this analysis is very plausible from a semantic point of view. [28] expresses an act of verbal communication: NP$_1$ corresponds to the 'deliverer' of the message, NP$_2$ to the 'recipient', and NP$_3$ to the 'content'. *Want*, on the other hand, expresses a relation between an 'experiencer' and a state of affairs or event: these correspond respectively to NP$_1$ and NP$_2$ of [31].

If [30] is indeed the deep structure of [28], then clearly one occurrence of *Bill* must be deleted during the transformational derivation. This can be effected by Equi, with [30] matching the structure index as follows:

[32]

$John_i$ Past tell	$Bill_j$		*it*	$Bill_j$	*brief* Guy_k	
1	2	3	4	5	6	7

We see now why the rule was formulated with parentheses round the VGp of term 3, indicating that it is optional: term 2 may be separated from term 4 by a VGp, as in earlier examples, or by nothing, as in the present example.

As before, Raising does not operate directly on the deep PM but on a structure derived by Extraposition. To generate [29], therefore, we first apply Extraposition to convert [31] into [33], which satisfies the structure index for Raising in the manner shown:

[33]

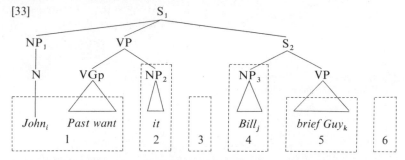

Since S_2 is already at the right in [31], the effect of Extraposition is simply to detach it from NP_2 and make it a daughter of S_1; this makes *it* a complete NP as required by term 2 of the Raising rule. The parentheses round VGp in the latter rule again allow for term 3 to be null, as in [33]. Notice, then, that when the higher verb is intransitive (like *seem*) Raising moves the S_2 subject into S_1 subject position, whereas when the higher verb is transitive (like *want*) it moves it into S_1 object position.

To justify the analysis here we need to show not only that the deep structure of [29] contains just one occurrence of *Bill*, located in S_2, but also that in surface structure *Bill* belongs in S_1. In the earlier example *John seemed to intimidate Bill* it was obvious that *John* was surface subject of *seem*, but in [29] we are not entitled simply to take it for granted that *Bill* is surface object of *want*. The arguments supporting the deep structures [30] and [31] are entirely parallel to those given for the *expect* and *seem* sentences; it will therefore be convenient to present these first, and then justify our claim about the surface structure.

(a) PASSIVIZATION OF THE COMPLEMENT CLAUSE

[34] *John told Guy to be briefed by Bill*

[35] *John wanted Guy to be briefed by Bill*

[35] derives from the same deep structure as [29], which accounts for the paraphrase relation. The deep structure of [34] on the other hand differs from that of [28] in having *Guy* in the NP_2 position – its terminal string is

[36] *John$_i$ Past tell Guy$_k$ it Bill$_j$ brief Guy$_k$*

This accounts for the difference in meaning: deliverer and content of the message are the same in each case, but in [28] the recipient is Bill, in [34] Guy. The derivations of [34] and [35] may be summarized as follows (the reader is invited to work through these to check that they give the correct results):

EXAMPLE	28	34	29	35
Deep structure	30	36	31	31
S_2 cycle	—	Passivization	—	Passivization
S_1 cycle {	Equi	Equi	Extraposition Raising	Extraposition Raising

(b) *There* INSERTION

[37] *John told a policeman to be at the meeting*
[38] **John told there to be a policeman at the meeting*
[39] *John wanted a policeman to be at the meeting*
[40] *John wanted there to be a policeman at the meeting*
~~John wanted it [a policeman be at the meeting]~~

[39] and [40] both derive from '*John Past want it* [$_S$ *a policeman be at the meeting*]$_S$'. In [40], *There* Insertion applies on the S_2 cycle, giving '*John Past want it* [$_S$ *there be a policeman at the meeting*]$_S$'; thus when Raising applies on the S_1 cycle it is the NP *there* that is affected. The deep structure of [37] is '*John$_i$ Past tell a policeman$_j$ it* [$_S$ *a policeman$_j$ be at the meeting*]$_S$'; if *There* insertion applies to S_2 here, Equi will not be able to apply on the S_1 cycle: there is no way of generating [38].

(c) SELECTIONAL RESTRICTIONS

[41] **John told his behaviour to shock Agatha*
[42] *John wanted his behaviour to shock Agatha*

The selectional violation in [41] shows that *John* and *Bill* in [28] must be deep structure clause-mates, as they are in [30] (NP_1 and NP_2). Conversely [31] does not have *John* and *Bill* in the same clause, correctly predicting that *want* imposes no constraints on what may occur in the position of *Bill*.

(d) FINITE COMPLEMENTS

[43] *John$_i$ told Bill$_j$ that he$_j$ should brief Guy$_k$*
[44] *?John$_i$ wanted that Bill$_j$ should brief Guy$_k$*

Tell is clearly functioning as a ditransitive verb in [43], which is a near-paraphrase of [28]; there is certainly no difference between them as far as the semantic roles of John, Bill, and Guy are concerned, and in particular Bill has one role with respect to the telling, and one with respect to the briefing. [44] is deviant for many speakers – but it is undoubtedly more acceptable as a variant of [29] than is *John wanted Bill that he should brief Guy; [44] is readily interpretable, and the role of Bill is understood to be the same as in [29].

It now remains to justify the claim that, in spite of the deep structure differences between [28] and [29], in surface structure *Bill* belongs in each case in S_1 not S_2: only if we can show this are we entitled to say that Raising applies in the derivation of [29]. The argument I shall give is based on the distribution of reflexive pronouns. These we have been accounting for by means of a transformation that replaces the second of two identical PMs by the appropriate reflexive form (*cf* Chapter 6): *John shaved himself* derives from '*John$_i$ Past shave John$_i$*', and so on. Now an important point about the Reflexivization transformation is that the identical NPs must be in the same clause – must be clause-mates in the sense defined above. This condition is established on the basis of innumerable examples where the clause boundaries are clear. Compare, for example:

[45] *John$_i$ persuaded himself$_i$* [$_s$ that Bill$_j$ was wrong]$_s$
[46] **John$_i$ persuaded Bill$_j$* [$_s$ that Mary$_k$ had deceived himself$_j$]$_s$
[47] **John$_i$ ignored the girl$_j$* [$_s$ who$_j$ had addressed himself$_i$]$_s$

John and *himself* are clause-mates in [45], but not in [46] and [47], which accounts for their deviance. We can now use this finding to decide the constituent structure in unclear cases. For many speakers, a sentence like *John wanted himself to get the job* is unacceptable: in this dialect, if the subjects of *want* and the complement clause are identical, Equi applies obligatorily, for *John wanted him to get the job* is also unacceptable if *him* is coreferential with *John*. This means that the clause-mate condition on Reflexivization does not bear directly on the analysis of *want* sentences like [29]; we can, however, use it indirectly by adducing such examples as

[48] *John believed himself to be ill*

In the absence of good reasons for the contrary analysis we here take the two *John*'s to be clause-mates at that stage in the derivation where Reflexivization applies – for otherwise we would have to give up the clause-mate condition. Now it is easy to show by appeal to points (a)–(d) above that *believe* enters into deep structures of the kind proposed for *want*, not *tell* – note the well-formedness of *John believed there to be a spy on the board*, the equivalence between [48] and *John believed that he was ill*, and so on. It follows that the deep structure of [48] will be '*John$_i$ Past believe it* [$_s$ *John$_i$ be ill*]$_s$'. We have thus shown that the second *John* is in S_2 in deep structure and S_1 at the stage of Reflexivization, and hence that it must have been raised. And if Raising applies in [48], we can assume that it applies in *John believed Bill to be ill* and [29] too, for otherwise it would have to be made subject to ad hoc and unmotivated restrictions. This concludes our analysis of [29], but it is worth pointing out that the facts just discussed provide a further strong argument for inserting reflexive pronouns by transformation rather than PS rule (*cf p* 89). For we have shown that in the derivation of [48] Raising applies before Reflexivization: the clause-mate condition does not apply at the level of deep structure and could not therefore be formulated as a condition on a putative PS rule inserting reflexives. This argument has the same form as that used above to justify a *There* Insertion transformation – *there* can be inserted into a structure resulting from Passivization but not into the corresponding deep structure.

Let us briefly review the results we have obtained. We have been concerned with sentences whose surface structures are of two main types, represented schematically in [49] and [50], where V_1 is active in voice and any auxiliary verbs are omitted.

[49] NP_1 V_1 *to* V_2 NP_2
[50] NP_1 V_1 NP_2 *to* V_2 NP_3

Two derivations have been proposed for each.

I: with *expect* as V_1 in [49], NP_1 and V_1 are deep structure clause-mates and Equi deletes the subject of V_2.
II: With *seem* as V_1 in [49], NP_1 is not a deep structure clause-mate of V_1 but is moved into the higher clause by Raising from subject position in the lower one.
III: With *tell* as V_1 in [50], NP_2 and V_1 are deep structure clause-mates and Equi deletes the subject of V_2.
IV: With *want* as V_1 in [50], NP_2 is not a deep structure clause-mate of V_1, but is moved into the higher clause by Raising from subject position in the lower one.

The fact that in (I) but not (II) NP_1 and V_1 are deep structure clause-mates explains why with *expect* but not *seem*, we get a change in meaning if we passivize V_2, interchanging its object with NP_1; why with *expect* but not *seem*, NP_1 cannot be moved round V_2 with *there* being substituted for it; and why with *expect* but not *seem*, there are selectional restrictions between NP_1 and V_1. Analogously for (III) and (IV). It is worth emphasizing that the close parallelism between the arguments supporting the (I) versus (II) contrast and those supporting the (III) versus (IV) contrast is a consequence of the analysis proposed: the 'raw facts' are different in the two cases. For example, the data show that *seem* but not *expect* can take *there* as surface SUBJECT and that *want* but not *tell* can take *there* as surface OBJECT: it is a merit of the analysis that it relates these two facts by showing that both follow from the Raising/Equi distinction. The postulation of these two rules thus enables us to bring order and unity to a wide range of superficially disparate phenomena, and for this reason we can justly claim that the analysis provides an explanation for these phenomena.

The deep structures proposed fall into three main classes, according as the higher verb is intransitive, transitive, or ditransitive:

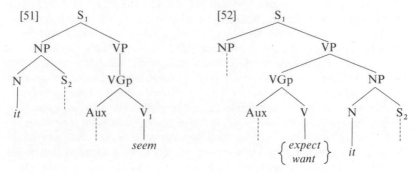

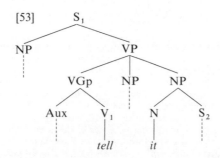

[49] is derivable from [52], as in (I), or from [51], as in (II); [50] is derivable from [53], as in (III), or from [52], as in (IV): *seem* fills the V_1 position in [51], *tell* that in [53], while both *expect* and *want* fill that in [52]. This then further explains why *seem* occurs in [49] but not [50], *tell* in [50] but not [49], while *expect* and *want* occur in both, witness

[54] *John expected Bill to brief Guy*
[55] **John seemed Bill to brief Guy*
[56] **John told to intimidate Bill*
[57] *John wanted to intimidate Bill*

Not all transitive verbs taking an infinitival complement in their object NP occur in both [49] and [50]:

[58] *John believed Bill to be right*
[59] **John believed to be right*
[60] *John tried to solve the problem*
[61] **John tried Bill to solve the problem*

I have already shown that *believe* enters into structure [52], not [53]; we can similarly see from a comparison of *try* with *expect* and *seem* that [60] must derive from [52], not [51]: *try* is like *expect* in excluding *there* from surface subject position, as in **There tried to be a policeman at the meeting*, and so on. We can, apparently, exclude [59] and [61] only by treating *believe* and *try* as 'exceptions' (see Chapter 10 for some discussion of the formal apparatus needed). There can be no denying that languages contain many exceptions. Thus the failure of the rules to block [59] and [61] in the same way as [56] and [55] respectively does not invalidate our analysis: it would do so only if there were a rival analysis providing a unitary explanation (and accounting no less satisfactorily for the other data we have considered). Just as we do not abandon our general rules for the formation of regular plurals like *cats*, *dogs* and *foxes* simply because they do not work for *geese*, *sheep* and *oxen*, so we do not abandon our Equi rule because it cannot apply in *believe* sentences or our Raising rule because it cannot apply in *try* sentences. Counterexamples and exceptions obviously constitute a challenge to an analysis, but do not of themselves invalidate it.

Notes

There is a large literature on complementation. The first major transformational study is Rosenbaum 1967; modifications to this are proposed in, among others, R. Lakoff 1968:12–72, Kiparsky and Kiparsky 1970, Stockwell *et al* 1973:502–99. Postal 1974 is a large book devoted almost wholly to a justification of the Raising rule. The Equi and Raising transformations play a considerable role in many theoretical discussions relating to rule ordering and other issues – see 12.3 below, G. Lakoff 1966*a*, McCawley 1970. Bresnan 1970 argues for introducing the complementizers by PS rules. It can be instructive to compare a transformational analysis of this area of the grammar with one written from a different theoretical standpoint, such as Palmer 1965:150–79, which is largely confined to a classification of surface forms; see also his later discussion of some problems in the transformational treatment (1973).

The analysis I have presented fails to account for the difference between (i) *John told Bill to mend the fuse* and (ii) *John promised Bill to mend the fuse*. *Promise*, like *tell*, is a ditransitive verb, so that both (i) and (ii) derive from a structure like [53] by the application of Equi. But whereas in (i) the S_2 subject is deleted under identity with *Bill*, the S_1 OBJECT, in (ii) it is deleted under identity with *John*, the S_1 SUBJECT. The NP in S_1 with which the complement subject is identical is often called the 'controller'; the problem of determining in some principled way which NP is the controller is discussed in Rosenbaum 1970, Postal 1970*b*, Jackendoff 1972:178–228. I have also glossed over the fact that some verbs may enter into more than one of structures [51–53]: *The rain threatened to disrupt the match* (where *threaten* = 'look ominously likely') derives from [51], *John threatened to sue Bill* (*threaten* = 'issue verbal threat') from [52], and so on.

The reader may have noted that Passivization, as formulated on *p* 73, cannot in fact apply to S_2 in PM [4], because there is no Aux constituent; the necessary adjustment could be made by enclosing term 3 of the rule in parentheses. But the assumption that the Tns element is absent from the deep as well as from the surface structure of non-finite clauses is somewhat questionable: see Chapter 14.

Chapter 9

Syntactic Structure and Illocutionary Force

9.1 Classification of sentences and of speech acts

In this section I want to introduce a distinction between the classification of
sentences and the classification of speech acts, and to consider the relations
between the various types of sentence and the various types of speech act that
can be performed in uttering them. Let us begin with the following very simple
examples:

[1]	MOOD	ILLOCUTIONARY FORCE
i *John died last week*	Declarative	Statement
ii *Where do you live?*	Interrogative	Question
iii *Stand still!*	Imperative	Command
iv *What a genius he was!*	Exclamative	Exclamation

There are clear syntactic differences having to do with the presence or absence
of the subject, its linear position, the presence or absence of special '*wh*' words
like *where* and *what*, and so on. These differences motivate the syntactic classification of [i–iv] as declarative, interrogative, etc: this is a time-honoured
and uncontroversial classification (at least as far as the first three are concerned), and for the moment I shall simply take it for granted. As noted in 5.1,
this dimension of classification is often referred to as 'mood', a term I shall
use in preference to the less specific 'sentence type'. Now suppose I use these
sentences in normal performance – the qualification 'normal' excludes cases
where I am practising elocution, testing a microphone, and so on. In uttering
[i–iv] I perform different kinds of acts: I respectively make a statement, ask a
question, give a command and make an exclamation. In uttering [i] I do
various other things as well as make a statement: I refer to John, I produce a
string of speech sounds, and so on, and these acts can also be regarded as
'speech acts'. Again, therefore, it will be helpful to have a more specific term
for the dimension of classification of speech acts along which we contrast
statement, question, etc: the term in standard use for this is ILLOCUTIONARY

FORCE. Accordingly we shall say that an utterance of [i] in an appropriate context has the illocutionary force of statement, and so on.

There are several reasons why it is important to distinguish between the mood categories declarative, interrogative, etc on the one hand, and the illocutionary force categories statement, question, etc on the other.

(a) In the first place, declarative, interrogative, imperative and exclamative provide for a more or less exhaustive syntactic classification of sentences, whereas there are very many more different types of illocutionary force than the four mentioned. This was one of the major themes of the philosopher J. L. Austin in his *How to do things with words*, the work in which the notion of illocutionary force was first introduced. Austin drew attention to such declarative sentences as

[2] *I name this ship the 'Queen Elizabeth'*
[3] *I bet you sixpence it will rain tomorrow*
[4] *I apologize*

observing that if one utters these in appropriate contexts one is doing something significantly different from what one does in uttering [1i]. If I utter [1i] I make a statement, but if I utter [2–4] what I do is name a ship, make a bet and apologize. Austin argued that it is a mistake to regard utterances of [2–4] as 'descriptions' or 'reports' of what the speaker is doing – as he wrote of another example (1962:6), 'When I say, before the registrar or altar, etc, "I do", I am not reporting on a marriage, I am indulging in it'. An important difference is that in [1i], but not [2–4], the question arises as to whether what I say is true. Clearly I can use [1i] to make a true statement or a false statement. But it does not make sense to ask whether an utterance of [2] is true: the sort of question that arises here is whether the speaker is the person authorized to perform the ceremony, whether 'Queen Elizabeth' is the pre-arranged name, and so on. If the speaker is not so authorized, then something will have gone seriously wrong with the speech act, but it will not have been 'false' in the way that an utterance of [1i] is false if John is still alive. There are many ways in which utterances can go wrong or be 'defective' besides being false – as when I say *Please open the door* though the door is already open or *When did you stop beating your wife?* though you have never beaten her. The point is, then, to distinguish between the syntactic mood category of a sentence and the function of an utterance in some speech situation, and to avoid the error of thinking that the only use to which a declarative sentence can be put is that of making a statement: one can promise, advise, congratulate, apologize, thank, marry, divorce, christen babies, sentence criminals, open buildings, close meetings, and so on.

(b) Secondly, the relation between the mood and illocutionary force categories is not one-to-many, as the above examples might seem to suggest, but many-to-many. That is, it is not just that sentences with the same mood can be used with differing illocutionary force – we also find that sentences of different mood can be used with the same illocutionary force. This many-to-many relation is evident from the following examples:

[5]	i *Report at the Guard-room at 0600 hrs*	[Imp]
	ii *I command you to report at the Guard-room at 0600 hrs*	[Decl]
[6]	i *Have a safe journey*	[Imp]
	ii *I wish you a safe journey*	[Decl]
[7]	i *Please pass the salt*	[Imp]
	ii *Would you mind passing the salt*	[Int]
[8]	i *Please accept my sincere apologies*	[Imp]
	ii *Will you please accept my sincere apologies*	[Int]
	iii *I apologize most sincerely*	[Decl]
[9]	i *Do let me take you to see 'Hamlet' on Friday*	[Imp]
	ii *Would you like to come and see 'Hamlet' on Friday?*	[Int]
	iii *I invite you to come and see 'Hamlet' on Friday*	[Decl]
[10]	i *Did you know the victim?*	[Int]
	ii *I ask you (again) whether you know the victim*	[Decl]
[11]	i *Hasn't she a marvellous voice?*	[Int]
	ii *What a marvellous voice she has!*	[Excl]

With the usual proviso about appropriate contexts, the examples in [5] will be commands, [6] wishes, [7] requests, [8] apologies, [9] invitations, [10] questions and [11] exclamations, whereas their classification as decl(arative), int(errogative), imp(erative) or excl(amative) is as shown at the right. We thus have the following pattern of relationships:

[12]

Imperative	Declarative	Interrogative	Exclamative

Command	Wish	Request	Apology	Invitation	Question	Exclamation

And clearly it would be a simple matter to find examples illustrating still other connections between the two sets of categories.

(c) A third reason for distinguishing the two sets of categories is that the mood classification applies (at least in part) to embedded sentences, as in

[13] *Bill thinks **that John died last week***
[14] *I know **where you live***
[15] *She remembers **what a genius he was***

The embedded clauses (in bold type) are respectively declarative, interrogative and exclamative, just like their independent clause counterparts, [1i], [ii] and [iv]. Yet in utterances of [13–15], no speech act function of the kind we have
in embedded sentences

been considering is associated with these embedded clauses. In [14] we have an interrogative inside a declarative, but we do not have a question inside a statement – an utterance of *where you live* does not here count as a discrete speech act and consequently has no illocutionary force at all. And this holds equally in a case like *I know who did it*, where *who did it* has the same internal structure as an independent clause: it may function as a question when it stands alone as a whole sentence, but not when it is embedded within the object of *know*. Imperatives are somewhat different from the other mood categories in this respect, for there are no embedded imperatives: I shall argue this point later in the chapter.

(d) Fourthly, the illocutionary force of an utterance depends on a variety of contextual factors, such as the beliefs, assumptions, intentions of speaker and addressee(s) and their relative social statuses, which will not always be expressed in the grammatical structure of the sentence uttered. Consider, for example, the following imperatives:

[16] i *Lend me a fiver*   ii *Have another beer*
      iii *Don't work too hard*   iv *Sleep well*

These would typically be used in contexts where the following differences in assumptions obtain (I use *S* and *A* as abbreviations for speaker and addressee): *A*'s sleeping well is not something *A* has voluntary control over, whereas he can choose whether or not to lend *S* a fiver, have another beer, avoid overworking; *A*'s lending *S* a fiver is something *S* wants rather than something that is primarily for the benefit of *A*, whereas his having another beer, not overworking, and sleeping well are in *A*'s interests; if *A* wants to have another beer, *S* will bring this about, whereas *S* is not in a position to bring it about that *A* sleeps well, avoids overworking or lends *S* a fiver. Given these assumptions, [16i] will be construed as a request, [ii] an offer, [iii] a piece of advice, [iv] a wish. But one can imagine contexts where at least some of these assumptions do not hold and where the illocutionary force is consequently different. For example, with [ii] the beer could belong to *A* and it could be *A* who is going to serve it: in this case [ii] would not be an offer. Or *A*'s not working too hard may be primarily in the interests of *S* and others who do not want their work to be shown to compare unfavourably with *A*'s: here [iii] might be taken as a request or order. Again, consider examples like:

[17] i *Come up to my flat and I'll show you my etchings*
      ii *Have another beer and you'll have a hangover tomorrow*
      iii *Speak to me like that again and I'll fire you*

The interpretation of these as invitation, warning and threat respectively depends on the following assumptions: (i) If *A* comes to *S*'s flat, *S* will be able to show *A* his (or her) etchings, and *S* believes *A* would derive benefit (pleasure, interest) from seeing them. (ii) *A*'s having another drink will result in *A*'s having a hangover tomorrow, and having a hangover will not benefit *A*. (iii) *A*'s speaking to S 'like that again' will result in S's firing A because S chooses to act in that way under such circumstances, and being fired will not benefit A. But again these assumptions are not necessary for the appropriate use of the sentences: if S believes that A cannot bear having to look at S's etchings, [17i] could be a threat designed to prevent A's coming to the flat rather than an invitation with the opposite aim.

Similarly, a crucial difference between a command and a request is that S is entitled to give a command only if he is in some kind of authority over A, and the recognition of this authority by S and A can be enough to give an utterance the force of a command even when the sentence used could in other contexts be construed simply as a request. *Be there at six*, say, would typically have the force of a command if spoken by colonel to sergeant, but the force of a request if spoken by brother to sister.

It is clear, then, that the illocutionary force of an utterance is not fully determined by the linguistic structure of the sentence uttered. Illocutionary force is similar in this respect to reference: the referent of a referring expression is not fully determined by the linguistic structure of that expression. Just as in 1.1 we distinguished between meaning and reference, so here we shall distinguish between meaning and illocutionary force. Meaning is a property of sentences or parts thereof, and accordingly falls within the province of a theory of linguistic competence; reference and illocutionary force are properties of utterances or parts thereof, and will not be directly and fully accounted for by a competence theory. But, to continue the analogy, just as reference is PARTLY determined by meaning, so too is illocutionary force. *Be there at six* may be used now as a command, now as a request, but it cannot be used to make a promise, statement, bet and so on. Thus a competence theory will not ignore illocutionary force, but will deal with it to the extent that it is determined by sentence structure rather than by purely contextual factors. And we can accordingly invoke notions like question not only in talking of the illocutionary force of utterances but also of the meaning of sentences – we will say that *What time is John arriving?*, for example, has question meaning, since a normal utterance of it will have question force.

One problem concerning the relationship between meaning and illocutionary force emerges from a consideration of pairs of examples like these:

[18] i *Would you like to have written a symphony like that?*
    ii *Would you like to open the door?*
[19] i *I want to write a biography of Leonard Bloomfield*
    ii *I want to know where you put the money*
[20] i *I should like to be an engine-driver*
    ii *I should like to thank you for your kind hospitality*
[21] i *We may stay as long as we like*
    ii *You may borrow this copy*

Although there are close structural resemblances between the members of each pair, there are significant differences in the way they would most likely be construed in normal use. In [18], [i] would be a question, [ii] a request; in [19], [i] would be an ordinary statement about the speaker's wants, whereas [ii] could well be equivalent to *Where did you put the money?;* in [20], [i] would again be a statement about the speaker, whereas [ii] would have the illocutionary force of thanking; and finally in [21], [i] would be a statement that we have permission to stay, while [ii] would typically be construed as the granting of permission. It is questionable, however, whether we should try to account for these facts by saying that [18ii] has a request meaning, and analogously for the others. It is clear, first of all, that we cannot exclude the interpretation of [18ii] as a yes/no question like [i], or the interpretation of [19ii] as a statement about the speaker's wants, again like [i], and so on. It might be objected that this point can be countered by saying that the [ii] sentences are simply ambiguous and should therefore be assigned two distinct meanings (and deep structures); but is this really an appropriate solution? Certainly the sentences do not exhibit the kind of ambiguity we find in such a clear and classic example as *I dislike visiting relatives* ('I dislike going to visit relatives' or 'I dislike relatives who visit me'). Here the ambiguity seems to arise from the chance combination of a number of unrelated and quite independently variable properties of the sentence: (a) *visit* belongs to the class of verbs which can be used with or without an expressed object and which can take animate NPs as both subject and object (contrast the unambiguous *I dislike doing crossword puzzles*); (b) *relatives* is not accompanied by a determiner or adjectival modifier (contrast *I dislike some visiting relatives, I dislike visiting your relatives, I dislike visiting elderly relatives*, etc). [18–21] are quite different: the fact that in [18] only [ii] can have the force of a request is due to the perfect aspect in [i], but this is not an independent matter: it is a crucial condition for a request that the action at issue be in the future (I clearly cannot request that in the past you wrote a symphony). The two interpretations of the *visiting relatives* example are on a par, each correlating with a distinct syntactic structure. But in the case of [18ii] it seems more reasonable to say that the question interpretation is primary, more basic than the request: it is a question by virtue of its LITERAL MEANING and a request only by IMPLICATION. *A* will construe [18ii] as equivalent to a request on the basis of inferences about *S*'s intentions in uttering it. If *A* would like to open the door, he would presumably comply with an explicit request to do so, and it is likely that in a given instance this would be the sole significance of the information that *A* would like to open the door. Moreover, *S*'s interest in *A*'s willingness to comply with such a request is likely to derive from his desire to have *A* open the door. Thus the utterance would typically lead *A* to infer that *S* wants him to open the door even though *S* has not explicitly requested him to do so. Similarly, I would suggest that [21ii] does not have the same literal meaning as *I hereby give you permission to borrow this copy*, even though the effect of uttering the two sentences might well be the same, given a context where *S* is assumed to be entitled to give such permission.

A particularly clear example of this distinction between literal meaning and implication arose in our early discussion of competence and performance in 1.1. I observed that a sentence like *I'm incredibly thirsty* might be construed in certain contexts as a request for a drink, but that this was not part of the meaning of the sentence – in the new terminology we would say that the request was simply implied. I further suggested that a competence grammar would deal with the meaning, but not the implication. It must be admitted, however, that examples like [18] create difficulties in the application of the competence-performance distinction. For what one feels intuitively to be an implication rather than part of the basic or literal meaning sometimes has an effect on the linguistic structure. Thus it is surely the regular use of the [18ii] type of construction to make requests that accounts for the occurrence of *please*, as in *Would you like to open the door please.* (*Please* can occur in ordinary questions as in *What time is it, please?*, a question being indeed a special kind of request, a request to give an appropriate answer; nevertheless in the *would you like* example, the *please* is associated with the request to open the door, not the request to answer the literal question.) Similarly with [21ii]: if the speaker is in fact using such a sentence to grant permission he may add a phrase like *with pleasure*, where it is clearly the speaker's pleasure that is involved, not the addressee's. Sentence [19ii] provides a third example. In a Black dialect of American English the fact that *I want to know* is used as a means of eliciting information would have the effect of making the Inversion rule apply to the complement sentence, giving *I want to know where did you put the money*, whereas *I told him where you put the money*, which does not seek information, has the uninverted order. Or again, imperatives like [17] that are equivalent to conditions may assume a form that they could not otherwise have: **Drink any more beer* is deviant if it stands alone, whereas the coordinated sentence *Drink any more beer and you'll have a hangover* is perfectly well-formed. Phenomena of this kind suggest that it will be necessary to extend the scope of generative grammar so as to take account of the implications of sentences in various types of context.

Let us now leave these cases where the illocutionary force depends on such implications and confine ourselves to the literal meaning of sentences. What aspects of syntactic structure determine that part of the meaning of a sentence which is relevant to illocutionary force? Mood is undoubtedly the most general of them – in emphasizing the distinction between mood and illocutionary force I have not sought to deny the important connections between them. Moreover, the contrast just drawn between what a sentence means and what an utterance of it implies in a given context will account to a significant extent for the many-to-many relationship between the two sets of categories noted in point (b) above. But it will not account for all departures from a one-to-one relationship – because mood is not the only aspect of syntactic structure relevant to illocutionary force. Among the others I shall mention here just one: the presence or absence of a PERFORMATIVE verb.

We can best see what is meant by a performative verb by considering such a contrast as that between

[22] *I apologize for the delay*
[23] *I shave after breakfast*

The very act of uttering [22] (in normal performance) constitutes an apology: I
'perform' the act of apologizing in uttering [22]. But to utter [23] is clearly not
to shave. *Shave* is accordingly non-performative, while *apologize* – like *name*
and *bet* in [2] and [3] – is performative. Others are *advise, command, congratulate, order, promise, thank* and so on (the number is quite large, though vastly
smaller than the number of non-performatives). A performative verb identifies a
particular kind of speech act that can be performed by virtue of uttering a
sentence containing the verb (and meeting certain syntactic conditions, mentioned very briefly below). Their function is to make explicit and precise the
illocutionary force of the utterance containing them. Thus we may contrast
*I command you to be there at six, I request you to be there at six, I beseech you
to be there at six* on the one hand, with *Be there at six* on the other. Here the
performative verbs *command, request, beseech* indicate explicitly how utterances of the sentences are to be construed, whereas the imperative mood of
Be there at six delimits the illocutionary force in a much more general way,
with contextual factors contributing to a narrower specification of the force.
Similarly, *I'll go and visit her* may be taken as a promise, but only by implication, whereas the performative in *I promise that I'll go and visit her* makes the
promise explicit.

Now the mere presence of the verb *apologize* in a sentence does not suffice
to make a normal utterance of it an apology: I do not make an apology in
uttering *John refused to apologize*. As well as distinguishing between performative and non-performative verbs, we need also to distinguish between performative and non-performative USES of a performative verb. In general a
verb can be used performatively only under the following conditions: (a) the
tense is present, not past; (b) the deep subject is first person; (c) the performative verb is not in an embedded clause; (d) there is no modal or aspectual
auxiliary; (e) there is no adverb of frequency. The following examples do not
contain a performative use of *apologize* because they conflict with the above
five conditions respectively: (a) *I apologized profusely;* (b) *John apologizes for
his absence;* (c) *John suggested that I apologize;* (d) *I have apologized;* (e) *I
always apologize.* None of these has the meaning of an apology. I should
emphasize that this account is quite rough; formulating explicitly the necessary
and sufficient conditions for the performative use of a performative verb poses
very considerable problems. The conditions are in fact primarily semantic
rather than syntactic: instead of saying that the deep subject must be syntactically first person, for example, we should say that it must refer to the
speaker or writer – note the performative use of *request* in *The management
requests that . . .*, and so on.

Let us now turn to mood. So far we have been simply taking the mood
categories for granted: it is now time to look at them more carefully. Or rather,
since there is not space to deal with them all, I shall examine the grammar of

interrogatives. My concern will be with such questions as these: How can we explicate the intuitive notion 'interrogative sentence' – what is it, precisely, that all interrogative sentences have in common? What differences are there between the deep and surface structures of such sentences, and what transformations apply in their derivation? How does the deep structure of interrogatives relate to meaning?

9.2 Interrogative mood

We may begin by noting that there is no single property of surface structure that will serve to define the class of interrogative sentences, so that any explication of the notion interrogative sentence must go deeper than the surface level. Consider, for example, the following three surface properties which are obviously determined in part by interrogative mood: the position of the subject, the presence of a '*wh*' word, and rising intonation.

(a) POSITION OF THE SUBJECT
Clearly the chief surface factor distinguishing interrogative *Can John swim?* from declarative *John can swim* is the position of the subject NP relative to the auxiliary verb. But this inverted order is neither a sufficient nor a necessary condition for interrogativeness. That it is not sufficient is shown by its occurrence in examples like *Only then did I realize my error* (declarative), *Don't you do that again!* (imperative), *What a furore would there be if this were made public!* (exclamative, though here the inverted order may be slightly archaic). That it is not a necessary condition is shown by its non-occurrence in certain types of interrogative: *Who can swim?*, *You're leaving already?* and the embedded clause of *I wonder **where I put it**.*

(b) '*Wh*' ELEMENTS
It is the presence of the special words *who* and *what* that marks *Who told him?* and *What politician said that?* as interrogatives in contrast to the declaratives *Someone told him* and *Some politician said that*. But again, many interrogatives do not contain such an element in surface structure, witness *Have you finished?*, *Did you give it to John or Peter?*. And '*wh*' words occur also in relative clauses, as in *The man who came to dinner stayed all night*, and exclamatives, as in *What chaos there was!*. ('*Wh*' is the standard mnemonic label for these forms, but it should be borne in mind that *how* also belongs to the class; phonologically, some begin with /h/, *eg: who, how, . . .*, others with /w/, *eg: what, when, ...*)

(c) RISING INTONATION
In speech it is the rising intonation that would normally distinguish interrogative *You've seen it?* from declarative *You've seen it;* here too, however, we note that interrogatives containing a '*wh*' word, even those with inverted order, do not necessarily have rising intonation.

Any of the three properties may serve as the sole distinguishing feature between an interrogative and a non-interrogative, but none of them will serve to characterize the class of interrogatives as a whole. For this we shall need to invoke the abstract morpheme Q, mentioned in Chapter 6: an interrogative sentence will be defined as one containing Q in its deep structure. The role of this element will emerge as the discussion proceeds.

There are two main types of interrogative, exemplified respectively in:

[24] *Did you give John the key?*
[25] *Who has taken my umbrella?*

In 5.3 I spoke of the first type as a 'yes/no interrogative'; there are, however, good reasons for regarding this as simply a special case of a more general category of 'disjunctive interrogatives', including also

[26] *Did you give John the key or did you keep it?*
[27] *Did you give John the key or did you not give John the key?*

The term 'disjunction' is used for a coordination where the coordinator is *or*: the claim is, then, that yes/no interrogatives derive from underlying disjunctions – in particular that [24] derives from (the structure underlying) [27]. We have already seen (7.2) that where two or more underlying coordinated clauses contain identical elements, these are optionally deletable. In disjunctive interrogatives, this rule will convert *Will you go now or will you go later?* into *Will you go now or later?*, *Is he alive or is he dead?* into *Is he alive or dead?* – and [27] into *Did you give John the key or not?*. The only special rule needed to derive structures like [24], therefore, is one which deletes *or not*. There is both syntactic and semantic evidence supporting this proposal. From a semantic point of view, the analysis accounts, obviously, for the paraphrase relation between [24] and [27]; we shall see below that it makes it easier to handle certain other semantic relations as well. The syntactic argument is that yes/no interrogatives are like overt disjunctives (*ie* those where the second clause is retained, at least in part, in surface structure) in that they (a) contain no *wh* element (in surface structure) when they occur in a non-embedded position, as in the above examples, but (b) are introduced by *whether* (or *if*) when they are embedded within a larger clause: compare *She doesn't know whether he is alive or dead* and *She doesn't know whether you gave John the key*. If we derive [24] from [27], these can be stated simply as properties of disjunctive interrogatives, whereas if we derived [24] independently we would need to state them twice, once for disjunctives, once for the 'yes/no' type, thereby losing a clear generalization.

I shall return to the analysis of disjunctive interrogatives when we have looked into the structure of the non-disjunctive type illustrated in [25] and the following:

[28] i   *What do they want?*   ii *What train did he catch?*
     iii *Why did she resign?*   iv *When did John arrive?*
     v   *Where does she live?*   vi *How does the device work?*

The kind of argument familiar from previous chapters establishes that the *what* of [28i] must occur in post-verbal position in deep structure. Such an analysis is necessary if we are to express generalizations about the transitivity of verbs and so on – note that it enables us, for instance, to exclude **What did John disappear?* by the same rule as excludes **John disappeared the money*. In deep structure, then, *what* will stand in the same grammatical relation to *want* as does *that book* in *I want that book*. Similarly, *what train, why, when, where, how* in [ii–vi] will originate in the VP, in the same position as such phrases as *the 10 o'clock train, for health reasons, yesterday, in New York, in a simple way* respectively. It follows that the grammar must include a transformation moving *what, what train*, etc to the front position in the clause – a rule that provides part of the formal basis for the intuition that these expressions have something in common. This common element may be represented (pending the introduction of further theoretical apparatus in Chapter 10) as a morpheme, symbolized *wh:* the fronting transformation can then be formulated in a general way to apply to phrases containing this morpheme.

The interrogatives [25] and [28] stand in a systematic relation to the following declaratives:

[29] *Somebody/someone has taken my umbrella*
[30] i *They want something*   ii *He caught some train*
    iii *She resigned for some reason* iv *John arrived at some time*
     v *She lives somewhere*   vi *The device works in some way*

This relation is called PRESUPPOSITION: [25] is said to presuppose [29], and so on. If I use [25] to ask a question, I shall be regarded as taking it for granted that somebody has taken my umbrella – clearly it would be anomalous to say *I know that no one has taken my umbrella, but who has taken it?*. This is undoubtedly part of the speaker-hearer's knowledge of his language, and must accordingly be accounted for in a generative grammar: we shall do so by giving rules relating sentences to their presuppositions. Presupposition is an important notion, and it is worth pausing very briefly to make some general observations about it.

One type much discussed by philosophers is associated with a certain class of referring expression. To use a standard example, we shall say that in a normal utterance of *The King of France is bald* it is presupposed that there is at the time of utterance just one King of France and it is asserted that he is bald. There are two reasons for distinguishing between the presupposition and the assertion here. (a) It provides a basis for differentiating between the above example and *The President of France is bald*. At the time of writing, neither of these is true, but they fail to be true in different ways: we can get a true statement by negating the second, but not the first. In the second case, the presupposition is true, the assertion false, whereas in the first the presupposition is false and in such circumstances, according to a common view, the question of the truth or falsity of the assertion simply does not arise. (b) Secondly, the distinction enables us to bring out the similarity between *The King of France is bald* and *Is the King of France bald?* or *Take this gift to the King of France:* they share the presupposition that there is presently just one King of France while differing in their illocutionary force. Presupposition and illocutionary force are thus separate and independently variable. There are differing views as to how the concept of presupposition should be explicated. Some writers take a presupposition of a sentence to express a proposition that must be true if an utterance of the sentence is to be a statement that is either true or false, a question that can be directly answered, a request that can be complied with and so on. Others regard a presupposition as expressing something that the speaker takes as already known, as information shared by the participants in the speech act. I shall not pursue this aspect of the matter any further: for our purposes a rough intuitive understanding of the notion will suffice.

The presuppositions of a sentence are determined by a variety of structural properties. In the example of the preceding paragraph the definiteness of the NP *the King of France* is one of the main determining factors (*cf* Chapter 15). In a case like *John regretted that Mary had seen the letter* the presupposition that Mary had seen the letter is attributable to a property of the verb *regret*, which contrasts in this respect with, say, *suggest:* in *John suggested that Mary had seen the letter* the speaker is not assumed to take it for granted that Mary had seen the letter. Our primary concern here is with the presuppositions that are attributable specifically to the interrogative properties of a sentence – with relating [25] and [28] to [29] and [30] respectively, and so on.

The statement of this relationship can be greatly simplified if we analyse *who, what, what train, why, when, where, how* as deriving from underlying '*wh some body/one*', '*wh some thing*', '*wh some train*', '*for wh some reason*', '*at wh some time*', '*wh some where*', '*in wh some way*'. There is then a constant and simple relation at the level of deep structure between [25], [28] and their presuppositions [29], [30]: the deep structures of the presuppositions do not contain the *wh* morpheme (nor the *Q* element) but are otherwise identical with those of the corresponding interrogatives. There is, moreover, a certain amount of syntactic evidence supporting some such analysis of the *wh* forms. This can be seen from the following sets of forms:

[31] i	*no man*	*nothing*	*no one*	*nobody*	*nowhere*
ii	*any man*	*anything*	*anyone*	*anybody*	*anywhere*
iii	*some man*	*something*	*someone*	*somebody*	*somewhere*
iv	*what man*	**whatthing*	**whatone*	**whatbody*	**whatwhere*
v		*what*	*who*	*who*	*where*

If we postulate rules substituting *what* for *whatthing*, *who* for *whatone* or *whatbody*, and *where* for *whatwhere*, we can account for the absence of the asterisked forms of [31] without sacrificing generality in our statement of the distribution in underlying structure of *thing, one, body, where*, and *wh some* (*what*). We shall be accounting for the occurrence of *what* instead of **whatthing*, *who* instead of **whatone*, etc, in much the same way as we account for the occurrence of *sheep* instead of *sheeps* or *went* instead of *goed*. There are three points to be noted here:

(a) Firstly *thing* and *body* in the above sets are to be distinguished from the forms spelt in the same way, but having different meanings, that occur in sentences like *There's a strange thing in the drive, They hid the body under the hedge*.

(b) Secondly, the parallel between the left-hand column, the forms with *man*, and the other columns suggests that *no*, *any* and *some* are basically determiners: the fact that *nothing*, *anything*, etc are pronounced as single words will be accounted for by a rule which incorporates determiner and noun into a single compound word when the noun is *thing*, *one*, etc. In this way we can handle *something*, *someone* and the like by means of the highly general PS rule 'NP → Det N', instead of having to introduce a rule 'N → Pre-noun Noun-stem', say, just for this handful of forms.

(c) The third point is that the neat pattern exhibited in [31] does not extend to all the *wh* forms, so that the force of the argument is clearly less than if it applied more generally. Nevertheless, the small-scale regularities of [31] are still worth stating, and the proposed analysis enables us to do this. Accordingly I tentatively adopt the proposal that all non-disjunctives contain a *wh* morpheme associated with *some* in determiner position (introduced by the rule 'Det → *wh some*').

Consider now the presuppositions of disjunctive interrogatives. The presuppositions of [26] and [27] are respectively:

[32] *Either you gave John the key or you kept it*
[33] *Either you gave John the key or you did not give John the key*

The latter type of presupposition has more significance than might at first appear. Suppose, for example, I say *Did you steal the money?*. This presupposes 'Either you stole the money or you did not steal the money': in asking the question I take it for granted that either you stole it or you did not steal it – and thereby conspicuously fail to take it for granted that you did not steal it. Or consider a classic example like *Have you stopped beating your wife?*. The properties of the verb *stop* are such that the two simple declarative sentences *You have stopped beating your wife* and *You have not stopped beating your wife* presuppose that you have been beating her. This must then also be a presupposition of the compound declarative sentence *Either you have stopped beating your wife or you have not stopped beating your wife*, and since the latter is the presupposition directly attributable to the interrogative structure of *Have you stopped beating your wife?*, the analysis shows how this too comes to carry the presupposition that you have been beating your wife.

Our rule for relating an interrogative sentence to its presupposition can be extended to cover disjunctives as well as non-disjunctives if we postulate a *wh* element in the underlying structure of the former with the same semantic role as it has in the latter. The difference would be that in non-disjunctives *wh* is associated with the determiner *some*, whereas in disjunctives it is associated with the coordinating conjunction. [25] and [27] would derive respectively from:

[34] *Q wh some one Pres have en take my umbrella*
[35] *Q wh either you Past give John the key or you not Past give John the key*

In both cases we get the presupposition by removing *Q* and *wh*, and the position of the *wh* further serves to indicate what it is that is being questioned. For [25] the presupposition is 'Someone has taken my umbrella', and the questioner is asking for an appropriate selection from the range of entities covered by *someone;* for [27] the presupposition is 'Either you gave John the key or you did not give John the key', and the questioner is asking for an appropriate selection from the range of clauses coordinated by *either-or*. More precisely, adopting the treatment of coordinators suggested in 7.2, [35] will itself derive from

[36] *Q wh or* [s *you Past give John the key*]s [s *you not Past give John the key*]s

with *wh* introduced by the rule 'Conj → *wh or*'. Notice that presuppositions provide further semantic evidence for our proposal to derive [24] from an underlying disjunction: under this analysis it is related to its presupposition by the same general rule as applies to [25] and [27], and indeed to all interrogatives.

The proposal to recognize a *wh* morpheme in the underlying structure of disjunctive interrogatives is, moreover, not without syntactic support. We have noted that disjunctives are introduced by *whether* (or its variant *if*) when in embedded position, and it is not unreasonable to regard *whether* as resulting from the fusion of *wh* plus *either*. This has phonological plausibility and would also account for the deviance of **She asked whether either you gave John the key or not.* Removing the *either* makes this well-formed: if *whether* derives from *wh either*, the deviance is shown to be due to the two occurrences of *either*, and the sentence is blocked in the same way as **Either either you gave John the key or not.* The difference between embedded and non-embedded disjunctives will then be handled by a transformation deleting *whether* (and by the Inversion rule operating only in the non-embedded construction). The syntactic similarity between [24] and *whether you gave John the key* is thus shown at the level of deep structure, where they are identical as far as their internal structure is concerned, and the difference between them is accounted for in the transformational component.

We have now arrived at an analysis where all interrogatives contain a *wh* in deep structure. This morpheme still cannot be used to define the class of interrogative sentences, however. We saw earlier that *wh* occurs in the surface structure of relatives and exclamatives; with relatives it is introduced by transformation (*cf* 7.3), but with exclamatives there is no reason to suppose that *wh* is not present in deep structure, so that even at this level its presence cannot identify the interrogative class. There is also another important reason why it cannot. Consider the following sentences:

[37] *What did John decide that he would buy?*
[38] *John decided what he would buy*

Despite the different surface positions of *what*, the underlying grammatical relation between it and *buy* is surely the same in both sentences: *what* is understood as object of *buy*. Yet [37] and [38] differ markedly in meaning: they have the meanings of question and statement respectively. At the level of deep structure we can represent the difference between them by having the *Q* morpheme in different positions:

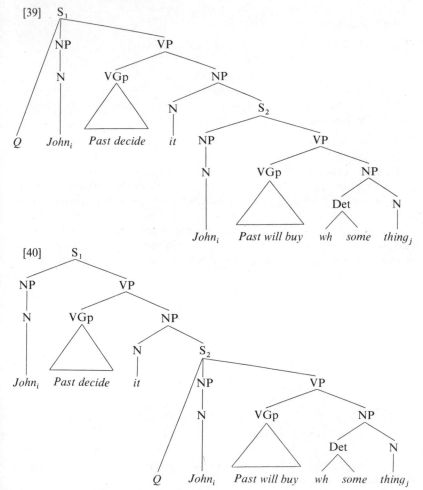

In [39] Q is in S_1, indicating that S_1 is the interrogative clause – and since S_1 is not embedded, this gives it its question meaning. S_2 in [39] is a finite complement clause of the type considered in 7.3. In [40] on the other hand, it is S_2 that is interrogative, having Q as daughter; but since S_2 is embedded its mood does not affect the illocutionary meaning of [38], which is determined by the structure of S_1, a declarative clause.

Complement clauses may thus be either declarative or interrogative. The mood of the complement – like the choice between the finite, infinitival and gerundive form – depends on the verb in the next higher clause (or on the adjective if the verb is *be*): (a) some verbs take declaratives but not interrogatives: *believe, expect, fear, hold, hope, insist, require, . . .*; (b) some take either declaratives or interrogatives: *determine, forget, know, observe, say, tell, . . .*; (c) a few take only interrogatives: *inquire, investigate, ...* The differences between the classes are exemplified in:

[41] i *She believes that he resigned because of his health*
     ii **She believes why he resigned*
[42] i *She doesn't know that he resigned because of his health*
     ii *She doesn't know why he resigned*
[43] i **She inquired that he resigned because of his health*
     ii *She inquired why he resigned*

Decide belongs to class (b): the complement is declarative in [37], interrogative in [38].

It follows that even if we discount exclamatives, the presence of *wh* in a clause does not suffice to make it interrogative: S_2 in [39] contains *wh* but is declarative. Every interrogative S dominates a *wh*, but there may be a non-interrogative S on the path joining them. Indeed, there is no limit to the number of declarative S nodes intervening between the interrogative S and the associated *wh*. There are, for example, two declarative complements in *Who did you say that Peter expected to win the prize?*, whose deep structure is roughly [44],

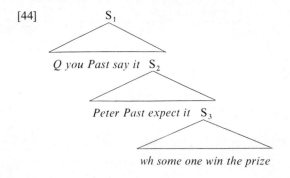

[44] S_1

          Q you Past say it S_2

               Peter Past expect it S_3

                    wh some one win the prize

and there would be no difficulty in constructing examples with greater depths of embedding.

To define and explicate the notion interrogative sentence, therefore, we need to refer to the abstract morpheme Q: an interrogative S is one that both dominates *wh* and immediately dominates Q in deep structure. The various functions performed in the grammar by this Q element are as follows:

(a) It serves as a 'trigger' for Inversion. Rule [45] of 5.3 (which was meaning-changing) must now be revised as in [45] (which is meaning-preserving):

$$[45] \text{ INVERSION: } Q - NP - \left\{ \begin{array}{l} Tns \left\{ \begin{array}{l} M \\ have \\ be \end{array} \right\} - \quad X \\ Tns \quad\quad - (not) \text{ V X} \end{array} \right\}$$

$$\begin{array}{cccc} 1 & 2 & 3 & 4 \quad \Rightarrow \\ 1+3 & 2 & \varnothing & 4 \end{array}$$

Condition: Q is not in an embedded clause

The condition blocks the application of the rule to interrogative complement clauses, so that we get *I forget whether she is coming*, not **I forget is she coming*. I have assumed that *Whether* Deletion applies before [45], and that in the generation of overt disjunctives like [26] and [27] there applies a transformation which copies Q into the second disjunct. (For the *not* in term 4, see *p* 80.) As noted earlier, Inversion is not confined to interrogatives, so that in a fuller version of the rule term 1 would have to be expanded to allow for certain negative and negative-like expressions such as *never*, *hardly*, *only then*, and so on. With Q as term 1 the rule is in general optional, for we find the uninverted order in both disjunctive and non-disjunctive interrogatives: *You've finished?*, *And after that you went where?*.

(b) Q marks the position to which the *wh* phrase is moved in the fronting transformation. Note that in [37/39] *what* is moved to the front of S_1, in [38/40] to the front of S_2. A first approximation to a formulation of this rule is:

$$[46] \text{ } Wh\text{-}Q \text{ FRONTING: } Q - X - [_{NP} \text{ } wh \text{ Y }]_{NP} - Z$$

$$\begin{array}{cccc} 1 & 2 & 3 & 4 \quad \Rightarrow \\ 1+3 & 2 & \varnothing & 4 \end{array}$$

These versions of [45] and [46] assume that they apply in that order. This permits a simpler formulation of [45] than if the order were reversed: note in particular that with the order as given [45] is applicable to all non-embedded interrogatives, including those with the *wh* phrase in subject position, like *Who has finished?*. Here [45] converts the deep structure '*Q wh some one Pres have en finish*' into '*Q Pres have wh some one en finish*', to which [46] applies, yielding again the original sequence '*Q wh some one Pres have en finish*'. There are certain problems involved in this derivation relating to the structure of the final PM (as the reader will be able to see by applying the principles for determining 'derived constituent structure' discussed in 12.3), and the correctness of the order [45] then [46] must remain somewhat questionable. What is fronted is of course not just the *wh* morpheme itself, but the whole phrase containing it (*eg: wh some thing* in [28i], *wh some train* in [28ii] and so on) – hence the variable Y and the NP brackets in term 3. Although the labelling of these brackets prevents the rule applying to disjunctives like [35], where *wh* does not begin a NP, this creates no problem because fronting is not needed in disjunctives: the *wh* will always be next to Q in any case. (Notice in this connection that in disjunctives it is not possible for there to be a declarative S node intervening between the interrogative S and the *wh*: there are no structures analogous to [39] and [44] but with the *wh* associated with *or*.) Although Q is a completely abstract unit, in the sense that it never has any phonological shape, its role in [46] provides evidence for its underlying position: the rule would have to be complicated if Q were introduced elsewhere than on the left of the subject.

(c) It is very likely that Q will figure in the rules assigning an intonation contour to sentences. However, there has not been enough work on the formulation of intonation rules for me to be able to say more on this point.

(d) Q will also play a role in the formal statement of the restrictions, mentioned above, on the mood of the clause functioning as complement to a higher verb (or adjective). We shall need to say, for example, that if *investigate* has an object NP consisting of '*it* S', that S must immediately dominate Q.

(e) Consider finally the semantic role of Q. We have seen that when it occurs in a non-embedded sentence it gives that sentence the illocutionary meaning of question. Yet this can be regarded, I believe, as a special case of a more general semantic function. In all interrogatives we are concerned with the appropriate selection from among either the clauses coordinated by *wh or* (in the case of disjunctives) or the entities or whatever covered by the *wh some* phrase. In questions, the speaker asks the addressee to make this selection; in complements the selection is at issue in some other way, depending on what the higher verb or adjective is. Thus in *I told him where I was going* the selection is the information I gave; in *I couldn't care less who he is* I express lack of interest in the selection; in *It is obvious why he resigned* the selection is said to be obvious; and so on. The position of the *wh* indicates the set from which the selection is made, and the position of Q indicates the clause where the selection is at issue.

To conclude this chapter let me return briefly to the applicability of the mood system to embedded clauses. The definition of interrogative that we have given allows for both embedded and non-embedded interrogatives, and the similarities between them that justify classifying them together on the mood dimension are clear. In both we have a major division between the disjunctive and non-disjunctive subtypes, and in the latter the types of phrase in which *wh* can occur are exactly the same – note, for instance, that clauses differing from [28] only in the non-application of Inversion and *Do* Support can occur as subject complements to *be clear, important, irrelevant, a mystery, obvious, . . .,* or object complements to *decide, determine, know, say, tell,* etc. Moreover, in the embedded type the *wh* phrase may originate in a lower clause than the one in which it appears in surface structure: the embedded counterpart of [37], for example, is found in *She doesn't know what John decided that he would buy*. The *Q* element is thus clearly needed in embedded as well as non-embedded clauses, and it is this that justifies the claim that both types of clause can be interrogative.

There are, however, no analogous reasons for extending imperative mood to complement clauses. In a sentence like *John told Bill to stand still* we shall not want to say that there is an embedded imperative. The sentence is like those discussed in Chapter 8, so that its underlying structure will be '*John$_i$ Past tell Bill$_j$ it [$_S$ Bill$_j$ stand still*]$_S$'. The embedded complement here is identical with that in the deep structure of *John expected/wanted/persuaded Bill to stand still* or *Bill expected/wanted/decided to stand still*, and there is no very significant relation between these and imperative constructions. The intuitive relationship between *Stand still!* and *John told Bill to stand still* is that the latter could (given the right circumstances) be used to report the speech act performed in the utterance of the former, but this is primarily due to the selection of *tell* in the higher clause rather than to the relation between the imperative and the embedded clause *Bill (to) stand still*. The syntactic function of the abstract morpheme *Imp* is to trigger the *You* Deletion transformation. As this rule applies only in non-embedded clauses, there is no motivation for having *Imp* in complement clauses.

Notes

Austin's notion of illocutionary force is further developed in, for example, Searle 1969:54–71. Katz 1972:441–52 discusses the scope of a theory of linguistic competence relative to illocutionary force. Gordon and Lakoff 1971 deals with the formal analysis of the implications of sentences like my [18ii], [19ii], etc. (Both Katz, and Gordon and Lakoff draw on important but largely unpublished work by Grice.) Ross 1970 proposes that all sentences contain a performative verb in underlying structure; for a different view on how illocutionary force should be accounted for within a TG framework, see Fraser 1973. On ambiguity, see Zwicky 1973, and on presupposition, Strawson 1964, Katz 1972:127–50, 1973a, Fillmore and Langendoen 1971 (papers by Garner, Keenan, R. Lakoff, Fillmore), Kempson 1974, Kartunnen 1973.

My discussion of interrogatives owes much to Katz and Postal 1964:79–120 (Katz 1972:201–27 further elaborates on the semantic aspects of the analysis). Baker 1970 shows that Katz and Postal fail to deal adequately with embedded interrogatives; Kuno and Robinson 1972 then argue for a modification of Baker's proposals. See also Stockwell *et al* 1973:600–32, and three descriptions of interrogatives within different theoretical frameworks: Bolinger 1957, Chafe 1970:309–45, Quirk *et al* 1972:387–402. There is some idealization in my account of the presuppositions of interrogatives: for a certain subclass of non-disjunctives the 'normal' presuppositions do not obtain. For example, one who says *Who wants some more coffee?* is quite probably seeking to elicit information as to whether anyone wants some more coffee (and if so who), rather than taking it as shared information that someone does – given a certain type of situation, *Who wants some?* and *Does anyone want some?* achieve the same effect.

Rule [46] does not cater for sentences like *With whom was she talking?*, where *wh* is not at the far left of the fronted phrase: see Ross 1967 for an important discussion of the theoretical issues involved here; Ross also deals with constraints on constructions like [37/39], where *Q* and *wh* belong in different underlying clauses. On the impossibility of giving a formal explication of the notion interrogative sentence in terms of surface structure, see Chomsky 1957:90–91, though I do not think his own proposal (that interrogatives be defined in terms of the Inversion rule) captures the notion satisfactorily, either.

Interrogatives, especially embedded ones, may be homonymous with relative clauses: the embedded clauses are relatives in *The man who came to dinner stayed all night* and *The cat wouldn't eat what Mary had put on the plate* (from *p* 104) but interrogative in *She asked who came to dinner* and *He couldn't have cared less what Mary had put on the table;* see Baker 1970:197–200, Huddleston 1971:234–43.

Stockwell *et al* 1973:633–71 gives an account of imperatives that does generalize to embedded clauses, like that in *I insist that he go*. An imperative can occur as a non-restrictive relative, as in *I expect to be a little late, in which case do go on ahead*. Notice that here utterances of the two clauses do count as separate speech acts, the first being a report or statement, the second a request or the like. This is typical of coordination rather than subordination, witness examples like *Come with us, or can't you spare the time?*, *It's your fault, and don't try to deny it*, etc, where we have sequences of different kinds of speech act. The behaviour of non-restrictive relatives in this regard lends some support to the proposal of 7.2 that they be derived from coordinate clauses.

Chapter 10

Syntactic Features and the Lexicon

In the *Syntactic Structures* version of the theory, PS rules were used to perform the three rather different kinds of function exemplified in [1–3].

[1] i $S \rightarrow NP\ VP$ ii $NP \rightarrow Det\ N$

[2] i $N \rightarrow \left\{ \begin{array}{l} N_{anim} \\ N_{inan} \end{array} \right\}$ ii $V \rightarrow \left\{ \begin{array}{l} V_{trans}\ /\ \underline{\quad}NP \\ V_{intrans}\ /\ \underline{\quad}\# \end{array} \right\}$

[3] i $Det \rightarrow \{the,\ some,\ \dots\}$ ii $V_{trans} \rightarrow \{annihilate,\ catch,\ \dots\}$

Rules like [1] express categorial immediate constituent structure: [i] analyses a sentence into two ICs, the first belonging to the category NP, the second to VP, and [ii] similarly says that a NP may have a Det and a N as its ICs. Rules like [2] effect a subclassification of the categories being rewritten. [i] is context-free, [ii] context-sensitive, subclassifying verbs according to their deep structure environment. ([i] is repeated from *p* 50; [ii] is a modified version of that given on *p* 44 – the modification follows from the different treatment of tense inflections introduced in 5.2.) Notice that one would not interpret [2i] as saying that a noun may have an animate noun as its IC, that a noun may be 'composed of' an animate noun, in the sense of IC structure and composition developed in structural linguistics. Finally, rules like [3] express class membership: *the, some,* . . . belong to the distributional class determiner, *annihilate, catch,* . . . to the class transitive verb.

It soon became apparent, however, that PS rules do not provide an appropriate formalism for expressing subclassification and class membership; Chomsky devotes a large part of *Aspects of the Theory of Syntax* to a discussion of the apparatus that he proposed should take over these functions. What makes PS rules inappropriate is the fact that the symbols they operate with have no internal structure. As we saw in Chapter 3, V_{trans} and $V_{intrans}$ are, from a formal point of view, unstructured atomic symbols: they have nothing at all in common and it would make no difference to the formal interpretation of the grammar if instead we wrote respectively 'T' and 'I'. The partial likeness between, say, the transitive verb *catch* and the intransitive verb *die* is expressed not in the V_{trans} and $V_{intrans}$ symbols but in the higher node V that dominates both these latter (*cf p* 45). Now this device of having separate nodes in the PM, a higher node corresponding to the primary class and a lower one to the sub-class, runs into difficulties when the primary class is subclassified along two or more dimensions which cut across each other.

Chomsky demonstrates this with the following example. Nouns in English must be subclassified as human versus non-human in order to account for the selection of *who* or *which* as relative pronoun: *who* is used when the antecedent is human (*the boy/girl/*table who was in the room*), *which* when it is non-human (*the table/*boy which was in the room*). We need also to subclassify nouns as 'proper' versus 'common' to account for the distribution of determiners: we can say *John has arrived*, but not *Boy has arrived*. (Plurals like *boys*, and 'mass' nouns like *coffee* or *gold*, also occur freely without a determiner, but this in no way invalidates the point: the distributional difference between *John* and singular *boy* suffices to justify the proper versus common subclassification.) Now these two dimensions are independent of each other, so that they yield a cross-classification, illustrated as follows:

[4]

	Proper	Common
Human Non-human	*John, Mary,* . . . *Egypt, Moscow,* . . .	*boy, girl,* . . . *table, ball,* . . .

In a theory allowing only atomic symbols, we would need some such set of PS rules as [5].

[5] i $N \rightarrow \{N_{proper}, N_{common}\}$
  ii $N_{proper} \rightarrow \{N_{proper/human}, N_{proper/non-human}\}$
  iii $N_{common} \rightarrow \{N_{common/human}, N_{common/non-human}\}$

These effectively distinguish *John, boy, Egypt* and *table*, but they do not provide a unitary definition of human nouns. Thus any rule involving human nouns will have to mention the two categories $N_{proper/human}$ and $N_{common/human}$ – we must say for example that the relative pronoun *who* is selected when the antecedent is either a $N_{proper/human}$ or a $N_{common/human}$. In other words, we cannot express the generalization that *who* occurs with a human noun as antecedent, but must say that it occurs under either of two conditions. This is the same kind of deficiency as appeared when we tried in Chapter 4 to use PS rules to differentiate active and passive constructions; this time, however, a different remedy is required. Notice that we could solve the particular problem just mentioned by writing '$N \rightarrow \{N_{human}, N_{non-human}\}$' instead of [5i], but this would of course make it impossible to refer to proper nouns except with an either-or disjunction. There is simply no way of writing PS rules to provide unitary definitions of all four subclasses of noun – human, non-human, proper and common.

What is needed is a formalism where the symbols do have internal structure.

Suppose, then, that instead of subtrees [6] and [7], which would be generated by [5], appropriately completed, we have subtrees [8] and [9].

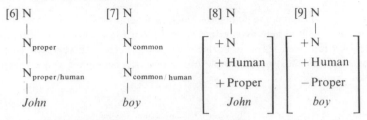

N in [8] and [9] immediately dominates a COMPLEX SYMBOL: reference may be made to the separate parts. This means that we can refer to the class of human nouns by the notation [+Human], which is interpreted as applying to any complex symbol containing the element '+Human', irrespective of what other elements it may contain.

A complex symbol consists of a morpheme plus a set of SYNTACTIC FEATURES. The complex symbol in [8], for example, contains the three syntactic features [+N], [+Human], [+Proper]. Each feature specifies a value along a particular dimension of classification, so that *John* and *boy* have the value '+' in respect of the dimension 'Human', *Egypt* and *table* the value '−'. The term 'feature' is in fact regularly applied to the dimensions as well as to particular values: one may speak of the feature [Human] (a dimension) or the feature [+Human] (a particular value) – it will be clear from the context and notation which sense is intended.

In order to introduce such complex symbols into the syntactic representations, Chomsky modified the form of the grammar in such a way that deep structures are now generated in two stages:

(a) First, a small set of PS rules generate PMs in which the terminal positions are filled by a special element, symbolized as Δ (delta), which serves simply as a place-holder for the lexical items that are inserted in stage two. Such PMs are referred to as PRE-LEXICAL STRUCTURES. A simple example is given in [10].

[10]

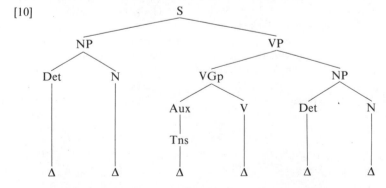

We thus include in the PS component of the grammar rules like 'Det → Δ', 'N → Δ', for each morpheme-category symbol.

(b) In the second stage, the deltas are replaced by complex symbols consisting of morphemes plus their associated syntactic features. This procedure will convert [10] into, say, [11] – or rather a filled-out version thereof, for I have included only an illustrative sample of the features belonging in the various complex symbols.

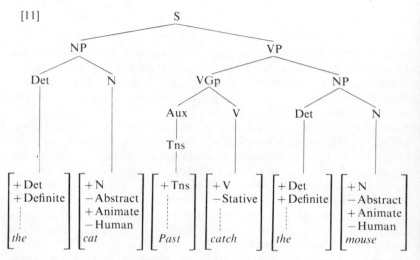

[11]

This is an approximate deep structure for *The cat caught the mouse* – or for *The mouse was caught by the cat*. (The [−Stative] feature in the complex symbol for *catch* represents the fact that *catch* denotes an action as opposed to a state; *know*, in contrast, would be specified as [+Stative]; *cf* 15.4.)

Technically, the process of replacing a Δ by a complex symbol plus lexical item is a transformational operation. We may then distinguish between LEXICAL TRANSFORMATIONS, which convert pre-lexical structures like [10] into deep structures like [11], and NON-LEXICAL TRANSFORMATIONS, which convert from deep to surface structure. The PS rules and lexical transformations jointly constitute what is called the BASE component of the grammar: these two sets of rules serve to generate the deep structures of the language. This gives the following organization of the syntax:

[12]

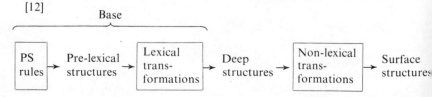

The syntactic derivation of a sentence will still include a sequence of PMs but the deep structure is no longer definable as the first in this sequence: it is, rather, the PM resulting from the last application of a lexical transformation. It remains the deep structures, of course, that form the input to the semantic rules. The PS rules now have in effect only the first of the three functions mentioned at the beginning of this chapter: they express IC categorial structure. In so doing, they assign an underlying linear order to the elements (the Δs in [10] are ordered from left to right) and define the underlying grammatical relations in a sentence (the constituent composed of the first two Δs in [10] is in the deep subject position, and so on).

There will clearly be a very large number of lexical transformations: one for each lexical item in the language. This set of rules may then be thought of as equivalent to a dictionary, or LEXICON as it is more often called. For each item there is a lexical entry specifying its semantic, phonological and syntactic properties. Here I shall deal only with the latter, which are represented in the form of features.

The syntactic information given in the lexicon must provide answers to three kinds of question about each item:

I: Whereabouts in deep structure can it occur? We shall say of *annihilate*, for example, that it can substitute for a Δ dominated by a V node that has a NP as sister (this corresponds to the information that *annihilate* is a transitive verb).

II: What are its inherent syntactic features? Under this heading we shall say that *boy* has the inherent features [+Human], [+Male], etc, that *catch* is specified [−Stative], and so on.

III: Is the item irregular or exceptional relative to any non-lexical transformation? Here we shall say, for example, that the verb *cost* blocks the application of Passivization, for a sentence containing *cost* as its main verb cannot undergo this rule even when its structure index is satisfied. Thus '*that book Pres cost a dollar*' satisfies the index for Passivization, but the rule must be prevented from applying so that we exclude **A dollar is cost by that book*: only the active, *That book costs a dollar*, is well-formed.

These three types of information are represented in the form of CONTEXTUAL, INHERENT, and RULE FEATURES respectively. Let us look at them in turn.

I. CONTEXTUAL FEATURES: Information of type (I) is equivalent to the structure index of the lexical transformation that substitutes an item for an occurrence of Δ. Thus the above information about *annihilate* means that a PM analysable as 'X—[$_v$ Δ]$_v$—NP—Y' can be transformed into one where *annihilate* plus its associated features occupies the position of Δ in term 2. Instead of representing the information in the form of a structure index, we break it down into a number of contextual features. There are three subtypes to be distinguished on the basis of the different kinds of condition that they impose on the location of the Δ to be replaced: CATEGORY, STRICT SUB-CATEGORIZATION and SELECTIONAL FEATURES.

IA. CATEGORY FEATURES: These specify the node immediately dominating the Δ. *Annihilate, frighten*, etc, will be marked as [+V], *ie* they may substitute for a Δ dominated by V. Similarly, *cat* has the category feature [+N], *the* [+Det], and so on. These features thus simply record what primary class an item belongs to, and there is such a feature corresponding to each of the categories that immediately dominate Δ.

IB. STRICT SUBCATEGORIZATION FEATURES: These specify nodes to the right or left of the Δ. *Annihilate* and *frighten*, for example, will be marked as [+ __ NP] indicating that they may substitute for a Δ occurring in the context of a following NP. The notation derives from that used earlier in context-sensitive PS rules, the '__' representing the position of the Δ to be replaced. The feature [+ __ NP] thus corresponds to the traditional concept 'transitive', [+ __ #] to 'intransitive'. It seems clear that an adequate grammar will need many features of this kind – certainly more than traditional grammar provides standard names for. For example, verbs like *put, throw, chase*, etc, will be distinguished from *kill, resemble*, and the like by virtue of their occurrence in such frames as '*He __ the cat out of the house'*; nouns like *fact* and *idea* differ from *man, disease*, etc, by being able to take a sentential complement (*cf: the idea/*disease that John was a coward*); adjectives like *clear* and *obvious*, but not *likely* or *possible*, occur in such frames as 'NP Aux *be __ to* NP' (*That John had seen it was obvious/*likely to everyone*); and so on.

I C. SELECTIONAL FEATURES: These involve reference to inherent features in complex symbols to the right or left of the Δ. We want, for example, to block the insertion of *frighten* as verb in a sentence where the object noun is inanimate, so as to exclude **The storm frightened the fact* and the like (*cf* Chapter 4). To do this we associate with *frighten* the selectional feature [− __[−Animate]]. The interpretation of the notation is slightly more complicated than is the case with strict subcategorization features: whereas the strict subcategorization feature (dimension) [__ NP] identifies a Δ immediately to the left of a NP node, the Δ identified by the selectional feature (dimension) [__ [−Animate]] is not necessarily adjacent to the complex symbol containing the inherent feature [−Animate], for there may be an intervening determiner, say, (thus in **I frightened the apple*, [−Animate] is an inherent feature of *apple*, not *the*). [Animate], however, is a feature of nouns, as opposed to determiners, prepositions, etc: we thus interpret [__ [−Animate]] as identifying a Δ such that the nearest noun clause-mate to the right is marked [−Animate]. Other examples of selectional features might be: [− __ [+Abstract]], a feature of verbs like *cut, wash, paint*, etc, which do not take abstract nouns as object (*He washed the apple/*sincerity*); [−[−Temporal] __], a feature of a verb like *elapse* which cannot occur with a non-temporal noun as subject (*Three weeks/*boys elapsed*); [−[−Animate] __], which characterizes verbs or adjectives that do not occur with inanimate subjects (*The boy/*carpet enjoyed the concert; The boy/*carpet was sad*); and so on.

Many morphemes of course have a variety of meanings, and it will often be the case that a selectional feature applies to one meaning but not another. For example, the impossibility of an abstract object applies to the verb *paint* with the sense 'apply paint to', but not 'create a representation in paint of' (*cf: He painted their agony*); similarly, *cut* cannot take an abstract noun as object when it means 'sever', but it can when it means 'reduce' (*He cut the pain*). Or again, we distinguish different senses of *sad* in, say, *sad people* and *sad films*, with only the first excluding inanimate subjects. In such cases I shall make the simplifying assumption that there are lexically distinct items with the same phonological form, *ie* homonyms – and similarly where the earlier types of contextual features are concerned, so that there will be several different lexical entries for the form *round*, for example, one where it has the category feature [+N] (as in *a round of drinks*), another [+V] (*He'll soon round the Cape*), and a third [+Adj] (*a round hole*), a fourth [+Prep] (*He went round the corner*), and so on. Ultimately, however, one would hope to develop a more sophisticated conception of the dictionary, incorporating the traditional distinction, if it can be made precise, between 'homonymy' and 'polysemy' – between the case of different words with unrelated meanings (such as *bank*, 'sloping margin of river' or 'establishment for custody of money') and the case of a single word with a range of related meanings (as in the above example with *sad*, and so on).

All three subtypes of contextual feature are binary (*ie* two-valued), with plus and minus as the values. Each contextual feature (dimension) identifies a certain contextual condition on Δ, and the positive value indicates that a lexical item so marked can substitute for a Δ meeting the condition in question, the negative value that it cannot. However, instead of including in each lexical entry a positive or negative value for each relevant contextual feature, we need mark only positive values for category and strict subcategorization features and negative values for selectional features, adding the general convention that any item that is not positively marked for a category or strict subcategorization feature is interpreted as having the negative value, and conversely for selectional features. This convention means that the entry for *frighten* will contain [+V] and [+ __ NP], but will not explicitly list [−N], [−Adj], [− __ #], [− __ NP NP] (assuming, for the sake of argument, that '__ NP NP' is the environment in which ditransitive verbs like *give, tell, show*, etc are inserted); and conversely the entry will contain [− __ [−Animate]] but will not list [+ __ [+Animate]] – and so on. The reason for choosing negative as the value to mark in the lexicon in the case of selectional features is as follows. We want to say that *cut, wash, paint*, etc may not take an abstract noun as object, rather than say that they must take a concrete noun, in order to account for cases like *He was cutting something*. For the pronoun *something* is not inherently either concrete or abstract: its distributional range covers both concrete positions (*He was cutting something*) and abstract positions (*Something wonderful is going to happen*). Thus we shall want to leave *something* unspecified for the feature [Abstract], which means that *cut* does not necessarily occur in the environment of a noun marked [−Abstract]. Assigning to *cut* the selectional feature [− __ [+Abstract]] allows it to be inserted before a noun specified as [−Abstract] or unspecified for abstractness.

The distinction between category, strict subcategorization and selectional features has been made on purely formal grounds – according as the feature specifies, respectively, a dominating category symbol, an adjacent category symbol (or string of symbols) or a feature of a complex symbol in the environment. On the basis of this formal distinction, we shall say, for example, that *John must with quickly, *John will die his brother to Mary and *John frightened the drawing-pin involve three different kinds of deviance: the first conflicts with the [−V] category feature of *with*, the second with the [− __ NP PP] strict subcategorization feature of *die*, the third with the [− __ [−Animate]] selectional feature of *frighten*. To some extent at least the formalism appears to capture an intuitively valid distinction: the sentences do seem to deviate from well-formedness in significantly different ways. In Chapter 16 I shall take up the question of whether selectional restrictions should in fact be regarded as syntactic.

II. INHERENT FEATURES: Features of the second of the three major types play a role in selectional restrictions or in certain non-lexical transformations, or in both. [Human], for example, is involved in various selectional restrictions (a verb like *speak* cannot take a non-human noun as subject, and so on) and also determines in part the choice of relative pronoun. The use of features in non-lexical transformations will be taken up in 11.2; in the present brief survey I shall mention only examples relating to selectional restrictions.

As will be clear from what has been said, selectional restrictions involve both inherent features and contextual (more specifically, selectional) features. We exclude *The child frightened the storm* by assigning to *storm* the inherent feature [−Animate] and to *frighten* the selectional feature [− __ [−Animate]]. Now we have been accounting for selectional restrictions by setting up inherent features for nouns, and contextual features for verbs and adjectives. In principle it would be possible to do it the other way round: to set up inherent features for verbs and adjectives, and contextual features for nouns; in practice however, it is easy to show that this is much less satisfactory than the first approach. Suppose, for example, we marked verbs like *frighten, anger, annoy*, with the inherent feature [+Emotion-evoking], and nouns like *carpet, water, sincerity*, with the contextual feature [− [+Emotion-evoking] __]. This would prevent the insertion of *sincerity* as object noun to *frighten*, and so on, thus serving to block the generation of *John frightened sincerity* and the like. But what of the selectional restriction holding between verbs like *enjoy, like, hate*, and their subject noun? Here we shall need to mark the verbs with the inherent feature [+Emotional-response], say, and to mark *carpet, water, sincerity* with the contextual feature [− __ [+Emotional-response]]. And again, adjectives like *happy, content, angry*, would be inherently marked [+Emotional-state], thus necessitating a further contextual feature [− __ [+Emotional-state]] for *carpet, water, sincerity*. The weakness of this second approach will now be apparent: it forces us to set up a whole array of contextual features defining exactly the same subclass of nouns. Thus instead of the single feature [− Animate] of the first approach, we now have [−[+Emotion-evoking] __], [− __ [+Emotional-response]], [− __ [+Emotional-state]] − a clear loss of generality, which is not compensated for by any saving in the features for verbs and adjectives. And the analogous restatement of selectional restrictions involving abstract nouns, human nouns and so on, will of course involve the same kind of loss in generality.

Inherent features are normally treated in the literature as binary, with plus and minus as values, just like contextual features. We saw above that such a formalism is well motivated for the latter, but it has certainly not been demonstrated that it is also justified in the case of inherent features. It is not clear, for example, that there is any principled basis for representing a certain feature as [−Abstract] rather than [+Concrete], say, or another as [−Male] rather than [+Female] or [Female Sex], and so on. The reader should therefore bear in mind that the plus-minus notation for inherent features is a somewhat arbitrary formalism: the theory is in need of considerable tightening in this area. There are severe limitations on what combinations of inherent features are allowable for a single lexical item − for example, no item could be marked as both [+Human] and [−Animate] or as [+Animate] and [+Abstract], and so on. Such interdependencies between features make it possible to simplify lexical entries by omitting features that are predictable from the presence of others − *eg* instead of including in the entries for *boy, girl, man, woman,* etc, all three features [+Human], [+Animate], [−Abstract], we can include just the first, and introduce a general convention whereby [+Animate] and [−Abstract] will be automatically added to any complex symbol containing [+Human]; the procedure involves what are known as 'redundancy rules' but there is no need for us to go into the formal structure of these.

III. RULE FEATURES: My initial example of the third type of syntactic information recorded in the lexicon was that *cost* is an exception to the Passivization rule. Notice that the deviance of **A dollar is cost by that book* is clearly attributable to a property of the verb *cost*, since *a dollar* and *that book* readily occur in passive sentences (*A dollar was stolen, John was impressed by that book*). Accordingly we mark *cost* with the rule feature [−Passivization], and introduce the general convention that a transformation T cannot apply to a sentence if the latter contains a complex symbol that includes the feature [−T].

Rules may be classified as GOVERNED or UNGOVERNED according as they do or do not have lexical exceptions. Passivization is thus a governed rule; other exceptions besides *cost* are *weigh* (in the sense 'have as weight' but not 'determine the weight of': *Martha weighs nine stone, *Nine stone is/are weighed by Martha; The nurse weighed the baby, The baby was weighed by the nurse*), *have* (again in certain senses only, *eg: *Two brothers are had by Mary*), and a few others. Another governed rule is Equi, if we assume it is ordered so as to apply before Raising. This can be seen from the deviance of sentences like

John believed to be right as opposed to *John believed himself to be right* (*cf*
p 125); the underlying structure here has the form '*John$_i$ Past believe it* [$_s$ *John$_i$*
be right]$_s$' and as this satisfies the index for Equi we shall apparently have to
mark *believe* (and also *assume, consider, know, . . .* , as opposed to the regular
expect, want, etc) with the rule feature [−Equi]. The *You* Deletion rule (*pp* 87,
187), on the other hand, is ungoverned: there is no verb which blocks its
application, being able to appear in an imperative like *You be careful!* but not
in the shorter type *Be careful!.* Similarly Reflexivization is an ungoverned rule:
whatever verb we substitute for *wash* in *I washed me,* the result will still be
deviant. I shall not pursue the distinction between governed and ungoverned
rules beyond this simple classification, but a deeper study would seek to
correlate the classification with other formal properties of rules.

The irregularities we have been considering involve items that block the
application of some rule. A different type of exception is one necessitating the
application of a rule that is normally optional. An example is *seem* with respect
to Extraposition. With most verbs taking finite subject complementation this
rule is optional, so that both *It finally emerged that John was right* (where
Extraposition has applied) and *That John was right finally emerged* (where it
has not) are well-formed; compare also *It amazed everyone that Mary got the
job* and *That Mary got the job amazed everyone,* and similar pairs with *anger,
annoy, matter, please, surprise* and many other verbs. With *seem,* however –
and also *appear* and *turn out* – only the extraposed construction is well-formed:
compare *It seemed that John was right* and *That John was right seemed.* A
second example is the verb *rumour,* which occurs (at least for many speakers)
only in passive sentences: *It was rumoured that John would resign* and *John was
rumoured to be a spy* are well-formed but not *They rumoured that John would
resign* or *They rumoured John to be a spy* – *rumour* must be marked in the
lexicon with a rule feature that makes the application of Passivization obligatory.

Not all cases are as simple as these. Consider the verb *say,* for example. The
passive *Jill was said to be a nymphomaniac* is well-formed, whereas the corresponding active is not: *They said Jill to be a nymphomaniac.* But this time it
would clearly be wrong to claim that Passivization is obligatory for *say* sentences, witness counterexamples like *They said that Jill was a nymphomaniac.*
What we need to say here is that Passivization is obligatory if Raising has
applied, otherwise optional. A different kind of complication arises with such
a verb as *try* in sentences like *John tried to solve the problem.* The Equi rule
must apply so as to exclude *John$_i$ tried for him$_i$ to solve the problem.* But we
need also to exclude *John tried for Bill to solve the problem,* which means that
we have to ensure that the structure index for Equi is satisfied – the subject of
try must be identical to the subject of the complement sentence that is object
of *try.* Now examples like *John tried not to be seen by the guests* show that this
constraint does not apply to deep structure, for the deep subject of the complement sentence here is *the guests,* not *John.* The constraint associated with
try, then, is that the early transformations must yield a structure that satisfies

the index for Equi at that stage in the derivation when this rule applies to the sentence containing *try* as main verb (see also 15.4). It will be apparent that the complexities mentioned in this paragraph (and many other examples could be given) show the need for a significantly more sophisticated formalism for representing type (III) information than I have here developed.

Notes

The major theoretical discussion of syntactic features is in Chomsky 1965:75–123 and 148–70. He makes two alternative proposals for the organization of the syntax. One is as I have presented it here: the PS rules generate prelexical PMs with Δ in the terminal node positions, and lexical transformations substitute lexical items plus their complex symbols for the various Δs. In the other, the rewrite rules generate pre-lexical PMs terminating in complex symbols, and lexical items are inserted by a rule which involves comparing the complex symbol associated with an item in the lexicon with those in the pre-lexical PM. Most of the discussion in *Aspects* is in fact devoted to the latter proposal, but in later works Chomsky adopts the one I have given here; some arguments for preferring it can be found in McCawley 1968*a*.

I have simplified slightly by ignoring the distinction Chomsky makes between 'lexical' morphemes (belonging to the large categories, N, V, Adj, etc) and 'grammatical' morphemes (such as *Past*, *and*, and the like); the latter he introduces directly by the PS rules, so that the terminal string of pre-lexical PMs will consist of Δs and grammatical morphemes, rather than Δs alone (1965:122). He offers little motivation for this treatment, however. The complex symbol inserted into a PM will contain the morpheme plus its inherent and rule features; there seems no reason to suppose that the contextual features should also be included in the complex symbol that is inserted, for they would simply duplicate information present elsewhere in the tree. (As McCawley 1968*a* points out, this is not a purely notational matter but involves empirical issues.) In PM [11], however, I followed the usual practice of including the category features [+N], [+V], etc in the complex symbols. The lexical transformations do not insert the semantic properties of items into the PMs, as they are assumed in the *Aspects* theory not to play any role in the syntactic derivation; this means, however, that the lexicon is not simply equivalent to a set of lexical transformations: the rules of the semantic component must also refer to the lexicon.

The major study on rule features is G. Lakoff 1965. On homonymy and polysemy, see Lyons 1968:405–7, McCawley 1968*b*:125–7, Katz 1972:68–70. Four points of terminology: (a) 'formative' has come to be widely used in place of the earlier 'morpheme'; (b) the set of PS rules is often referred to as the 'categorial component' of the syntax; (c) 'complex symbol' is commonly applied just to the set of features, rather than to the combination of these plus the morpheme; (d) although substitution of a complex symbol for Δ is strictly speaking a transformation, it is clearly one of a very special kind and the reader should be prepared to find 'transformation' quite commonly used, even in post-*Aspects* literature, in the sense of 'non-lexical transformation'. It is not quite true to say that the determining factor in the choice between *who* and *which* is the feature [Human]. *Which* can be used of babies, and *who* of animals in certain circumstances – when they are referred to by name, *who* seems in fact obligatory, as in *Tiger, who/*which was miaowing loudly, wanted to be let in*. The choice does not depend solely on physical properties of the referent: the way the speaker thinks of or treats the referent is also relevant.

Chapter 11

Phonology and Morphology

11.1 The phonological form of morphemes

The model of grammar that Chomsky proposed in *Syntactic Structures* is shown schematically in [1], with [2] giving an illustrative sample of morphophonemic rules.

[1]

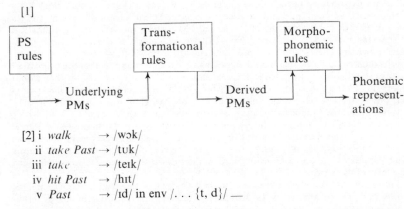

[2] i *walk* → /wɔk/
  ii *take Past* → /tʊk/
  iii *take* → /teɪk/
  iv *hit Past* → /hɪt/
  v *Past* → /ɪd/ in env /... {t, d}/ —

The morphophonemic rules specify the phonological realization of morphemes. They are ordered, so that for example [ii] applies before [iii]: [ii] says that the sequence *take Past* is together realized as /tʊk/ and then [iii] gives the realization of any occurrence of *take* not dealt with by [ii], *ie* any occurrence not immediately to the left of *Past*. Rule [v] states that *Past* is realized as /ɪd/ when it occurs after /t/ or /d/; this is a context-sensitive rule with 'in env' ('in the environment') being used instead of the oblique of context-sensitive PS rules (*cf* Chapter 3) because the oblique here has its other standard use of enclosing phonological units. Rule [v] handles the past tense of regular verbs ending in /t/ or /d/: irregular ones are dealt with by rules ordered earlier in the series, like [iv].

The main innovation in [1] was in the conception of syntactic structure; in a number of other respects it reflects views on the organization of a linguistic description, on the 'design of a language', prevailing among neo-Bloomfieldian scholars: (a) The rules relating morpheme sequences to their phonetic realizations were divided into two distinct sets, morphophonemic rules converting from morpheme sequences to phoneme sequences, and phonetic rules converting the latter to their phonetic realizations. (b) Of these two sets, only the morphophonemic rules were held to fall within the scope of the systematic linguistic description. I do not intend to suggest by this that the phonetic rules were not included in published grammars of the time. My concern is rather with their theoretical status: phonetics was commonly held to fall outside the domain of linguistics proper and phonetic representations were often characterized as 'impressionistic' rather than 'scientifically' accurate. (c) The statement of the relation between syntactic forms and meaning likewise did not belong within the formal linguistic description itself. I have already discussed the abandonment of this last point, and will not comment further on it here.

Points (a) and (b) were based on the distinction between phonetics and phonology, a distinction on which great emphasis was placed in neo-Bloomfieldian linguistics. Whereas phonetics was concerned with the detailed description of all articulatory, acoustic and auditory properties of the speech signal, phonology dealt only with those properties that were DISTINCTIVE or CONTRASTIVE. I observed in 1.1 that no two utterances are absolutely identical in purely physical terms, but that physically different utterances may nevertheless count as the same from a linguistic point of view. Different utterances counting as linguistically the same were said to be in FREE VARIATION, those counting as linguistically different to be in CONTRAST. For example, two pronunciations of *It's near the rat*, with the final consonant released in one, unreleased in the other, are in free variation, whereas pronunciations with a final alveolar and a final velar are in contrast: *It's near the rat* versus *It's near the rack*. (In this example, the free variants are not differentiated in the standard orthography, whereas the contrasting pronunciations are; this is typical but does not apply in all cases: pronunciations of *It's near the boy* and *It's near the buoy* are not in contrast, whereas there are contrasting pronunciations corresponding to the one written form *They read 'The Times'*, the past and present tenses of *read* contrasting in speech but not in orthography.) At the phonological level, free variants would have identical representations and contrasting utterances different ones. The difference between free variation and contrast provided a principled basis for determining how much phonetic detail to account for in a linguistic description: just enough to differentiate between contrasting utterances. Once one started representing the difference between free variants there was, it was argued, no non-arbitrary stopping place: the amount of phonetic detail incorporated would depend on the training, experience, perception of the phonetician, the particular practical aims he had in view, and so on. This is why a linguistic description of an utterance was regarded as including a phonological representation but not a phonetic one. The main task of phonological analysis was to establish the inventory of minimal distinctive units, the PHONEMES, and to describe their possible combinations, their distribution (phonology was accordingly often referred to as 'phonemics'). The contrast between *It's near the rat* and *It's near the rack*, for example, would be accounted for by setting up /t/ and /k/ as different phonemes, whereas the difference between the released and unreleased final stops in free variant pronunciations of *It's near the rat* would be ignored, the two sounds being treated simply as different manifestations or realizations of the one phoneme /t/.

The role of the morphophonemic component was to relate morpheme sequences to their phonemic form. The main reason why a special component of the grammar was needed for this purpose was that morphemes could not be regarded as simply composed of phonemes, could not therefore be represented directly as sequences of phonemes. Consider, for example, the past tense endings in regular verbs like *died, laughed* and *started*. These endings were regarded as differing not only at the phonetic level, but also at the phonemic, where they were analysed as /d/, /t/, and /ɪd/ respectively. Replacing the voiceless stop of *laughed* with its voiced counterpart yields a deviant form (*/lafd/), rather than a contrasting one, so that there is strictly speaking nothing distinctive about the voicelessness here. But the distinctiveness principle was interpreted in such a way that if a given phonetic difference was distinctive in SOME instances it would be treated as phonemically relevant in ALL instances (an interpretation summed up in the slogan 'once a phoneme, always a phoneme'). The contrast between, say, *A bit was made* versus *A bid was made* justified treating the difference of voiceless and voiced alveolar stops as distinctive, with /t/ and /d/ different phonemes therefore, and the voiceless and voiced alveolars were then regarded in all their occurrences as realizations of /t/ and /d/ respectively. Now if the three endings of *died, laughed* and *started* are composed of different phoneme sequences, one cannot without contradiction maintain both that they are instances of the same morpheme and that a morpheme is simply composed of a sequence of (one or more) phonemes. It would be unsatisfactory to analyse them as different morphemes for the reasons given in 2.2: the choice between the endings is determined by the phonological properties of the preceding phoneme and is thus not appropriately handled as a choice between different syntactic units. It was, then, the conception of the morpheme as composed of phonemes that was rejected, with the more complex relationship between the two levels being handled in the morphophonemics.

The past tense endings in *died, laughed, started* and other regular verbs are an example of phonologically determined alternation: the choice between the three phonemic forms, the 'alternants', is determined, as we have said, by the phonological context. Allowance was also made for a morpheme to have different phonemic realizations that are not phonologically determined. Suppose we compare the choices between /d/, /t/ and /ɪd/ in these regular past tense forms, /ɪz/ and /ən/ in the plurals *foxes* and *oxen*, /bɪt/ and /bɪd/ in *A bit was made* versus *A bid was made*. In the first set the following two conditions obtain: (I) There is no contrast in meaning between the forms, the choice between them being determined by the context in which they occur. (II) The determining factor in the context is phonological. In the choice between /ɪz/ and /ən/, condition (I) obtains, but not (ɪɪ) – /ən/ is determined by the particular morpheme *ox*, not by the phoneme sequence /ɒks/ (which also occurs in *fox*). In the choice between /bɪt/ and /bɪd/, neither condition obtains. The /ɪz/ versus /ən/ case was generally held to be more like /d/, /t/ and /ɪd/ than like /bɪt/ versus /bɪd/, and was consequently also handled as a purely morphophonemic choice: /ɪz/ and /ən/ were analysed as realizations of the same morpheme, /bɪt/ and /bɪd/ as realizations of different morphemes. The analysis of *foxes* and *oxen* as '*fox Plur*' and '*ox Plur*' was generalized to cover *men* as '*man Plur*', *sheep* (in *The sheep are . . .*) as '*sheep Plur*', so that the morpheme came to be conceived of as a quite abstract unit often related very indirectly to phonemic form. The grammar contained two types of basic unit, morphemes and phonemes, each type being primitive in the sense that it is not definable in terms of the other.

The first modifications to model [1] involved the rejection of points (a) and (b) above, the separation of morphophonemic and phonetic rules, and the exclusion of the latter from the formal grammar. The result is [3].

[3]

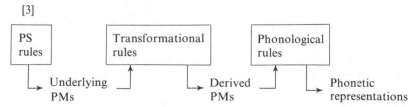

This is not the place for a detailed discussion of arguments against the neo-Bloomfieldian conception of the phoneme, but it is relevant to our concerns to consider the reasons for abandoning rules like [2] and the consequent change in the relation between syntactic and phonological form. The rules in [2] can be regarded as a fairly straightforward and faithful formalization of the kind of statement typical of neo-Bloomfieldian morphophonemics. Now, as observed in 1.5, the adoption of a formalized, generative approach focuses attention on the question, What is the appropriate form for grammatical rules and representations if the grammar is to match the data adequately and express the regularities in the language in general statements? Considered from this point of view it is apparent that the appropriate form for phonological representation is not a sequence of atomic, unstructured units, such as phonemes, but a sequence of complex symbols, each consisting of a set of phonological features. Instead of representing *dent* as /dɛnt/, we will give it as a sequence of four complex symbols, the first containing such features as [+Consonantal], [+Stop], [+Alveolar], [+Voiced], and so on. The reason for using a feature notation in generative phonology is the same as in syntax (indeed, it was introduced first into phonology and then extended to do analogous work in syntax). If we represent *start*, *plod* and the like as sequences of phonemes ending in /t/ and /d/ respectively, our rule for the morpheme *Past* will have to say that in regular verbs it is realized as /ɪd/ after either /t/ or /d/ (*cf* [2v]), whereas if we use a feature notation we can give a unitary definition of the determining context in the form $\begin{bmatrix} +\text{Alveolar} \\ +\text{Stop} \end{bmatrix}$. The contrast is more striking, but not different in principle, with the realization of *Past* as /t/: if the context is given in phonemic terms, we need a disjunctive listing of /p/, /k/, /f/, /s/, etc, instead of the general definition [−Voiced]. The fact that segments are classified with respect to properties like voicing, place of articulation, manner of articulation, etc, has been recognized from the earliest days of phonological theory, and the use of feature representations simply allows the various classes to be referred to formally in the rules in a direct way rather than by a disjunctive listing of the members. The status of notations like '/t/', '/d/' and so on will be like that of 'subject', 'object', etc in syntax: shorthand devices useful in informal discussion but playing no role in the formal grammar, hence non-primitive terms as opposed to primitive ones like '[+Alveolar]' or 'NP'.

Nor is there any reason for having special primitive symbols for morphemes. We can dispense with rules like [2i] (whether the right-hand side is given in phonemic or feature notation) if we introduce the morpheme into the PM directly in its phonological form. We have seen that the lexicon is equivalent to a set of transformations that substitute a lexical item plus its syntactic complex symbol for some occurrence of Δ: all we need, then, is to represent morphemes in the lexicon in their phonological form. This means that in PM[11] of Chapter 10 the notation '*cat*' is to be interpreted as a non-primitive symbol, a purely informal abbreviation for the corresponding phonological representation, where the first segment is specified as [+Consonantal], [+Stop], [+Velar], [−Voiced], and so on.

The morpheme is here conceived of as composed of phonological units, a conception which, as we saw above, was decisively rejected in the neo-Bloomfieldian model because of the phenomenon of alternation. How then can this phenomenon be reconciled with a compositional relationship between syntactic and phonological units? Let us take the example of *wife*, which ends with a voiced fricative when it occurs before the morpheme *Plur*, in *wives*, and with a voiceless one elsewhere. First consider how the alternation can be expressed if we revert to the morphophonemic rules of model [1]; we shall need the following rule:

[4] $wife \rightarrow \begin{cases} /\text{waɪv}/ \text{ in env } \_\_\_ Plur \\ /\text{waɪf}/ \end{cases} \begin{matrix} \text{i} \\ \text{ii} \end{matrix}$

(As before the ordering is crucial, so that [ii], giving the realization of *wife* when it occurs elsewhere than before *Plur* can be formulated as a context-free rule.) Again, this formalizes a quite common way of handling the alternation in neo-Bloomfieldian morphophonemics, where /waɪv/ and /waɪf/ were often spoken of as the 'allomorphs' of the morpheme *wife*. The trouble with [4] is that we shall need a similar pair of subrules for *calf, knife, leaf, life, loaf,* etc: we have to state what is really the same alternation as many times as there are morphemes in which it occurs. If the grammar is to express formally the fact that *wife, calf, knife*, . . ., do exhibit the same alternation, it must state it in a single general rule, not a multiplicity of separate particular ones like [4].

The fact that expressing the alternation as holding between allomorphs /waɪv/ and /waɪf/ had the undesirable consequence that separate alternations had to be stated for each of the above morphemes was recognized by some neo-Bloomfieldian scholars. They proposed that instead of saying that *wife* has two allomorphs, it should be analysed as /waɪF/, where /F/ is a 'morphophoneme', a unit intermediate between morpheme and phoneme. /F/ would then be realized phonemically as /v/ or /f/, depending on the context, and since /F/ would constitute the final segment of each of *wife, calf, knife*, . . ., the alternation could be stated in a single rule applying to /F/ rather than separate ones applying to the different morphemes. Notice, however, that the same alternation of voiced and voiceless segments as we find between /v/ and /f/ occurs also between /z/ and /s/ in *houses* versus *house* and /ð/ and /θ/ in *mouths* versus *mouth*. If we set up special morphophonemes /S/ and /Θ/ and write a separate realization rule for each of /F/, /S/, /Θ/ we shall still be failing to express the alternation in its proper generality. The example again demonstrates the need for representations in the form of features, not atomic segments. What we want, then, is a rule along the lines of [5].

$$[5] \quad \begin{bmatrix} -\text{Voiced} \\ +\text{Fricative} \end{bmatrix} \rightarrow \begin{bmatrix} +\text{Voiced} \\ +\text{Fricative} \end{bmatrix} \text{ in env } \underline{\quad} Plur$$

We take the final segment of the morphemes *wife, calf, house*, etc, to be 'basically' voiceless, *ie* to be specified as [− Voiced] in the lexical entry: thus no special rule is required corresponding to [4ii], any more than to [2i], and so on. Rule [5] states that a voiceless fricative is replaced by its voiced counterpart when it occurs just before the morpheme *Plur*. The one rule covers all the examples cited.

It does not, however, apply to all morphemes ending in a voiceless fricative – compare *cliff, cliffs; horse, horses; month, months;* etc. This indeed was the major motivation for recognizing /F, S, Θ/ as special morphophonemes: the difference between *wife* and *cliff* was handled by analysing them as /waɪF/ and /klɪf/ respectively. But once it is accepted that segments must be analysed into features, it is clear that there can be no place in the formal grammar for unstructured symbols like /F/, and consequently we shall need some other way of differentiating between *wife* and *cliff*. A plausible approach is to invoke the notion of irregularity and rule government alluded to in Chapter 10: *wife, house*, etc, are irregular with respect to plural formation in comparison with regular *cliff, horse*, etc, just as *cost* is irregular with respect to Passivization in contrast to regular *buy, sell*, etc. [5] will accordingly be a governed rule, applying only to morphemes having the plus value of the associated rule feature.

We can now return to the question, How can the conception of the morpheme as composed of phonological units be reconciled with the phenomenon of alternation? The answer is simply that we allow for more than one level of phonological representation. In the derivation of a sentence like *Shall I invite their wives?* the morpheme *wife* will be represented at one level with a final voiceless fricative and at another with a voiced one, with rule [5] relating one to the other. The parallel with syntax is evident: just as the syntactic structure of a sentence is described in terms of a series of syntactic representations ranging from more to less abstract and related by syntactic rules (transformations), so is its phonological structure described in terms of a series of phonological representations related by phonological rules. And just as in syntax the deep structure may differ markedly from the surface structure but is essentially the same kind of formal object, a PM, so the underlying phonological structure may be quite abstract in comparison with the final representation, but both will analyse the sentence into a sequence of segments consisting of sets of phonological features.

There is no reason why the final phonological representation should contain only as much information about the pronunciation of a sentence as is recorded in a neo-Bloomfieldian phonemic analysis. There are two reasons for claiming we should go beyond the latter. First, there is much else that is determined by general rules, and hence properly included within a systematic linguistic description. For example, voiceless stops are aspirated in word initial position, as in *team, kin,* etc, but not after /s/, as in *steam, skin;* the choice between aspirated and unaspirated stops is not 'distinctive', but nor is it random: a pronunciation of *team* with an unaspirated stop would be deviant. Of crucial significance here is the fact that this aspiration does not occur in all languages (not in French, for example): a general rule specifying the pronunciation of English surely belongs in a grammar of English. Secondly, the difference between free variation and contrast cannot in general be handled satisfactorily by treating free variants as 'linguistically the same', *ie* as having identical representations at all levels. This is because there is more than one kind of free variation. Pronunciations of *It's near the rat* with released and unreleased final stops are phonetic free variants, whereas *Give it to the girl that John's talking to* and *Give it to the girl John's talking to* are syntactic free variants. No one has ever suggested that the latter pair be represented identically at all levels: the presence or absence of *that* cannot be simply ignored in their syntactic and phonological description. Free variation here cannot be a relation between different utterances of the same linguistic unit: it is a relation between different linguistic units such that they have the same representation at the semantic level and different ones at the final phonological level. In the particular example cited the difference is introduced by the optional transformation of *That* Deletion, so that the sentences differ also at the level of surface syntax. This account generalizes naturally to the phonetic free variants. They will have identical representations at the underlying phonological level (and hence also at the syntactic and semantic levels) but not at the final level, the difference here being due to the optionality of the phonological rule releasing final voiceless stops. The output of the rules will accordingly give more phonetic information than a neo-Bloomfieldian phonemic analysis – but it will not give all the information that would be included in the skilled phonetician's detailed transcription of a particular utterance: the grammar is still dealing with sentences (competence) as opposed to individual utterances of them (performance). Accordingly it will specify only those aspects of the pronunciation that are systematic rather than due simply to performance factors – for this reason the final output is referred to as a SYSTEMATIC PHONETIC REPRESENTATION.

The principle of distinctiveness now applies not to the final phonological output of the grammar (as in model [1]) but – in a modified form – to the underlying phonological level, the SYSTEMATIC PHONEMIC REPRESENTATION. If two sentences are phonetically contrastive (like *It's near the rat/rack*) they will have different underlying phonological representations, but there is no requirement that because the final stops of *bit* and *bid* have to be differentiated at this level in terms of voicing those of *laughed* and *died* must be too: in the latter case the voicing is predictable by a general rule rather than being an inherent lexical property of the tense morpheme. For this and other reasons, the underlying phonological representation tends to be considerably more abstract, *ie* further removed from the phonetic representation, than the neo-Bloomfieldian's phonemic level.

Model [3] involves as radical a departure from the neo-Bloomfieldian approach in phonology as [1] had in syntax. Both versions of generative grammar, however, retain the sharp division between syntax and the 'lower' component (morphophonemics in [1], phonology in [3]). This division can be regarded as self-evident in [1], for there the basic units of syntax, the morphemes, were represented by primitive symbols that were completely non-phonological: phonological units were introduced into a derivation by morphophonemic rules like [2], applying after the completion of the transformational derivation. But this is no longer so in [3], where phonological material is introduced by syntactic rules (by lexical transformations and also by certain non-lexical ones, such as Passivization and *Do* Support) so that the distinction between syntactic and phonological rules cannot be defined simply in terms of the absence versus presence of phonological units in the rule. [3] assumes both that there is a formally well-defined distinction between the two types of rule and also that they are ordered in such a way that all the syntactic rules apply before all of the phonological ones. These assumptions may be valid, but I think it is fair to say that they have not as yet received very thorough justification.

11.2 Morphology

Model [1] above differs strikingly from traditional views on the design of language, where the grammar (understood in a sense which excludes phonology) is divided into three components: syntax, INFLECTION (or accidence) and DERIVATION (or word-formation). Inflection deals with variation in the form of words depending on such properties as tense, mood, aspect, voice, person, number, etc, for verbs; number and case for nouns; and so on. The classical method of specifying the various inflectional forms of a word is to tabulate them in a PARADIGM; the paradigms for two Latin nouns, for example, are given in [6].

[6] i

	Singular	Plural	ii	Singular	Plural
Nominative	*mensa*	*mensae*		*dominus*	*dominī*
Vocative	*mensa*	*mensae*		*domine*	*dominī*
Accusative	*mensam*	*mensās*		*dominum*	*dominōs*
Genitive	*mensae*	*mensārum*		*dominī*	*dominōrum*
Dative	*mensae*	*mensīs*		*dominō*	*dominīs*
Ablative	*mensā*	*mensīs*		*dominō*	*dominīs*

Latin nouns are grouped into 'declensional classes' according as their inflectional forms follow the model of, say, *mensa* ('table'), a first declension noun, *dominus* ('lord, master'), a second declension noun, and so on; verbs are divided into 'conjugational classes' on a similar basis. The syntax will deal with the conditions determining the selection of the various cases (that the nominative case is used when the noun is in subject position, and so on), whereas the inflectional component specifies what form a noun takes when it appears in the nominative or the vocative or whatever, and similarly with other inflectional properties.

The third component of the grammar, derivation, describes the formation of words from more elementary words by 'compounding' (as in *blackbird* from *black + bird*), 'affixation' (*disable* is formed from *able* by prefixing *dis-*, *payment* from *pay* by suffixing *-ment*), and so on. Derivation is typically much less systematic than inflection. Inflections generally apply to all members of a major part of speech category or to a large and independently definable subclass – *eg* tense applies to the whole class of verbs, number to the subclass of 'count' nouns; exceptions like *used* (in *He used to live here*, etc), which has no present tense, or *must*, which has no past, are said to be 'defective' in that they have incomplete paradigms. Derivations, however, are much more restricted: the forms that can take *dis-* or *-ment*, for example, are not independently definable but have to be listed. Moreover, as noted above, inflections are of direct syntactic relevance in a way that derivations are not: third person singular present tense verbs, for example, constitute a syntactic subclass in that they differ distributionally from other verbs, but nouns formed by the suffix *-ment* do not: *embarrassment*, *payment*, *punishment*, *statement*, *treatment*, etc, do not constitute a class differing distributionally from all other nouns. Inflection and derivation are commonly subsumed under the more general term MORPHOLOGY: this deals with the form of words, while traditional syntax is concerned with the way words can combine to make sentences.

It is the concept of 'word', then, that provides the basis for the division between syntax and morphology. In the neo-Bloomfieldian view of the design of language, the word played a much reduced role. Apart from phonology, the major components here are grammar and morphophonemics, and the word is not regarded as the basic unit of either of these. As for the grammar, the structure of words, just like that of phrases, clauses or sentences, is held to be describable in terms of immediate constituent analysis and the distributional classification of constituents. For example, *ungentlemanly* is divisible into the ICs *un* and *gentlemanly*, the latter being then analysed into *gentleman* and *ly*, with *gentleman* finally broken down into the ICs *gentle* and *man; un* belongs to the class of morphemes that can be prefixed to adjectives (it is to permit this generalization that we divide first into *un* and *gentlemanly*, not *ungentleman* and *ly*), and so on: the basic or minimal grammatical unit is accordingly not the word but the morpheme. And as for the morphophonemics, the word is not the maximum unit of relevance. The environment determining the realization of the morpheme *Plur* as /ən/, /ɪz/, /s/, /z/, etc, is part of the same word as *Plur*, but there are also alternations depending on the shape of neighbouring words, not neighbouring morphemes within the same word. For example, the definite and indefinite articles (leaving aside instances where they are heavily stressed) are realized as /ði/ and /ən/ when the following word begins with a vowel and as /ðə/ and /ə/ elsewhere. Similarly in French we find *vieil*, as in *un vieil ami* ('an old friend'), rather than *vieux*, as in *un vieux soldat* ('an old soldier'), when the following word begins with a vowel. The traditional model does not cater satisfactorily for this kind of alternation: /ə/ and /ən/ are not different inflectional forms of a single word (like *take* and *taken*), nor is /ən/ a different word from /ə/, derived from it by suffixation (like *hearten* from *heart*).

Some versions of the neo-Bloomfieldian model retained a word-based syntax-morphology division within the grammar, but morphology dealt only with the morphemic structure of words, not with their phonological form as in traditional grammar; most of traditional grammar's inflectional morphology was handled in the morphophonemic component. The first version of transformational grammar took over the basic neo-Bloomfieldian division between grammar and morphophonemics, but not the lesser one between syntax and morphology; the terminology, however, was changed, with 'syntax' extended to cover the earlier 'grammar' and 'grammar' extended to cover the whole description. The minimal unit of the syntax was accordingly the morpheme, not the word.

It is apparent, however, that not all inflectional properties can be appropriately formalized as morphemes. For the morpheme is a SEGMENTAL unit: it occupies a distinct position in linear structure. This means that different linear arrangements of the same set of morphemes count as distinct representations. For example, the representations '*John Past see Mary*', '*John see Past Mary*', '*Mary see Past John*', '*Mary Past John see*' are all formally distinct (according to the grammar of Chapter 5, the first two are the terminal strings of the deep and surface structures respectively of *John saw Mary*, the third is the surface string of *Mary saw John* and the fourth is not well-formed at any level). But consider now the syntactic properties of a form like *am*. This is traditionally analysed as the first person singular present indicative of *be*, and there is no doubt that this is essentially correct. The five separate components are justified by the fact that they are independently variable: *am* contrasts with *is* as first person versus third, with *are* as singular versus plural, with *was* as present versus past, with *were* as indicative versus subjunctive, and with *have* as a form of *be* versus a form of *have*. If we treated each component as a morpheme, however, we should create for ourselves completely unreal problems concerning their relative linear order: Does '*First-Person*' precede or follow '*Singular*'? – and so on. Any order we assigned here would almost certainly be purely arbitrary, an artefact of the formal apparatus without any empirical motivation, rather than representative of any significant property of the form. We can avoid such arbitrariness by making use of syntactic features and representing *am* at the level of surface structure in the form of a complex symbol along the lines of [7].

[7]
$$\begin{bmatrix} \text{First Person} \\ \text{Singular Number} \\ \text{Indicative Mood} \\ \text{Present Tense} \\ be \end{bmatrix}$$

There is no ordering among the separate parts of a complex symbol, so that it would not count as a different representation if we wrote Singular Number above First Person – any more than it would if we used blue ink instead of black. The non-segmental nature of features thus makes them a much more suitable device than the morpheme for handling the properties at issue in the present example. Person, Number, Mood and Tense are to be interpreted as feature dimensions in [7], with First, Singular, Indicative and Present their respective values: I leave open here the question of whether the traditional analysis should be revised to incorporate binary plus-minus features.

To generate [7] and the like we need to extend somewhat the formal apparatus introduced in Chapter 10. It is clear that we shall not want to insert the complex symbol [7] into deep structure by means of a lexical transformation. For the person and number features of the verb are agreement features (the verb agrees with the subject in the sense that it takes the same values for these features as the subject) – and the subject in question is not the deep structure subject. This is apparent from examples like *The letters were written by John* or *The boys seem to like it*, where the verbs agree with the plural NPs that become subject by Passivization and Raising respectively. What we need, then, is a non-lexical transformation, ordered to apply after these latter rules, which will insert the appropriate person and number features into the complex symbol of the verb. Notice that the verb agrees not with a given noun but with the whole NP that functions as subject, witness examples like *John and Mary are/*is here*, where plural *are* agrees with the coordinate NP *John and Mary*, not with the separate singular nouns. It seems likely that to handle agreement we shall need to allow for syntactic features to appear on non-terminal as well as terminal nodes – in particular to allow [Person] and [Number] to be associated with a NP node. The values of these features would be determined by working up from the bottom of the subtree dominated by the NP, taking account of properties of the relevant nouns and combining values where NPs are coordinated (distinguishing the conjunctive and disjunctive types because of the difference between *John and Mary are* . . and *John or Mary is* . . .), and so on.

An example similar to [7] is provided by the personal pronouns. *We* and *us* will be alike in all respects except case, which we shall regard as a feature not a morpheme category, for again we do not want to analyse *us* into a linear sequence of units. The value of the [Case] feature for a given pronoun will be determined not in the base rules but in the transformational derivation, just like those of [Person] and [Number] in the verb and for the same reason – they depend on the structure obtaining after such rules as Passivization and Raising have applied (compare *John saw us/*we* versus *We/*us were seen by John*). Ordering Passivization before Subject-Verb Agreement and Case Marking enables us to express the former in its proper generality – the differences in case and verbal person and number in *She has seen them* versus *They have been seen by her* do not have to be accounted for in the Passivization rule itself but are handled by later independent rules; as observed in our original discussion of Passivization (Chapter 4), we could not achieve this generalization if Passivization were formalized as a rule operating on sentences, as distinct from their more abstract syntactic representations.

There are two further points to be made about representations like [7]. Firstly, it is clear that the realization rules that eventually specify the phonetic form of sentences cannot operate simply on sequences of morphemes (plus their categorial IC structure): in [7] we shall need a rule that gives a phonological representation for the whole complex of components. Secondly, in between the many clear examples where we have no hesitation in analysing an element as segmental (a morpheme) or non-segmental (a feature) there is a residue of borderline instances where the correct choice is uncertain. On the one hand, there can be no question of representing *has been* as a single complex symbol containing the morpheme *be* together with the features [+Perfect], [Third Person], etc: we need a minimum of two syntactic segments because the *has* and *been* are not always contiguous (witness '. . . has often been . . .'). On the other hand, *am* is clearly not to be represented as a sequence of five segmental units, as observed above. It is much less clear, however, whether *am* should be represented as a single complex symbol as in [7], or as a sequence of two, a stem *be* followed by an 'ending' comprising the person, number, mood and tense features. Segmentation of regular verb forms like *dies, died*, etc, is motivated on phonological grounds and this lends some support for a stem plus ending analysis generalized to all verbs. As far as syntactic arguments are concerned, the discussion of Chapter 5 showed that we cannot regard tense as a deep structure property of the verb it accompanies in surface structure, for the auxiliary *be* that carries the tense element in the surface structure of passives does not figure in the deep structure. This provides some justification for treating the tense element as segmentally separate from the verb stem, and it will be clear that our handling of the auxiliary *do* also depended crucially on such an analysis. However, it is possible that the major claims of Chapter 5 could equally well be formalized in an analysis in which tense was a feature of the VGp, with a transformation lowering it at an appropriate stage of the derivation into the complex symbol of the first verb in the VGp, to yield surface representations like [7]. I shall not attempt to decide the matter here: we cannot hope to resolve this kind of issue without a much more rigorous specification and justification than is currently available of the range of operations involving features that are allowed by the theory. Many aspects of the feature formalism remain obscure, and I have not thought it worthwhile, therefore, to give here explicit formulations of any rules in which features figure.

Turning now very briefly from inflection to derivation, we note that derived words can typically be segmented fairly straightforwardly into morphemes, as in *un-gentle-man-ly*, *tele-graph-ic*, *read-able*, etc, and often, as with the first two of these examples, assigned a layered IC structure. However, there are enormous restrictions, as observed above, on which morphemes can combine with which (*unroughmanly*, *televisionic*, etc, are not well-formed); and the meaning of derived words, moreover, is often not fully predictable from the meanings of their parts: *gentleman* is not synonymous with *man who is gentle*, nor does *readable play* mean the same as *play which is able to be read*. It seems inevitable, then, that a large proportion of derived words will have to be entered as such in the lexicon and inserted into PMs as wholes instead of being generated by rules operating on syntactically independent parts in the way that phrases like *a gentle man* are. The units listed in the lexicon we accordingly speak of as lexical items rather than morphemes; many lexical items are single morphemes, but many others are morphemically complex. Some indeed consist of more than one word: these are the traditional idioms – *to pull . . .'s leg* (in the sense of 'tease'), *to kick the bucket* ('die'), and so on. As noted in our earlier discussion of the latter example (*p* 30) we need to assign internal syntactic structure in such cases: the point I am making here is that this structure must be specified directly in the lexicon.

The morpheme concept was an innovation of structural linguistics, and it is clear in retrospect that it was considerably overworked in the neo-Bloomfieldian and early transformational models. Its role in the *Aspects* model is significantly reduced, for now it is but one of three different types of basic unit: morpheme, feature and lexical item. The morpheme remains the minimal segmental unit of syntax, but allowance is now made for non-segmental units and for non-minimal segmental units with a structure individually specified in the lexicon. Much of traditional grammar's derivational morphology will now be handled in the lexicon but although the change from *Syntactic Structures* to *Aspects* has brought the theory somewhat closer to traditional views on the design of language, there has been no return to a word-based syntax-morphology distinction: the word is still not the basic unit of syntax.

Notes

Harms 1968 and Schane 1973 are introductory textbooks on the phonological component of a TG; two important primary sources are Chomsky and Halle 1968, Postal 1968. Chomsky 1962:132–5 gives a brief early statement of reasons for rejecting model [1] and rules like [2]. For a neo-Bloomfieldian view on the design of a language, see Hockett

1954, 1961. Robins 1959 argues for a return to a word-based model. A good general introduction to morphology is Matthews 1974; see also his more detailed study of inflection (1972). On the treatment of inflection in TG, see Chomsky 1965: 170–84; and of derivational morphology, Chomsky 1965: 184–92, 1970a and the review of the latter in McCawley 1974b. The problem of idioms is discussed in Weinrich 1966, Fraser 1970, Katz 1973b. On subject-verb agreement, see Morgan 1972, Quirk et al 1972: 359–67. Stockwell et al 1973 make considerable use in the syntax of complex symbols without any accompanying phonological form – the latter is added after the operation of the non-lexical transformations in what is called a 'second lexical look-up'.

Chapter 12

The Interpretation and Ordering of Rules

12.1 A static interpretation of generative rules

Up to this point we have been interpreting the rules of a generative grammar as in effect instructions for constructing derivations of sentences. We start with the given string #S#, apply PS rules to get a PS derivation, convert this into a pre-lexical PM, apply lexical substitution transformations to change this into a deep structure, run through the syntactic transformations to arrive at the surface structure, and finally apply the phonological rules so that we end up with a phonetic representation, a sentence. In line with this interpretation our description has been couched in dynamic, or process, terminology. Thus we have spoken of 'rewriting' one symbol as a string of symbols, of 'substituting' a lexical item for an occurrence of Δ, of 'deleting' elements or 'moving' them from one position in the tree to another – of 'Passivization', 'Reflexivization', 'Subject Raising' and the like. But the question arises, What is the empirical content of this dynamic interpretation? A process surely involves time: it is a change from an earlier state to a later state – what is the time-scale along which Passivization, for example, takes place?

Real time is clearly involved in : (a) language change, (b) language learning, (c) linguistic performance. But these are not what a generative grammar aims to describe. No one is claiming that *They seem to like it* derives historically from *They to like it seem* or that the child first learns the latter, subsequently replacing it by the former. Nor is the generative grammarian claiming to describe the mental processes that take place in the time it takes to produce or understand an utterance in actual performance. It would be wildly implausible, for instance, to suggest that a speaker first constructs in his mind a pre-lexical tree structure and then decides what lexical items he is going to insert – *ie* what he is going to talk about; or that in *They seem to like it* he goes through some mental process of moving *they* around *seem*, and so on. From the beginning of generative grammar, Chomsky has made it clear that he is not claiming that in producing an utterance a speaker mentally works his way progressively through the rules.

What a generative grammar describes is a state: the (ideal) speaker-hearer's knowledge of his language at some particular point in time. We are thus faced with the problem of justifying our use of process terms in describing something which is not a process. We can resolve this problem by showing that the grammar has in fact a purely static interpretation; it will then follow that the process terminology does not reflect anything inherent in the grammar itself, but is merely a convenient stylistic device for talking informally about the grammar.

Let us consider first the case of PS rules. In the dynamic interpretation we take these rules to be instructions for constructing a derivation consisting of a sequence of lines (strings of symbols), the first being #S#, the last a string of Δs flanked by #. Here we begin with #S#, scan the rules for one with S on the left, say 'S → NP VP', and apply this, writing down #NP VP# as the second line of the derivation – and so on. In the static interpretation we are not concerned with how a PS derivation is constructed but rather with the conditions that a sequence of lines must satisfy in order to qualify as a PS derivation in the language. Consider, for example, the simplified PS rules [1] and the sequence of lines given in [2].

[1]			[2]	
i	S → NP VP		#S#	i
ii	VP → VGp (NP)		#NP VP#	ii
iii	VGp → Aux V		#NP VGp#	iii
iv	Aux → Tns (M)		#NP Aux V#	iv
v	NP → (Det) N		#NP Tns V#	v
vi	N → Δ		#N Tns V#	vi
vii	V → Δ		#Δ Tns V#	vii
viii	Tns → Δ		#Δ Tns Δ#	viii
ix	M → Δ		#Δ Δ Δ#	ix
x	Det → Δ			

To qualify as a PS derivation, the sequence must satisfy the following conditions:

I: Line [i] must be #S#.

II: The only difference between each adjacent pair of lines is that where the higher one has A, the lower one has B, where A is a variable for a single symbol, B for a string of one or more symbols.

III: For each adjacent pair of lines differing as in (II), there is in the grammar a PS rule (or subrule) of the form 'A → B'.

It is clear that [2] satisfies these conditions, given the grammar in [1]. (I) is straightforward. As for (II), the only difference between the first pair of lines is that where [i] has S, [ii] has NP VP; between the second pair that where [ii] has VP, [iii] has VGp; and so on. As for (III), the difference between the first pair is sanctioned by the rule 'S → NP VP', that between the second pair by the subrule 'VP → VGp'; and so on. Notice that in both interpretations the lines of the derivation are arranged in a sequence, but in the static interpretation it is not a temporal sequence. We simply have #S# at one end of the sequence, and every other line will be a certain number of lines away from #S#. In this interpretation, then, the PS rules simply specify the permitted differences between adjacent lines in a derivation: there is no 'changing' one line into another.

We can deal with transformations in an analogous way. In the dynamic interpretation they were conceived of as instructions for constructing transformational derivations, each consisting of a sequence of phrase markers, $PM_1, \ldots, PM_n$. PM_1 was obtained from the PS derivation, then PM_2 derived from PM_1 by the application of a transformation, and so on. In the static interpretation we are again concerned not with constructing derivations but with the conditions that a PM sequence must meet in order to qualify as a transformational derivation in the language. The general conditions are these:

I: For each pair of adjacent PMs, PM_i and PM_{i+1}, there is in the grammar a transformation such that PM_i satisfies the structure index and PM_{i+1} differs from PM_i in the way specified in the structure change. Thus given a grammar containing rule [3], PMs [4-5] would qualify as an admissible pair.

[3] *You* DELETION: *Imp — you — VP*
$$\begin{array}{cccc} 1 & 2 & 3 & \Rightarrow \\ 1 & \varnothing & 3 & \end{array}$$

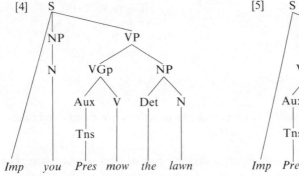 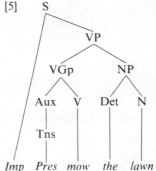

The 'structure change' would thus more appropriately be called 'structure difference': a transformation specifies the permitted differences between adjacent PMs in a derivation.

II: The last PM in the sequence, PM_n, must not satisfy the index of any obligatory transformation. (If it does, the sequence will at most be part of a derivation.)

III: The first PM in the sequence, PM_1, must be 'based' on a PS derivation: I leave it to the reader to make this precise by reinterpreting the account of *pp* 37-8 in terms of differences between formal objects instead of operations performed upon them.

There are also conditions relating to the ordering of rules: I will add these in 12.2. I have spoken of one PM as the first, but again this has no temporal implications: the 'first' PM in a transformational derivation is simply defined as the one that is based on the PS derivation; the others are then numbered in terms of their distance from this one.

The main point, then, is this: we can interpret PS rules and transformations as defining admissible differences between consecutive stages in syntactic derivations. In this account there is no process, no time-scale: the ordering of the consecutive stages involves not time but level of abstraction, with the deep structure being more abstract than the surface structure, and so on. Having established that the rules specify static conditions rather than dynamic operations, we can continue to use the process terminology, secure in the knowledge that what we say can be translated into an empirically equivalent static formulation: the choice of one formulation over the other is then simply a matter of stylistic convenience. The price we must pay for the greater ease of expression provided by the process terminology is constant vigilance against being led into false inferences. In addition to the danger of mistaking the grammar for a performance rather than a competence model, there is the more subtle danger of assuming that there is some kind of unidirectionality in the rules: transformations, for example, simply relate pairs of PMs – the arrow notation should not lead us to think that they work unidirectionally from deeper to less deep, or that deep structure has some kind of priority over surface structure. Similarly one should beware of the term 'determine': in saying, for example, that deep structure determines meaning, there is again no question of deep structure having any temporal or logical priority, and we could equally well say that meaning determines deep structure. The content of the claim made in the *Aspects* theory that deep structure determines meaning is this: that there are semantic rules directly relating meaning to deep structure but not to any other level of syntactic structure – meaning relates to surface structure only indirectly, via deep structure and the syntactic transformations. For example, there is no semantic rule relating the question meaning of *Have you finished?* to the auxiliary verb + subject surface order: rather this surface order is related by syntactic transformation to the deep structure *Q you have finished* (or more precisely *Q wh or you have en finish you not have en finish*) which is in turn related to the meaning by a semantic rule which interprets the element *Q*.

12.2 Extrinsic rule ordering

We shall see that EXTRINSIC ORDERING has greater significance for transformations than for PS rules, but as the latter are formally so much simpler it will be convenient to deal with them first so that the issues involved in rule ordering can be seen more easily. I shall begin by considering PS rules from a dynamic point of view, as instructions for constructing derivations and then shift to the static interpretation of 12.1.

We can distinguish two theories concerning the organization of the PS component of the grammar. In one, the rules are numbered consecutively, and the procedure for constructing derivations takes this numbering into account:

this is what is meant by saying that the rules are extrinsically ordered. The construction of derivations proceeds roughly as follows (where *n* is a variable ranging over the rule numbers):

[6] Procedure when the rules are extrinsically ordered:

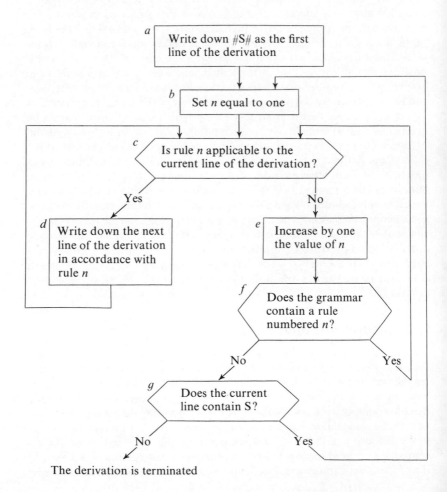

In the second theory there is no such numbering of the rules, and derivations are constructed according to the following procedure (again given only roughly):

[7] Procedure when the rules are not extrinsically ordered:

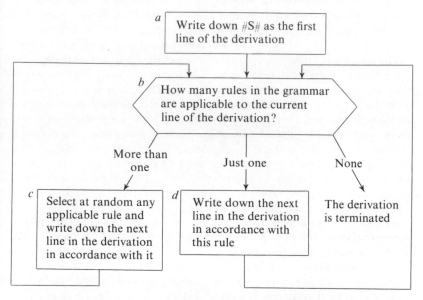

Let us consider what effect the choice between these procedures has on the set of PS derivations that can be constructed from a given grammar. Continuing with the simple grammar given in [1] above, we note that each of the following, suitably completed, can be constructed by procedure [7], but only the first two by [6].

[8] #S#	[9] #S#	[10] #S#	i
#NP VP#	#NP VP#	#NP VP#	ii
#NP VGp NP#	#NP VGp NP#	#N VP#	iii
#NP Aux V NP#	#NP Aux V NP#	#N VGp NP#	iv
#NP Tns M V NP#	#NP Tns M V NP#	#N VGp N#	v
#N Tns M V NP#	#NP Tns M V N#	#N Aux V N#	vi
#N Tns M V N#	#N Tns M V N#	#N Tns M V N#	vii
. . .	. . .	. . .	
#Δ Δ Δ Δ Δ#	#Δ Δ Δ Δ Δ#	#Δ Δ Δ Δ Δ#	xiii

The difference between [8] and [9] depends on which NP in line [v] is rewritten by the 'NP → N' rule: procedure [6] leaves this open. The reason why procedure [6] will not produce [10] is that the rule which relates lines [ii] and [iii] is ordered after the one relating lines [iii] and [iv], and so on. The static interpretation of PS rules I gave in 12.1 holds for the case where there is no extrinsic ordering, and thus corresponds to [7]. Extrinsic ordering is to be interpreted as imposing an ADDITIONAL condition on what sequences of lines are admissible as PS derivations: that the rule sanctioning a given pair of adjacent lines (in the way specified in condition (III)) must not have a higher number than any rule sanctioning an earlier pair of lines (I simplify by ignoring sentence recursion, catered for in box *g* of [6]). It follows that every PS derivation generated by a grammar where the rules are extrinsically ordered will be generated by a grammar containing the same rules without such ordering, but not conversely.

The extrinsic ordering theory contains formal apparatus not available in the other theory: it attributes to the speaker-hearer a tacit knowledge not just of the rules themselves but also of their numbering. The burden of proof thus rests with the advocate of the extrinsic ordering theory: he must show that this additional apparatus is empirically justified. Here it is worth disposing of one factor which does not constitute such justification. It can be argued that [6] is computationally simpler than [7] inasmuch as if a computer were programmed to construct derivations it would take more time to use [7] than [6]. This is because step *b* of [7] involves comparing the current line of the derivation with every rule in the grammar, whereas step *c* of [6] involves only a single comparison. But when we adopt a static interpretation of the rules we can see that this has no significance. The processes involved in the construction of a derivation do not correspond to anything in what we are trying to describe, which is a state. The greater 'economy' of [6] has, therefore, no empirical import, and cannot count as an argument in favour of extrinsic ordering. The function of extrinsic ordering is to block certain sequences of lines (such as [10]) which would otherwise be generated as PS derivations. The only valid way to justify extrinsic ordering, therefore, is to show that there are empirical reasons for excluding such derivations.

In the case of [10] this cannot be done. For [8–10] all define exactly the same PM, *viz*

[11]

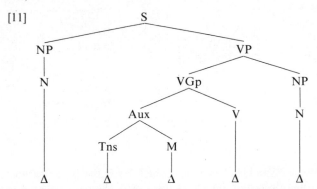

(the pre-lexical structure of *John may see Mary*, etc). The three derivations are accordingly wholly equivalent, and there is no reason to accept two and reject the third.

In early work it was assumed that the PS rules were extrinsically ordered. In the case of context-sensitive rules, such ordering did serve a useful function. Consider, for example, the restrictions on preverbs combining with *not* discussed on *p* 87; extrinsic ordering of subrules enables us to handle these in the following way:

[12]   Preverb   → $\left\{ \begin{array}{l} \text{Preverb}_{pos} \, / \, not \, \underline{\quad} \\ \text{Preverb}_{pos}, \, \text{Preverb}_{neg} \end{array} \right\}$ i ii

Preverb$_{pos}$ → {*always, often,* . . .}   iii

Preverb$_{neg}$ → {*never, scarcely, seldom,* . . .}   iv

If Preverb occurs after *not* it will automatically be rewritten as Preverb$_{pos}$ by subrule [i], so that **He does not never/scarcely/seldom speak* will be blocked. If Preverb does not follow *not*, [i] will not be applicable and it will be rewritten as either Preverb$_{pos}$ or Preverb$_{neg}$ by subrule [ii], so that all of *He always/often/ never/scarcely/seldom speaks* will be generated. Extrinsically ordering [ii] after [i] enables us to formulate [ii] as a context-free subrule instead of specifying all contexts other than '*not* __'. The ordering thus enables us to handle the notion 'everywhere else': Preverb will be rewritten as in [ii] when it occurs in any other environment than that given in [i].

When we restrict the PS component to context-free rules, however, as proposed in Chapter 10, there ceases to be any need for the extra apparatus provided by extrinsic ordering. I shall henceforth assume, therefore, that these rules are not so ordered.

The term 'extrinsic' is used to distinguish the type of ordering we have been looking at from what is called INTRINSIC ORDERING. The latter is ordering that simply follows from the content of the rules themselves. For example, it is clear that in any derivation constructed from grammar [1] by procedure [7] the Aux rule cannot apply until after the VGp rule: this is because it is only through an application of the latter that the symbol Aux can get into the derivation. Similarly the VGp rule cannot apply until after the VP rule, and so on. We accordingly say that the VGp rule is intrinsically ordered before the Aux rule, and so on. The point to bear in mind is that extrinsic ordering involves more than this: it is ordering for which we have to make special provision by assigning numbers to the rules, with these numbers forming an integral part of the formal grammar.

Before leaving the PS component, we should observe that the abandonment of extrinsic ordering here makes possible a significant revision of the function of PS rules. Instead of taking them to be rewrite rules expressing conditions on well-formed PS derivations, we can regard them as stating 'node-admissibility conditions' on pre-lexical PMs. That is, we dispense with PS derivations, ordered sequences of strings of symbols, and interpret a rule like 'S → NP VP' as admitting as part of a well-formed pre-lexical PM a subtree in which S immediately dominates NP as left daughter and VP as right daughter. A pre-lexical PM is then admitted as the first PM in a well-formed transformational derivation if and only if every subtree in it is sanctioned by a PS rule in this way. This revised conception of PS rules, proposed in McCawley 1968*a*, overcomes a problem created by a certain type of recursive rule. Consider the 'NP → NP S' rule that we need for the deep structure of restrictive relative constructions (*cf* 7.3). **Interpreted as a rewrite rule, it admits [13] as part of a well-formed PS** derivation; interpreted as a node-admissibility condition, it directly admits [14] as part of a well-formed pre-lexical PM.

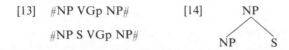

[13]   #NP VGp NP#   [14]   NP

       #NP S VGp NP#   NP   S

The trouble with [13] is that it does not correspond to a unique subtree, for the procedure of Chapter 3 does not enable us to determine whether S should be joined to NP or to VGp: this information is given in the PS rule but not in the PS derivation, and we can consequently avoid indeterminacy in such cases only by relating the PM directly to the PS rules, as in McCawley's interpretation of the latter.

Let us now consider transformational rules in terms of the notions of extrinsic and intrinsic ordering. Here the situation is different, for this time we can show the need for the extra apparatus provided by extrinsic ordering. There are a number of cases in the rules considered in earlier chapters where we have relied crucially on such ordering to prevent the generation of unwanted surface structures. I shall give three examples:

(a) Affix Hopping and *Do* Support (as given on *pp* 74 and 78). Suppose the base rules generate the terminal string '*they Pres will see Mary*'. This satisfies the structure index for *Do* Support, but clearly the rule must not be allowed to apply or else the grammar will generate the deviant sentence **They do will see Mary*. We prevented this derivation by extrinsically ordering *Do* Support after Affix Hopping. The above string thus first undergoes Affix Hopping, to become '*they will Pres see Mary*'; this now does not satisfy the index for *Do* Support and consequently no *do* is inserted.

(b) Reflexivization and *You* Deletion. Given a structure terminating in a string like '*Imp you$_i$ wash you$_i$*' we must use extrinsic ordering to ensure that Reflexivization applies before *You* Deletion, for if the latter applied first the conditions for the former would not be met (there would not be a pair of identical NPs), and we would thus end up with the deviant sentence **Wash you!* If there were no extrinsic ordering, so that a transformation could apply at any stage in a derivation when its index was met, the grammar would generate both *Wash yourself* and *Wash you*. Extrinsically ordering Reflexivization before *You* Deletion has the effect of excluding from the set of well-formed derivations any sequence of PMs where *You* Deletion applies first, and consequently there will be no derivation for **Wash you*.

(c) Passivization and Subject-Verb Agreement. As I emphasized in discussing Subject-Verb Agreement on *p* 168, the NP that determines the person and number of the verb is not the deep subject but the subject at a fairly late stage in the derivation, witness examples like *John was/*were arrested by the police*, *The police were/*was criticized by John*. Although I have not given an explicit formulation of the Agreement rule, it seems clear that its index will be satisfied by the deep structure of the above sentences and that we shall therefore need some way of preventing the rule from applying until after Passivization has interchanged the subject and object NPs: extrinsically ordering it after Passivization does precisely this.

The rules introduced earlier also involve a good deal of intrinsic ordering. Two examples will suffice:

(d) Passivization and Inversion. The main steps in the derivation of *Why was John arrested by the police?* will be essentially as follows:

[15] i   *Q the police Past arrest John why.*   [by Base rules]
     ii *Q John Past be en arrest by the police why.*   [by Passivization]
     iii *Q Past be John en arrest by the police why.*   [by Inversion]
     iv *Q why Past be John en arrest by the police.*   [by *Wh-Q* Fronting]

Affix Hopping (applied twice) and *Q* Deletion then yield '*why be Past John arrest en by the police*' – I ignore syntactic features, the analysis of *why* and other non-pertinent factors. Now the deep structure PM, terminating in [i], satisfies the index for Inversion as well as for Passivization. Suppose we apply Inversion directly to [i]: the result will be '*Q Past the police arrest John why*'. This, however, does not satisfy the index for Passivization given on *p* 73, for there is no longer an Aux between the NP and the V. Accordingly Passivization cannot apply, and the endpoint of the transformational derivation will be the active '*why do Past the police arrest John*'. It follows from the way we have formulated the rules, then, that the only way of generating *Why was John arrested by the police?* is for Passivization to apply before Inversion. It is important to see that the ordering here is intrinsic, and different from that in (a)–(c). Extrinsic ordering is used to block certain unwanted derivations that would be generated if the rules were allowed to apply freely, *ie* at any stage when their structure index was satisfied. But there is no question of needing to block derivations in the present example, no question of having to add special conditions on the application of transformations beyond those expressed in their structure indices.

(e) Passivization and *You* Deletion. A somewhat different type of case emerges in the derivation of a sentence like *Don't be caught by the police!*. In deep structure the *you* that is understood here will be object, not subject. This means that the deep structure will not satisfy the index for *You* Deletion, namely '*Imp — you — VP*'. Only after Passivization has moved *you* into subject position can

You Deletion apply. Thus the ordering Passivization then *You* Deletion follows from the way the rules are formulated: we do not need extrinsic ordering here because the correct order of application is guaranteed by the structure indices of the rules.

However, cases like (a)–(c) do provide convincing evidence for having some extrinsic ordering in the transformational component. Certainly in (b) and (c) it seems impossible that any viable reformulation of the relevant rules could eliminate the need for extrinsic ordering. It is inconceivable, for example, that the Agreement rule might fail to refer crucially to the NP in subject position, and since this position can be occupied by different NPs at different stages in a derivation we cannot pick the right one by means of the structure index of the rule: we need the extra device of being able to determine extrinsically the stage in the derivation at which the rule applies.

Let us suppose there is total extrinsic ordering of the transformations. The rules will then be numbered consecutively and within a single cycle all applications of a given rule will precede all applications of all rules with a higher number. Ignoring the qualifications needed to deal with the cyclic principle, we can add to the three given in 12.1, the following two conditions that a sequence of PMs must satisfy in order to qualify as a transformational derivation:

IV: If the pairs $PM_i - PM_{i+1}$ and $PM_j - PM_{j+1}$, where i is less than j, are admitted according to condition (I) by transformations T_a and T_b respectively, the sequence is not accepted as a well-formed derivation if T_a has a higher number than T_b. (This formulation allows for the case where T_a and T_b are the same, and thus for successive applications of a rule like Affix Hopping.) It is in terms of condition (IV) that we will block *They do will see Mary*, with $T_a = Do$ Support and $T_b = $ Affix Hopping, or *John were arrested by the police*, with $T_a = $ Subject-Verb Agreement and $T_b = $ Passivization.

V: If the pair $PM_i - PM_{i+1}$ is admitted according to condition (I) by transformation T_a, the sequence is not accepted as a well-formed derivation if PM_i satisfies the index of an obligatory transformation T_b which has a lower number than T_a. This condition blocks sequences like that corresponding to *Wash you*, where *You* Deletion has applied to yield a structure that does not satisfy the index for Reflexivization ($= T_b$).

This assumption of total extrinsic ordering was adopted in probably all the work done in the first ten years or so of transformational grammar, and in much of the more recent work too. It should be borne in mind, however, that the assumption goes beyond what is directly justified by evidence of the kind presented in (a)–(c) above. The fact that there are cases where extrinsic ordering must be invoked to block unwanted derivations does not establish that there must be TOTAL extrinsic ordering. This has been used as an argument for restricting in various ways the role of extrinsic ordering in the grammar.

Examination of these proposals falls outside the scope of an introductory text, however, and here I shall simply leave open the choice between total and partial ordering of the syntactic transformations.

12.3 The transformational cycle

I stated in 7.1 that the transformations apply cyclically, beginning with the most deeply embedded S in the tree and working progressively upwards until the root S is reached. If S_j is dominated by S_i, then the transformations apply in turn to the part of the tree dominated by S_j before they apply to the part of the tree dominated by S_i. We are now in a position to present arguments in support of this claim.

One classic form of argument is to find a pair of Transformations T_a and T_b such that in one derivation T_a must apply before T_b and in another T_b must apply before T_a: it is then shown that the cyclic principle allows this to be reconciled with a fixed extrinsic ordering of the rules. An example is provided by the rules Subject Raising and Reflexivization applying in the derivations of [16] and [17], whose deep structures are given in [18] and [19].

[16] *Mary believed herself to be ill*
[17] *John believed Mary to be deceiving herself*

A crucial condition for Reflexivization, as noted on *p* 123, is that the two identical NPs be clause-mates at the stage in the derivation when the rule applies. In [18] the two *Mary*'s, NP_1 and NP_2, are in different clauses; thus before Reflexivization can apply, Raising must move NP_2 into S_1, to make it a clause-mate of NP_1. In [19], on the other hand, NP_1 and NP_2 are clause-mates to start with, but cease to be when Raising moves NP_1 into S_1; Reflexivization must therefore apply before this movement takes place. Thus in the derivation of [16], Raising

[18]

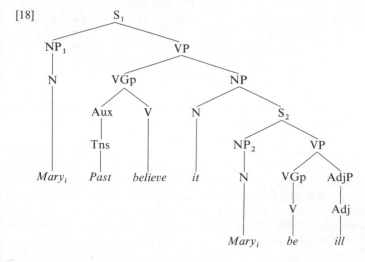

[19]

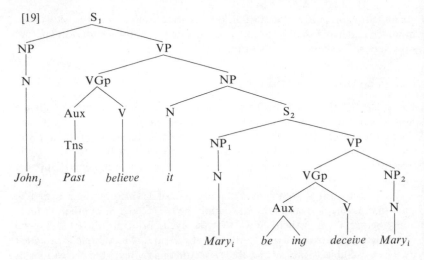

must precede Reflexivization, and in the derivation of [17] Reflexivization must precede Raising. The cyclic principle makes this compatible with an extrinsic ordering of the rules. In [16] both rules clearly apply on the same cycle, that of S_1, establishing that Raising is ordered before Reflexivization; the fact that in [17] Reflexivization applies on the earlier S_2 cycle then explains why in this derivation it applies before Raising.

A second form of argument is to find a derivation involving two applications of a rule T_a that must be separated by an occurrence of a different rule T_b: again the cyclic principle reconciles such a situation with an extrinsic ordering of the rules. An example is the derivation of [20]: its deep structure is essentially [22] and the crucial ordering of rules is given in [21].

[20] *Mary didn't want to appear to be trying to influence the boss*

[21] i Equi applies to S_3, deleting *Mary* (NP_4)
    ii Raising applies to S_2, making *Mary* (NP_3) subject of S_2
    iii Equi applies to S_1, deleting *Mary* (NP_3)

[i] deletes NP_4 under identity with NP_3 and thus must precede [ii], whose effect is to move NP_3 out of S_2: if [ii] applied first we would get '*Mary$_i$ appears be ing try it Mary$_i$ influence the boss*' which does not satisfy the index for Equi (see p 112), so that [i] would be blocked. Similarly [ii] must precede [iii] because Equi can only delete the subject of S_2 if it is identical to NP_1, *Mary*, and S_2 has *Mary* as subject only when Raising has applied to it. The example establishes, therefore, that it is not possible for all applications of Equi to precede all applications of Raising, or vice versa. And the cyclic principle defines precisely the conditions under which the application of one rule must occur between two applications of another rule.

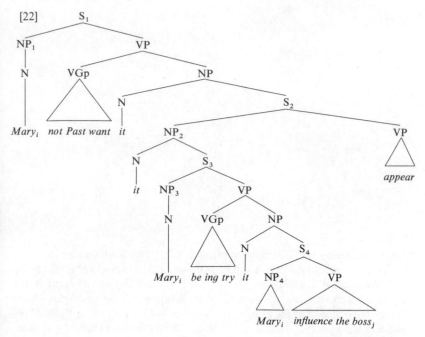

There are, however, certain phenomena that cannot be handled under the assumption that the cyclic principle regulates the application of all transformations. Consider, for example, the Inversion rule that applies in the derivation of certain interrogative clauses. We have to account for the fact that non-embedded interrogatives may undergo the rule, while embedded ones may not. Thus we have to derive [23] and [24], but not [25].

[23] *What can you say?*
[24] *I don't know what you can say*
[25] **I don't know what can you say*

Simplified deep structures for [23] and [24] are as follows:

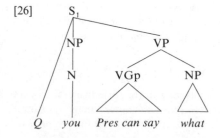

[27]

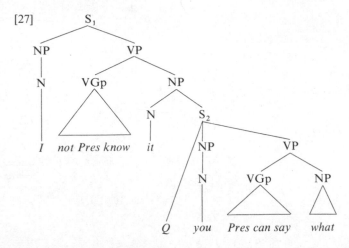

Now let us assume that Inversion applies cyclically like Reflexivization, Equi, Raising, etc. Then in the derivation of [23] from [26] it would apply on the S_1 cycle: [26] contains only one S node, so that there will be just one cycle. But if we formulate the rule in such a way that it can apply on the S_1 cycle in [26] it will clearly be able to apply also on the S_2 cycle in [27], given that S_2 of [27] is identical with S_1 of [26] (this identity follows from the arguments of 9.2). And if Inversion applies to S_2 in [27] we generate the deviant sentence [25]: we therefore reject our assumption that Inversion applies cyclically. The argument thus involves the following steps: (a) The applicability of Inversion to a clause is not fully determined by the internal structure of the clause. (b) It accordingly cannot apply during the cycle of the interrogative clause itself, for this cycle deals with just that part of the tree dominated by the interrogative S. (c) It cannot apply on the next cycle after that of the interrogative S because there may not be one. (d) The conclusion is, then, that Inversion cannot be handled in the transformational cycle.

To deal with this kind of problem it has been proposed that in addition to the cyclic rules, which apply in the way I have described, there should be a set of 'post-cyclic' rules which apply after the completion of the cycle for the topmost S: Inversion would then belong to this set. I shall not develop this notion here, however, nor various other restrictions on the cyclic principle that have been proposed. It must be emphasized that there is a great deal of uncertainty at present regarding the general principles governing the order of application of transformations, not to mention the specific ordering of individual rules.

12.4 Derived constituent structure

In this section I want to consider certain aspects of the formalism for transformational rules that have been glossed over in earlier chapters. In many examples I have saved space by giving transformational derivations in the form of a sequence of terminal strings rather than as a sequence of PMs, but it is essential for an understanding of the theory to bear in mind that transformations relate pairs of PMs, not simply pairs of morpheme-strings. The reason for saying that transformations operate on full PMs not morpheme-strings is evident from examples like

[28] *John Past see Mary*
[29] *The boss Pres may have en find the letter*
[30] *John Past be angry*

Passivization can apply to [28] and [29], although they have no morpheme in common, but cannot apply to [30] although this is more like [28] than is [29] in terms of the morphemes it contains. Clearly, then, the applicability of the rule is determined by the tree structure – transformations are, in Chomsky's phrase, 'structure-dependent'.

We have seen that a transformation contains a structure index and a structure change. The former defines the conditions that must be satisfied by a PM if it is to qualify as input to the rule. The latter specifies the DERIVED CONSTITUENT STRUCTURE, the form of the output PM. The formalism for the index is based on the notion of analysability discussed in 5.2, and I need not here add to that account: my concern will be with the structure change.

The change effected by a rule involves one or more ELEMENTARY TRANS-FORMATIONAL OPERATIONS. These are of three main types: deletion, substitution and adjunction. Let us look at them in turn.

(a) DELETION
Here part of the input tree structure is simply missing in the output PM. A rule involving just one such operation is *You* Deletion, [31]; its effect is illustrated in [32], the structure for *Close the door!*.

[31] *Imp — you — VP*
$$\begin{array}{ccc} 1 & 2 & 3 \Rightarrow \\ 1 & \varnothing & 3 \end{array}$$

[32]

[32] gives the input PM; the broken-line boxes show how it is analysed in terms of the index of [31]. The $\varnothing$ indicates that box 2 is empty in the output PM. Notice, however, that if only box 2 were deleted, we should have an ill-formed PM, one containing a category symbol (N) in a terminal position: thus the circled nodes in [32] must also be deleted. The general convention for determining the derived constituent structure resulting from deletion stipulates, therefore, that the operation delete not only the part of the tree identified in the rule

itself, but also any category symbols that would otherwise appear in the terminal string.

(b) SUBSTITUTION

The Raising rule, as formulated earlier and repeated here, involves one operation of substitution and one of deletion.

[33] X — [$_{NP}$ *it*]$_{NP}$ — (VGp) — [$_S$ NP — Y]$_S$ — Z
　　　1　　　2　　　　3　　　4　　5　　6 ⇒
　　　1　　　4　　　　3　　　∅　　5　　6

[34]

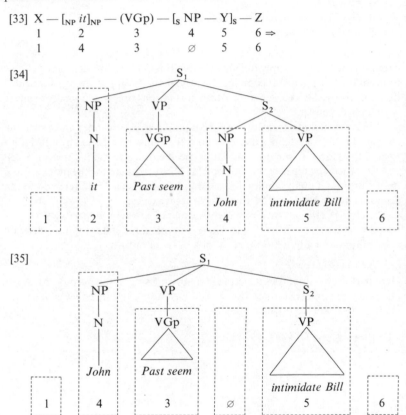

[35]

[34] and [35] give the input and output PMs in the derivation of *John seemed to intimidate Bill* (see p 113). As always, the numbered terms are identified by reference to the input. The position occupied by box 2 in [34] is occupied in [35] by box 4: this difference is effected by the substitution operation and is expressed in the rule by writing 4 beneath 2. The position occupied by box 4 in [34] is empty in [35]: this difference is effected by the deletion operation and is expressed as before by writing ∅ beneath 4. A rule involving substitution alone is Pronominalization, as when the *it* of *I was told that John wrote the book but I don't believe it* is substituted for the underlying repeated sentence *that John wrote the book*.

(c) ADJUNCTION

There are two subtypes of this operation known as SISTER-ADJUNCTION and CHOMSKY-ADJUNCTION. The Inversion rule involves one operation of sister-adjunction and one of deletion. Omitting various alternatives allowed in the structure index (see *p* 78 for the full rule), [36] relates PMs [37] and [38] in the derivation of *Have you seen John?*.

[36] Q — NP — Tns *have* — X
     1   2   3   4 ⇒
   1+3 2   ∅   4

[37]

[38]

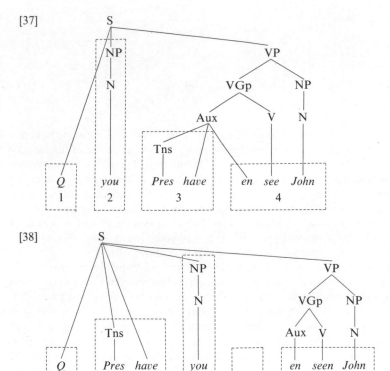

Term 3 is sister-adjoined to the right of term 1: in [38] Tns and *have* occur as right sisters to Q – this is expressed in the rule by means of the plus symbol. The position occupied by term 3 in [37] is empty in [38], and this is expressed in the familiar way by the ∅ symbol.

Chomsky-adjunction and deletion are involved in the Affix Hopping rule. As in [36] I omit alternatives irrelevant to the illustrative example, the derivation of *John vexes Mary*:

[39] X — Tns — V — Y
        1   2   3   4 ⇒
        1   ∅   3#2 4

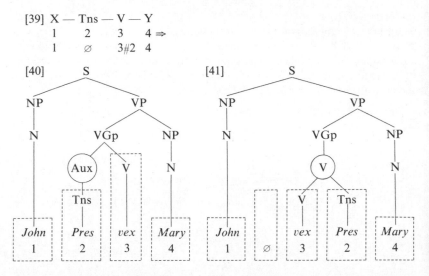

Here the Tns element is Chomsky-adjoined to the right of term 3 of the structure index: this operation is symbolized by # (clearly a different use of this symbol from that where it marks a sentence boundary). The effect of Chomsky-adjunction is to create a new node dominating the adjoined terms and having the same label as the term to which the shifted element is adjoined: this new node is the circled V in [41]. The position occupied in [40] by term 2 is empty in [41], as indicated in the rule by the deletion symbol. Note that the circled Aux node of [40] is also missing from [41]: this is in accordance with the convention for deleting terminal category symbols, mentioned above.

The main motivation for adopting Chomsky-adjunction in the present example is that the verb plus its various affixes behaves like a verb as far as the phonology is concerned – the rules for the assignment of stress will not work satisfactorily unless *vexes* has the constituent structure shown in [41]. The argument here depends on the segmentation of verbs like *vexes* into two morphemes, which I suggested in 11.2 was not necessarily correct; however, there are other examples where Chomsky-adjunction is needed, as in the generation of subtrees like [19–21] on *p* 99, or in such rules as Topicalization, which will be discussed in 15.2.

Adjunction may be to the right, as in [36] and [39], or to the left; an example of the latter is the rule introducing the infinitival complementizer *to*, which is Chomsky-adjoined to the left of the VGp.

Over the years the set of elementary transformational operations has been modified in various ways. Early work had recognized a special operation of permutation, interchanging the position of two adjacent terms: such interchanges are now handled by a combination of adjunction and deletion, as in [36]. Chomsky-adjunction was not introduced until 1966, and earlier work tended to allow daughter as well as sister-adjunction, though without systematic differences of notation. (Daughter-adjunction is illustrated in the pair [13i] and [ii] on *p* 51: one respect in which [i] differs from [ii] is that *be* and *en* have been adjoined as daughters to Aux – compare the Chomsky-adjunction treatment of this below.) There are considerable problems still outstanding concerning this matter, and the general principles underlying the formalization of transformations. One problem worth mentioning here concerns the effect of introducing new morphemes into a tree by substitution or adjunction (note that my examples [33], [36], [39] all involve the movement of elements already present in the input PM, not the introduction of new morphemes). The classic example is Passivization:

[42] $\quad$ X — NP — Aux $\quad$ — $\quad$ V $\quad$ — $\quad$ NP — Y
$\qquad$ 1 $\quad$ 2 $\qquad$ 3 $\qquad\qquad$ 4 $\qquad\qquad$ 5 $\qquad$ 6 ⇒
$\qquad$ 1 $\quad$ 5 $\qquad$ 3#*be en* $\quad$ 4 $\quad$ *by*+2 $\qquad$ 6

According to the principles I have given, this would convert [43] into [44].

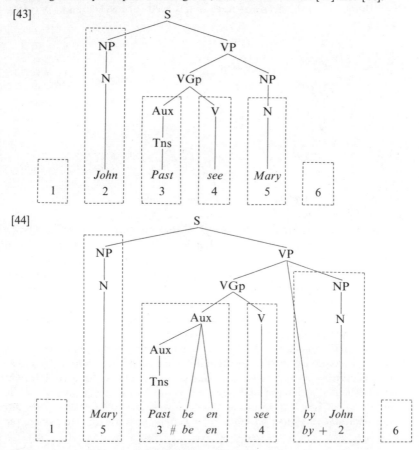

[43]

[44]

Term 5 has been substituted for term 2, and vice versa; *be* and *en* have been Chomsky-adjoined to the right of term 3, *by* sister-adjoined to the left of term 2. Yet [44] is surely not the derived constituent structure we want: it fails to show that *by John* is a constituent (of any kind, let alone a PP). Our strong intuition that it should be one is borne out by constructions like *It was by John that Mary was seen*, for note that corresponding to *She laid by some money*, where *by some money* does not form a constituent, there is no **It was by some money that she laid*. There are various ways in which this deficiency might be overcome. One would be to write '[$_{PP}$[$_{Prep}$ *by*]$_{Prep}$ 2]$_{PP}$' instead of simply '*by*+2' in [42]; other proposals will be found in the works referred to in the notes: I shall leave the matter open at this point but will comment further in Chapter 13 on the kind of issue involved here.

12.5 Surface structure constraints

The apparatus we have introduced will allow the base rules to generate PMs which do not form the deep structure of any well-formed sentence. A typical example is

[45]

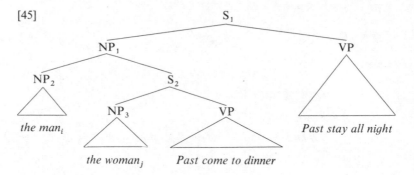

NP$_1$ is expanded by the rule 'NP → NP S' that introduces restrictive relative clauses (see 7.2), and if the NP$_3$ position were occupied by *the man$_i$* we would have the deep structure for *The man who came to dinner stayed all night*. But the rules that generate S$_2$ are not sensitive to the context in which S$_2$ occurs, and therefore there is no way to guarantee that S$_2$ will dominate a NP that is identical with NP$_2$.

Extending the power of the base rules so that they could exclude structures like [45] would involve an enormous increase in their complexity. One reason why this is so is that in a well-formed relative construction the relative pronouns may derive from NPs occupying indefinitely many different positions in underlying structure. This is because the relativized NP may be in a complement clause embedded within the relative clause, without there being any limit to the depth of embedding. For example, the deep structure of *They sacked the girl whom John said that Mary had told Peter to appoint* is roughly [46], where the first occurrence of *the girl* (the antecedent) is in S_1 and the second (the one that is relativized) is in S_4.

[46]

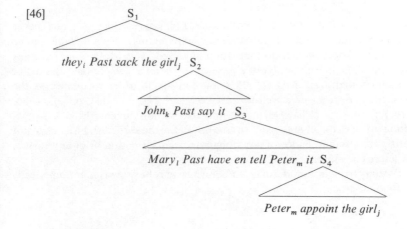

The situation here is closely analogous to that discussed in 9.2, where we saw that the *wh* phrase associated with an interrogative clause may also be embedded indefinitely deeply within it. To have the base rules generate the above while excluding one with *Peter appoint the boy* as S_4 would require a massive revision of the formalism for lexical insertion.

Instead Chomsky proposed that the base rules should continue to develop each S independently of its context and that derivations containing PMs like [45] should be blocked at the level of surface structure. This can be achieved quite simply. Each S will be flanked by a pair of boundary symbols: #S# is the given initial line for PS derivations, and the rules introducing S will introduce # too – we merely revise the 'NP → NP S' rule to read 'NP → NP #S#'. We then write the Relativization rule in such a way that it deletes the boundary symbols flanking the relative clause. Thus instead of the structure index given as [27] on *p* 102, we will have, essentially:

[47] W — [$_{NP}$ NP — # — X — NP — Y — #]$_{NP}$ — Z
    1   2   3   4   5   6   7   8
    Condition $2 = 5$

The rule will substitute a relative pronoun for term 5, adjoin it as left-sister to term 4, and delete terms 3 and 7. PM [45] (amended to include #) does not satisfy this index because of the lack of identity between terms 2 and 5. Consequently the boundary symbols flanking S_2 will remain throughout the derivation. We then stipulate that no PM containing an internal occurrence of # qualifies as a well-formed surface structure.

This stipulation is a SURFACE STRUCTURE CONSTRAINT, a condition on the well-formedness of surface structures. It can be stated by using a structure index:

[48] $\#X - \# - Y\#$

No sequence of PMs, $PM_1, \ldots, PM_n$, where PM_n satisfies this index, qualifies as a transformational derivation. Notice that [48] contains a structure index but no structure change: there is no 'operation' involved. This fits in quite naturally with our static interpretation of a generative grammar, where the rules define conditions that a sequence of PMs must satisfy in order to qualify as the syntactic derivation of a well-formed sentence. The introduction of surface structure constraints like [48] means only that we must amend the general condition (II) given on p 174 to read: (II) the last PM in the sequence, PM_n, must not satisfy the structure index of any obligatory transformation or of any surface structure constraint.

We thus arrive at a model of grammar which may be shown diagrammatically as follows:

[49]

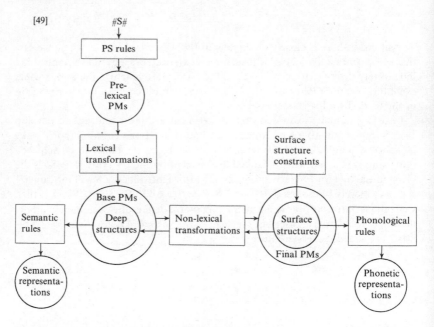

The base rules (*ie* the PS rules plus the lexical transformations) define a set of base PMs, which are mapped by the syntactic transformations on to a set of final derived PMs. The surface structure constraints admit a subset of these as surface structures. The deep structures are then defined as the subset of base PMs that are transformationally linked with the surface structures. Thus [45], for example, belongs to the set of base PMs, but not to that subset of them that qualify as deep structures, since it is not transformable into a well-formed surface structure. The non-lexical transformations accordingly have two major functions: (a) They map the base PMs on to the final derived PMs (this is shown in [49] by the left-to-right path through the transformations); (b) They define the deep structures as those base PMs which map on to well-formed surface structures (the right-to-left path). Chomsky uses the metaphor of a 'filter' for this latter function: only a subset of the base PMs are transformed into surface structures, the remainder being 'filtered out'. This filtering function reinforces the need for the static, 'bi-directional' interpretation of transformations emphasized in 12.1. Deep structures are not definable by the base rules alone, just as surface structures are not definable by surface structure constraints alone: the grammar defines the set of PM sequences that constitute transformational derivations, and deep and surface structures are then defined in terms of these derivations. There is no question of the deep structures 'coming first' in any temporal or logical sense. In Chapter 4 we saw that it is not possible to define the well-formed surface structures directly by PS rules; transformational grammar defines them to a large extent indirectly by having base rules generate abstract structures which are transformed into derived structures, but the need for constraints like [48] shows that we cannot dispense altogether with rules that refer directly to surface structure.

Notes

The filtering function of transformations is introduced in Chomsky 1965:137–141, a passage which deals also with the 'static' interpretation of generative grammar; on the latter see also Chomsky 1970b and G. Lakoff 1971:232–3. The distinction between intrinsic and extrinsic ordering is defined in Chomsky 1965:223; in this work Chomsky takes the PS rules to be extrinsically ordered. Burt 1971 is very largely devoted to determining the ordering of a considerable number of transformations. Arguments against complete extrinsic ordering of transformations are given in Ringen 1972 and Koutsoudas 1972. On cyclic and non-cyclic rules see G. Lakoff 1966a, McCawley 1970, Postal 1972; the classical arguments for the cycle rely quite heavily on an assumption of total extrinsic ordering of transformations – for more recent discussion see Kimball 1972 (papers by Kimball, Grinder and G. Lakoff), Bach 1974:110–25. An early account of derived constituent structure can be found in Bach 1964:70–82 and a recent formal treatment in Kimball 1973:38–47; see also Ross's discussion of 'tree-pruning' (1967:24–64). The term 'Chomsky-adjunction' is introduced in Ross 1967:142 n12. 'Output condition' is an alternative term for 'surface structure constraint'. The example given in [48] is presumably universal; examples specific to particular languages can be found in Ross 1967, 1972, Perlmutter 1971.

If Affix Hopping is reformulated as effecting Chomsky-adjunction, appropriate category symbols will have to appear in the rule in place of *have* and *be*, for clearly we could not have a derived structure in which the latter appeared as non-terminal nodes; in general there are a number of fairly technical problems involved in adapting the original analysis of the auxiliary to the *Aspects* theory, but as I shall be proposing a radical reanalysis in Chapter 14 I shall not deal with these matters. On the problem of the derived constituent structure of passive sentences, see Chomsky 1957:73–4, 1965:103–6; in the latter he proposes to differentiate passives from actives in deep structure: *Mary was seen by John* is analysed as '*John Past see Mary by Passive*', where *Passive* is a purely abstract morpheme like *Q*, *Imp*, etc (except that it has no direct semantic interpretation). See R. Lakoff 1971 for a discussion of this and other suggested analyses of the passive.

Chapter 13

Universal Grammar

In the preceding chapters we have been developing a framework of theoretical concepts in terms of which we can account for a range of natural language data in an insightful and explanatory way. Although these concepts have been motivated and exemplified by reference to English, they are of much wider applicability: concepts like deep structure, transformation, syntactic feature are needed, it is claimed, in the description of any natural language. The central goal for the theory of generative grammar is to give a precise specification of the form that grammars of particular languages may take, to define the notion 'possible grammar'. This study of the conditions that must be satisfied by the grammar of any natural language Chomsky calls UNIVERSAL GRAMMAR.

The task of stating the conditions that a grammar must meet may be broken down into two subtasks. First, we must define the set of SUBSTANTIVE UNIVERSALS, the minimal primitive elements that may figure in the grammar – features like [Voiced] in phonology, categories like NP and V or features like [Human] in syntax, and so on. Secondly, we must specify how the substantive universals may combine in various types of rules, how the rules are organized into components, what principles govern the order of application of rules, and so on: these conditions are FORMAL UNIVERSALS. The *Aspects* theory claims as formal universals, for example, that the grammar is divided into the three major components, semantics, syntax and phonology, that the syntax is itself divided into a base, consisting of a set of PS rules and a lexicon, plus a (non-lexical) transformational subcomponent; that the PS rules can rewrite just one category symbol at a time and are context-free; that the transformations involve one or more of the elementary operations of Chomsky-adjunction, sister-adjunction, deletion and substitution, and operate according to the cyclic principle, and so on.

Progress in developing a theory of substantive universals clearly depends on providing a satisfactory basis for the identification of elements across the grammars of different languages: what grounds are there for identifying 'verb' in English with 'verb' in French, Urdu, Basque or whatever, for example? It is in the field of phonology that much the most progress has been made in answering questions of this kind. Features like [Voiced], [Stop], etc can be defined in articulatory (or, in some cases, acoustic or auditory) terms, independent of any particular language, so that there is no problem in identifying [Stop] in one language with [Stop] in another. A great deal of work has been devoted to defining a suitable set of such features for use in the phonological description of a wide range of languages. It is claimed (in the theory of phonology associated with TG) that the features figuring in the abstract underlying phonological representations are drawn from the same set as those in the systematic phonetic representations, so that all phonological features are ultimately definable in universal phonetic terms.

As for semantics, plausible candidates for the status of substantive universals might be such concepts as 'Human', 'Physical Object', and so on, but so little is known about the nature of semantic representations that it would be inappropriate to pursue the matter here. One point that is nevertheless worth emphasizing is that the semantic universals are likely to be highly abstract: in particular we shall not find complete identity between the meanings of sentences in different languages. For example, there is no sentence in French that has exactly the same meaning as English *I saw my cousin this morning:* in French it would be necessary to specify the sex of the cousin (*mon cousin* if male, *ma cousine* if female), and conversely French does not express the semantic contrast between *I saw* and *I have seen*, and so on. Languages are often spoken of as 'codes', but one must bear in mind that the 'messages' are not independent of the language: the rules of the grammar not only relate the messages to their corresponding signals, they also define the set of well-formed messages in the language.

As far as syntax is concerned, the theory of substantive universals will need to give universal definitions for the categories NP, V, etc, and for those features that are either inherent (in the sense of Chapter 10), such as [Animate], [Stative], [Person] (in pronouns), or are introduced by non-lexical transformation, such as [Case] – we shall see below that contextual features and rule features are specified in the theory of formal universals. It seems that the definitions of the substantive universals will need to be of two kinds: some will be based on the role the element plays in the syntactic rules and the structures they generate, others on the meaning associated with the element. Consider, for example, the deep structures generated for simple sentences by PS rules of the kind we have proposed. These structures will contain a single occurrence of VGp and from one to perhaps four occurrences of NP, as in the underlying PMs for *John died* (one NP), *John saw Bill* (two), *John gave the book to Bill* (three), *John sold the car to Bill for £100* (four). This kind of pattern will doubtless be found in all languages: the category occurring just once can then be identified as VGp and the category from one to, say, four occurrences as NP. (In Chapter 14 I shall be calling in question the validity of the VGp category: if it is discarded, what has just been said will need to be reformulated with V substituted for VGp.) It might then be possible to define N by reference to the structure of NP. For example, if the PS rule expanding NP is of the form 'NP → (A)B(C)', with a single obligatory element and various optional ones on the right, then we could define N as the one obligatory element. An alternative approach to the definition of noun (for it is very questionable whether the NP rule will always be of the above form) is to invoke semantic criteria and to define noun as the word-class containing among its most basic members (*ie* those consisting of a single morpheme) words denoting physical objects. And certainly in the case of inherent features like [Animate], [Stative], [Person] it would seem clear that there could be no way of identifying them across different languages that did not appeal to meaning.

There are two important points to be made in clarification of the theory of substantive universals. Firstly, the universal definitions of syntactic categories and features do not provide criteria for determining whether any arbitrary expression in a language belongs to a certain category or has a certain feature: what they provide is a basis for identifying elements across languages. In my discussion of the independence of syntax in 2.1 I took the category noun as an example, arguing that it was a class of words grouped together on the basis of shared distributional rather than semantic properties – in particular, that many nouns (*arrival, insanity,* and the like) do not denote physical objects. This argument is not in dispute – the present proposal is to use the criterion of denoting physical objects not as a condition for assigning a word to the class noun but as a condition for assigning the label 'noun' to one of the major distributional classes in a language. There is then no need to insist that the definition is valid only if every member of the class denotes a physical object: the point is that monomorphemic words in English denoting objects do belong in the same major distributional class, a different one from those denoting actions, etc, and the same holds in French, German, and so on, and this therefore provides a principled basis for using the same category in the grammars of these different languages. My discussion in 5.2 of the use of the non-primitive terms voice, tense, aspect and mood should be interpreted along similar lines. Or take the example of gender in a language like French. We divide French nouns into two subclasses to account for inflectional differences in modifying determiners and adjectives, as in *mon vieux père* ('my old father') versus *ma vieille mère* ('my old mother') : the choice between *mon* and *ma, vieux* and *vieille* is determined by the gender of *père* and *mère.* (In English, of course, determiners and adjectives are not inflected for gender and I shall in fact be arguing in Chapter 16 that there is no syntactic gender at all in English.) *Mon* and *vieux* are traditionally said to agree in gender with the noun *père* that they modify: this account could be formalized by assigning inherent gender features to nouns and having an agreement transformation that copies them into determiners and adjectives. Now French nouns denoting male humans or animals typically belong to a different gender class from those denoting females, and this provides the basis for assigning them the features [Masculine Gender] and [Feminine Gender] respectively and identifying these features with those figuring in the grammars of, say, German or Latin, even though these languages differ from French in having a third gender, neuter. But there are many masculine and feminine nouns in French (and likewise in German, Latin, etc) which do not denote males and females respectively, so that the definition of [Masculine Gender] in universal grammar does not enable us to predict that French *livre* ('book') is masculine:

this has to be stated as an idiosyncratic property of *livre* in the lexicon of French grammar. There is obviously no one-to-one correlation in these languages between the syntactic property of gender and the semantic property of sex, so that it is not possible in general to predict the former from the latter – but this does not mean that there is no significant correlation at all. There are in fact languages where gender and sex bear no significant correlation; in such cases however, we shall not use the feature-values [Masculine Gender], [Feminine Gender], but terms based on whatever semantic properties the system does correlate with (*eg* shape, size).

This brings me to my second general point concerning substantive universals. There is a stronger and weaker sense in which we might claim that an element is universal. In the strong sense, an element is universal if it figures in the grammar of every language – it seems very likely that the categories S, NP and V will be universals of this kind. In the weaker but nonetheless important sense, an element is universal if it is definable in general linguistic theory, *ie* independently of its occurrence in any particular language. It is in this sense that [Masculine Gender] and many other elements (including noun, perhaps) are universal. It would be a mistake to admit only the strong kind of universal: the fact that an element does not figure in every grammar does not mean that it is completely idiosyncratic to a single language.

Early work in structural linguistics, especially in America perhaps, tended to stress the differences between languages rather than their likenesses. Linguists working on Amerindian languages, for example, were struck by the enormous differences between them and the familiar Indo-European languages and by the futility of trying to describe them in terms of the standard inflectional paradigms of Latin or Greek. They insisted on the principle that each language should be 'described in its own terms', a principle enunciated as a corrective to what was seen as the tendency of traditional grammar to force one language into the mould of another, to transfer grammatical categories from Latin, say, to languages to which they are not appropriate. An often-quoted example of this practice is the postulation in many traditional grammars of English of distinct dative and accusative cases in the noun paradigm. We have seen (*p* 166) that Latin nouns are inflected for case; the case in which a noun appears in a given sentence is determined in part by its function in the clause (nominative case being associated with 'grammatical' subject or predicative function, accusative with direct object, dative with indirect object, etc) in part by idiosyncratic properties of the 'governing' verb or preposition (*ūtī* 'to use' takes an object in the ablative, *meminisse* 'to remember' in the genitive, *nocēre* 'to harm' in the dative; the verb *ūtī* is traditionally said to 'govern' the ablative, and so on: the transformationalist's concept of rule government involves a generalization from this usage). Now it is important to distinguish between the concepts of grammatical function and case inflection. In *John gave Mary money*, for example, *John*, *Mary* and *money* differ in grammatical function but not in case inflection. As far as case inflection is concerned, Modern English has only a distinction between genitive *John's* and non-genitive *John*, except in personal pronouns where nominative *I* contrasts with accusative *me;* nevertheless one finds many traditional grammars where *Mary* in the above is analysed as dative, *money* as accusative. This could be defended if cases were defined as grammatical functions rather than inflections (*cf* 15.3), but then it will not do to say that *John* is in the same case, nominative, in *John died* and *I am John*, which is what the grammars in question do say. Similar examples can be found in the English verb paradigm, where a future tense is often set up alongside present and past; where *I be* and *I were* are classified as present and past subjunctive, though the relationship between them is quite different from that between present and past indicative *I am* and *I was* (*cf p* 80); where six distinct person-number forms are recognized in each tense-mood combination, *eg* present subjunctive (*I*) *be*, (*you*) *be*, (*he*) *be*, (*we*) *be*, (*you*) *be*, (*they*) *be*, although in English (unlike Latin, say), person is relevant to the form of the verb only in the singular of the indicative; and so on. Traditional grammars vary in the extent to which they fall into this kind of error, but it was certainly prevalent enough to warrant the criticisms of structural linguists. If the principle that a language should be described in its own terms means simply that we should avoid such errors, it is clearly valid and important. But it was often interpreted to mean more than this – that the descriptive categories used in the grammar of a given language should be defined uniquely for that language, with only a handful of the most abstract concepts (such as phoneme, morpheme, construction and the like) being defined in general linguistic theory. In this view, the practice of using the same terms (*eg* noun, past tense, etc) in the grammars of different languages – a practice more or less invariably adopted – would be simply a matter of mnemonic convenience, having no systematic import or theoretical backing. It is the task of a theory of substantive universals to go beyond this, to provide a sound theoretical basis for the cross-linguistic identification of grammatical terms.

I have said that the theory of universal grammar specifies the conditions that individual grammars must meet; in so doing it can be thought of as defining a class of languages – the class consisting of all languages that can be generated by a grammar meeting those conditions. 'Language' here is to be understood in a technical sense: a language is the set of formal derivations generated by a grammar. For example, the grammar consisting of the PS rules 'S → AB', 'A → {*c, d*}', 'B → {*e, f*}', generates a language in this sense (one containing just four derivations), and so do the various grammars presented in Chapters 3 and 5. We will speak of such a language as an actual natural language if the grammar generating it provides a description meeting conditions of external and internal adequacy of some language in the everyday or pre-theoretical sense of the term. Now in elaborating his theory of universal grammar the linguist must aim to ensure that the class of languages it defines both contains all natural languages (task I) and excludes everything which is not a 'possible' natural language (task II). In a much-quoted remark that expresses the structuralists' emphasis on the diversity of languages in its most extreme form, Martin Joos spoke of the 'American (Boas) tradition that [natural] languages could differ without limit and in unpredictable ways' (1957:96). If interpreted literally, this would be to claim that there are no constraints on what is a possible natural language – which is clearly false. We can be quite confident we shall never come across a natural language where a positive sentence and the corresponding negative are the mirror image of each other (*ie* contain the same elements but in reverse order), or where the linear order of morphemes in every sentence is determined by their length, with the shortest morpheme first and the longest last, and so on – and a satisfactory theory of universal grammar must accordingly exclude such languages from the class it defines.

In this book we have been primarily concerned with task I, or rather one special case of it, that of trying to get the class of languages defined by the theory to contain English. We began our investigation of formal models of grammar by considering one with a minimum of formal apparatus, a context-free PSG. We saw, however, that English was not among the languages generable by such a grammar and accordingly elaborated the model to allow for context-sensitive rules, thereby extending the class of languages defined by the general theory. Then in Chapter 4 we showed that English was still not included within this wider class, and this led us to add transformations to the formal apparatus made available by the general theory for use in particular grammars; and we continued in this way in subsequent chapters, adding progressively more and more apparatus – syntactic features, complex symbols, surface structure constraints, and so on. But if the theory is to provide a real understanding of the nature of human language, it cannot neglect task II, and in recent years generative grammarians have given a good deal more attention to the problem of constraining as tightly as is consistent with achieving task I the class of languages defined by the theory. Development of a theory of substantive universals is clearly a move in this direction: if individual grammars have to draw their primitive symbols from a stock defined in universal grammar, the class of possible languages will be much more highly constrained than if each grammar can use an arbitrary and ad hoc set of primitives, unrelated to those in other grammars. But we need to elaborate the theory of formal universals too.

The 'unnatural' languages mentioned above – one with positives and negatives as mirror images, the other with morphemes ordered according to length – are effectively excluded by the formal universals of the theory we have presented, for such languages cannot be generated by grammars consisting of rules with the properties we have discussed. Nevertheless, the rules we have allowed for include many that are thoroughly implausible as candidates for inclusion in the grammar of a natural language. If a transformation is simply a rule relating one PM to another, we can imagine any number of quite absurd transformations – for example, one converting PM [13i] on *p* 51 into PM [30] on *p* 120 – and the theory of transformations ought to be constrained so that such absurdities are automatically disallowed. Here I shall briefly review three ways in which one might attempt to restrict the range of permitted transformations.

(a) Consider first the question of deletions. Suppose we included in our grammar of English a rule with the structure index 'Det — Adj — N — VP' and a structure change deleting the second term. The effect would be that a sentence like *A man arrived* could be derived from as many different deep structures as there are adjectives that can modify *man:* the grammar would be claiming that the sentence was ambiguous according as it meant 'an old man arrived', 'a young man arrived', 'a clever man arrived', and so on. Notice that linguistic theory makes a sharp distinction between ambiguity and lack of specificity (or vagueness), a distinction not always maintained in the everyday, pre-theoretical use of these terms. A sentence is ambiguous, according to a given grammar, if it is paired with two or more different semantic representations, whereas it is non-specific relative to a certain semantic property if its semantic representation does not contain a particular value for that property. Given this understanding of the terms, it is clear that an adequate grammar of English should treat *A man arrived* as non-specific, not ambiguous, as regards the type of man, and that the proposed adjective deletion rule must therefore be rejected. Moreover, it ought to be rejected as a matter of principle, *ie* by the general theory, because this kind of ambiguity is simply not found in natural languages. What we need is to exclude transformations that delete material that is not 'recoverable'. We cannot insist on unique recoverability because there are in fact cases of ambiguity resulting from genuine deletion transformations – the comparative construction *I like Tom more than Bill* is a clear example – but we must be able to prevent the pairing of one surface structure with arbitrarily many different deep structures through the operation of a single deletion. A first attempt towards excluding non-recoverable deletions might be to restrict deletions to cases meeting one or other of two conditions: that the deleted element is stipulated in the rule to be identical to some other term in the structure index, or that the rule delete a terminal element specifically mentioned in the structure index. Equi meets the first condition: it is the identity between the second and fifth terms in the structure index that makes the complement subject NP in *John wanted to go* uniquely recoverable as *John*. Similarly it is the identity condition that ensures recoverability in Coordination Reduction (*John and Mary saw Bill* derives from *John saw Bill and Mary saw Bill* not *John saw Bill and Mary went to pieces*) and Comparative Reduction (the ambiguity in the above example is due to the fact that there are two different underlying structures in which the identity condition is satisfied, those corresponding to *I like Tom more than I like Bill* and *I like Tom more than Bill likes Tom:* note that in determining identity we discount agreement features, such as distinguish *like* from *likes* in this example). The second condition is met in rules like *You* Deletion or *That* Deletion: here it is of course the identification of the element in the rule itself that ensures recoverability – *Stand up!* can be derived from the structure underlying *You stand up!* but not *The boy who said that stand up!*. One would expect that there should be further constraints on what elements can be deleted in this second type of rule (we shall hardly find a rule specifying the deletion of such a form as *exhilarating*, for example) but it remains to be seen whether this intuition can be made precise and formalized. In other respects, the proposal to limit deletions to those meeting one of the above two conditions is undoubtedly too restrictive: the present discussion has been simply illustrative of the kind of approach needed.

(b) Consider, secondly, the question of what new structure can be created by transformation. According to the rough account of the elementary transformational operations sketched in 12.4, only Chomsky-adjunction can create new non-terminal nodes, and these must be identical to one of their daughters in the derived structure. It would seem that this restriction must be relaxed at least to the extent of allowing for a morpheme introduced by non-lexical transformation to be assigned to the appropriate syntactic category – for example, in the derived structure resulting from *There* Insertion, *there* must be a NP in order that the Interrogative Inversion rule can apply (*cf p* 116). But should the restriction be relaxed even further? I spoke earlier of the problem of getting a satisfactory derived constituent structure for the *by* phrase in passive sentences. If we state the relevant part of the structure change as merely '$by + 2$', the result is an unsatisfactory PM like [44] on *p* 191. But if we wrote '$[_{PP}[_{Prep} by]_{Prep} 2]_{PP}$' instead, we would be adopting a significantly less constrained theory of transformations than one in which labelled brackets cannot appear in a structure change except where they enclose exclusively terminal elements, as in the *there* example – and in adopting this less constrained theory we would also make available a vast range of quite unnatural rules. Critics have complained that works written within the TG framework are often inexplicit about derived constituent structure. There is no doubt that this charge has some validity, especially as applied to the early literature (*cf p* 190), but the problem is only superficially one of explicitness. It is not difficult to achieve explicitness as such, for one needs only to adopt a formalism for transformations where input and output are given in the form of labelled bracketings. But this would be to leave the notion of transformation far too unconstrained, and hence unsatisfactory in terms of task II above. The question raised by the Passivization example is whether we can obtain an adequate derived structure without abandoning very general constraints on transformations that seem otherwise well supported. I shall return to the example in Chapter 15, in the context of a discussion of the NP and PP categories.

(c) A third type of constraint on transformations involves the role and interpretation of variables. Consider, for example, the Relativization rule, whose structure index was given on *p* 102 as

$$[1] \ W \ — \ [_{NP} \ NP \ — \ [_S \ X \ — \ NP \ — \ Y]_S]_{NP} \ — \ Z$$
$$1 \qquad 2 \qquad 3 \qquad 4 \qquad 5 \qquad 6$$

where terms 2 and 4, the antecedent and the NP to be relativized, are identical. The effect of the rule is to replace 4 by a relative pronoun and move it to the front of the relative clause, *ie* to adjoin it to the left of term 3. The variables W and Z allow for the NP consisting of terms 2–5 to occupy any position in its clause: relative clauses occur in NPs functioning as subject, direct object, object of a preposition, and so on. Similarly X and Y allow for the relativized NP to occupy any position in the embedded clause. The variables are clearly necessary if the rule is to be expressed in its proper generality: obviously we do not want to write one rule for the case where the relativized NP is subject, another for the case where it is direct object, and so on. How then are we to prevent the rule applying to a structure like

[2]

I met	*the baker$_i$*	*she said Ed and*	*the baker$_i$*	*were twins*	
1	2	3	4	5	6

to yield *I met the baker who she said Ed and were twins?* We might consider adding special conditions to the structure index, stipulating that term 3 must not end with a conjunction coordinating part of term 3 with the NP of term 4. But it turns out that this limitation on Relativization is simply a special case of a highly general constraint. Exactly the same limitation applies to the variable in term 2 of *Wh-Q* Fronting (*p* 143): '*Q she said Ed and who were twins*' satisfies the index as given, but the resultant *Who did she say Ed and were twins?* is deviant. The variables in term 5 of Relativization, term 4 of *Wh-Q* Fronting and term 6 of Passivization likewise cannot begin with a conjunction coordinating part of the element in question to the preceding term, witness *I met the baker who she said and Ed were twins*, *Who did she say and Ed were twins?*, *The food was provided by Bill and drink* (from *Bill provided the food and drink*), and so on. And the application of similar rules in other languages is limited in the same way. Thus instead of adding special conditions to particular rules in particular grammars we shall formulate a universal constraint to the effect that no transformation may move an element from inside a coordinate structure to a position outside that structure. This 'Coordinate Structure Constraint' is just one of a number of constraints proposed in an important study by John Ross (1967) on the operation of transformations containing variables in their structure index. These constraints (or at least some of them, including the above) belong to universal grammar, constituting part of our definition of a possible natural language: the claim is that there will be no natural language containing derivations in which they are violated.

Let us turn now to the kind of constraint that the theory of formal universals might impose on the form of contextual features and on the government of transformations by rule features. Contextual features specify which occurrences of Δ a lexical item may substitute for, and accordingly we need to define as narrowly as possible the factors that determine lexical insertion. We saw in Chapter 9 that verbs and adjectives are subclassified according to whether they take a declarative, an interrogative or either as sentential complement, and this shows that insertion of a lexical item in one clause may be dependent on the structure of another clause, *ie* that elements mentioned in contextual features need not be clause-mates of the Δ to be replaced. But there are surely severe limits on this kind of phenomenon: we shall not find the structure of a relative clause in the subject NP affecting lexical insertion in a relative clause embedded in the object NP, and it is plausible to suggest that this possibility should be excluded by the general theory, and similarly in many other cases. As for rule government, our original example, Passivization, was of a rule governed by the lexical item in the main verb position in the clause on whose cycle the rule is potentially due to apply: how typical is this of rule government in general? That the governing item belongs in the clause on whose cycle the rule potentially applies is likely to hold true in all cases: it is a reasonable hypothesis that no natural language will have a rule of Passivization, say, that is blocked if the subject NP contains a relative clause having a special subclass of verb – where *The man who came to dinner stole the silver*, but not *The man who ran to Paris stole the silver* could be Passivized. A second constraint we might hypothesize is that the items governing a given rule must occur in a single position, thus excluding the possibility of a rule being dependent both on what the lexical verb is and on what the lexical noun in the subject NP is, and so on. A stronger version of this constraint would be that only the (main) verb can govern a transformation. It is unclear whether either of these last two constraints can be accepted: we shall see in the following chapters that the grammar we have so far been assuming for English is in conflict with them, but this does not mean that they are invalid – it may be that the fault lies in the grammar, and it can be argued that there are independent grounds for revising the grammar in such a way that the conflict is resolved (*cf pp* 217–8). The construction of particular grammars and the development of the general theory must naturally proceed simultaneously and interdependently, and since the former are currently extremely fragmentary and tentative, discussion of such constraints on rule government, and of other formal universals, will inevitably be highly speculative at present. But the point I want to emphasize here is that in constructing a grammar for a particular language we must bear in mind task II as well as task I, so that in choosing between different ways of analysing a language we shall prefer, other things being equal, that analysis which is compatible with the most highly constrained set of formal universals.

In justifying our claims about the form that grammars should take, we have drawn heavily on the notion of a linguistically significant generalization. We noted at the outset that it is not sufficient for a grammar to achieve external adequacy, to match the data: it must also express the regularities, the linguistically significant generalizations underlying the data. It is largely in order to permit this that we have established various levels of structure intermediate between the semantic and the phonetic, and various theoretical constructs for representing the structure at these levels. Consider, for example, the kind of phenomena that motivates the distinction between the phonetic and phonemic levels. At the phonetic level, the initial stops of *pill, team, kin*, etc, must be represented as aspirated, whereas the second segments of *spill, steam, skin* are unaspirated. But these are not idiosyncratic properties of these particular lexical items (as it is an idiosyncratic property of *pill* that it begins with a voiceless bilabial stop): voiceless stops in English are REGULARLY aspirated in initial position, but unaspirated after /s/. Entering items in the lexicon in an abstract phonemic form rather than their systematic phonetic form enables us to express these facts in a clear and explicit way: aspiration is not represented in stops at the phonemic level, and is thus not stated separately for each relevant lexical item but is accounted for by a general rule relating the phonemic level to the phonetic. Similarly we recognize a level of syntax where forms like *cats, dogs, foxes, oxen, men* are represented as containing a shared plural element even though it is not identifiable by any shared phonetic element, in order that we can formulate a general rule of subject-verb agreement, for example: we want to be able to show that *The cats is here*, *The oxen is here*, etc, are deviant for the same reason, instead of excluding them by separate rules. And it is the same kind of consideration that motivates the distinction between deep and surface structure: we want to be able to state a general rule accounting for the deviance of both *The storm frightened the fact* and *The fact was frightened by the storm* instead of treating them as violations of distinct, independent rules, and similarly with imperative *Pamper myself!* and declarative *You don't pamper myself*, and innumerable other examples.

We also invoke the notion of generalization in choosing between rival grammars conforming to the same set of universal conditions and equivalent in respect of external adequacy. For example, given a grammar G_1 where *will* is analysed as a modal auxiliary and a grammar G_2 where it is analysed as a future tense marker, we prefer G_1 over G_2 because it permits us to exclude *John will can swim* and *John may can swim* by a general rule prohibiting non-coordinate combinations of modals, because it permits a more general account of tense backshifting, and so on. Or again, we prefer a grammar where the PS rules introduce Tns as the left-most element in the Aux constituent over one which introduces it directly into its surface structure position because this enables us to express the generalization that a VGp may contain just one tense inflection. Numerous other examples of this form of argument have arisen in the preceding chapters as we discussed the choice of one analysis over another.

The question then arises as to whether this aspect of the evaluation of grammars can be made sufficiently precise and explicit to be performed by a 'mindless robot' (*cf p* 16). Chomsky has argued that in addition to specifying the conditions that particular grammars must meet, universal grammar should also provide an evaluation procedure permitting a mechanical choice between rival grammars that are alike in external adequacy. This would involve developing a system of notation such that we could measure – for example, by counting the number of symbols – which of two grammars attains the greater level of generality. Consider again the example mentioned above: the generalization that a VGp may contain just one tense inflection. I argued that this (and also the generalizations that perfective *have* and progressive *be* are accompanied by the inflectional morphemes *en* and *ing* respectively) is directly expressed by the rules [23] on *p* 70 – especially [23v]: 'Aux → Tns (M) (*have en*) (*be ing*)' – but not by rules [26] on *p* 71. Now notice that the latter rules, repeated here as [3], are no simpler, in terms of the number of symbols used, than [4].

[3] i $VGp \rightarrow (M)\ (Perf)\ (Prog)\ V$ [4] i $VGp \rightarrow (M)\ (Perf)\ (Prog)\ V$

ii $V \quad \rightarrow VS \begin{cases} Tns\ /\ NP\ \_\_ \\ /\ M\ \_\_ \\ en\ /\ Perf\ \_\_ \\ ing\ /\ Prog\ \_\_ \end{cases}$ ii $V \quad \rightarrow VS \begin{cases} Tns\ /\ NP\ \_\_ \\ /\ M\ \_\_ \\ en\ /\ Perf\ \_\_ \\ ing\ /\ Prog\ \_\_ \end{cases}$

iii $Prog \rightarrow be \begin{cases} Tns\ /\ NP\ \_\_ \\ /\ M\ \_\_ \\ en\ /\ Perf\ \_\_ \end{cases}$ iii $Prog \rightarrow be \begin{cases} en\ /\ NP\ \_\_ \\ Tns\ /\ M\ \_\_ \\ /\ Perf\ \_\_ \end{cases}$

iv $Perf \rightarrow have \begin{cases} Tns\ /\ NP\ \_\_ \\ /\ M\ \_\_ \end{cases}$ iv $Perf \rightarrow have \begin{cases} /\ NP\ \_\_ \\ ing\ /\ M\ \_\_ \end{cases}$

v $M \quad \rightarrow MS\ Tns$ v $M \quad \rightarrow MS\ Tns$

Let us call the language generated by a grammar containing [4] 'pseudo-English' – for clearly it cannot be identified with real English: the rules will generate morpheme strings corresponding to *could having seen, could was seeing, been seeing, have been seeing,* but not *was seeing, has been seeing,* and so on. Pseudo-English differs from real English precisely by virtue of the fact that the generalizations that (in non-embedded non-coordinate declarative sentences) the VGp contains exactly one tense element, that perfect *have* is accompanied by *en*, progressive *be* by *ing*, hold for real English but not for pseudo-English. There is therefore a clear sense in which we can say that pseudo-English is more complicated, less regular than real English. But [3] is no simpler than [4] in terms of the number of symbols used. This then lends some plausibility to Chomsky's suggestion that the number of symbols in a set of rules might be taken as a formal measure of the amount of generalization expressed therein: the fact that [3] fails to express the above generalizations about real English correlates with the fact that the rules contain the same number of symbols as those that generate a language for which the generalizations do not hold.

Most of the work attempting to develop a mechanical evaluation procedure has been in the field of phonology and remains somewhat controversial: I shall accordingly not pursue the matter further here. But given the crucial role that 'significant generalizations' play in arguments over rival models of grammar and over rival grammars conforming to the same model, it is clearly important to find an explicit basis for determining whether or not a generalization is in fact expressed by a certain grammar.

We noted earlier that Chomsky takes a generative grammar of a language to be an explicit description of the ideal speaker-hearer's linguistic competence, his intrinsic (or tacit) knowledge of the language. He also uses the term grammar for this linguistic competence itself: in this usage we will say that the speaker-hearer possesses, or has 'internalized', a grammar of the language. 'Grammar' is thus applied either to the linguist's description or to the mental reality that it purports to describe.

At this point the question arises as to how the speaker-hearer comes to be in possession of his internalized grammar. Provided a child has no relevant serious physical or mental handicap and is exposed to the ordinary use of language, he will attain mastery of the essence of the language by the age of about six. People obviously differ in the proportion of the total vocabulary they learn, in the extent to which they acquire mastery of the written language or of the more formal styles of the spoken language, and so on. Nevertheless, the major syntactic, phonological, and semantic rules are acquired by all children (with the above proviso) by a fairly early age: they will all have passive constructions as well as actives; negatives as well as positives; interrogatives and imperatives as well as declaratives; coordinate, relative and complement constructions as well as simple sentences. Insofar as transformations like *Do* Support, Affix Hopping, Subject Raising, Equi, Coordination Reduction and Restructuring, and others discussed in this book are valid for any speaker's internalized grammar of English, they are valid for that of everyone beyond early childhood. This relative uniformity and speed of acquisition is independent of the amount of formal instruction the child receives and to a very significant extent independent of his level of intelligence. Children of quite low intelligence control these constructions, so that learning one's native language is very different from learning mathematics, history and the like.

Conversely, attempts to teach a human language to even the most intelligent of non-human animals have proved unsuccessful. And no other species has developed a communication system that does not differ in quite fundamental ways from human language: there is, for example, no other system that allows for the communication of indefinitely many different messages by combining elements drawn from an inventory of discrete units (*cf p* 3).

These facts argue that the human child is genetically endowed with a special capacity for acquiring a language, a capacity unique to the human species: Chomsky refers to it as the child's innate LANGUAGE-ACQUISITION DEVICE. What can we infer about the structure of this device? The upper limit on what it might contain is set by the diversity of natural languages. No child is genetically endowed to learn English rather than Russian, say: which language we learn is determined by the environment in which we grow up. Anything that is specific to a given language must be learnt; it cannot be attributed to the innate language-acquisition device. The lower bound on the latter's content is set by the requirement that it account for the relative uniformity and speed with which children acquire their grammars. Our discussion of the form of grammars has inevitably been highly fragmentary and programmatic, but enough has been said to make it clear that a complete generative grammar of a language will be enormously complex and abstract. Chomsky argues that it is out of the question that from the limited performance data available to him a child would so quickly learn such a grammar if he did not tacitly know in advance the principles determining the form a grammar may take. How, for example, could a child possibly

LEARN the principle of the transformational cycle? (Note again that there is no evidence of children of low intelligence acquiring grammars constructed on non-cyclic principles.) Chomsky proposes instead that we attribute to the child an innate tacit knowledge of the form of grammars – an innate knowledge of universal grammar. This would reduce his learning task to that of learning the properties specific to the language spoken in his community (or, as Chomsky puts it, determining which of the possible natural languages is being used): he would not have to learn that transformations apply cyclically, and so on, for he would know this to start with.

The fact that one who knows a language can produce and understand sentences he has never used or heard before establishes that we do not learn sentences as atomic units: what we learn is an abstract system of rules underlying the sentences. Learning these rules involves a large amount of trial and error, as is evident from the many errors that children make. The child can be thought of as unconsciously formulating hypotheses about the grammar on the basis of the data he is exposed to – the child who says *Daddy buyed it* has learnt the rule for the realization of *Past* in regular verbs but has not yet learnt that *buy* is irregular. Now Chomsky's point is that the child's innate knowledge of universal grammar serves to guide and constrain this process of hypothesis formation: he will only entertain hypotheses involving rules meeting the conditions on 'possible rules' that are specified in universal grammar. As an example (though not one Chomsky himself uses) consider the relationship between pairs of sentences like *John ran away* and *Away ran John*. The latter derives from the former by two transformations: one moving *away* to front position (this may be a special case of Topicalization – see *p* 229) and a rule of Subject Postposing, moving the subject NP to the right of the VGp. The fact that there are two separate rules involved is clear from the existence of intermediate forms like *Away John ran* and of constructions to which Subject Postposing but not Topicalization has applied, such as '. . . *the drawer, out of which were hanging several old socks*', where *out of which* is moved not by Topicalization but by the ordinary *Wh* Fronting rule that applies obligatorily to relative clauses. It is possible, however, that a child might come across the *Away ran John* construction before *Away John ran*, etc. Now it happens that *John ran away* and *Away ran John* are mirror images in terms of their analysis into words, but the theory of universal grammar we have developed does not admit rules which systematically convert a structure into its mirror image: such rules cannot be expressed in terms of the formalism of TG. On the basis of Chomsky's claim that the child has innate knowledge of universal grammar, of what a possible rule is, we would accordingly predict that a child exposed to sentences like *John ran away*, *Away ran John*, *Tom fell down*, *Down fell Tom* will not subconsciously formulate a mirror-image rule leading to errors like **Away ran dog the*.

I should emphasize that Chomsky's claim that the study of universal grammar is equivalent to the study of the child's innate language-acquisition device is highly controversial. There are two main areas of dispute. One has to do with the identification of the linguist's grammar with the speaker-hearer's internalized grammar – for it is clearly crucial to Chomsky's arguments about learnability that the speaker-hearer acquires a grammar of the type specified by the generative grammarian. The argument here, then, is over the psychological reality of current generative grammars. Chomsky's proposals concerning the general form of grammars and the choice between competing grammars are dictated by the desire to provide for the expression of the maximum amount of linguistically significant generalization: are we entitled to assume that the child constructing his internal grammar gives as much weight to this principle as the linguist? The second disagreement is over the validity of attributing to the innate device the full structure of universal grammar: it is one thing to accept the need for a specific language-learning capacity, quite another to accept that it involves an innate knowledge of universal grammar. The reader can follow up these matters in the works cited in the notes; Chomsky himself attaches great importance to this aspect of his work, saying that the intellectual justification for linguistic research is to be found in the information provided by universal grammar concerning innate intellectual structure (1966b:591).

Notes

See Chomsky 1965:27–62, 1968, 1972c:13–46 for his views on universal grammar and innate intellectual structure; for criticism, see Matthews 1967, Putnam 1967, Derwing 1973. The papers by Campbell and Wales, and Marshall, in Lyons 1970 survey work on child language and animal communication systems. Some general studies of universals outside the TG framework are Greenberg 1963, 1966, Hockett 1958:541–86, Householder 1971:24–42. On noun as a universal, see Robins 1952, Chomsky 1965:113–18, Lyons 1966, 1968:317–33; on gender, see Lyons 1968:283–8, Palmer 1971:97–106. Curme 1931–5 is an example of a traditional grammar open to the charge that it fails to describe the language 'in its own terms' – cf his treatment of case and the verb paradigm. Early work in mathematical linguistics on various models of grammar was mostly confined to a study of their weak generative capacity, and one will therefore frequently find the term language applied to the set of sentences (rather than full derivations) generated by a grammar. On the importance of placing maximum constraints on the formal apparatus available for use in particular grammars, see Chomsky 1972a:66–70, Peters 1972a, Bach 1971 (which argues the need for restrictions on the substantive content of transformations in addition to formal constraints – see also Bach 1974:265–77). Constraints on deletion transformations are discussed in Katz and Postal 1964:79–84, Chomsky 1965:144–5 and 177–81; for other constraints, see Chomsky 1973.

Chapter 14

A Reconsideration of Auxiliary Verbs

According to the fragments of grammar presented in Chapters 5 and 8 sentences like those in [1] will be assigned very different underlying structures from those in [2].

[1] i *The sugar was dissolving*   [2] i *The sugar began to dissolve*
    ii *Ed may like Jill*   ii *Ed seems to like Jill*

In [1] there is just one main verb in each, *dissolve* and *like*; *be* and *may* are not main verbs but part of the auxiliary. [2i] and [ii], on the other hand, each contain two main verbs and thus two clauses. Rough deep structures for [1i] and [2i] will be [3] and [4], and those for the other two will differ in a similar way.

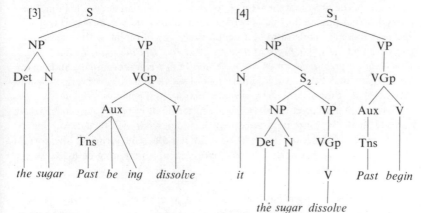

It is clear from these differences that a great deal of weight is attached to the distinction between auxiliary verbs and main verbs; in this chapter I want to look more closely into the nature of this distinction.

The traditional notion of an auxiliary is that of a verb used to form a tense, mood, aspect, voice, etc, of another verb – *be* is used to form the passive voice, *have* the perfect aspect, and so on. I shall have more to say about this definition later; at this stage it is sufficient to note that it does not provide a clear basis for distinguishing [1] from [2]. For if we analyse *was dissolving* as the progressive aspect form of *dissolve*, why should we not treat *began to dissolve* as its 'ingressive' aspect form? (It is in fact so analysed in some traditional grammars, and *begin, start, continue, keep, cease, stop*, etc, are frequently referred to as 'aspectual' verbs.) And if *may* in [1ii] expresses a mood of possibility, why should we not say that *seem* in [2ii] expresses a mood of 'appearance'?

Let us therefore turn to the syntactic properties which do clearly distinguish *be* and *may* on the one hand from *begin* and *seem* on the other. There are four types of construction that are relevant to their differentiation: those in which the Inversion transformation applies; negatives; emphatic positives; and certain anaphoric constructions. Only a fairly small set of verbs can carry the tense inflections in these constructions – compare *Was the sugar dissolving?* versus **Began the sugar to dissolve?*, *They **haven't** seen it* versus **They **stopn't** working, John **CAN** swim* versus *John **LIKES** to swim* (the latter is well-formed, but not an emphatic denial of *John doesn't like to swim*), *Ed **may** resign and so **may** Tim* versus **John **lives** in London and so **lives** Jill*. The four constructions define virtually the same class of verbs – the qualification 'virtually' is needed because of the doubtful status of sentences like *?Ed **mayn't** like Jill*, which are judged unacceptable by many speakers, although *may* can clearly carry the tense inflections in the other three constructions. Notice that it is the contracted negative with *n't* that is relevant here: *Ed may not like her* is obviously well-formed, but so is *Ed seems not to like her*, etc. For convenience I will refer to the verbs that can carry the tense inflections in (some or all of) these constructions by means of the pre-theoretical term, 'class I verbs'. It will be recalled that these four constructions are the ones in which the dummy auxiliary *do* occurs (*cf p* 77), and that there are constraints on which verbs can combine with *do* in them – compare *Did the sugar **begin** to dissolve?* versus **Did the sugar **be** dissolving?*, *Tom **didn't try** to understand* versus **Tom **didn't can** understand*, and so on. Verbs that can combine with *do* here I shall speak of as 'class II verbs'. *Be* and *may* in [1] are thus class I verbs, *begin* and *seem* in [2] class II.

Having differentiated the two classes in terms of criteria that can be made quite explicit, we must next go on to consider what significance we should attach to the distinction, how we should handle it in terms of the formal apparatus that we have established. Two general points may be made before we turn to the question of formalization.

(a) Most verbs belong exclusively to class I or class II, but the way we have defined them does not logically rule out the possibility of a verb belonging to both classes. And there are indeed a few such verbs. *You needn't come* and *You don't need to come* are both well-formed, as are *He daren't contradict her* and *He doesn't dare to contradict her*, so that *need* and *dare* belong to both I and II. The picture is complicated by differences between dialects, styles and contrasting uses of a given verb. *Ought* belongs to class I in the standard dialect but to class II in certain non-standard ones, as in *You didn't ought to have done that*. With *used* we have both *He usedn't to go* and *He didn't use to go*; the latter will not normally be found in formal styles but is common in spoken informal ones. As for *have:* in its use as the perfect aspect marker it belongs exclusively to class I (**Do you have seen it?*); in its 'possession' and 'obligation' senses it belongs to both (*Have you enough money?* and *Do you have enough money?*, *Have you to go?* and *Do you have to go?*) but with regional dialect preferences, British English, for example, tending to treat it as class I, American English as class II; and in cases where it is more or less equivalent to *take* it belongs exclusively to class II in all dialects (*John didn't have a swim this morning,* not **John hadn't a swim.*)

(b) The differences on which the classification is based are very much idiosyncratic to English: classes defined on this basis can hardly be claimed as universals. Notice in particular that it would not be satisfactory to identify I and II with the classes of auxiliary and main verb respectively (which, traditionally at least, are regarded as universal categories). The principal objection to such an identification is that *be* and *have* (in its possession and obligation senses in some dialects at least) belong to I even when there is no other verb in the clause (and no ellipsis of a verb): *Isn't Canberra the capital?*, *Have you any brothers?*. The traditional notion of auxiliary presupposes that there is a main verb to which the auxiliary is subordinated: auxiliary and main verb are essentially functional notions rather than purely categorial ones.

Bearing these two points in mind, let us see how we can handle the two classes in a formal grammar. In the grammar we have been working with so far, class II corresponds quite straightforwardly to the category V – but we have not established any single category matching class I. Our rules for Inversion and *Not* Placement included a disjunctive listing {M, *have, be*}, and we may assume that the same disjunction would occur in the rules relating to the emphatic positive and anaphoric constructions. The rules allow for the generation of both *Have you the money?* and *Do you have the money?* since the underlying PM can be analysed in two different ways that satisfy the structure index for Inversion, as given on *p* 78 (the modifications that we subsequently made to our original PS and transformational rules for interrogatives do not affect the point at issue here).

[5]   [6]

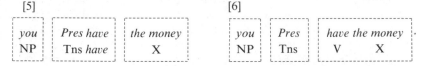

This means that either *Pres have* is fronted or *Pres* alone, in which latter case the *Do* Support rule will apply. The grammar will not generate **Do you have seen it?*, because aspectual *have* is not analysable as a V: it is within the Aux constituent. Two problems arise here, however. Firstly the rules will incorrectly generate **Had you a swim?*: somehow we must distinguish those uses of *have* which belong exclusively to class II from those which belong to either class. Secondly, in extending the grammar to cover copulative constructions (see

15.5) we must ensure that it generates *Are you happy?* but not **Do you be happy?*.
Chomsky's solution to this second problem is to assign *be* (except in its uses
as progressive or passive marker) to the category 'Copula', a distinct primary
category, rather than a subcategory of verb – but this means that it will no
longer be the case that the constituent V is common to all VPs.

This brings us to a more general observation about the grammar: that it
does not contain a category matching the traditional part of speech 'verb'. We
cannot, of course, simply take it for granted that the traditional category is a
valid one; however, it can be shown that the failure to recognize a category of
verb does in fact lead to loss of generality. This is evident from the structure
index for Affix Hopping (*p* 74) where the third term is given as a disjunctive list,
{M, *have*, *be*, V}. Instead of saying that the affixes are moved round a following
verb, we have to say that they are moved round a following element if it is
either a modal, or *have*, or *be*, or a V. The fact that M, *have*, *be*, and V behave
alike with respect to this rule shows that they do share a significant syntactic
property, one that distinguishes them from nouns, adjectives, etc: it is this
property of taking the tense inflections that motivates the recognition of the
traditional category of verb.

Now in *Syntactic Structures* Chomsky did not give the Affix Hopping rule in
the form in which I have presented it; what he had instead was as follows
(except for minor and irrelevant differences in notation and choice of symbols):

[7] X— Af — v — Y
    1   2   3   4 ⇒
    1   ∅   3+2   4

where Af is any Tns or is *en* or *ing* and v is any M or V, or *have* or *be*.

The status of 'Af' and 'v', however, was left unexplained: they were introduced
and defined in a purely ad hoc way to simplify this particular rule. Chomsky
has since described them as notational devices equivalent to syntactic features –
recall that features were formally introduced only in the *Aspects* version of the
theory. In accordance with this interpretation, we may adjust the structure
index to read 'X — [+Affix] — [+Verb] — Y'. In the same spirit, Chomsky
introduces a feature [+Aux] common to the modals, *be* and *have* (except in its
'take' sense), so that it is no longer necessary to give a disjunctive listing of these
in the rules of Inversion, *Not* Placement, etc. All traditional verbs will now have
the feature [+Verb], class i verbs will be marked [+Aux], class ii [+V]. In
I had finished and *John had a swim*, *have* is marked [+Aux] and [−Aux] respectively, while the *have* of *You have enough money* can have either the plus or the
minus value of the feature. Moreover we no longer need the special category
'copula', for *be* can now be assigned to V without leading to the generation of
*Do you be happy? and the like. This is because V will no longer figure in the
Inversion rule, whose index will now read (roughly):

[8] NP — $\begin{Bmatrix} \text{Tns}\,[+\text{Aux}] — & \text{X} \\ \text{Tns} & — [-\text{Aux}]\,\text{X} \end{Bmatrix}$

At this point we must look more carefully at the nature of the three features [Verb], [Aux] and [V]. In terms of the classification given in Chapter 10, [V] is a straightforward category feature: items specified as [+V] are those that can replace a Δ immediately dominated by the category V. But [Aux] is not a category feature: Chomsky's choice of symbol here is very misleading. In *John is angry*, *be* is marked [+Aux] but is not dominated by Aux; and in *John may have been ill*, *may* is not a DAUGHTER of Aux and does not even stand in the 'is a' relation to Aux. The role of the [Aux] feature is to distinguish those forms which undergo fronting in the Inversion rule from those which do not (and to make analogous distinctions for negative constructions, and so on). [Aux] thus does the work of a rule feature, although it is not in fact formalized as one; and the same holds for [Verb].

The modifications we have made to the original grammar affect it in two principal ways. Firstly, by providing for the exclusion of *John hadn't a swim*, they improve it in terms of external adequacy. Secondly, they remove the need for disjunctive listings of categories and morphemes in various transformational rules. It would be a mistake, however, to assume that this necessarily involves a gain in internal adequacy. In replacing {M, *have*, *be*, V} by [+Verb] we have simply shifted the ad hoc listing from the Affix Hopping rule to the lexicon; since there is no other property shared by all items specified as [+Verb], adding this feature to the grammar does not capture any new generalization. It is important not to be misled by the formalism in such cases: merely adding a lexical feature to all items having a certain syntactic property does not of itself secure an increase in generality, in internal adequacy.

I began this chapter by drawing attention to the striking differences between the deep structures attributed to sentences like [1] on the one hand and [2] on the other. In seeking justification for these analyses, we adduced various syntactic properties which differentiate between the principal items concerned, *be* and *may* in [1], versus *begin* and *seem* in [2], or more generally between what we have been referring to by the pre-theoretical terms class I verbs and class II verbs. Yet what has emerged from the subsequent discussion is that the constituent structure differences between the deep structures proposed for [1] and [2] have little or no relevance to the formal differentiation of class I verbs from class II. In the original version, the rules of Inversion and *Not* Placement did mention the CATEGORIES M and V but they also listed the MORPHEMES *have* and *be*: the rules applied to these quite independently of what node they were dominated by. And in the amended version the differences between classes I and II are handled by means of the FEATURE [Aux], and items marked [+Aux] can occur in a variety of quite different positions in the PM. Our conclusion must be that the differences between classes I and II do not provide any real justification for distinguishing [1] from [2] in terms of CONSTITUENT STRUCTURE. The non-primitive term 'auxiliary verb' can be defined in this analysis as an item marked [+Verb] and dominated by the constituent Aux. But we cannot claim that this provides any genuine insight into the notion unless we can furnish solid arguments for establishing an Aux constituent in the first place.

The analysis distinguishes progressive *be* as an auxiliary verb from ingressive *begin* as a main verb, but the Aux constituent plays no part in the rules accounting for the differences in the syntactic properties of the two verbs.

There is a further syntactic property differentiating between *may* and *seem* (but not *be* and *begin*): the modals are always finite. It is this restriction that excludes the possibility of a sequence of two modals (**John may must have gone, *John will can swim soon*), for the next verb after a modal must be an infinitive. It follows, then, that the VGp is non-recursive: there is an absolute upper bound of four auxiliaries in any one VGp. The construction exemplified in [2], on the other hand, is not subject to this constraint, so that if we analysed *seem, begin,* etc, as auxiliaries it is doubtful whether there would be any linguistic limit to the number of auxiliaries permitted in a single VGp (*cf: John may have seemed to have been beginning to lose his grip*). This restriction on the distribution of modals undoubtedly provides a criterion for distinguishing them from *seem, begin,* etc, and for delimiting a VGp unit. But it is one thing to provide a classificatory criterion, quite another to show that the property in question justifies handling the two classes as distinct categories occupying quite different positions in underlying constituent structure. It is not the case that all clauses must contain a finite verb: why, therefore, should we implicitly attach such significance to this property of the modals (especially when we note that it does not in fact apply to all dialects, witness such forms as *He'll no can come*)?

Given these doubts about the analysis proposed for [1] and [2], let me now introduce an alternative, one where they have deep structures of the same general form. It would not do to generalize PM [3] to cover sentences like [2], for this would mean making Aux recursive in some way and losing the straightforward solution we gave in Chapter 8 to the problem of accounting for the relation between pairs like *Ed seems to like Jill* and *It seems that Ed likes Jill.* Our proposal will be, therefore, not that *begin* and *seem* belong in the Aux constituent, but that there is no Aux constituent – that progressive *be* and *may* are intransitive verbs taking an embedded complement sentence as underlying subject. Deep structures for [1i] and [2i] will then be essentially as shown in [9], those for [1ii] and [2ii] as in [10] (I simplify at this stage by omitting the tense element).

[9]

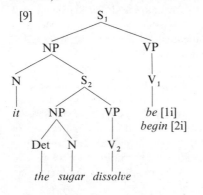

[10]

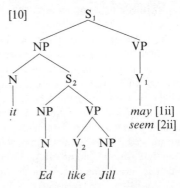

For convenience I shall refer to this as the 'new' analysis (of auxiliaries) in contrast to the 'old' analysis discussed earlier (in either its original version or the one involving the features [Aux] and [Verb]). The new analysis gives a more abstract deep structure to [1] than the old one, in that there will be more steps in the progression from deep to surface structure. But the extra steps do not require new rules: they are covered by those already set up to handle [2]; in particular, Extraposition and Subject Raising will now apply in [1] as well as [2]. Let us now review in turn some of the arguments that can be advanced in support of the new analysis.

(a) Firstly (and very briefly), it clearly permits a simplification of the PS rules, in that we can now dispense with the categories VGp, Aux and M.

(b) Secondly, we can dispense with the ad hoc feature [+Verb], giving the third term of the Affix Hopping rule as the category V. This represents an improvement over the grammar of Chapter 5 in respect of internal adequacy in a way that simply replacing {M, *have*, *be*, V} by [+Verb] does not: in both versions of the old analysis the elements round which the affixes are moved have nothing else in common, whereas in the new analysis they are just those forms that are daughters of the category V. Suppose we had a language identical to English except that *be* did not carry the affixes but *it* did: in this pseudo-English *It did be raining* and *Ited rain?* would be well-formed, *It was raining* and *Did it rain?* deviant. The old analysis could be modified to handle this pseudo-English without any complication at all of the rules: in the original version we merely substitute *it* for *be* in the Affix Hopping rule, and in the feature version we merely change the values of [Verb] for *be* and *it* in the lexicon. In the new analysis on the other hand, we would need to complicate the rules quite significantly: *be* would have to be marked as an exception (the only one) to Affix Hopping and the third term would have to be given as the disjunction {V, *it*}. There can be no doubt that pseudo-English is considerably more irregular than real English, and the fact that only the new analysis shows this to be the case demonstrates that it is expressing a significant generalization not captured in the old analysis.

(c) We noted above that [Aux] does the work of a rule feature. A third advantage of the new analysis is that it permits [Aux] to be formalized as a rule feature much more naturally than the old analysis. For all [+Aux] items will now be under the immediate domination of V, and the rules in question (Inversion, etc) can be said to be governed by the verb – just like Passivization and so on. In the old analysis, however, [+Aux] items do not occur in any unique position in a tree. Although we have not investigated the formalism for rule government in any serious way, it is clear that formalizing [Aux] as a rule feature under the old analysis requires a much less tightly constrained theory of rule government than under the new; it follows from the discussion of Chapter 12 that a theory in which rules are governed by items occurring in a fixed position in the PM will be preferred, other things being equal, over one which allows the governing item to occur in any position. This third point clearly relates to (b): in the old analysis it is quite arbitrary and fortuitous that the [+Aux] items should be the modals, *have* and *be*, rather than, say, the modals, *the* and *it*, whereas in the new analysis the [+Aux] items are a sub-category of verbs.

(d) Fourthly, the new analysis permits a more general account of comple-mentizers. One dimension of classification distinguishes four types of non-finite construction: infinitive with *to*, bare infinitive, *ing*-form and *en*-form (*cf p* 67). The choice between them is determined, roughly, by the preceding or higher-clause verb, but we find each of them selected now by a class I verb, now by a class II:

[11] i *He ought to go*	[12] i *He wants to go*
ii *They may go*	ii *He let them go*
iii *It was raining*	iii *It kept raining*
iv *He was killed*	iv *He got killed*

However we account for the presence or absence of the morphemes *to, ing* and *en*, it is clear that the rules will be more general under the new analysis. Under the old analysis, for example, the *ing* of [iii] is introduced in [11] and [12] by quite different rules, so that it is an arbitrary coincidence that the same mor-pheme occurs in both; in the new analysis, the two sentences will have the same underlying structure, save only for the contrast between *be* and *keep* as the higher clause verb: *ing* can thus be introduced by a single rule.

(e) I pointed out above that there is a certain amount of overlap between classes I and II: in some cases an item belongs to both within a single dialect, in others it belongs to I in one dialect, II in another. In the new analysis the I versus II distinction is handled purely in terms of rule features: *Do you need to tell him?* and *Need you tell him?* will have the same deep structure. The variation between them is due to the fact that *need* optionally accompanies Tns in the fronting effected by Inversion, whereas *can* obligatorily accompanies it and *want* is blocked from doing so. In the old analysis, however, the two sen-tences would presumably have quite different deep structures, with *need* a daughter of V in the former and of M in the latter. It might be argued that this is not a necessary consequence of the old analysis: an alternative would be to take *need* as a V in both, accounting for the variation in the same way as that between *Do you have enough money?* and *Have you enough money?*. But this would reduce still further the role of the category M in the grammar. Note for instance that in *Need he go?* there is no *s* ending (*cf: *Needs he go?*): if we do not take *need* as a modal here we lose the generalization that all the items that have no special third person singular forms are modals. And most studies of English that have a modal category do in fact include *need* in those uses where it has the properties of a class I verb.

(f) *Dare* is likewise normally included in the class of modals when used with class I properties – and note again the lack of a distinct third person singular form in these uses: *Dare/*dares he tell the truth?*. Yet in other respects *dare* is like the transitive verbs taking object complementation that we discussed in Chapter 8, witness

[13] i *John daren't escort Mary*
  ii *Mary daren't be escorted by John*
[14] **There daren't be a policeman among the guests*
[15] **The stone daren't move*

[13i] and [ii] are clearly not paraphrases, and [14] and [15] are deviant – compare the corresponding *expect* sentences ([1], [9], [14] and [22] of Chapter 8). If *dare* is analysed as a modal there will be no principled way of deriving [13ii] except from the same deep structure as underlies [i], and no way of blocking [14] and [15] that is not totally ad hoc – note that there are no other cases of selectional restrictions holding between NP and M in a 'NP M . . .' construction. But if *dare* is analysed as a verb taking an infinitival clause as object complement, the facts of [13–15] follow naturally from the analysis established in Chapter 8: taking *dare* as a modal leads to a striking loss in generalization. The facts of [13–15] reinforce the point that the distinction between classes I and II is a fairly superficial one, and consequently cannot be used to motivate any differentiation between them in terms of underlying constituent structure.

(g) A further difficulty with the old analysis has to do with constituent bracketing. Consider first [16].

[16] i *They ought to have finished the job by then*
  ii *They expect to have finished the job by then*

In the old analysis *ought to have* and *ought to have finished* are surface structure constituents while *expect to have* and *expect to have finished* are not, yet there is no phonological evidence to suggest any difference in surface bracketing. Note also the evidence provided by sentences like

[17] i *Ed says Jill may have been lying, which she may have been*
  ii *Ed says Jill may have been lying, which she may have*
  iii *Ed says Jill may have been lying, which she may*
[18] i *Ed may arrive this evening, in which case we'll be O.K.*
  ii *Ed hopes to arrive this evening, in which case we'll be O.K.*

In [17] *which* serves as a relative pronoun standing for *lying, been lying* and *have been lying* respectively. In the new analysis these will all be constituents in derived structure, which makes it easier to account for the fact of their relativization than in the old analysis, where they are not constituents. In [18] *Ed arrive this evening* is in some sense antecedent for the expression *in which case*. In the new analysis, but not the old, *Ed arrive this evening* is a deep structure constituent of both [i] and [ii], and again this will permit a more uniform treatment of the two examples.

(h) My next point has to do with the role and distribution of time expressions. Consider the following examples:

[19] i *John intended leaving last night*
   ii *John now intends leaving tomorrow*
  iii *Yesterday John still intended leaving tomorrow*
[20] i *John was leaving last night*
   ii *John is now leaving tomorrow*
  iii *Yesterday John was still leaving tomorrow*

[19i] is ambiguous between the interpretation 'at some unspecified time in the past John intended that he would leave last night' and 'John intended last night that he would leave at some unspecified time'. In the first interpretation *last night* specifies the time of leaving, in the second the time of the intention. Now the main verb status of *intend* is not in dispute, so that there will be two clauses in the structure of [19], the higher one having *intend* as verb, the lower one *leave*. A natural way of accounting for the ambiguity of [19i] is to have two different underlying structures: the one corresponding to the first interpretation will have *last night* in the *leave* clause, the other in the *intend* clause. Examples like [19ii] and [iii] support this: by putting *tomorrow* in the *leave* clause and *now* [ii] or *yesterday* [iii] in the *intend* clause, we avoid having incompatible or contradictory time expressions within a single clause, and provide for a straightforward relation between syntactic structure and semantic interpretation. Observe now [20], containing the so-called progressive auxiliary. I noted earlier (*p* 65) that there are two main uses of the '*be ... ing*' construction: most often it indicates that the action/state is being considered not in its totality, but at some intermediate point or period between its beginning and end (as in *John was just leaving as I arrived*); but it is also used to indicate that the action/ state is planned, scheduled or arranged in some way – and this is the sense I am concerned with here, so that in discussing [20i] I shall ignore the 'intermediate point' interpretation. With this proviso it will be agreed that the relation of [i] to [ii] to [iii] is the same in [20] as in [19]. For example, [20i] is ambiguous according as it means 'at some unspecified time in the past John was scheduled to leave last night' or 'last night the schedule was that John should leave at some unspecified time'. (There may well be intonational differences in readings of [19i] and [20i] corresponding to the different interpretations, but this serves only to support the point that we need to provide two different analyses of each.) Now in the new analysis we can handle [20] in just the same way as [19]: in the first interpretation of [20i] *last night* belongs in the *leave* clause, in the second in the *be* clause, and so on. But this solution is not available in the old analysis: there we would have to account for the ambiguity in [20i] and for the co-occurrence of the time expressions in [20ii] and [iii] in a quite different way than in [19]. Again, then, we find that the new analysis can express generalizations that are lost in the old.

Where *be ... ing* has the 'intermediate point' rather than the 'schedule' sense, we do not have ambiguities like that in [i] nor combinations of time expressions as in [ii] and [iii]. But the same applies with constructions involving other semantically aspectual verbs, such as *begin, keep, stop*, etc: there is no ambiguity in *The rain began to ease off an hour ago* according as *an hour ago* is associated with *begin* or *ease off*, and *Yesterday John kept leaving tomorrow* is clearly deviant. Verbs taking complement clauses as subject or object fall into two subclasses: those like *intend, want, expect*, which allow a time adverbial in the complement clause; and those like *begin, keep, stop*, which do not. This division cuts across that between our classes I and II, for class I *be* belongs with *intend* in its schedule sense, but with *begin* in its aspectual sense, and *intend* and *begin* are both class II verbs.

(i) My final argument has to do with the interaction between the dimensions which in Chapter 5 I labelled 'tense' and 'perfect aspect'. There they were treated as quite independent dimensions because of the existence of the four different combinations, past perfect (*had seen*), present perfect (*has seen*), past non-perfect (*saw*), present non-perfect (*sees*). If we look beyond the surface forms, however, we find a number of important similarities between the 'tense' element *Past* and the 'perfect aspect' marker *have*. Consider first examples like

[21] i *I know that John is in Paris now*
    ii *I know that John was in Paris last week*
[22] i *I know John to be in Paris now*
    ii *I know John to have been in Paris last week*

The contrast between *is* and *was* is here paralleled by that between *to be* and *to have been*. *Past* can occur only in finite clauses: in non-finites *have* is used instead. A second similarity is evident in the phenomenon of 'backshifting' in indirect reported speech (*cf* 5.1). A present tense form like *lives* in *Mary lives in Sydney* may be backshifted to an indirect speech past tense, as in *John said that Mary lived in Sydney*. But suppose the direct speech is already in the past tense, as in *Mary died of cancer*: the backshifted version of this is *John said that Mary had died of cancer*. Thus in some cases backshifting is marked by *Past*, in others by *have*. Thirdly, note the interplay between *Past* and *have* in

[23] i *John could speak fluent French at that time*
    ii *John may have gone yesterday*
    iii *You needn't have come until tomorrow*

In [i] we have a straightforward past tense of *can*: we are talking about the ability John had in the past. [ii] is equivalent to *Perhaps/maybe John went yesterday*; note that the past time expression *yesterday* is associated with the activity of going rather than with the modality of possibility, so that in the new analysis, where *may* and *go* belong in separate clauses, *yesterday* will be in the *go* clause – and since this is non-finite, the pastness is marked, as in [22], by *have*. [iii] is only superficially like [ii], for it is equivalent not to *You don't need to have come until tomorrow* but rather to *You didn't need to come until tomorrow*: the past time component is associated with *need* not *come*. Contrary to surface structure appearances, then, [iii] is more like [i] than like [ii]. The surface difference between [i] and [iii] results from the fact that *can* is able to combine with the inflection *Past* whereas *need* is not (more precisely, not when it is used as a class I verb), witness * *You neededn't come until tomorrow;* because the past time component in [iii] cannot be expressed by the morpheme *Past* it is expressed by *have*. There is, finally, a fourth similarity. Semantically we can make a distinction between past, present and future time, but the contrast between present and future time is not marked inflectionally, as noted in 5.1 – compare *If he is here now . . .* versus *If he is here tomorrow . . .*, or *He goes to London every week* versus *He goes to London tomorrow*, and so on. As far as the finite verb is concerned, then, we have a contrast between past and non-past. And the same holds for non-finite constructions, where *have* simply contrasts with its absence, and where the form without *have* may be used either for present time, as in [22i], or for future time, as in *I expect John to be in Paris tomorrow*. These four similarities suggest strongly that *Past* and *have* (in some of its uses, at least) are different surface manifestations of a common underlying element, a deep past tense element. The old analysis makes a fundamental distinction between finite and non-finite constructions, with only the former selecting for tense – it accounts for the difference between *Past* and *have* but not for their deeper likeness.

At this point let us return to the traditional idea of an auxiliary as a verb used to form a tense, mood, aspect, voice, etc, of another verb – the main verb. Its function is regarded as being essentially the same as an inflection: just as the past tense of a verb is marked by an inflection, so its 'future tense' is marked by use of the auxiliaries *shall* and *will*. In Latin, passive voice is marked inflectionally in the imperfective aspect, as in *amor* 'I am loved', and by an auxiliary (plus the 'past participle' inflection) in the perfective, as in *amatus sum* 'I have been loved'. The traditional paradigm for the verb accordingly contains not just single-word forms like *took, takes*, etc, in English or *amo, amor*, etc, in Latin, but also forms consisting of two or more words – so-called 'periphrastic forms' – like *will take, has taken, has been taken*, etc, in English or *amatus sum*, etc, in Latin. Some writers use the term 'inflection' in a broad sense that includes all forms in the paradigm, while others restrict it to the one-word forms in such a way that *took* but not *will take* is an inflected form of *take;* it is this second usage that I have adopted here. However, whether the periphrastic forms are handled under the heading of inflection or not, *will take, has taken*, and the like are generally regarded in traditional grammar as 'forms of the verb *take*' just as *took, takes*, etc, are. ('*Take*' is to be understood here as a 'lexical item' in the sense in which this term was introduced in 11.2. Traditional grammar uses the term 'word' instead, but this creates some difficulty in talking about forms like *has taken:* if we say both that this form consists of two words and that it is the third person singular present perfect of the word *take*, we are using 'word' in two different senses; I shall therefore restrict 'word' to the first and use 'lexical item' for the second. We thus distinguish between the WORD *take*, which occurs in *They take the bus* but not *They took the bus*, and the LEXICAL ITEM *take*, which occurs in both.)

What is the significance of this traditional manner of speaking – of saying that *will take, has taken*, etc, are forms of the lexical item *take?* Tense, aspect, voice and so on are clearly being treated as in some sense properties of the main verb. Now within the framework of generative grammar that we have developed it is important to distinguish between the surface structure location of the marker of some property and its underlying 'scope'. For example, in *I daren't leave* and *I mustn't leave* the negative marker *n't* is located in the same surface position in the two sentences, but its scope is quite different: the first means 'It is not the case that I dare leave', but the second does not mean 'It is not the case that I must leave' – it means not that there is no obligation on me to leave, but that there is an obligation on me not to leave. In *the King of Spain's daughter* the possessive or genitive case inflection is located in surface structure in the word *Spain's* but its scope is the NP *the King of Spain* not the noun *Spain*. Similarly with passive voice: the auxiliary *be* and the inflection that we have been representing as *en* are located near the main verb, but voice affects the organization of the clause as a whole, not just the verb, as is clear from our formalization of Passivization. So too with mood and aspect: in *John may win the match* the mood of possibility applies to John's winning the match, not just to 'winning', and in *John was mowing the lawn* what was in progress was John's mowing the lawn. It is this interpretation that is formalized in the new analysis. The markers of mood and aspect are treated as verbs taking complement clauses as subject, so that in [9], for example, aspectual *be* and *begin* are shown to be more directly related to the complement sentence *the sugar dissolve* than to the verb *dissolve*. (I should add that the analysis would more directly formalize the interpretation of aspect as a property of a clause if we dropped the *it* from the underlying structure of complement constructions, as suggested on *p* 108.) In the new analysis the auxiliary verbs of traditional grammar will in general be simply intransitive verbs taking subject complementation, but there will be no implication that such verbs are in any sense subordinate or secondary relative to another verb, as there is in the traditional notion of auxiliary – rather the contrary if anything, for in [9] and [10] the aspectual and modal verbs are in the higher (thus 'main') clause, *dissolve* and *like* in the lower ('subordinate') one. *Was dissolving* is not the realization of any deep structure constituent – nor indeed of a surface structure constituent. If this analysis is correct it will make no real sense to say that *was dissolving* is a progressive form of the verb *dissolve*, just as it makes no real sense to say, for example, that *desired to leave* is a desiderative form of *leave*.

A natural extension of the analysis is to treat tense in like manner, *ie* as an underlying property of a clause rather than of a verb. For past tense, for example, we shall set up an underlying intransitive verb: this past tense verb is sometimes realized in surface structure as *have*, and sometimes it is lowered into its complement clause, appearing as an inflection attached to the verb of that clause, the inflection we have been representing as *Past*. The notion of inflection is itself in need of explication – but this would require a much more careful study of the rules relating surface syntactic structures to their phonetic realizations than there is space for here. However, our discussion of *have* and *Past* has suggested that from the point of view of syntax inflection is a surface structure concept. The passive in Latin, mentioned above, lends support to this conclusion, and so too do various other constructions, such as the comparative and superlative adjective constructions in English. Note, for example, that the comparative is marked by the inflection *er* as in *taller* or the separate word *more* as in *more reasonable*: the choice depends on the phonological structure of the adjective.

The items defined as auxiliary verbs in the old analysis do not constitute a semantic class: there is no semantic property in terms of which we can set them off from other items. This is evident from the fact that *dare* and *need* belong to both auxiliary and main verb classes in this analysis without any corresponding difference in meaning, that in the more-or-less synonymous *I must leave* and *I have to leave*, *must* is an auxiliary but *have* is not (the *have* of obligation will not be classified as a modal because it is not restricted to finite forms, witness *I will have to leave*, *I've had to refuse it*), and so on – recall the discussion of the modals in 5.1. For this reason the new analysis is preferable from a semantic point of view: the new deep structures are more uniformly related to representations of the meaning than are the old. Notice, for example, that a pair of sentences like *John may be in Paris now* and *It is possible that John is in Paris now*, which are near-paraphrases, have thoroughly different deep structures under the old analysis, but very similar ones under the new, where they will both contain the clause *John is in Paris now* as subject complement – and analogously for *I must leave* and *I have to leave* or *You needn't go* and *You don't need to go*. Nevertheless, it would be misleading to characterize the new analysis as 'semantically based' in contrast to the old as 'syntactically based': most of the arguments for the new analysis given above are of the same general kind as those used earlier to support various proposals concerning underlying syntactic structures.

The new analysis remains quite controversial – and it certainly has not been formulated and developed as explicitly as the old. It was first put forward in the late sixties, and in general was accepted by those who subsequently developed the theory of generative semantics, whereas those who retain the concept of a syntactic deep structure typically retain some version of the old analysis – though I think it fair to say that there has been little published argument in the latter's defence.

Notes

The interpretation of 'v', etc, as features is proposed in Chomsky 1972*a*:65. The most important primary source for the 'new' analysis is Ross 1969*a; cf* also Hofmann 1966; Huddleston 1969. That tense too should be handled in terms of underlying intransitive verbs is the thesis of McCawley 1971. It is arguable whether, in their non-epistemic uses, the modals should be treated in the new analysis as intransitive, transitive or even di-transitive; this issue is discussed in Newmeyer 1970, Jacobs and Rosenbaum 1971:78–82, R. Lakoff 1972, Huddleston 1974. Boyd and Thorne 1969 discuss the role of the modals in determining illocutionary force. Some defence of a modified version of the old analysis can be found in Jackendoff 1972:76–82. An example of a traditional paradigm for the English verb, containing both periphrastic and simple forms, can be found in Curme 1935:327–33; Curme treats the periphrastic forms under 'inflection', in contrast with, for example, Sweet 1891:242.

Chapter 15

Grammatical Functions

We have been distinguishing notions like subject, object, predicate, etc, as grammatical relations or functions in contrast to categories like S, NP, VP, etc, treating only the latter as primitive concepts of the theory: the functions are defined in terms of categories and their position in PMs, with the definitions applicable in principle to any PM in a transformational derivation. In this chapter I want to look further into the syntactic and semantic properties of the main functional elements in the clause and their treatment within a transformational framework.

15.1 Ellipsis

There is traditionally said to be ELLIPSIS of an element when it is 'understood' but not expressed – in imperative *Go away!*, for example, there is ellipsis of the subject *you*. We may begin by distinguishing two major types according to whether or not the missing elements are 'recoverable' by virtue of their identity with other elements in the same sentence (this distinction is related to that made on *p* 202 in the discussion of admissible types of deletion transformation). The first type has already been sufficiently analysed. In *John expected to intimidate Bill*, for example, the surface structure contains no subject for *intimidate*, but *John* from the higher clause is understood as subject of *intimidate* as well as *expect;* we accounted for these facts by having two occurrences of *John* in underlying structure with a deletion transformation, Equi, removing the lower one, so that it does not appear in surface structure. In this section I shall concentrate on the second type of ellipsis, that where there is no relation of identity between covert and overt elements in the sentence.

Very often elements that are not present in surface structure are recoverable from the meaning of the verb. For example, the verb *eat* denotes an action that inherently involves two entities, one performing, the other undergoing, the action; there need be no surface NP corresponding to the 'undergoer', but in a sentence like *John was eating* we nevertheless understand that SOMETHING was being eaten. Generalizing from [1–3] below we note that *eat* can occur either with or without an expressed object, *die* only without, *find* only with.

[1] i *John ate*   ii *John ate something*
[2] i *John died*   ii **John died something*
[3] i **John found*   ii *John found something*

A significant semantic difference between [1i] and [2i] is that [1i] entails [1ii] while [2i] does not entail [2ii]. As far as the syntax is concerned, there are two ways in which we might handle [1i]. One is to say that there is an object NP in deep structure and that it is deleted during the course of the transformational derivation; I shall refer to this as the 'transformational' formalization of ellipsis. The other is to say that [1i] has no object even in deep structure; this leaves it to the semantic component to handle the fact that eating is understood to involve two entities, and I shall accordingly speak of it as the 'semantic' solution to ellipsis. In this second analysis, *eat* must be listed in the lexicon with the strict subcategorization features of both intransitive and transitive verbs: [+ __ #] for [1i] and [+ __ NP] for [ii]. In the transformational solution, *eat* has only the second of these – but instead of the first it must be assigned a rule feature, [+ Unspecified Object Deletion], to distinguish it from *find*, so that we can generate [1i] but not [3i]. One can imagine variants of this solution depending on what the underlying object is postulated to be; one proposal commonly adopted is to represent it simply as Δ. The transformational and semantic solutions would then assign to [1i] the syntactic deep structures [4] and [5] respectively.

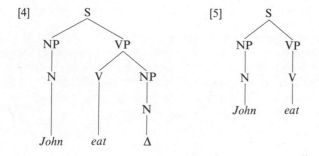

[4]   S   [5]   S
     /   \   /   \
   NP   VP   NP   VP
    | / \ | |
    N   V   NP   N   V
    | | | | |
    | | N   *John*   *eat*
  John *eat* Δ

(I omit many non-crucial details, including the tense element.) In [4] the right-most Δ introduced by the PS rules into the pre-lexical structure is unaffected by any lexical transformation: the analysis says that there is a deep structure object but that it is not lexically specified. This Δ is later removed by the Unspecified Object Deletion transformation, and the grammar will contain a surface structure constraint blocking any derivation in which the final PM contains a Δ. This means that although '*John Past find* Δ' is generated by the base rules (assuming we retain the 'old analysis' of tense) it does not qualify as a deep structure because it is not paired with any well-formed surface structure . (*cf* 12.5). The transformational solution formalizes a quite common and traditional view of the difference between [1i] and [2i]: that whereas *die* is a genuine intransitive verb, *eat* is inherently transitive, being merely 'used intransitively' in [1i]. PM [4] provides a better input to the semantic component than [5] inasmuch as it contains NPs corresponding to the two entities conceptually involved. But although some version of the transformational solution is adopted in virtually all transformational studies, there has been surprisingly little syntactic argumentation given in its support. Moreover, if the transformational analysis is used here, the question arises as to why it is not normally adopted in all cases where an element is understood but not specified. For example, *John died* entails *John died at some time* just as much as [1i] entails [ii], but the standard practice is not to analyse *John died* as containing a Δ time element in its deep structure.

One analogous case of ellipsis where there is some syntactic evidence for the transformational solution is that of passive sentences like *John was killed*. This will be derived from underlying '*Δ Past kill John*' by Passivization (giving '*John Past be en kill by Δ*'), followed by Unspecified Passive Agent Deletion, an obligatory and ungoverned rule which removes the '*by Δ*'. Suppose that, instead, we left it to the semantic component to handle the ellipsis here. The deep structure would then be simply '*Past kill John*' (with an amended Passivization rule applying obligatorily). This solution involves revising the PS rules in such a way that the deep subject NP is no longer obligatory – and this leads to loss of generalization in the rules for VP, for we would need to block the selection of an intransitive VP in a sentence containing no subject NP: although '*John Past die*' is a possible deep structure, '*Past die*' is not. Instead of a single general context-free rule for the VP, we would need separate rules depending on whether or not there was a subject NP.

Somewhat different from the ellipsis of [1i] is that exemplified in *John refused*. This too is understood transitively, but whereas in *John ate* it is left quite vague what it was that John ate, in a normal utterance of *John refused* the speaker takes it for granted that the addressee will be able to identify uniquely and correctly what John refused. The difference is in effect the same as that between an indefinite and a definite NP, as in

[6] i *I've found something*   [7] i *I've found it*
    ii *I can hear a train*   ii *I can hear the train*

where the object NPs are indefinite in [6], definite in [7]. In [7] the speaker presupposes that the addressee knows what *it* refers to, knows which train he has in mind, whereas no corresponding presuppositions are associated with the indefinite NPs *something* and *a train*. Definite NPs may be marked by a definite determiner, *the, this, that*, etc, by a definite pronoun, *I, you, he, she, it*, etc, by a proper noun, and so on – in *John is coming this evening* the addressee is assumed to know which of the vast number of people called *John* and which evening are being referred to. The identification may be made on the basis of the preceding linguistic context (*A bus came. But it was full*) or of the non-linguistic situation (*Put it over here*, where *it* refers, say, to the thing the addressee is carrying, or *The Vice-Chancellor is talking tonight*, where the subject NP refers to the Vice-Chancellor of the university with which the speaker and/or addressee have some connection). Similarly in ellipsis the missing element may be identified from the linguistic context (*I offered him a fiver but he refused* [sc the fiver]) or the situation (*Don't touch* [sc those papers, or whatever]). The deletion of such a definite object (with or without a preceding preposition or 'pro-verb' *do*) is governed, as is evident from the contrast in well-formedness between *He refused* [sc it], *He agreed* [sc to it], *I told him* [sc that], *I blame John* [sc for it], *I made him* [sc do it] on the one hand and on the other **I gave him* [sc it], **I wanted* [sc it, or to do it], **I offered him a stick but he wouldn't use*, and so on.

It is obvious, therefore, that simply postulating deep structure Δs falls far short of providing an adequate account of how such elliptical sentences are understood. Notice, for example, the different ways in which we reconstruct the covert deep subjects of *Passengers are requested to remain in their seats until the plane has stopped, I want to be left alone, John was killed.* The first we would normally interpret as 'I/we request . . .': although the sentence is in the passive voice *request* is used performatively (*cf* 9.1). The second is equivalent to 'I want to be left alone by everyone, or people in general'. In the third who or what killed John may be left quite vague or be recoverable from the context, as in, say, *The gangster fired and John was killed.* But it is a formidable task to go beyond the anecdotal discussion of a few examples like these to an explicit statement of systematic rules; the context clearly plays a large role in determining interpretation, and it is arguable how far the rules for reconstructing ellipted elements fall within the province of a competence grammar. The examples will give some idea of the problem of explicating the notion 'recoverability' in terms of formal constraints on deletion transformations along the lines of Chapter 13.

15.2 Logical, grammatical and psychological subjects

I have spoken of the traditional distinction between logical and grammatical subject: in a passive sentence like *Bill was seen by John*, *John* would be the logical, *Bill* the grammatical subject. Recognition has commonly been given also to a third type, the 'psychological' subject, such that in [8i] *Mary* is logical and grammatical subject but *economics* psychological subject, whereas in [ii] *Mary* functions as subject in all three senses.

[8] i *Economics Mary just can't understand*
　　ii *Mary just can't understand economics*

Within a transformational framework [i] will be derived from (the structure underlying) [ii], so that in deep structure *economics* will be in object position. A possible formulation of the rule concerned is [9], which would give [10] as the rough derived constituent structure of [8i].

[9] TOPICALIZATION　　　X — NP — Y
　　(Optional)　　　　　　　1　　2　　3　⇒
　　　　　　　　　　　　　2#[1　　∅　　3]

[10]

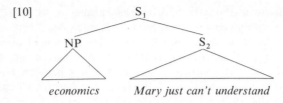

economics   Mary just can't understand

The structure change specifies that term 2 is Chomsky-adjoined to the left of the whole sentence: this creates the new node S_1 in [10]. Chomsky-adjunction is used rather than sister-adjunction so that in surface structure the whole sentence will have two ICs, *economics* and *Mary just can't understand*, which matches the phonological phrasing better than a three-IC analysis into *economics* and *Mary* and *just can't understand*. In accordance with the formal specification of Chomsky-adjunction, the whole sentence and its second IC are assigned to the same category. Within the TG framework there appears to be no descriptive objection to this – though clearly it would not be satisfactory in a PSG model, where the surface structures are generated directly by PS rules. In general, TG requires far fewer different category labels than PSG: notice, for example, that in Chapter 3 we had to distinguish between verb and verb stem in order to avoid generating strings like '*catch Past Past Past ...*', whereas in Chapter 5 verb stem was not needed as a primitive term. This point is of some importance, given the need to constrain as narrowly as possible the range of admissible transformations – *cf* the earlier discussion on limiting the kind of new structure that can be created (*p* 203).

Examples can be found where logical, grammatical and psychological subjects are all different, as in *A deduction of that size he certainly couldn't have been allowed by the tax inspector*. We can still define the logical subject as the NP daughter of S in deep structure, but the NP daughter of S in surface structure will now be the definition of the psychological rather than grammatical subject (except that it must be qualified so as not to apply to a clause in the position of S_2 in [10]: *Mary* will be psychological subject of [8ii] but not of [i]). Whether there is any level between deep and surface structure which it would be appropriate to select for the definition of grammatical subject remains to be seen. In *Are there many brands being manufactured now?*, *many brands* is subject at the stage of Subject-Verb Agreement, *there* at the stage of Inversion, and it seems pointless to insist on choosing one of these as grammatical subject: it is not clear that there is any significance attaching to the notion of a unique grammatical subject, distinct (at least potentially) from logical and psychological subjects.

Of the two non-syntactic notions of actor and topic that are commonly invoked in discussions of the function subject, actor correlates more closely with logical than with psychological subject, while the converse holds for topic. For example, in *John was chased down the street*, the actor corresponds to the logical subject but is not expressed in surface structure owing to the application of Unspecified Passive Agent Deletion; *John* is the psychological subject and the sentence is surely about John rather than the unspecified actor: it expresses the event from the point of view of what happened to John rather than of what some unspecified actor did. The same applies in [11], already cited in 3.1.

[11] i *This violin is easy to play sonatas on*
   ii *Sonatas are easy to play on this violin*

These derive from the same deep structure, roughly '*It* [$_S$ Δ *play sonatas on this violin*]$_S$ *Pres be easy*'. A governed rule that we may call Object Raising (to suggest its resemblance to the familiar Subject Raising transformation) moves a NP out of a complement clause into the position of subject in the higher clause – the NP that is affected may be the direct object of the complement clause, as in [ii], or the object of a preposition, as in [i]. The difference in psychological subject here does seem to correspond to a difference in topic; the logical subject of the complement clause has the role of actor, but is again unspecified and transformationally deleted – it clearly does not form the topic of either sentence. However, neither the correlation between topic and psychological subject nor that between actor and logical subject is one-to-one as is evident from the examples of 2.1.

15.3 Case grammar

The definitions of the non-primitive functional notions subject, object, etc, specify: (a) the category of the expression having the function in question – NP for subject and direct object, VP for predicate (assuming the PS rules we have been working with so far), and so on; (b) its position in the PM. According to Chomsky's proposals, the position is specified by giving just the immediately dominating node – S for subject and predicate, VP for direct object. Or rather he suggests that such specification should be sufficient at the level of deep structure, whereas it may be necessary to give further detail at later levels. For example, I argued above that the psychological subject cannot be satisfactorily defined simply as a NP daughter of S in surface structure. As a second example (though not one that Chomsky himself discusses), consider the syntactic functions in sentences like [12i], which we will assume to derive from the structure underlying [ii] by a transformation of Indirect Object Formation converting PM [13] to [14] (where tense is again omitted).

[12] i *John gave Bill the money*
   ii *John gave the money to Bill*

(One reason for deriving [14] from [13] rather than vice versa is that *to* is not the only preposition involved in such pairs – compare *He found her a job* versus *He found a job for her*. Some verbs can occur with either preposition, so that *Write me a letter* alternates with *Write a letter to me* while *Write me a cheque* alternates with *Write a cheque for me;* we could scarcely formulate a meaning-preserving transformation that would convert '*Write* NP NP' into the '*Write* NP PP' construction.) In [13] the VP has only one NP daughter, so that *the*

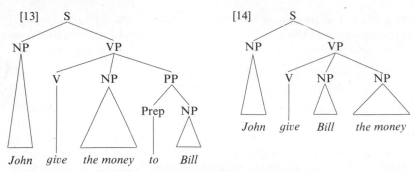

money satisfies the definition for direct object; in [14], however, there are two NP daughters, which means that if functions are to be defined at this level we shall need to take account of linear sequence as well as immediate domination. The term 'indirect object' is most often used in traditional grammar in such a way that *Bill* is the indirect object in both [12i] and [ii], but it does not seem possible to capture this sense in a definition of the form proposed by Chomsky: the surface structure difference between the sentences excludes a unitary definition at this level, and if [13] is the deep structure it is difficult to see how a definition of the standard form could distinguish *Bill* in [12] from, say, *the doctor* in *He sent his son to the doctor*, where *to the doctor* is traditionally analysed as a directional adjunct not an indirect object. A different usage of the term indirect object, typical of modern structuralist grammars, is that where it is applied to *Bill* in [12i] but not [ii] (it was this usage I had in mind in calling the above transformation Indirect Object Formation). The indirect object in this sense can be formally defined as the first of two NP daughters of VP – but it will not be a deep structure function and it will have no semantic significance.

In an interesting series of papers beginning in the mid-sixties Charles Fillmore develops the idea that subject and direct object, as defined by Chomsky, are likewise not deep structure functions and that the functions we should recognize at this level are of a quite different kind, namely semantic roles, or 'cases', such as agent, experiencer, goal, source and so on. Chomsky's definitions crucially involve (a) the distinction between the categories NP and PP, for both subject and direct object positions are filled only by NPs; (b) the division of a sentence into the constituents NP and VP, from which it follows that subject and direct object NPs are not sisters, only the former being a daughter of S. Fillmore argues that neither the NP–PP distinction nor the NP–VP division has any semantic significance, that neither has relevance at the level of deep structure.

There are several reasons for thinking that the presence versus absence of a preposition before a NP is a fairly superficial distinction. Firstly, we find many pairs of sentences containing the same verb and the same NPs with the same semantic values but in different linear arrangements and with accompanying differences in prepositions. [12] is such a pair, but there are others involving the direct object [15–16] or subject [17–18].

[15] i *Tim blamed the crash on Bill*   ii *Tim blamed Bill for the crash*
[16] i *He provided food for them*   ii *He provided them with food*
[17] i *Tim rented the flat to Ed*   ii *Ed rented the flat from Tim*
[18] i *Val benefited from the decision*   ii *The decision benefited Val*

In [15] the presence or absence of *on* before *Bill* and *for* before *the crash* depends simply on which of the NPs comes first, but does not affect our interpretation of the semantic role associated with the NPs; the same goes for [16–18] and other similar pairs. Secondly, there are pairs like

[19] i *John resembles Bill*   ii *John's resemblance to Bill*
[20] i *Ted rejected Bill*   ii *Ted's rejection of Bill*

In both [19] and [20], [i] is a clause, [ii] a 'nominalization', with the nouns *resemblance* and *rejection* formed by adding a suffix to the corresponding verb. The presence or absence of the prepositions *to* and *of* before *Bill* is determined by the choice between nominalization and clause, but again it has no effect on their semantic roles. A third type of pair is exemplified in

[21] i *Ed is seeking employment*
     ii *Ed is looking for employment*
[22] i *The course comprises ten lectures*
     ii *The course consists of ten lectures*

The two sentences in each pair are (more or less) paraphrases; the presence or absence of a preposition is this time determined by the particular verb selected but is, as before, of no semantic significance.

Let us turn now to the division of a sentence into NP and VP, with the functions subject and predicate respectively. The traditional basis for this division is the idea that the subject is what the sentence is about and the predicate says something about the subject. I have already observed that this is a somewhat elusive distinction but that to the extent that topic does correspond to subject it is the psychological subject, the subject in surface, not deep, structure that is involved. Some syntactic evidence for dividing a sentence like *John found the key* into two ICs, *John* and *found the key*, rather than three, *John*, *found* and *the key* is provided by the intonation associated with coordinate constructions:

[23] *John found the key and opened the door*
[24] *Reinhardt produced, and Huston directed, the film of Crane's novel*

In [23] the intonation is the same as that where *and* coordinates what are clearly complete constituents, as in, say, *John found the key and the padlock*, where the status of *the key* and *the padlock* as constituents of the underlying coordinated sentences is uncontroversial. But [24] has a quite different intonation, which is used in examples where the linked items are clearly not constituents of the underlying sentences, as in *Mary wants, and I hope she gets, the deputy chair-*

manship: there is no question of the highest IC division in *I hope she gets the deputy chairmanship* being between *I hope she gets* and *the deputy chairmanship*. These facts argue that *found the key* is a complete constituent in *John found the key* – as it is in the VP analysis. But this argument applies to that stage in the derivation at which Coordination Reduction and Restructuring take place: we saw in 7.2 that there are strong reasons for not having coordinate VPs generated directly by the PS rules and that such transformations as Passivization must apply before Coordination Restructuring (because of examples like *John wandered into the field and was attacked by the bull*). The fact that *found the key* is a constituent at this level does not establish that it is one in deep structure. Other things being equal, we shall of course carry over into deep structure the constituent division we have established at this later level: for every difference we make between the levels a transformation is needed to relate them, and thus each such difference must be justified. But in the present example other things are not equal: Fillmore maintains that there are grounds for rejecting the NP–VP division in deep structure.

What we have been regarding as the deep subject is like the object in that both are associated with a variety of different semantic roles and, more importantly, the same semantic role may be associated with the subject of one verb and the direct (or prepositional) object of another. Consider, for example:

[25] i *Jill slapped Ed*	[26] i *I crumpled the letter*
ii *Jill underwent surgery*	ii *I wrote the letter*
iii *Jill heard an explosion*	iii *I have two brothers*
[27] i *The concert pleased John*	[28] i *Bill received £5 from Tim*
ii *John liked the concert*	ii *Tim gave £5 to Bill*

[25] illustrates the different semantic roles of the subject, [26] those of the object. [25i] is a simple example where the subject expresses the actor (or 'agent' as, following Fillmore, I shall henceforth call it): Jill clearly performed some action here – but not in [ii] or [iii]. In [ii] her role is that of 'patient', in the sense of the one on whom the action is performed; in [iii] that of 'experiencer' of the sensation of hearing: to hear an explosion is not to 'do' something. In [26i] the letter is patient: I performed the crumpling action on the letter; but [ii] is different, for here the letter did not exist prior to my writing it – in [i] my action affects the letter, in [ii] it creates it. [26iii] expresses a purely static relation, with my brothers being neither affected nor created; there is in fact very little content expressed in the *have:* the nature of the relation is given in the noun *brother*. The traditional semantic basis for the term 'transitive' verb is that the action 'passes over' from agent to patient, but as usual this account does not hold for anything like all transitive verbs: not all subjects are agents and not all objects are patients. [27i] and [ii] are very similar in meaning, and in particular the semantic roles associated with *John* and *the concert* are essentially the same in both despite the differences in respect of the subject and direct object functions: John is the experiencer of the pleasure/enjoyment, while the

concert is the cause or stimulus. Similarly in [28]: in both [i] and [ii] Bill is the
recipient or 'goal', Tim the 'source' – the sentences report the transfer of £5
from Tim to Bill. [17] is very like [28], except that the different arrangement of
source and goal is not there accompanied by any change in the verb.

The point of these examples – and many others could be added – is that as
far as semantic role is concerned no special significance attaches to the subject,
that there is no reason for taking one role in a clause and setting it aside from
a constituent formed by the verb together with all the other roles accompanying
it. Fillmore proposes a deep structure in which the semantic roles are represented directly, and at such a level (considerably more abstract, or 'deeper',
than that envisaged by Chomsky) there will accordingly be no VP constituent,
no subject and direct object functions: these functions will be definable only at
later stages in the derivation.

The various roles are known as CASES – hence the term 'case grammar' for
this version of transformational theory. As we have seen, 'case' is traditionally
used for one of the dimensions along which nouns are inflected in various
languages. The main semantic correlates of the case inflections are semantic
roles of the type we have been considering. For example, in the Latin equivalent
of *The master gave the servant the money*, the NP expressing the thing trans-
ferred (the money) would be in the accusative, the source (the master) in the
nominative, the goal/recipient (the servant) in the dative (the term 'dative'
being in fact etymologically related to the verb *dare*, 'to give'). It is this kind of
correlation that provides the basis for Fillmore's extension of the term 'case'
to cover the underlying semantic roles. The correspondence between semantic
role and case inflection is generally complex and indirect, however. In Latin,
for example, the choice of inflection is not fully determined by semantic role:
the NP that is moved into subject position by Passivization takes the nominative inflection while the corresponding NP in the active counterpart is in the
accusative and as noted on *p* 199 the case inflection of an object NP depends on
idiosyncratic properties of the governing verb, and so on.

Systems of case inflections vary greatly from language to language, and some
languages have no case inflections at all. In English, for example, where there
is no dative inflection, the recipient/goal in an active sentence with *give* is
marked by its position before the direct object, as in [12i], or by the preposition
to, as in [12ii]. But while the inflections (and other markers – prepositions,
linear position, etc) differ across languages, Fillmore claims that the underlying semantic roles, the deep cases, are universal. Determining just what the
set of cases is poses formidable problems, of course, and not surprisingly
Fillmore has frequently modified his inventory and definitions during the
course of his work and other scholars adopting this framework have suggested
their own modifications. In a recent paper he proposed a set of nine, Agent,
Experiencer, Instrument, Source, Goal, Place, Time, Path and Object (for
which I will substitute the term 'Neutral', reserving object for the sense in
which we have been using it earlier in this section). Rough definitions of some
of these are as follows (Fillmore 1970:116):

[29] AGENT : the instigator of the event
      EXPERIENCER : the entity which receives or accepts or experiences or
          undergoes the effect of an action
      INSTRUMENT : the immediate physical cause of an event
      SOURCE : the place from which something moves
      GOAL : the place to which something moves
      NEUTRAL : the entity that moves or changes or whose position or
          existence is in consideration

In deep structure a sentence has two ICs, which Fillmore calls Modality and
Proposition; the latter consists of the verb plus the cases, while the former
contains tense, mood, aspect and negative elements modifying the sentence as
a whole. Each case consists of a NP and a case marker, symbolized K (for
'Kasus') and filled (at least in English) by a preposition. For example, [30i–iii]
will have the deep structures [31–33] respectively.

[30] i *John opened the door with the key*
     ii *The key opened the door*
    iii *The door opened*

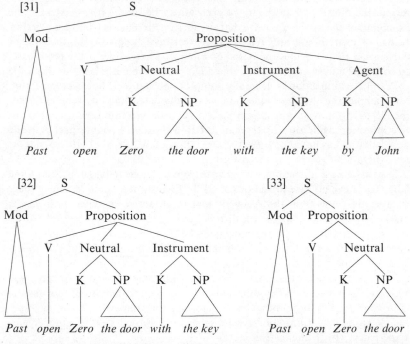

These structures show directly that in spite of surface differences *the key* has
the same semantic role in [i] and [ii], and *the door* in [i–iii]. There are no subjects
or objects in [31–33]; the subject is formed by adjoining one case as left daughter

of S and deleting the K element and the case-label, and similarly the object is formed by selecting one case as immediate right sister of V and deleting its K and case-label. [30i] will derive from [31] by Subject Formation, Object Formation and a rule attaching *Past* to the verb, giving [34] as surface structure.

[34]

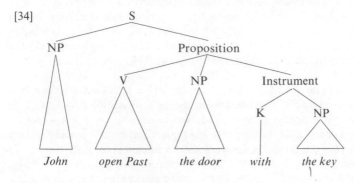

(Object will now be a NP daughter of Proposition, rather than of VP, as in Chomsky's definition.)

I have been speaking of agent, experiencer, etc, as semantic roles, and one apparent advantage of case grammar is that it provides deep structures that are intuitively more illuminating from a semantic point of view than those we find in Chomsky's version of the theory. For example, it enables us to express the difference between *Jill slapped Ed* and *Jill heard an explosion* by analysing *Jill* as agent and experiencer respectively and the similarity between *The concert pleased John* and *John liked the concert* by analysing *John* as experiencer in both, and so on. But in introducing the cases into deep structure Fillmore is claiming that they have syntactic significance as well. This claim is based on such points as the following:

(a) NPs in the same case, but not in different ones, may be coordinated: compare *John and Bill opened the bottles* (agent + agent) versus **John and the corkscrew opened the bottles* (agent + instrument). An analogous constraint holds for comparative constructions: *John opened more bottles than Bill* versus **John opened more bottles than the corkscrew*.

(b) Case is one of the major factors determining subject and object selection. For example, other things being equal, if the proposition contains an agent, this becomes subject (as in [30i]); if there is an instrument but no agent, the instrument becomes subject (as in [ii]) and so on. If there is a neutral not selected as subject, it will become object (as in [30i] or *Bill received £5 from Tom*, etc). There are two reasons for the 'other things being equal' qualification. Firstly, subject and object may be affected by later transformations like Passivization, as in *The door was opened with the key by John;* however, this simply means that we must continue to allow a sentence to have different subjects and objects at different stages in its derivation: it is the original subject and object that are selected on the basis of case. Secondly, some verbs are exceptions to the regular pattern in that they require or optionally allow some case other than the normal one to be selected as subject or object. For example, *rob* requires that the source rather than the neutral case become object – compare *John robbed Jill of all her money* versus *John stole all Jill's money from her*; *blame* allows either neutral or goal as object, as in [15i] and [ii] respectively; *look*, as in *Ed is looking for employment*, blocks the rule of Object Formation, so that the neutral element retains its preposition (whereas the synonymous *seek* is regular); and so on.

(c) Case is likewise one of the chief determinants in the choice of preposition (or, in some languages, case inflection and/or postposition). Typically, the prepositions for instrument, agent, goal, source are *with*, *by*, *to*, *from* respectively, and so on. Again, there are several qualifications to be made. Firstly, prepositions may be deleted or inserted in the transformational derivation; for example, Subject Formation and Object Formation delete prepositions, while Passivization inserts *by*. Secondly, verbs may be marked in the lexicon as taking special prepositions – it is an idiosyncratic property of *blame*, for example, that it selects *for* for the neutral case, *on* for the goal. Thirdly, some prepositions clearly make an independent contribution to the meaning, as opposed to simply marking case. Obvious examples are place and time prepositions: in *The book lay on/beside/near/underneath/in the tray* the preposition choice is limited, but by no means fully determined, by the place case of *the tray*.

(d) There may be no more than one occurrence of any case within a single proposition (except with coordination); the cases thus provide a suitable framework in which to state the strict subcategorization features of verbs. For example, *open* will be entered in the lexicon as insertable in the environment of a neutral, optionally accompanied by agent and/or instrument, *receive* in the environment of goal, neutral and source, and so on. Fillmore attaches crucial significance to the principle that each nominal element in the proposition must be in a different case, but certain difficulties arise in applying this principle. In the first place, there are clauses expressing the exchange of goods. If we say that in *John sold the car to Ed* and *Ed bought the car from John*, *the car* is neutral, *Ed* goal and *John* source, on the grounds that the car passes from John to Ed, how shall we analyse *John sold the car to Ed for £500*, *Ed bought the car from John for £500*, *Ed paid John £500 for the car*, where there is also transfer of £500 in the opposite direction? A second difficulty arises with pairs like

[35] i *The hors d'oeuvres preceded the soup*
    ii *The soup followed the hors d'oeuvres*

The relationship between [i] and [ii] here is like that in [27] and [28], except that in [35] it seems hardly possible to differentiate in a non-ad hoc way the roles of *the hors d'oeuvres* and *the soup* in [i] while still assigning the same case to *the soup* and the same to *the hors d'oeuvres* in the two sentences.

A serious evaluation of case grammar would require a much more thorough examination of points (a)–(d) than there is space for here – and I think it is fair to say that Fillmore's own treatment of them remains somewhat speculative. It is a formidable task to provide satisfactorily rigorous definitions of the cases – those quoted above are quite rough and vague. One major difficulty is to determine an appropriate level of generality for them. Consider the verbs *rob* and *criticize*, for example. One might propose that the roles combining with *rob* are 'culprit', 'loser', 'loot', and with *criticize* 'critic', 'offender', 'offence'; Fillmore writes as follows of this suggestion (1970: 116):

> It seems to me, however, that this sort of detail is unnecessary, and that what we need are abstractions from these specific role descriptions, abstractions which will allow us to recognize that certain elementary role notions recur in many situations, and which will allow us to acknowledge that differences in detail between partly similar roles are due to differences in the meanings of the associated verbs.

At one extreme, where culprit, loser, loot, etc, are established as cases, the interpretation of the roles associated with a verb is expressed directly in the case labels. At the other extreme, where we have subjects and objects rather than cases in the deep syntactic structure, the interpretation of the roles depends wholly on the meaning of the verb. Fillmore's proposal is for something in between: the case label makes some contribution to the interpretation, with further detail being derived from the meaning of the verb. It remains to be seen whether points (a)–(d) above provide a principled basis for sharing the burden of interpretation between the case labels and the meaning of the verb.

I observed earlier that Chomsky's definitions of subject and object depend crucially on the distinction between NP and PP, and on the division of a sentence into the ICs NP and VP: the claim that both of these were relatively superficial was one of the main motivations for Fillmore's proposal to change the form of deep structure representations. However, this claim is independent of case grammar, in that accepting the claim does not necessitate accepting case theory. Leaving aside those prepositions that make an independent contribution to meaning (*cf* 15.5 below), one can imagine having the presence or absence of prepositions in examples [15–22] and so on handled in the transformational component, like the choice of case inflection. Moreover it may be that just as it is unnecessary for the transformation adding case inflections to introduce any new category label into the derived tree (a case-inflected NP is still a NP), so the transformation adding prepositions need not introduce any special label – it may be sufficient to Chomsky-adjoin the preposition to the NP, with prepositional phrase being no longer a primitive term, no longer a distinct category from NP. (If this still speculative proposal can be shown to be workable, it would solve the problem of the derived constituent structure of the *by* phrase in passive sentences – *cf p* 203.) Secondly, McCawley (1970) has argued on syntactic grounds against a subject-predicate division in deep structure, proposing representations like [36] instead of [37] (tense is again omitted).

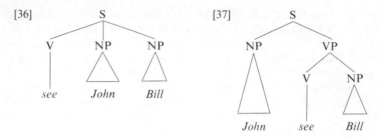

His thesis is that a number of transformations, such as Passivization, *There* Insertion, Subject Raising, can be significantly simplified if the verb is on the left until a fairly late stage in the derivation; the grammar will of course then need a special Subject Fronting rule – but it will not need an Inversion rule to move the verb to initial position in interrogatives, etc. We can still apply the functional terms subject and object to *John* and *Bill* respectively in [36], but the definitions will have to be amended to differentiate between them in terms of linear position, not dominating node. The traditional classification of verbs as intransitive, transitive and ditransitive is based on the number of objects they take: none, one and two respectively. NPs preceded by a preposition do not count as objects for the purposes of this classification (or at least not in general: there is some equivocation over the indirect object), so that *consist*, for example, as in *The course consists of ten lectures*, is classified with verbs like *exist*, as in *God exists*, as intransitive, rather than with transitive verbs like *see*, as in *John saw Bill*. In a grammar where the subject is not set aside in deep structure from the rest of the sentence and where the presence or absence of prepositions is handled for the most part by transformations, a more natural classification will be based simply on the number of NPs the verb combines with (*ie* has as sisters) in deep structure. Accordingly, we shall speak of one-place verbs (*eg: exist*), two-place verbs (*eg: see*), three-place verbs (*eg: give* in *Ed gave Jill a present*) and four-place verbs (*eg: buy* in *Tom bought the car from Bob for £100*).

15.4 A note on agents and causatives

Case grammar provides a neat solution to the problem of accounting for the relation between pairs of sentences like

[38] i *The temperature increased*
    ii *John increased the temperature*

The temperature is neutral in both, *John* agent in [ii], and *increase* is listed in the lexicon with a strict subcategorization feature specifying that it occurs with a neutral and optionally an agent. How can pairs like [38] be handled in a grammar where the deep structure nominal functions are subject and object rather than cases? One solution, proposed in fact earlier than Fillmore's, is to analyse [ii] as containing an abstract causative verb taking a complement sentence as its deep object, roughly as in [39].

[39]

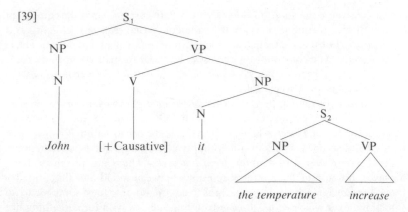

The constant relation between *the temperature* and *increase* in the two sentences is accounted for by having *the temperature* deep subject of *increase* in both; the verb of the higher clause is abstract in the sense that it has no phonological form and is obligatorily deleted in the course of the transformational derivation.

A type of construction relevant to the choice between the two solutions is exemplified in [40].

[40] i *The new recruit marched to the guard-room*
     ii *Sgt Jones marched the new recruit to the guard-room*

Fillmore would analyse *the new recruit* as agent in [i], but it cannot be assigned to this case in [ii] because of the requirement that there be only one occurrence of a given case within a single clause (and if there is just one agent in [ii] it must surely be *Sgt Jones*). If the relation between [i] and [ii] is judged to be the same in [40] as in [38], this must count as an argument for the abstract causative solution, where the two pairs are handled alike, as against the case solution, where they cannot be.

Consider also the contrast in acceptability between

[41] *I persuaded John to help me*
[42] **I persuaded John to suffer from diabetes*

You can only persuade someone to do something over which he has some measure of control or choice: hence the anomaly of [42]. It is arguable how far this notion can be specified in linguistic terms, but most of the TG literature assumes that to some extent at least it falls within the province of a competence grammar, and sentences like [42] are normally regarded as deviant. One widely adopted way of differentiating between them is in terms of the inherent feature [Stative], with *suffer* having the '+' value, *help* the '−' value, and *persuade* having a selectional feature excluding it from occurrence with a complement sentence whose verb is marked [+Stative]. The [Stative] feature thus distinguishes verbs expressing states from those expressing activities, 'doing' verbs – note that *He helped me*, but not *He suffered from diabetes*, would be a perfectly normal answer to the question *What did he do?*. In case grammar the equivalent to the inherent feature [Stative] will be the contextual feature [__Agent], and *persuade* will be excluded from occurring with a complement that does not have a deep agent. (The constraint on *persuade*, however formalized, applies to the *persuade to* construction, not *persuade that*: *I persuaded John that he suffered from diabetes* is quite acceptable.)

The same constraint applies to other verbs: *advise, command, order, remind, request, tell, urge*, etc, in the construction 'NP *advised* NP *to* ...'; *attempt, choose, condescend, forget, remember, try*, etc, in the construction 'NP *attempted to* . . .'; and so on. It is often said to apply also to imperative constructions: compare *Help me!* with **Suffer from diabetes!*. There are problems here, however, because of the complex relations between mood and illocutionary force. We can agree that it is anomalous to command or request someone to do something over which he has no control, but one can wish for something not subject to control and wishes can be expressed in an imperative, as in *Sleep well!* or *Have a safe journey!*. (As noted in 9.1, the fact that sleeping well is not something one can choose to do is undoubtedly one of the factors determining the interpretation of *Sleep well!* as a wish.)

A more general problem arises with sentences like:

[43] *John appeared to be enjoying the party*
[44] *John tried to appear to be enjoying the party*
[45] *I persuaded John to be vaccinated against tetanus*

[43] will be analysed, according to the criteria of Chapter 8, as having the deep structure '[$_{NP}$ *it* [$_S$ *John be ing enjoy the party*]$_S$]$_{NP}$ *Past appear*'. Clearly 'appearing' is not something that can be 'done' by the proposition expressed in the subject NP, so that *appear* will be specified as [+ Stative] or, in the case approach, as [− __ Agent]. How then can we account for the interpretation of [44], where John is understood to have tried to 'do' something. The analysis with the abstract higher verb (which will be marked as [−Stative] as well as [+Causative]) could be extended to cover this situation: the object complement of *try* would have *John* as subject, the abstract causative as verb and *it* plus the structure underlying [43] as object. Similarly in [45], where the complement of *persuade* will be roughly '*John* [+Causative, −Stative] *it* [$_S$ Δ *vaccinate John against tetanus*]$_S$'. It is difficult to see how invoking the notion of an agent case can obviate the need for an abstract causative in such constructions − it is clear, for example, that *John* cannot be agent in the *vaccinate* clause itself: the agent for this clause is the unspecified vaccinator. It seems likely that agent should be treated as a non-primitive term (definable perhaps as underlying subject of a certain class of verbs) rather than a primitive, as in case grammar.

The motivation for the abstract structures we have been postulating has been essentially semantic, so that it might be argued that the phenomena in question would be more appropriately handled in the semantic component than in the syntax. In this view the deep structures of [38i] and [ii] would differ only trivially from their respective surface structures (*eg* in respect of the position of *Past*), so that the deep function of *the temperature* would be subject in [i], object in [ii]. It would still be possible to maintain the *Aspects*-theory principle that it is the functions in deep structure that determine meaning, given the sense of 'determine' explained on *p* 175, for the rules leading to the semantic interpretation would take the deep structure as input – though the less difference there is between deep and surface functions, the less interest there is in the claim that it is the former that determine meaning. Moreover, it is clear that relational or functional notions of some kind must play a part in semantic structure: whatever system we devise for representing meanings, we shall somehow need to distinguish the roles associated with *John* and *Bill* in *John saw Bill*, and so on. And if we have functions in semantic structure and functions in syntactic surface structure, the question arises as to where we draw the line between syntax and semantics, as to how 'deep' the syntactic deep structure should be: this is the major issue dividing the current rival versions of TG, and the Extended Standard Theory and Generative Semantics. The introduction of abstract verbs, as in [39], was one of the first major steps towards the latter theory, where ALL elements in underlying structure are abstract (non-phonological), and where there is no level intermediate between the semantic and surface syntactic representations that can be regarded as marking a division between semantics and syntax.

15.5 Verbs, adjectives and nouns

In surface structure, verbs and adjectives differ in a number of obvious ways; two major (and related) differences are as follows: (a) A verb, but not an adjective, can carry the tense inflections – *John smiled* versus **John happied*. (b) A verb, but not an adjective, can combine with one or more NPs or PPs to form a complete, non-elliptical sentence – *They love music* versus **They keen on music*. On the basis of such differences, verb and adjective have traditionally been regarded as different parts of speech, and this view has been carried over into the grammar we have been assuming so far, where they are different categories in both deep and surface structure.

There are, however, some significant similarities between verbs and adjectives: several important subclassificatory dimensions apply to them both. Consider first strict subcategorization. According to the proposal made at the end of 15.3, verbs will be strictly subcategorized as to the number of deep structure NPs ('places') they take. Now the distinction between one- and two-place verbs is matched by that between one- and two-place adjectives: compare *The grass is green* versus *Ed is keen on football*. The traditional classification into intransitives and transitives, based as we have seen on the number of NP objects, does not bring out this similarity, for the second NP in a two-place adjectival construction is usually preceded by a preposition, as in the above example or *John is fond of animals*, *John is eager for recognition*, and so on. The usual pattern is for the second place to have a preposition after an adjective but not after a verb – compare *John likes animals*, *John wants recognition*, etc. However, just as there are some exceptional verbs that take a preposition (*eg: consist of*), so we find a few adjectives used without a following preposition: *The stamp is worth £5, Ed is like his father*, and so on. If we adopt the case theory, the strict subcategorization will be based not on the number of places but on the particular array of cases in the deep structure environment, but the similarity between verbs and adjectives remains. For clearly the semantic roles of *John* and *animals* are the same in *John is fond of animals* and *John likes animals*, and analogously with *Ed is like his father* and *Ed resembles his father*. Notice further that verbs and adjectives are also alike in being subclassified according as a particular place (or case) can be filled by an embedded complement clause, and if so whether it is declarative or interrogative – witness *That John was ill surprised/*shaved me, That John was ill was obvious/*oblong. I wonder/*believe why he came, I am uncertain/*glad why he came*, and so on.

Turning from strict subcategorization to inherent features, we may observe next that the feature [Stative] applies to adjectives as well as verbs: compare [41] and [42] above with *I persuaded John to be tactful/*tall*. This feature also has some relevance to progressive aspect: we saw in 5.1 that verbs are subclassifiable according as they can or cannot occur (normally) in the progressive, and again this difference is found with adjectives – compare *John is learning/*knowing Greek* and *John is being obstreperous/*slim*.

Thirdly, verbs and adjectives are subclassified by some shared selectional features. For example, both *enjoy* and *happy* are incompatible with an inanimate subject: hence the anomaly of **The key enjoyed the concert, *The key was happy*, and so on.

Finally we find some rule features shared by verbs and adjectives: a number of governed rules impose a subclassification on both. For example, just as Subject Raising can apply on a cycle where the verb is *appear* or *seem* but not *emerge* or *matter* (*John seemed/*mattered not to like her*), so it can apply with *certain* or *likely* but not *obvious* or *possible* (*John is likely/*possible to arrive*, from '*It [sJohn arrive]s is likely/possible*'), and so on. Object Raising similarly occurs with adjectives like *easy, hard, impossible*, but also with at least one verb, *take* – compare *The letter took an hour to write*, where the rule is applied, with *It took an hour to write the letter*, where it is not. And as implied above, rules determining insertion or deletion of prepositions subclassify both verbs and adjectives – *look* differs from *seek* in the way that *similar* differs from *like* (*cf: John is similar to his father*).

There is at present no general agreement as to how these undisputed similarities between verbs and adjectives should be handled in formal terms. Chomsky himself maintains that the theory of syntactic features allows them to be expressed without any need for modification of the underlying constituent structures that we have been assuming so far. Others have argued that verbs and adjectives should be merged into a single deep structure category, with the differences between them being handled in the transformational component. Under this analysis, the copula *be* that occurs in *John is happy* and the like will be introduced transformationally, by a rule we may call *Be* Support, to suggest its affinity with *Do* Support. *Do* is introduced to carry a tense inflection that has not been affixed to a verb, and the suggestion now is that *be* similarly serves as a semantically empty carrier of verbal inflections that cannot be affixed to any of the elements in the deep structure of the clause. The difference between verbs and adjectives will then be formalized not in terms of a distinction of primary categories, V versus Adj, but of rule features, [−*Be* Support] versus [+*Be* Support]. The proposal is of the same formal nature as that discussed in Chapter 14 whereby the auxiliaries and main verbs of Chapter 5 would be merged into a single category and be differentiated solely in terms of rule government.

Be is of course not the only verb to fill the blank position in the surface structure construction 'NP __ Adj': others are *appear, become, feel, grow, look, prove, seem*, and so on; with *be* these make up the class commonly known as copulative verbs. If we analyse *John was happy* as having *happy* as the underlying 'verb' (extending this term to cover the new more general category) with *be* introduced transformationally, how shall we deal with *John appeared/became/ . . . happy?* We have already seen that *appear* can take a complement sentence as deep subject, so that *John appeared to like Jill* derives from (roughly) '*It* [s *John like Jill*]s *Past appear*'. Similarly *John appeared to be happy* will derive from '*It* [s *John happy*]s *Past appear*': *be* is inserted on the cycle of the complement sentence by the same rule as applies in the simple sentence *John was happy*, but for the rest the transformational derivation is the same. All we need to derive *John appeared happy* from the same deep structure is a rule of *To Be* Deletion applying on the *appear* cycle. This rule is governed: it cannot apply to *John ceased to be happy*, for example. Not all the copulative verbs occur in structures with an overt infinitival verb in the complement: **John became to like Jill* is clearly deviant, for example (though note that this gap in the distribution of *become* is filled by *come: John came to like Jill* – and conversely we cannot delete the *to be* of *John came to be happy*, without also changing *come* to *become*). Reanalysing the traditional copulative verbs (other than *be*) as verbs taking a complement sentence as underlying subject (or object in one or two cases, *eg: feel*) has semantic plausibility, but makes of course for significantly more abstract deep structures.

Let us turn now to nouns, considering them first as they occur in predicative position, as in *John's appointment was a **surprise***. These exhibit some of the same resemblances to verbs as do adjectives. Firstly, we can distinguish between one- and two-place nouns: *The child was a **boy*** versus *The candidate was a **son** of the prime minister*, where *boy* takes a single NP (*the child*) and *son* relates two (*the candidate* and *the prime minister*). The second NP in such constructions always has a preposition or else is in the possessive case: *Jill was sister to Ed* or *Jill was Ed's sister*. Secondly, predicative nouns are subclassifiable in terms of the feature [Stative], witness *John is being a martyr/*diabetic*. Thirdly, they impose selectional restrictions on their accompanying NPs in the same way as verbs and adjectives: compare *His niece/*nephew is a nymphomaniac*. Predicative nouns (unlike adjectives) also resemble verbs in that they normally agree in number with the subject NP – *The child was a boy, All the children were boys*. Such similarities support the further extension of the category 'verb' to include predicative nouns too. Notice, moreover, that the more conservative (less abstract) analysis, where *be* is taken as the underlying verb in these constructions, faces the problem of how to capture the traditional distinction between the predicative and direct object functions in *The child was a boy* and *The child saw a boy* respectively: if *a boy* is analysed as a NP daughter of VP in the former it will satisfy the definition of object.

What, now, of nouns functioning as the head of a subject or object NP, as in *The king died, They caught the assassin?* Bach 1968 has argued that in deep structure these nouns are in fact also in predicative position and thus belong to the category verb too: he derives *the king* via an intermediate structure of the form (roughly) '*the one who was king*'. One of his arguments is based on the structure of NPs like *a heavy smoker*. The account we gave in 7.2 of pre-nominal (or 'attributive') adjectives like *pretty* in *a pretty girl* does not work for these: *a heavy smoker* (at least in its most likely interpretation) is not equivalent to *a smoker who is heavy*. A more appropriate source would be *one who smokes heavily*, so that some pre-nominal adjectives would derive from adverbs. Treating nouns like *king* as underlyingly predicative then allows us to generalize this analysis to constructions like *the former king* (from *the one who was formerly king*), *the alleged assassin* (*the one who was allegedly the assassin*), *the putative father* (*the one who was putatively the father*), and so on.

When we turn to other traditional word classes, we again find resemblances to verbs or adjectives. Those prepositions that have independent meaning, for example, are from a semantic point of view like two-place verbs – compare *The box contains lots of toys* and *Lots of toys are in the box* (where the *be* could be regarded as simply the carrier of the verbal inflections, just as in *John was happy*), or *The rain caused them to cancel the match* and *They cancelled the match because of the rain*. The same holds for various adverbs and conjunctions, witness pairs like *It is possible that John has left* and *John has possibly left* (and recall also our discussion of *John may have left*). Such resemblances have led some scholars to extend still further the category verb – to the point where, in the generative semantic theory, the only primary categories postulated are S, NP and V.

Notes

A general study of grammatical functions can be found in Lyons 1968:334–99. Chomsky 1965:68–74 discusses the treatment of grammatical functions in the *Aspects* theory, and his 1970 paper proposes some extensions to that account. Case theory is developed in Fillmore 1968*a*, *b*, 1970, 1971, Stockwell *et al* 1973; see also Jackendoff 1972 and, for some criticism, Mellema 1974. Halliday 1967–8 and 1970 discusses the English clause functions within the framework of 'systemic grammar'.

One difference between active and passive constructions is that the logical subject can be left unspecified in the latter but not, in general, in the former: this is doubtless a significant factor in determining the choice between them in actual performance – textual studies show that the majority of passive clauses contain no *by* phrase. In some of these passives it is arguable whether there really is a logical subject 'understood' – *cf* Huddleston

1971:104–8. Shopen 1973 argues against handling ellipsis by deletion transformations. The rule of Object Raising is often called *Tough* Movement (*tough* being one of the adjectives that govern it); for discussion, see Postal and Ross 1971. Just as subject or object can be raised in complement constructions, so either can be deleted under identity with a higher NP: in addition to Equi (Subject Deletion) applying in *The patient is eager to see the doctor*, we need an Equi Object Deletion rule for *The patient is ready for the doctor to see*, etc.

On the inclusion of adjectives within the verb category, see G. Lakoff 1966*b* (where the feature [Stative] is introduced) and for a contrary view Chomsky 1970*a*. The extended concept of verb corresponds quite closely to the logician's concept of 'predicate': the logician commonly speaks of *exist, mortal, man*, etc, as 'one-place predicates', *love, fond, sister*, etc, as 'two-place predicates', and so on – a different use of 'predicate' from that where it is paired with 'subject'. Abstract causative verbs are introduced in G. Lakoff 1965; for a different treatment, see Chomsky 1970*a*, Jackendoff 1972, Fodor 1974. Fillmore 1970 allows his agent case to combine with another, claiming that in *John bought the car from Bill*, for example, *John* is both agent and goal, while in *Bill sold the car to John*, the agent combines with source in *Bill*. On the notion of agent, see Cruse 1973; also Haas 1973*b*. 'Agent' as a deep case should be distinguished from 'agent' as the NP in a passive sentence corresponding to the subject of the active counterpart: *John* is agent in the first sense but not the second in *John hit Bill*, and vice versa in *The message wasn't understood by John*. Berman 1974 argues against [36] and Jackendoff 1973 against the merging of PP and NP.

The distinction between categories and functions is sometimes partially obscured in practice. Fillmore's cases, for example, are intended as functional concepts but are formalized as categories – he himself admits this to be unsatisfactory (1971). Chomsky too (1965:107) makes the questionable assumption that concepts like Duration, Direction, Place, Frequency are syntactic categories and introduces some rather suspect categories in order to distinguish the predicative and direct object functions.

Chapter 16

Syntax and Semantics

It has been a recurrent theme in Chomsky's work that syntactic structure can and should be described independently of meaning. In the first version of the theory, as we have seen, semantics was held to fall outside the domain of generative grammar altogether: semantics was concerned with the use rather than the form of sentences. The task of a grammar was to generate 'all and only the grammatical sentences of the language' and to describe the structure of each, and Chomsky emphasized the non-semantic nature of the concept of a grammatical sentence and the various concepts needed in the structural descriptions (concepts like phoneme, morpheme, constituent, noun, verb, subject, transformation, kernel string, and so on). Katz and Fodor's paper of 1963 extended the domain of generative grammar to include semantics, but left intact the rest of the theory, including the autonomy of syntax: semantics simply took over where syntax left off. The paper was highly programmatic and can hardly be said to have shed any significant new light on the problem of explaining how the syntactic structure of a sentence determines its meaning: its importance lies rather in the fact that it did extend the generative model so as to provide in principle for a set of explicit rules associating sentences with their semantic interpretation. Subsequent investigation within this enlarged framework of the relations between syntactic structure and meaning suggested that (non-lexical) transformations make no contribution to meaning, so that in the *Aspects* model the input to the semantic rules consists solely of syntactic deep structures. It must be remembered, however, that in the study that provided the main evidence for this view Katz and Postal (1964) argued that in all the cases they examined there were purely syntactic reasons for formulating the rules in such a way that the transformations were meaning-preserving. In principle, then, the autonomy of syntax was retained in the *Aspects* theory even though the model had been expanded to include a semantic component, and in work done within this framework arguments based on such semantic notions as sameness or difference of meaning would not be accepted as sole justification of a proposed syntactic analysis.

One important departure from this principle, however, appears to have been the introduction of referential indices, for I am not aware of any published attempts to provide syntactic justification for their use in syntactic representations: their function was to permit transformations like Reflexivization to meet the semantic condition of being meaning-preserving (*cf pp* 89–90). Unless independent syntactic evidence can be adduced for having any given transformation meet this condition, the autonomy of an *Aspects*-model syntax is necessarily diminished.

In recent work Chomsky has given up the requirement that (non-lexical) transformations preserve meaning and returned to the idea of a completely autonomous syntax. Some of the crucial data that called into question the validity of the Katz-Postal hypothesis are exemplified in [1] and [2].

[1] i *Many MPs weren't in the House*
    ii *There weren't many MPs in the House*
[2] i *Many arrows didn't hit the target*
    ii *The target wasn't hit by many arrows*

[1i] and [ii] do not have the same meaning. I could without inconsistency assert [i] and deny [ii]: it would be appropriate to do so, for example, if half the MPs were present in the House, half absent. The difference in meaning can be described in terms of the 'scope' of the negative element. In [ii] the quantifier *many* is inside the scope of the negative, *ie* part of what is being negated – compare 'It is not the case that many MPs were in the House' or 'Not many MPs were in the House'. In [i], on the other hand, *many* is outside the scope of the negative: the MPs who were not in the House are quantified, positively, as many – compare 'Many were the MPs who were not in the House'. Syntactically, however, we have argued that dummy *there* is not present in deep structure but is inserted by (non-lexical) transformation. And if we derive [i] and [ii] from the one deep structure '*many MPs not Past be in the House*', with *There* Insertion applying in [ii] but not [i], then we clearly cannot maintain that this rule is meaning-preserving.

Much the same holds for [2], except that here the situation is complicated by variation in stress and intonation. For clarity of exposition I shall confine my attention at this stage to the most usual readings, with the main stress falling on the final word, *target* in [i], *arrows* in [ii]. With this proviso, we have the same meaning-difference as in [1]. [2i] asserts that many arrows failed to hit the target, so that *many* is outside the scope of *not;* [ii] denies that many hit, and has *many* inside the scope of *not* (*cf* 'Not many arrows hit the target'). Again it follows that if [ii] is derived by Passivization from the same structure as underlies [i] this transformation cannot be meaning-preserving. We find equivalent meaning-differences attributable to the two Raising rules. In *Many MPs didn't seem to understand it*, where Subject Raising applies, *many* is outside the scope of the negative (like [1i], the sentence makes a negative assertion about many MPs), whereas in *It didn't seem that many MPs understood it* the *many* is inside the scope of the negative; similarly in *Many errors weren't easy to see* versus *It wasn't easy to see many errors*, with Object Raising applying in the former but not the latter.

The four examples have it in common that in each case the transformation reverses the linear order of *many* and *not:* in [1] and [2] *many* is moved to the right of *not* and in the Raising examples *many* is moved to the left of *not*. And in all four cases, whether *many* falls within the semantic scope of *not* is determined by their relative position in surface structure, not deep structure. For this reason Chomsky proposes that instead of having all the rules of semantic interpretation operate on deep structure, some should take the surface structure as input. The semantic relation between *MPs* and *in the House* is constant in [1], as is that between *arrows*, *hit* and *target* in [2]: this aspect of the meaning will still be determined by a rule taking the deep structure as input; the role of the new type of semantic rule will be to specify various other aspects of meaning – in this instance the scope of a negative. This extension in the range of the semantic rules is reflected in the name given to the revised model: the 'Extended Standard Theory'.

I should emphasize that linear position in surface structure is not the only factor determining the scope of *not*. *Many went walking when it wasn't raining* and *When it wasn't raining many went walking* do not exhibit the above meaning-difference: the semantic rule must take into account whether *many* and *not* are clause-mates and, if they are not, which is in the main clause, and so on. Another relevant factor is stress and intonation – which brings us back to [2]. If [ii] is read with nuclear stress on *many*, the quantifier will be taken to fall outside the scope of the negative, and if [i] is read with a fall-rise intonation, and nuclear stress on *many* as well as *target*, the quantifier will be inside the scope of *not:* the interpretive rule specifying the semantic scope of the negative will accordingly have to take account of this aspect of phonological structure. (I should add that there appears to be some dialect variation here – not all speakers accept that both [2i] and [ii] can have the two interpretations.)

The relaxation of the condition that the semantic rules operate only on deep structure makes it possible to handle certain aspects of meaning that had earlier been regarded as falling outside the domain of semantic theory. We have so far been regarding pairs like *Bill saw Joe* and *Joe was seen by Bill* or *Ed gave the key to Tim* and *Ed gave Tim the key* as semantically identical. They are certainly equivalent as far as basic semantic relations like entailment, consistency, etc, are concerned (*cf p* 91), but there are nevertheless important differences in their use that should be accounted for in a description of the speaker-hearer's linguistic knowledge. Consider the examples

[3] i *Did Bill give the map to John?*
   ii *Did Bill give John the map?*
  iii *Was John given the map by Bill?*

again read with the main stress falling on the final lexical item, *John*, *map* and *Bill* respectively. Now suppose we have a context where it has been established that Bill gave the map to someone and I want to find out whether this person was John: in this context it would be appropriate for me to use [i] but not [ii] or [iii]. The claim is not of course that this is the only context where [i] is appropriate, but that in this context only the first of the three sentences is appropriate – and that this is something the speaker-hearer tacitly knows about these sentences. Likewise, if I know that Bill gave John various things, [ii] but not [i] or [iii] is an appropriate sentence to elicit whether the map was among them; and if John's having been given the map is established, [iii] is an appropriate question for finding out whether Bill was the one who gave him it. Chomsky proposes that this aspect of meaning be described in terms of the notions of presupposition and focus, where the presupposition consists of the information taken to be already shared by speaker and addressee, the focus that which is being asked for (in a question), asserted (in a statement) and so on. (These presuppositions about [3] are in addition to the type discussed in the analysis of interrogatives in 9.2, and it is arguable whether both can properly be subsumed under a single concept: presupposition is certainly in need of further explication.) [3i] would allow a number of distinct interpretations on this dimension – with the presupposition being 'Bill gave the map to someone' in one, 'Bill did something' in another, 'Something happened' in a third. What is common to the meanings of [i–iii] will be handled by the old type of semantic rule operating on the deep structure, which is the same for all three; the meaning differences relating to presupposition and focus, on the other hand, will be determined by the new type of rule that takes account of surface constituent structure and stress.

Although the coverage of the model as a whole has thus expanded in the change from *Aspects* to the Extended Standard Theory, the domain of the syntactic component has contracted significantly. Various phenomena that were earlier handled in the syntax are now handled in the semantics; the main example is anaphora.

ANAPHORA is an important concept, so that it is worth pausing briefly to discuss it in more or less pre-theoretical terms before turning to its treatment within the TG framework. We may begin with a simple example like *Ed hurt himself*, where *himself* is said to be anaphorically related to *Ed:* it is by virtue of this relation that *himself* is understood as referring to Ed. The two terms in the relation are known as the ANAPHOR (*himself*) and the ANTECEDENT (*Ed*). In this example, anaphor and antecedent are coreferential, but this condition does not hold for all types of anaphora. In *Joe wore a blue tie, Tim wore a red one*, for example, *tie* is antecedent to the anaphor *one*, for it is again by virtue of this relation that *one* is understood here as equivalent to *tie*, but *tie* and *one* are not coreferential (they are not in fact referring expressions at all: it is the full NPs *a blue tie* and *a red one* that refer). The anaphoric relation may cross sentence boundaries, as when you ask '*Where's Bill?*' and I reply '*He's upstairs*' with *he* anaphoric to *Bill*, and there may be ambiguity over the identification of the antecedent – *Ed told Tom he had won* is ambiguous according as *Ed* or *Tom* (or a preceding NP) is antecedent to *he*. The traditional term 'antecedent' suggests that this element precedes the anaphor; this is the most usual situation, but under certain structural conditions (very roughly, when the anaphor is in a clause subordinate to the one containing the antecedent) the reverse order is possible. Thus *she* can be anaphoric to *Mary* in *When she got home Mary lit the fire*, but not in *She can have the money if Mary wins*. All the anaphors cited above are pronouns, but it must be emphasized that (a) not all pronouns are anaphoric, and (b) not all anaphors are pronouns. *Somebody* and *something*, which do not have antecedents, are examples of non-anaphoric pronouns; so too are *I* and *you*, for they refer directly to speaker/writer and addressee(s), rather than by virtue of an anaphoric relation to an antecedent. *He* and *she* are most often anaphoric to some antecedent, but they can also be used non-anaphorically, as when I go to bring in the milk and say *He's only left one pint*, with *he* referring directly to the milkman. Point (b) is exemplified in *Ed ran faster than he had ever done before*, where *run* is antecedent to the verb *do*, or *Jill said the key was in the box but I couldn't find it there*, where *in the box* is antecedent to *there*, traditionally classified as an adverb. A cover-term for *there, do, he,* etc, is 'pro-form'.

There are two other major types of anaphora besides that where a pro-form is used as anaphor: one involves ellipsis, the other the use of a definite determiner such as *the*. Ellipsis is anaphoric when the missing elements have antecedents. In *I'll help you if I can* the anaphora relation holds between the antecedent *help you* and what we may informally call a 'zero' anaphor: here too it is by virtue of this relation that we understand the *if* clause as equivalent to *if I can help you;* similarly in *If I can, I'll help you*, where the antecedent follows. The anaphoric ellipsis of *John enjoys bribing people*, where *John* is antecedent to the covert subject of *bribe* may be contrasted with the non-anaphoric ellipsis of *Bribing people is wrong*, where there is no antecedent. The anaphoric use of *the* is exemplified in *A man and a woman got on the bus; the man was wearing military uniform:* here we shall say that the indefinite NP *a man* is antecedent to the anaphor *the man*, a definite NP. Again, not all definite NPs are anaphoric – recall the discussion of examples like *The Vice-Chancellor is talking tonight* in 15.1 (and as observed above *I* and *you*, which are definite, are never used anaphorically; nor are definite NPs consisting of a proper noun, like *John*). In what follows I shall simplify by considering only pro-form and zero anaphora: these are sufficient to illustrate the theoretical issues.

In the *Aspects* model, anaphora is handled by transformations effecting substitution (in the pro-form type) or deletion (in the case of ellipsis). The substitution or deletion is dependent on the affected elements being identical with some specified term of the structure index (as in Equi, *p* 112). On the face of it this approach appears to offer a simple formal explication of the notion 'antecedent' and a natural way of handling both the semantic and the syntactic properties of anaphora. As for the semantics, if *John shaved himself* is derived from '*John_i Past shave John_i*', the understood identity between the shaver and the one shaved is accounted for by the deep structure identity of the two NPs, and similarly if *I'll help you if I can* is derived by deletion of *help you* all the elements necessary for the interpretation of the *if* clause will be present in the deep structure of the clause itself. As for the syntax, appropriate ordering and formulation of the rules enables us to state the conditions under which the anaphor may precede the antecedent and to predict the form of the anaphor –

zero in *Ed tried to escape*, reflexive pronoun in *Ed believed himself to be ill*, non-reflexive pronoun in *Ed believed that he was ill* (recall that the clause-mate condition on Reflexivization does not apply at the level of deep structure), and so on.

There are, however, a number of objections that can be made to this approach. Consider first the way it will handle the choice between the various third person singular pronouns. To handle such data as *The boy hurt himself/*herself*, *The girl hurt herself/*himself*, inherent gender features are assigned to nouns and the Reflexivization rule takes account of the gender feature on the noun in the NP undergoing substitution. But this means that to generate both *My cousin hurt himself* and *My cousin hurt herself* we need to treat *cousin* as ambiguously male or female: in a model where transformations are meaning-preserving, the difference in meaning expressed by *him* versus *her* cannot be introduced by Reflexivization itself but must be attributed to the underlying NP which the pronouns replace. It follows that a sentence like *My cousin is here* has to be analysed as AMBIGUOUS as to the sex of the cousin, whereas what the grammar ought to say is surely that the cousin's sex – like the speaker's, or like the cousin's marital status, etc – is simply left UNSPECIFIED (see *p* 202 for this important distinction). The *Aspects* approach forces us to treat English as having a system of syntactic gender with choice of pronoun determined by the gender feature of the antecedent, instead of having the choice directly express relevant properties of the referent.

A second objection to the *Aspects* approach to anaphora has to do with the referential indices. These enable us to distinguish the deep structures of *John hurt himself* and *John hurt John* (respectively '$John_i$ Past hurt $John_i$' and '$John_i$ Past hurt $John_j$'), etc, but this device will not work for pairs like

[4] i *All the ministers praised themselves*
    ii *All the ministers praised all the ministers*

We cannot say that the two NPs in [ii] are non-coreferential: in the most likely (if not the only possible) interpretation they refer to the same set of people, in which case '*all the ministers_i* Past praise all the ministers_j' cannot be the deep structure. Yet if [i] and [ii] are both derived from '*all the ministers_i* Past praise all the ministers_i', Reflexivization ceases to be meaning-preserving, for the sentences are clearly not paraphrases. Analogous remarks hold for pairs like *Only Ed voted for himself* versus *Only Ed voted for Ed;* the latter is ambiguous according as the two NPs are coreferential or not, but even when they are the sentence differs in meaning from the first: the first but not the second would be falsified by Tim's having voted for Tim, the second but not the first by Tim's having voted for Ed. The same problem arises with non-reflexive pronouns or zero anaphors – *cf: Both candidates say they will reduce taxes* versus *Both candidates say both candidates will reduce taxes* or *Everyone wanted to vote* versus *Everyone wanted everyone to vote*. I have suggested that the introduction of referential indices was not justified on syntactic grounds: their function was to allow the transformations to meet the semantic condition of being meaning-preserving – but the above examples show that they cannot in fact do this. They have accordingly been abandoned in the Extended Standard Theory. Whether two expressions are coreferential or not is no longer shown directly in the syntactic representations but is determined by the new type of semantic rule.

Now once the burden of accounting for the coreferential aspects of anaphora has been shifted from the syntactic component to the semantics, the question arises as to whether it would not be more economical to have the semantic rules handle all aspects of anaphora. This indeed is the treatment that Chomsky now tentatively advocates. Anaphoric pro-forms are inserted directly into deep structures instead of by later substitution rules, and anaphoric ellipsis is no longer handled by deletion: in the deep structure of *John wanted to go* the deep subject of *go* is left unspecified and instead of a syntactic rule of Equi NP Deletion there will be a semantic rule of Δ Subject Interpretation. In *Aspects* the base rules already had to provide for the insertion of the pronouns *he*, *she*, etc, in their non-anaphoric uses: the revised analysis thus allows for a uniform syntactic treatment of these forms. It also avoids the necessity of treating *cousin* (and scores of similar words) as ambiguous: the difference in meaning in *My cousin hurt himself/herself* can be determined directly from the pronouns, so that no gender features are needed on *cousin*. Various other arguments for the revision can be found in the works cited in the notes.

One consequence of the revision is that many deviant sentences which were earlier analysed as syntactically ill-formed will now be analysed as syntactically well-formed but semantically ill-formed. Thus *The man tried to kill herself (from 'the man Past try it Δ kill herself') will not violate any syntactic rule: the deviance will be accounted for in the semantics: *herself* is marked as co-referential with Δ and Δ with *the man*, so that the deviance lies in referring to a single entity by means of expressions attributing incompatible properties to it. Similarly both *John is studying law and Tom medicine* (p 98) and *John died and Tom medicine* will be generated as syntactically well-formed, the latter being marked as semantically deviant because there is no antecedent for the zero anaphor.

This has serious implications for the delimitation of the domain of syntax. In *Syntactic Structures*, as we have seen, a major task of the grammar, consisting of syntax plus morphophonemics, was to generate the set of grammatical sentences in the language. Chomsky adopted the working assumption (1957:13) that we have independent knowledge of whether a sentence is grammatical or not through native speaker judgments of acceptability: one test of the grammar's adequacy will thus be whether the sentences it generates match those judged acceptable by native speakers. He acknowledged, however, that the assumption was in fact too strong (1957:103), and the subsequent development of the distinction between competence and performance allows for discrepancies between grammaticality (a concept in competence) and acceptability (performance). Nevertheless, judgments of linguistic acceptability still provided for a preliminary or pre-theoretical delimitation of the domain of syntax (plus morphophonemics). Hence the treatment of selectional restrictions as syntactic in nature: granted that sentences like *The man elapsed* or *John frightened sincerity* are unacceptable, we shall need to set up syntactic rules to exclude them (for the deviance is clearly not morphophonemic). In *Aspects* Chomsky devoted considerable attention to refining the syntactic apparatus for handling these restrictions (*cf* Chapter 10 above), and in general the addition of the semantic component had not at this stage had any appreciable effect on the domain of syntax. He did, however, raise the possibility that it might be better to handle such restrictions in the semantics, and subsequent argument has shown that this is in fact so. A major point is that selectional restrictions cannot properly be regarded as holding between pairs of lexical items, as is assumed in the *Aspects* formalism: *The person who begat John is pregnant* exhibits the same anomaly as *John's father is pregnant*, although the well-formedness of *That person is pregnant* shows that the deviance of the first is not attributable to any inherent lexical properties of *person.*

Now if we shift first selectional restrictions, then the treatment of anaphora, from the syntax to the semantics, the discrepancy between the sentences defined by the grammar as syntactically well-formed and those judged acceptable by native speakers will be so enormous that these judgments can no longer be taken to provide a pre-theoretical delimitation of the domain of syntax (plus phonology). And indeed I think it is fair to say that in the Extended Standard Theory it is virtually impossible to give any significant pre-theoretical account at all of the domain of syntax: which facts concerning the distribution of forms will be handled by syntactic rules and which by semantic rules will be decided by comparison of alternative formal analyses to see which achieves the greater measure of generalization.

Let us now turn briefly to a different, and rival, line of development: one where the domain of syntax, instead of being contracted, was progressively expanded. This expansion has indeed already been exemplified in the last two chapters. The revised analysis of auxiliaries considered in Chapter 14 involved deep structures that were both further removed from the surface structures (*ie* transformationally related to them via more intermediate steps) than in the *Aspects* analysis and also intuitively closer to a representation of the meaning. The introduction of abstract causative verbs (15.4) and the merging of verbs, adjectives, nouns, etc, into a single category (15.5) likewise increase the distance between deep and surface structure while decreasing that between deep structure and meaning.

Such a deepening of deep structure was also proposed as part of an alternative solution to the problem posed by examples like [1] and [2] above. In discussing these we tacitly assumed that *many MPs* and *many arrows* were NPs in deep as well as surface structure; but if we give up this assumption and extend still further the category of verb so as to include *many* and *not*, we can give different deep structures to the non-synonymous sentences. For example, PMs along the lines of [5] and [6] (extended to include tense) might be proposed as deep structures for *Many arrows didn't hit the target* (=[2i]) and *The target wasn't hit by many arrows* (=[2ii]) respectively.

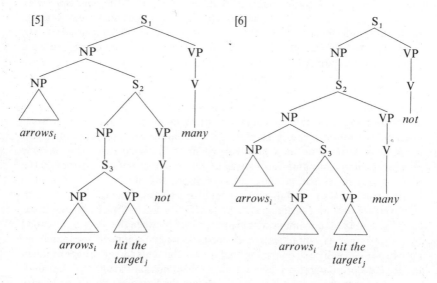

S_2 is a relative, S_3 a complement clause in [5], vice versa in [6] (I omit the *it* from the complement constructions). The scope of the negative can be determined directly from these structures – it is the clause constituting the subject NP of which *not* is predicated. Thus *many* is outside the scope of *not* in [5] (*cf* 'The arrows which didn't hit the target were many'), inside in [6] (*cf* 'That the arrows which hit the target were many is not so'). The fact that at least the first of these two glosses is a more or less acceptable sentence (if somewhat archaic-sounding) lends plausibility to the analysis of *many* as a verb, given that we have already argued for analysing adjectives as verbs; *not* (or *be not*) does not occur as a surface predicate but the verb *fail*, as in *The audience failed to appreciate his jokes* and *His jokes failed to be appreciated by the audience*, has much the same meaning as *not* and, like *not* in [5] and [6], is a one-place verb taking subject complementation. Positing these abstract deep structures does not of itself suffice to save the Katz–Postal hypothesis: it is also necessary to ensure that the structures are mapped into the right sentences. Thus if we confine ourselves to readings of [2i] and [ii] with normal intonation and nuclear stress on *target* and *arrows* respectively, [5] must be mapped into [i] not [ii] and [6] into [ii] not [i]. Lakoff (1971) proposes to achieve this by means of a rule saying, roughly, that if *not* and *many* are clause-mates in surface structure (and the sentence has normal stress and intonation) the one which comes first must be the one that belongs in the higher clause in deep structure. This is a new type of rule but like other syntactic rules is to be interpreted as a condition that must be met by a well-formed derivation (*cf* 12.1) – the transformations will map [5]

into final derived PMs corresponding to both [2i] and [ii] but the derivation containing [5] and the final PM for [2ii] will be inadmissible by virtue of the new rule.

In the *Aspects* model, the deep structure is a level intermediate between the semantic representation and the surface structure: it is related to the former by rules of semantic interpretation and to the latter by transformations. The progressive increase in the abstractness of deep structures proposed by some of those working within this model ultimately led to the claim that there is no justification for a level of deep structure distinct from the semantic level – that the first PM in the transformational derivation of a sentence is its semantic representation. This gives us the theory known as 'Generative Semantics', advocated by Lakoff, McCawley, Postal, Ross and others. The term 'generative' here contrasts with 'interpretive' and has a narrower sense than that in which we have been using it so far (as in 'a generative grammar', one which is fully explicit and formalized). Interpretive rules relate one level of representation to another while generative rules define conditions on well-formedness at a single level. In both the *Aspects* theory and the Extended Standard Theory the semantic component is interpretive in this sense, for the semantic representations are specified by rules operating on (hence 'interpreting') syntactic structures – the generative rules are in the syntactic component, where the PS rules, for example, directly specify the well-formed pre-lexical structures. 'Generative Semantics' is thus so called because the semantic rules are generative: they directly define the set of well-formed semantic representations; the latter are mapped into surface structures by a single set of syntactic transformations, interpretive rules. All three theories aim to provide for the description of a 'state' (*cf* 12.1), so that there is still no question of one level being assigned any temporal priority over another.

If, as the generative semanticists claim, the underlying PMs are to serve as semantic representations, they will need to be much more abstract still than those we have been considering. Most obviously, the terminal elements will not be morphemes (or complex symbols containing morphemes), but will be drawn from the set of primitive semantic elements defined in universal grammar. In the first place, it is evident that the phonological properties of morphemes have no place in semantic representations – the feature [+Velar] that characterizes the initial phonological segment in *cat*, for example, is not a component of meaning. Secondly, morphemes do not in general express minimal semantic concepts. One meaning of *bachelor*, to take a standard example, can be broken down into the components 'human', 'male', 'of marriageable status' (one would not apply the term *bachelor* to a five-year old or to a pope) and 'never having had a wife'; *buy* involves the transfer of money or whatever from buyer to seller in exchange for the transfer of goods from seller to buyer; *malinger* means something like 'pretend to be sick in order to avoid work'; and so on. A grammar must contain rules that pair complexes of phonological units (lexical items) with complexes of semantic units, and these will be interpretive rules in the sense defined above, *ie* they will relate one level of representation (where the terminal elements are semantic) to another (where they are, at least in part, phonological).

This much is not in dispute. The major claims that distinguish Generative Semántics from the Extended Standard Theory (and *Aspects*) are: (a) that the structures containing semantic elements are of the same general form as those containing lexical items, *ie* PMs with the non-terminal nodes labelled with category terms, S, NP and V; (b) that the semantic PMs are related to the surface structure PMs by a single set of transformations, such that there is no systematic significance attaching to any intermediate level that would constitute a boundary between semantics and syntax.

As for point (a), it is clear that semantic representations must impose a layered constituent structure on the terminal elements. This is evident from our discussion of the semantic scope of the negative in examples like [1] and [2]. The semantic representations of [1i] and [ii] will both contain a negative, but the semantic constituent with which it enters into construction is that corresponding to *MPs were in the House* in [i] and to *many MPs were in the House* in [ii]. Similarly the contrast between *John said Bill claimed Ed was a spy* and *John claimed Bill said Ed was a spy* makes clear the need for a bracketing type of structure: the semantic structure for *claim* is part of a larger constituent combining with that for *say* in the first sentence, vice versa in the second. Classic IC ambiguities like *old men and women* provide further demonstration of the point: the two semantic structures will have to be differentiated in a way which shows that 'old' is predicated of the men in one case and of both the men and the women in the other.

It is equally obvious that if we are to state rules that distinguish well-formed semantic structures from deviant ones, the constituents will have to be assigned to distributional categories: the semantic structure of *many MPs were in the House* is distributionally quite different from that of *not* or *the House*. It remains to be seen whether the three categories S, V and NP are adequate for this task, though we may note in passing that they correspond respectively to the logician's 'proposition', 'predicate' and 'argument', well-established notions in discussions of the logical structure of sentences. S is used for a constituent consisting of a V combining with one or more NPs, and V is the category of the minimal elements expressing properties of or relations between the terms designated by the NPs. A NP may consist of an embedded complement S or a 'variable' (optionally accompanied by a restrictive relative S); for example, *John believes that Ed is ill* expresses a relation between some entity that bears the name *John* and the proposition 'Ed is ill'. The term variable is used here because the specific entity referred to will vary with the circumstances of the speech situation, as noted in our early discussion of reference in 1.1. Using 'x', 'y', etc, for the variables, we can bring out the difference in meaning between the above examples *Only Ed voted for himself* and *Only Ed voted for Ed* by representing them as containing the propositions 'x voted for x' and 'x voted for y' respectively: the first asserts that 'x voted for x' is true only where x is Ed, the second that 'x voted for y, where y is Ed' is true only where x is Ed.

The most dubious aspect of claim (a) has to do with the question of linearity: in addition to assigning a categorized IC structure to the terminal elements, a PM also assigns a linear order. The linearity of phonetic representations has its justification in the temporal sequence of the speech signal, but it is unclear what properties of meaning can similarly provide justification for the alleged linearity of semantic representations. The syntactic representations that mediate between the 'outer' levels of phonetics and semantics must clearly be both linear and hierarchical, phonetic representations are linear but not hierarchical, and there is some *prima facie* plausibility in the view that semantic representations should be hierarchical but not linear.

Consider now claim (b). If semantic representations are in the form of PMs, a considerable amount of restructuring will have to take place before that stage in the derivation where lexical items are inserted – because the constituents in PMs containing lexical items will very often not match the constituents in semantic structure. We can see this by contrasting a pair of sentences like

[7] *Val slept for an hour*
[8] *Val lent Tim the car for an hour*

In [7] *for an hour* specifies the duration of Val's sleeping, whereas in [8] what lasted an hour was Tim's having use of the car, not Val's granting him permission to use it. The difference in what (generalizing from the discussion of negation) we may call the 'scope' of the durational specifier accounts for the contrast in well-formedness between *Val slept until tomorrow* and *Val lent Tim the car until tomorrow:* in the former the incompatible past tense and future time adverbial both apply to the sleeping, whereas in the latter one applies to the giving of permission, the other to the ensuing state. We can gloss *lend* here as something like 'give permission to have use of' but it is apparent that this complex of semantic elements cannot form a constituent at the level of semantic representation, for the semantic unit expressed as *for an hour* must there enter into construction with a constituent that includes the 'have use of' component of *lend* but excludes the 'give permission' component. The semantic elements expressed in *lend* no more form a constituent in semantic structure than do the words *give permission to use* form one in syntactic structure in the sentence *Val gave Tim permission to use the car for an hour.* It is evident, therefore, that in the derivation of [8] the earliest PM containing the morpheme *lend* will differ markedly in constituent structure from the semantic representation and hence that restructuring rules will be needed to relate them.

The question then arises as to whether these rules have the same formal properties as those we have been accepting as syntactic transformations. If a transformation is simply a mapping of one PM onto another, then it will follow by definition that the rules will be transformations; the question is of interest only in the context of the programme discussed in Chapter 13, where I stressed the importance of imposing the strongest possible formal constraints on what is admitted as a transformation. The generative semanticists argue that the constraints holding for *Aspects*-type transformations also apply to the rules relating semantic PMs to the PMs containing lexical items – that these rules are likewise subject to the conditions on the role of variables mentioned in Chapter 13, and so on.

A serious investigation of claims (a) and (b), and more generally of the relative merits of Generative Semantics and the Extended Standard Theory, would take us well beyond the limits set by the aims of this book. At present there is a great deal in each theory that remains vague and speculative, and it would be foolish to attempt to decide between them on the basis of a cursory comparison; it is inevitable, therefore, that we should conclude without resolving the issue of the delimitation of the field of syntax. My objective in this book has been to give the reader an understanding of as much as possible of the earlier work so that he will have the necessary background to go on to the more advanced studies dealing with these current issues of controversy.

Notes

Major sources for the Extended Standard Theory are Chomsky 1970*a*, *b*, 1972*a*, Jackendoff 1972; and for Generative Semantics G. Lakoff 1970, 1971, McCawley 1973, 1974*a*, *b*, Postal 1970*a*   many other references are given in these works. On the challenge to the Katz–Postal Hypothesis, see Partee 1971*a*, *b*. On anaphora, see Kuroda 1968, Langacker 1969, G. Lakoff 1968, Ross 1969*b*, Postal 1971. For discussion of the presupposition-focus contrast within a different theoretical framework, see Halliday 1967–8. The distinction between generative and interpretive rules is made in Chomsky 1965:16 and 135–7.

Bibliography

Journals and periodicals are abbreviated as follows:

CLS   *Papers from the Regional Meetings of the Chicago Linguistic Society*,
        Chicago University: Linguistic Society
FL   *Foundations of Language*, Dordrecht: Reidel
HER   *Harvard Educational Review*, Cambridge, Mass
JL   *Journal of Linguistics*, Cambridge: UP
Lg   *Language*, Baltimore: Linguistic Society of America
LI   *Linguistic Inquiry*, Cambridge, Mass: MIT Press
Lingua *Lingua*, Amsterdam: North-Holland
MLAT   Reports to the National Science Foundation on *Mathematical Lin-
        guistics and Automatic Translation*. Harvard: The Computation
        Laboratory of Harvard University
MSLL   *Monograph Series on Languages and Linguistics*. Washington:
        Georgetown UP
PAS   *Proceedings of the Aristotelian Society*, London: Methuen
Synthese *Synthese*, Dordrecht: Reidel
TPhS   *Transactions of the Philological Society*, Oxford: Blackwell
Word   *Word*, New York: Linguistic Circle

Note: all the mimeographed works cited are currently obtainable from
    Indiana University Linguistics Club, Bloomington, Indiana.

ALLEN, R. L. (1966) *The verb system of present-day American English*, The
    Hague: Mouton
ALLEN, W. S. (1957) *On the linguistic study of languages*, Cambridge: UP. Also
    in P. D. Strevens (ed), *Five inaugural lectures*, London: Oxford UP, 1966
ANDERSON, S. R. and KIPARSKY, P. (eds) (1973) *A festschrift for Morris Halle*,
    New York: Holt, Rinehart & Winston
AUSTIN, J. L. (1962) *How to do things with words*, Oxford: Clarendon Press
BACH, E. (1964) *An introduction to transformational grammars*, New York:
    Holt, Rinehart & Winston
    (1968) 'Nouns and noun phrases', in Bach and Harms 1968
    (1971) 'Syntax since *Aspects*', *MSLL* 24, 1–17
    (1974) *Syntactic theory*, New York: Holt, Rinehart & Winston
BACH, E. and HARMS, R. T. (eds) (1968) *Universals in linguistic theory*, New
    York: Holt, Rinehart & Winston

BAKER, C. L. (1970) 'Notes on the description of English questions: the role of an abstract question morpheme', *FL* 6, 197–219

BAZELL, C. E. (1964) 'Three misconceptions of "grammaticalness"', *MSLL* 17, 3–9

BERMAN, A. (1974) 'On the VSO hypothesis', *LI* 5, 1–37

BEVER, T. (1970) 'The cognitive basis for linguistic structures', in J. R. Hayes (ed), *Cognition and the development of language*, New York: Wiley

BLOOMFIELD, L. (1933) *Language*, New York: Holt, Rinehart & Winston

BOLINGER, D. L. (1957) *Interrogative structures of American English*, Publications of the American Dialect Society, Alabama: UP

(1967a) 'Imperatives in English', in *To Honor Roman Jakobson*, Vol 1, The Hague: Mouton

(1967b) 'Adjectives in English: attribution and predication', *Lingua* 18, 1–34

(1968) 'Judgments of grammaticality', *Lingua* 21, 34–40

BOYD, J. and THORNE, J. P. (1969) 'The semantics of modal verbs', *JL* 5, 57–74

BRESNAN, J. W. (1970) 'On complementizers: toward a syntactic theory of complement types', *FL* 6, 297–321

BURT, M. K. (1971) *From deep to surface structure: an introduction to transformational syntax*, New York: Harper & Row

CAMPBELL, R. and WALES, R. (1970) 'The study of language acquisition', in Lyons 1970

CHAFE, W. L. (1970) *Meaning and the structure of language*, Chicago: UP

CHOMSKY, N. A. (1957) *Syntactic structures*, The Hague: Mouton

(1961a) 'On the notion "rule of grammar"', in R. Jakobson (ed), *On the structure of language and its mathematical aspects*, Providence: American Mathematical Society. Also in Fodor and Katz 1964

(1961b) 'Some methodological remarks on generative grammar', *Word* 17, 219–39

(1962) 'A transformational approach to syntax', in A. A. Hill (ed), *Proceedings of the Third Texas Conference on Problems of Linguistic Analysis in English, 1958*, Austin: Texas UP. Also in Fodor and Katz 1964

(1965) *Aspects of the theory of syntax*, Cambridge, Mass: MIT Press

(1966a) *Topics in the theory of generative grammar*, The Hague: Mouton. Also in Sebeok 1966

(1966b) 'The current scene in linguistics: present directions', *College English* 27, 587–95. Also in Reibel and Schane 1969

(1968) *Language and mind*, New York: Harcourt, Brace & World

(1970a) 'Remarks on nominalization', in Jacobs and Rosenbaum 1970. Also in Chomsky 1972b.

(1970b) 'Deep structure, surface structure and semantic interpretation', in R. Jakobson and S. Kawamoto (eds), *Studies in general and oriental linguistics*, Tokyo: TEC Corporation for Language Research. Also in Steinberg and Jakobovits 1971 and Chomsky 1972b

(1972a) 'Some empirical issues in the theory of transformational grammar', in Peters 1972b. Also in Chomsky 1972b

(1972b) *Studies on semantics in generative grammar*, The Hague: Mouton

(1972c) *Problems of knowledge and freedom*, London: Fontana

(1973) 'Conditions on transformations', in Anderson and Kiparsky 1973

CHOMSKY, N. A. and HALLE, M. (1968) *The sound pattern of English*, New York: Harper & Row

CRUSE, D. A. (1973) 'Some thoughts on agentivity', *JL* 9, 11–24

CURME, G. O. (1931) *Syntax*, Boston: Heath
(1935) *Parts of speech and accidence*, Boston: Heath

DERWING, B. L. (1973) *Transformational grammar as a theory of language acquisition*, Cambridge: UP

DIK, S. C. (1968) *Coordination*, Amsterdam: North-Holland

DINGWALL, W. O. (ed) (1971) *A survey of linguistic science*, Maryland: University Linguistics Program

DOUGHERTY, R. C. (1970–1) 'A grammar of coordinate conjoined structures', *Lg* 46, 850–98 & 47, 298–339

FILLMORE, C. J. (1968a) 'The case for case', in Bach and Harms 1968
(1968b) 'Lexical entries for verbs', *FL* 4, 373–93
(1970) 'Types of lexical information', in F. Kiefer (ed) *Studies in syntax and semantics*, Dordrecht: Reidel. Also in Steinberg and Jakobovits 1971
(1971) 'Some problems for case grammar', *MSLL* 24, 35–56

FILLMORE, C. J. and LANGENDOEN, D. T. (eds) (1971) *Studies in linguistic semantics*, New York: Holt, Rinehart & Winston

FODOR, J. D. (1974) 'Like subject verbs and causal clauses in English', *JL* 10, 95–110

FODOR, J. A. and GARRETT, M. (1966) 'Some reflections on competence and performance', in J. Lyons and R. J. Wales (eds), *Psycholinguistic papers*, Edinburgh: UP

FODOR, J. A. and KATZ, J. J. (eds) (1964) *The philosophy of language*, Englewood Cliffs, NJ: Prentice-Hall

FRASER, B. (1970) 'Idioms within a transformational grammar', *FL* 6, 22–42
(1973) 'On accounting for illocutionary forces', in Anderson and Kiparsky 1973

GLEITMAN, L. R. (1965) 'Coordinating conjunctions in English', *Lg* 41, 260–93. Also in Reibel and Schane 1969

GORDON, D. and LAKOFF, G. (1971) 'Conversational postulates', *CLS* 7, 63–84

GREENBAUM, S. and QUIRK, R. (1970) *Elicitation experiments in English*, London: Longman

GREENBERG, J. H. (ed) (1963) *Universals of language*, Cambridge, Mass: MIT Press
(1966) *Language universals*, The Hague: Mouton

HAAS, W. (1973a) 'Meanings and rules', *PAS* 73, 135–56
(1973b) 'Rivalry among deep structures', *Lg* 49, 282–93

HALLIDAY, M. A. K. (1967–8) 'Notes on transitivity and theme in English', *JL* 3, 37–81 & 199–244; 4, 179–215
(1970) 'Language structure and language function', in Lyons 1970

HARMS, R. (1968) *An introduction to phonological theory*, Englewood Cliffs, NJ: Prentice-Hall

HARRIS, Z. S. (1951) *Methods in structural linguistics*, Chicago: UP. Republished 1960 as *Structural linguistics*

HOCKETT, C. F. (1954) 'Two models of grammatical description', *Word* 10, 210–33. Also in Joos 1957
(1958) *A course in modern linguistics*, New York: Macmillan
(1961) 'Linguistic elements and their relations', *Lg* 37, 29–53

HOFMANN, T. R. (1966) 'Past tense replacement and the modal system', *MLAT*, 17

HOUSEHOLDER, F. W. (1971) *Linguistic speculations*, Cambridge: UP
(1973) 'On arguments from asterisks', *FL* 10, 365–76

HUDDLESTON, R. D. (1969) 'Some observations on tense and deixis in English', *Lg* 45, 777–806
(1971) *The sentence in written English*, Cambridge: UP
(1974) 'Further remarks on the analysis of auxiliaries as main verbs', *FL* 11, 215–29

HUDSON, R. A. (1970) 'On clauses containing conjoined and plural noun-phrases in English', *Lingua* 24, 205–53

JACKENDOFF, R. S. (1972) *Semantic interpretation in generative grammar*, Cambridge, Mass: MIT Press
(1973) 'The base rules for prepositional phrases', in Anderson and Kiparsky 1973

JACOBS, R. A. and ROSENBAUM, P. S. (eds) (1970) *Readings in English trans-formational grammar*, Waltham, Mass: Ginn
(1971) *Transformations, style and meaning*, Waltham, Mass: Xerox Publishing Co

JESPERSEN, O. (1909–49) *A modern English grammar on historical principles*, Copenhagen: Munksgaard; and London: Allen & Unwin

JOOS, M. (1957) *Readings in linguistics*, Washington: American Council of Learned Societies. Republished 1966 by Chicago UP

KARTUNNEN, L. (1973) 'Presupposition of compound sentences', *LI* 4, 169–93

KATZ, J. J. (1964) 'Semi-sentences', in Fodor and Katz 1964
(1972) *Semantic theory*, New York: Harper & Row
(1973a) 'On defining "presupposition"', *LI* 4, 256–60
(1973b) 'Compositionality, idiomaticity and lexical substitution', in Anderson and Kiparsky 1973

KATZ, J. J. and FODOR, J. A. (1963) 'The structure of a semantic theory', *Lg* 39, 170–210. Also in Fodor and Katz 1964

KATZ, J. J. and POSTAL, P. M. (1964) *An integrated theory of linguistic descrip-tions*, Cambridge, Mass: MIT Press

KEMPSON, R. (1974) 'Presupposition: a problem for linguistic theory', *TPhs for 1973*, 29–54

KIMBALL, J. P. (ed) (1972) *Syntax and semantics*, Vol 1, New York: Seminar Press
(1973) *The formal theory of grammar*, Englewood Cliffs, NJ: Prentice-Hall

KIPARSKY, P. and KIPARSKY, C. (1970) 'Fact', in M. Bierwisch and K. Heidolph (eds), *Progress in Linguistics*, The Hague: Mouton. Also in Steinberg and Jakobovits 1971

KLIMA, E. S. (1964) 'Negation in English', in Fodor and Katz 1964

KOUTSOUDAS, A. (1971) 'Gapping, conjunction reduction, and coordinate deletion', *FL* 7, 337–86
(1972) 'The strict order fallacy', *Lg* 48, 88–96

KRUISINGA, E. (1925) *A handbook of present-day English*, Utrecht: Kemink en Zoon

KUNO, S. and ROBINSON, J. J. (1972) 'Multiple wh questions', *LI* 3, 463–87

KURODA, S. Y. (1968) 'English relativization and certain related problems', *Lg* 44, 244–66. Also in Reibel and Schane 1969

LABOV, W. (1971) 'Methodology', in Dingwall 1971

LAKOFF, G. (1965) *On the nature of syntactic irregularity, MLAT* 20. Published commercially as *Irregularity in syntax*, New York: Holt, Rinehart & Winston 1970

(1966a) 'Deep and surface grammar', Mimeographed

(1966b) 'Stative adjectives and verbs in English', *MLAT* 17, 1–16

(1968) 'Pronouns and reference', Mimeographed

(1969) 'Presuppositions and relative grammaticality', in Todd 1969. Also published as 'Presuppositions and relative well-formedness' in Steinberg and Jakobovits 1971

(1970) 'Linguistics and natural logic', *Synthese* 22, 151–271. Also in D. Davidson and G. Harman (eds), *Semantics of natural languages*, Dordrecht: Reidel, 1971

(1971) 'On generative semantics', in Steinberg and Jakobovits 1971

LAKOFF, G. and PETERS, S. (1966) 'Phrasal conjunction and symmetric predicates', *MLAT* 17. Also in Reibel and Schane 1969

LAKOFF, R. (1968) *Abstract syntax and Latin complementation*, Cambridge, Mass: MIT Press

(1971) 'Passive resistance', *CLS* 7, 149–62

(1972) 'The pragmatics of modality', *CLS* 8, 229–46

LANGACKER, R. W. (1969) 'On pronominalization and the chain of command', in Reibel and Schane 1969

LEES, R. B. (1961) *The grammar of English nominalizations*, Bloomington: Indiana University Publications in Folklore and Linguistics; and The Hague: Mouton

LEES, R. B. and KLIMA, E. S. (1963) 'Rules for English pronominalization', *Lg* 39, 17–28. Also in Reibel and Schane 1969

LYONS, J. (1966) 'Towards a "notional" theory of the "parts of speech"', *JL* 2, 209–36

(1968) *Introduction to theoretical linguistics*, Cambridge: UP

(ed) (1970) *New horizons in linguistics*, Harmondsworth: Penguin

MCCAWLEY, J. D. (1968a) 'Concerning the base component of a transformational grammar', *FL* 4, 243–69

(1968b) 'The role of semantics in a grammar', in Bach and Harms 1968

(1970) 'English as a VSO language', *Lg* 46, 286–99

(1971) 'Tense and time reference in English', in Fillmore and Langendoen 1971

(1973) *Grammar and meaning*, Tokyo: Taishukan

(1974a) 'Syntactic and logical arguments for semantic structures', in O. Fujimura (ed), *Three dimensions of linguistic theory*, Tokyo: TEC Corp.

(1974b) Review of Chomsky 1972b, *LI* 5

MATTHEWS, P. H. (1965) 'Some concepts in word-and-paradigm morphology', *FL* 1, 268–89

(1967) Review of Chomsky 1965, *JL* 3, 119–52

(1972) *Inflectional morphology*, Cambridge: UP

(1974) *Morphology*, Cambridge: UP

MELLEMA, P. (1974) 'A brief against case grammar', *FL* 11, 39–76

MORGAN, J. L. (1972) 'Verb agreement as a rule of English', *CLS* 8, 278–86

NEWMEYER, F. (1970) 'The root modal: can it be transitive?', in J. M. Sadock and A. Vanek (eds), *Studies presented to Robert Lees by his students*, Edmonton: Linguistic Research Inc

PALMER, F. R. (1965) *A linguistic study of the English verb*, London: Longman
(1971) *Grammar*, Harmondsworth: Penguin
(1973) 'Noun phrase and sentence: a problem in semantics/syntax', *TPhS for 1972*, 20–43

PARTEE, B. H. (1971*a*) 'On the requirement that transformations preserve meaning', in Fillmore and Langendoen 1971
(1971*b*) 'Linguistics metatheory', in Dingwall 1971

PERLMUTTER, D. M. (1971) *Deep and surface structure constraints in syntax*, New York: Holt, Rinehart & Winston

PETERS, S. (1972*a*) 'The projection problem: How is a grammar to be selected?', in Peters 1972*b*
(ed) (1972*b*) *Goals of linguistic theory*, Englewood Cliffs, NJ: Prentice-Hall

POSTAL, P. M. (1964*a*) 'Underlying and superficial linguistic structure', *HER* 34, 246–66. Also in Reibel and Schane 1969
(1964*b*) 'Limitations of phrase-structure grammars', in Fodor and Katz 1964
(1964*c*) *Constituent structure*, Bloomington: Indiana University Publications in Folklore and Linguistics; and The Hague: Mouton
(1968) *Aspects of phonological theory*, New York: Harper & Row
(1970*a*) 'On the surface verb "remind"', *LI* 1, 37–120. Also in Fillmore and Langendoen 1971
(1970*b*) 'On coreferential complement subject deletion', *LI* 1, 439–500
(1971) *Cross-over phenomena*, New York: Holt, Rinehart & Winston
(1972) 'On some rules that are not successive cyclic', *LI* 3, 211–22
(1974) *On raising*, Cambridge, Mass: MIT Press

POSTAL, P. M. and ROSS, J. R. (1971) 'iTough movement si, tough deletion no!', *LI* 2, 544–6

POUTSMA, H. (1914–29) *A grammar of late modern English*, Groningen: Noordhoff

PUTNAM, H. (1967) 'The "innateness hypothesis" and explanatory models in linguistics', *Synthese* 17, 12–22

QUIRK, R., GREENBAUM, S., LEECH, G. and SVARTVIK, J. (1972), *A grammar of contemporary English*, London: Longman

QUIRK, R. and SVARTVIK, J. (1966) *Investigating linguistic acceptability*, The Hague: Mouton

REIBEL, D. A. and SCHANE, S. A. (eds) (1969) *Modern studies in English: readings in transformational grammar*, Englewood Cliffs, NJ: Prentice-Hall

RINGEN, C. (1972) 'On arguments for rule ordering', *FL* 8, 266–73

ROBINS, R. H. (1952) 'Noun and verb in universal grammar', *Lg* 28, 289–98
(1959) 'In defence of WP', *TPhS*, 116–44

ROSENBAUM, P. S. (1967) *The grammar of English predicate complement constructions*, Cambridge, Mass: MIT Press
(1970) 'A principle governing deletion in English sentential complementation', in Jacobs and Rosenbaum 1970

ROSS, J. R. (1967) *Constraints on variables in syntax*, Mimeographed
(1969*a*) 'Auxiliaries as main verbs', in Todd 1969
(1969*b*) 'Guess who', *CLS* 5, 205–39

(1970) 'On declarative sentences', in Jacobs and Rosenbaum 1970

(1972) 'Doubl-ing', *LI* 3, 61–86. Also in Kimball 1972

SCHANE, S. A. (1973) *Generative phonology*, Englewood Cliffs, NJ: Prentice-Hall

SEARLE, J. R. (1969) *Speech acts*, Cambridge: UP

SEBEOK, T. A. (ed) (1966) *Current trends in linguistics*, Vol 3, The Hague: Mouton

SHOPEN, T. (1973) 'Ellipsis as grammatical indeterminacy', *FL* 10, 65–78

SMITH, C. S. (1964) 'Determiners and relative clauses in a generative grammar of English', *Lg* 40, 37–52. Also in Reibel and Schane 1969

STEINBERG, D. D. and JAKOBOVITS, L. A. (eds) (1971) *Semantics*, Cambridge: UP

STOCKWELL, R. P., SCHACHTER, P. and PARTEE, B. H. (1973) *The major syntactic structures of English*, New York: Holt, Rinehart & Winston

STRAWSON, P. F. (1964) 'Identifying reference and truth-values', *Theoria* 30, 96–118. Also in Steinberg and Jakobovits 1971

SWEET, H. (1891) *A new English grammar*, Vol 1, Oxford: Clarendon Press

THOMPSON, S. A. (1971) 'The deep structure of relative clauses', in Fillmore and Langendoen 1971

TODD, W. (ed) (1969) *Studies in philosophical linguistics*, series 1, Evanston, Ill: Great Expectations Press

TWADDELL, W. F. (1960) *The English verb auxiliaries*, Providence: Brown UP

WALL, R. E. (1971) 'Mathematical linguistics', in Dingwall 1971

WEINREICH, U. (1966) 'Explorations in semantic theory', in Sebeok 1966. Also published as separate book, The Hague: Mouton, 1972

ZWICKY, A. (1973) Review of J. G. Kooij: *Ambiguity in natural language*, *Lingua* 32, 95–118

Index

abstract verb, 240–3, 247
acceptability, 15, 254–5
accidence, 165
active voice, 26, 47–53, 60–1, 72, 82, 91
adjective, 104, 110, 243–5, 247
adjunction, 187, 189–92
Affix Hopping, 73–5, 78–81, 180–2, 189–190, 195, 214–15, 217
agent, 48, 228, 235–43, 247
agreement, 25–6, 168–9, 171, 181–2, 198, 202, 206, 230
Allen, R. L., 80
Allen, W. S., 18
allomorph, 162–3
alternation, 160–4, 167
ambiguity, 11, 18, 85, 91, 132, 145, 202, 253
anacoluthon, 2
anaphora, 77–8, 212, 251–5
antecedent, 102, 251–4
aspect, 65–6, 80, 198, 223
Aspects of the Theory of Syntax, 21, 89, 91, 95, 170, 248–60
attributive adjective, 246
Austin, J. L., 128, 145
auxiliary constituent/verb, 57, 78, 81, 211–225

Bach, E., 195, 210
backshifting, 62–4, 221
Baker, C. L., 145–6
base, base PM, 150–94
Bazell, C. E., 22
be, 67, 244–5
Berman, A., 247
Bever, T., 22
binary feature, 153–5, 168
Bloch, B., 33
Bloomfield, L., 28, 33
Boas, F., 200
Bolinger, D. L., 22, 92, 110, 145

Boyd, J., 225
Bresnan, J. W., 126
Burt, M. K., 195

Campbell, R., 22, 210
case, 26, 109, 166, 169, 199–200, 232–40, 244, 247
categorial component, 157
category (grammatical/syntactic), 25, 40–1, 97, 230
category feature, 151–4
causative construction, 240–3
Chafe, W. L., 145
Chomsky, N. A., 1, 2, 7, 13, 15, 19, 21–3, 33, 35, 37–8, 46, 55–6, 80–1, 82, 89, 91–2, 95, 146, 147, 149, 157, 158, 170–1, 172, 187, 193, 195, 196, 206–10, 214–15, 224, 231–2, 235, 244, 246–7, 248–55, 260
Chomsky-adjunction, 189–92, 195, 203
clause, 96–7, 109
clause-mate, 118–19, 123
common noun, 148–9
comparative construction, 85, 202, 224
competence, 1–9, 12, 15, 22, 131, 133, 165, 175, 207, 229, 254
complement clause, 101, 106–9, 111–26, 142, 144–5, 192, 221, 256
complementizer, 107, 109, 126, 218
complex symbol, 149, 157, 168
complexity, 7, 90
code, 197
conjoining, 109
conjugation, 166
constituent, 40
context-free grammar/rule, 44, 179
context-sensitive grammar/rule, 44, 152, 158, 179
contextual feature, 151–5, 204–5
contrast, 159–65
controller, 126

copula, copulative verb, 214, 244–5
coordination, 7, 93–101, 106, 109–10, 136, 140, 146, 168, 202, 204, 233–4, 237
coreference, 6, 18, 89–90, 251–4
correctness (*vs* well-formedness), 12
Cruse, D. A., 247
Curme, G. O., 18, 210, 225
cycle, *see* transformational cycle

data, 17–19, 22, 25
daughter node, 39
declarative, 25, 53–4, 68, 82, 127–34, 142
declension, 166
deep structure, 52, 55, 83–91, 150–1, 175, 192–5, 206, 250
defective verb, 166
defining (*vs* naming), 60–1, 69, 198
definiteness, definite NP, 138, 228–9, 252
deletion, 187–90, 201–3, 210, 226–9
derivation (of words), 165–6, 170–1
derived constituent structure, 186–92, 195, 203
Derwing, B. L., 22, 210
determination, 175
deviant sentence, 9, 12–15
dictionary, 83; *see also* lexicon
Dik, S. C., 109
discontinuous constituent, 56
discovery procedure, 21
discreteness of units, 3–4
disjunctive interrogative, 136, 139–40, 143
distinctiveness, 159, 165
distribution, 24, 29–30, 96–7
do, 28–9, 77–80, 144, 165, 169, 180, 182, 212, 245
domination, 38–9, 46
double-base transformation, 95
Dougherty, R. C., 109
duality of patterning, 33

elementary transformational operation, 187–92, 203
ellipsis, 226–9, 247, 252
embedding, 93–110, 129–30, 144–5, 146
emphatic positive, 77–8, 212
en-form, 49, 67, 218
epistemic meaning of modals, 69
Equi NP Deletion, 111–26, 155–7, 184–5, 202, 254
evaluation of grammars, 17–22, 206–7
exceptions, 20, 56, 126, 151, 155–7, 166
exclamative clause, 127–9, 135, 140
Extended Standard Theory, 21, 243, 250–260
external adequacy, 17–19, 45

Extraposition, 108, 113, 121, 156
extrinsic ordering, 175–83, 195

Fillmore, C. J., 145, 232–41, 246–7
filtering role of transformations, 195
finiteness, 60, 66–8, 109, 119, 122–3
finite state grammar, 35
focus, 251
Fodor, J. A., 22, 83, 248
Fodor, J. D., 247
form (linguistic), 22–3
formal (*vs* notional) grammar, 33
formal universal, 196, 201–5
formative, 157
Fraser, B., 145, 171
free variation, 159–65
function (grammatical/syntactic), 25, 41–2, 46, 83–5, 151, 199–200, 226–47

Garner, R., 145
Garrett, M., 22
gender, 198–9, 210, 253
generalization, *see* linguistically significant generalization
generalized transformation, 95
generative grammar/rules, 16–17, 37, 161, 172–5, 257, 260
Generative Semantics, 21, 243, 257–60
gerund, gerundive construction, 67, 109
Gleitman, L. R., 109
Gordon, D., 145
governed rule, government, 155–6, 163, 199, 204–5, 217
grammatical morpheme, 157
grammatical relation, *see* function
grammatical sentence, 14, 22, 254
grammatical subject, 26, 229–31
Greenbaum, S., 22
Greenberg, J. H., 210
Grice, H. P., 145
Grinder, J. T., 195

Haas, W., 22, 247
Halle, M., 16, 170
Halliday, M. A. K., 246, 260
Harms, R., 170
Harris, Z. S., 22, 33
Hockett, C. F., 33–4, 170, 210
Hofmann, T. R., 224
homonymy, 67, 153, 157
Householder, F. W., 22, 210
Huddleston, R. D., 92, 110, 146, 224–5, 246
Hudson, R. A., 109

idealization, 3, 6, 22
idiom, 30, 170, 171
illocutionary force, 127–46, 225, 242
immediate constituent structure, 40, 147, 151, 167
Imp morpheme, 87–8, 145
imperative, 53–4, 68, 82, 87–8, 91, 92, 127–33, 145, 146, 156, 242
implication, 132, 145
indicative mood, 69–70, 80
indirect object, 231–2
infinite set of sentences, 7, 94
infinitive, 67, 80, 109
inflection, 67, 71, 165–71, 200, 212, 222–4
inherent feature, 151, 152, 154–5
ing-form, 67, 109, 218
internal adequacy, 17–21, 41, 45, 50
interpretive rules, 257, 260
interrogative, 25, 69, 75–80, 82, 85, 88, 127–46, 185–6
intransitive, *see* transitivity
intrinsic ordering, 179–83, 195
Inversion, 76–80, 85, 116, 133, 140, 143–4, 146, 181, 185–6, 212–15, 230
irregularity, *see* exceptions *and* rule feature
'is a' relation, 40
it, 108, 256

Jackendoff, R. S., 92, 126, 225, 246–7, 260
Jacobs, R. A., 225
Jespersen, O., 16, 18
Joos, M., 200

Kartunnen, L., 145
Katz, J. J., 22, 83, 88–91, 92, 145, 157, 171, 210, 248, 260
Katz-Postal hypothesis, 88–90, 249–57, 260
Keenan, E. L., 145
Kempson, R., 145
kernel sentence/string, 82–3, 90–1, 95
Kimball, J. P., 46, 81, 195
Kiparsky, P. & C., 126
Klima, E. S., 92
knowledge of language *vs* knowledge of world, 15
Koutsoudas, A., 109, 195
Kruisinga, E., 18
Kuno, S., 145
Kuroda, S. Y., 110, 260

Labov, W., 22
Lakoff, G., 21, 22, 109, 126, 145, 157, 195, 247, 256–7, 260
Lakoff, R., 126, 145, 195, 225

Langacker, R. W., 260
Langendoen, D. T., 145
language, 200, 210
language acquisition, 208–10
Lees, R. B., 92
lexical item, 170, 222–3
lexical (*vs* grammatical) morpheme, 157
lexical transformation, 150, 157
lexicon, 151–7, 170
linear ordering, 39, 151, 167–8, 259
linguistically significant generalization, 19–20, 84, 205–7
logical subject, 26, 229–31, 246
Lyons, J., 33, 80, 109, 157, 210, 246

McCawley, J. D., 21, 109, 126, 157, 171, 180, 195, 224, 239, 257, 260
main verb, 57, 211–25
Marshall, J. C., 210
Matthews, P. H., 46, 171, 210
meaning, 4–6, 18–19, 22, 23–30, 91, 131–2; *see also* syntax *vs* semantics
meaning-changing *vs* meaning-preserving transformations, 87–91, 249, 253–4
meaningfulness, 13–14, 30
Mellema, P., 246
modal auxiliary/VGp, 68–70, 211–25
mood, 61, 68–70, 80, 85, 127–46, 198, 223, 242
Morgan, J. L., 171
morpheme, 27–33, 39, 157, 158–65, 167–71
morphology, 165–71
morphophoneme, 163
morphophonemic component/rule, 31–3, 36, 39, 52, 88, 158–65, 166

naming (*vs* defining), 60–1, 69, 198
negation, 77–80, 82, 85–7, 92, 212–14, 249–50, 255–7
Neo-Bloomfieldians, 35, 55–6, 158–67, 170
Newmeyer, F., 225
node, 38
node admissibility condition, 179–80
nominalization, 233
non-finite clause/verb, 66–8, 109
non-terminal symbols, 36
not, see negation
notional (*vs* formal) grammar, 33
noun, 23–5, 40, 197–8, 210, 245–6

obligatory transformation, 75, 182
object (direct), 42, 83–5, 227–8, 231–40, 247
Object Raising, 231, 244, 247, 249–50
optional transformation, 75, 82, 90

ordering of rules, 158, 174, 175–86, 195
output condition, 195

Palmer, F. R., 33, 80, 109, 210
paradigm, 166
paraphrase, 11, 91
Partee, B. H., 260
Particle Shift, 91
passive, Passivization, 26, 47–53, 56, 60–1, 72–5, 77–81, 82, 84, 91, 99, 114–15, 117, 121–2, 126, 151, 155–6, 165, 168–9, 181–2, 191–2, 195, 203, 204, 205, 223, 228–9, 239–40, 246, 249
past participle, 48–9, 67
past tense, 31–4, 48–9, 61–4, 160–1, 221–2
perfect aspect, 66, 221–2
performance, 1–9, 12, 15, 22, 133, 165, 172, 175, 254
performative verb, 133–4, 145
periphrastic form, 222, 225
Perlmutter, D. M., 195
permutation, 190
Peters, S., 109, 210
phoneme, phonemic level, 31, 159–65, 205–6
phonetic level/representation, 10, 159–65, 205–6
phonology, 11, 29–33, 158–65, 170
phrase marker, 37, 39–42
phrase structure derivation, 36, 45, 109, 172–80
phrase structure grammar, 35–56, 72, 80, 82, 84–5
phrase structure rule, 35–46, 76, 82, 85, 88, 90–1, 95, 147–8, 151, 173–80
plural number, 33–4, 160–1, 163
polysemy, 153, 157
possessive construction, 41, 109, 223
Postal, P. M., 21, 46, 56, 88–9, 92, 109, 126, 145, 170, 195, 210, 247, 248, 257, 260
post-cyclic transformation, 186
Poutsma, H., 18
predicate, 42, 232–40, 247
predicative noun, 245, 247
pre-lexical structure/phrase-marker, 149, 157
preposition, prepositional phrase, 232–3, 238–40, 246, 247
prescriptive grammar, 3, 12
present participle, 67
presupposition, 137–40, 145, 228, 251
preverb, 87, 179
primitive (vs non-primitive) term, 42, 46, 60

process, 7, 172–5
pro-form, 252–3
progressive aspect, 64–6, 220
projection rule, 83
Pronominalization, 188
pronoun, 188, 252–3
proper noun, 148–9
psychological subject, 229–31
Putnam, H., 210

Q morpheme, 136, 141, 143–6, 181
question, 127–45
Quirk, R., 22, 34, 80, 109–10, 145, 171

Raising, see Subject Raising
realization, 32, 158
recoverability of deletions, 202, 226–9
recursion, 93–110, 178, 180
redundancy rule, 155
reference, referent, referring expression, 4–6, 131, 137
referential indices, 89, 92, 248–9, 253–4
reflexive, Reflexivization, 53–4, 89–90, 92, 102, 123–4, 156, 180, 182–4, 186, 249, 253
relation, see function
relative clause/pronoun, Relativization, 8, 12, 101–7, 110, 135, 140, 146, 148, 192–4, 203–4, 219, 256
restrictive vs non-restrictive relative clause, 106
rewrite rule, 38, 179–80
Ringen, C., 195
Robins, R. H., 171, 210
Robinson, J. J., 145
root meaning of modals, 69
root (node), 38
Rosenbaum, P. S., 108, 126, 225
Ross, J. R., 21, 109–10, 145–6, 195, 204, 224, 247, 257, 260
rule feature, 151, 155–7, 163, 204–5, 215, 217–18, 244
rule schema, 94, 100

Schane, S. A., 170
Searle, J. R., 145
selectional feature, 151–5, 244
selectional restrictions, 14, 49–50, 89, 102, 104–5, 118–19, 122, 152–4, 219, 244–5, 255
semantic representation, 10, 83, 257–60
semantics, see meaning and syntax (vs semantics)
sentence (vs clause), 96–7, 109
sentence (vs utterance), 2–9, 127, 165